Zürl
Modern English
for the
Automotive Industry

Karl-Heinz Zürl

Modern English for the Automotive Industry

Englisch für die Aus- und Weiterbildung von Ingenieuren
Aktuelle und zukünftige Themen aus der Automobilindustrie

3., aktualisierte Auflage

Mit zahlreichen Bildern

Dipl.-Ing. Karl-Heinz Zürl
http://www.zuerl.com
zuerl@zuerl.com

Bibliografische Information Der Deutschen Bibliothek

Die Deutsche Bibliothek verzeichnet diese Publikation in der Deutschen Nationalbibliografie; detaillierte bibliografische Daten sind im Internet über http://dnb.ddb.de abrufbar.

ISBN 3-446-40187-3

Die Wiedergabe von Gebrauchsnamen, Handelsnamen, Warenbezeichnungen usw. in diesem Werk berechtigt auch ohne besondere Kennzeichnung nicht zu der Annahme, dass solche Namen im Sinne der Warenzeichen- und Markenschutz-Gesetzgebung als frei zu betrachten wären und daher von jedermann benutzt werden dürften.

Dieses Werk ist urheberrechtlich geschützt.
Alle Rechte, auch die der Übersetzung, des Nachdrucks und der Vervielfältigung des Buches oder Teilen daraus, vorbehalten. Kein Teil des Werkes darf ohne schriftliche Genehmigung des Verlages in irgendeiner Form (Fotokopie, Mikrofilm oder ein anderes Verfahren), auch nicht für Zwecke der Unterrichtsgestaltung, reproduziert oder unter Verwendung elektronischer Systeme verarbeitet, vervielfältigt oder verbreitet werden.

© 2005 Carl Hanser Verlag München Wien
www.hanser.de
Projektleitung: Jochen Horn
Herstellung: Renate Roßbach
Umschlaggestaltung: MCP • Agentur für Marketing – Communications – Production, Holzkirchen
Einbandbilder: DaimlerChrysler AG, Adam Opel AG
Druck und Bindung: Druckhaus „Thomas Müntzer" GmbH, Bad Langensalza
Printed in Germany

Vorwort (Preface)

Liebe Leser, das Ihnen vorliegende englischsprachige Buch mit deutschen Übersetzungshilfen bietet Informationen über praxisnahe, aktuelle sowie zukunftsorientierte Themen aus der Automobilwelt.

Sie haben sich für ein Buch entschieden, welches weder ein ausgesprochenes Lehrbuch noch ein reines Sachbuch ist. Dieses Buch entstand im Zuge von Sprachkursen, welche sich nach dem Bedarf der Mitarbeiter und Manager der Automobilindustrie und deren Zulieferer richten. In der Aus- und Weiterbildung wird das Werk Studenten, Technikern, Ingenieuren und Managern eine Hilfe sein. Die Vokabeln und Texte sind für Fahrzeugbau-, Maschinenbau-, Wirtschafts-, Marketing- und DV-Personal gleichermaßen interessant und lehrreich.

Ich habe als Maschinenbau- und Wirtschaftsingenieur in mehreren Bereichen von Unternehmen, u. a. in der Kunststoff- und Automobilindustrie, gearbeitet (zuletzt einige Jahre in verschiedenen Projekten der Produktentwicklung und Fertigung von Automobilen mit Auslandsaufenthalt). Interessante Gebiete aus der Automobilwelt, kombiniert mit meinem Wissen aus meinen Tätigkeiten habe ich in diesem Buch zusammengefasst.

Geschriebenes wurde mit Bildern und Grafiken ergänzt, und jedes Kapitel in mehrere Abschnitte gegliedert. Die Texte sind einfach und übersichtlich gestaltet. Eine möglichst unkomplizierte Satzkonstruktion wurde verwendet; dies erleichtert das Verständnis.

Das Werk besteht aus mehreren interessanten Lehreinheiten, die übersichtlich gegliedert sind. Die ersten Kapitel enthalten Basisinformationen über den Markt, der Unternehmens-, Marketing- und Planungsstrategien. Die weiteren Themen decken den Bereich von Styling bis zum Service ab. Am Ende des Buches befindet sich ein ausführliches Vokabelverzeichnis in Deutsch/Englisch und Englisch/Deutsch. Dieses Buch eignet sich sowohl für den Sprach- und Sachunterricht als auch für das Selbststudium und als sprachliche Referenz.

Die Lektüre ist für jeden geeignet, der über ein Grundwissen an Englisch oder einige Jahre Schulenglisch verfügt. Mit diesem Buch sparen Sie Zeit, indem Sie gleichzeitig Ihren Sprachwortschatz erweitern und Wissenswertes über aktuelle und zukünftige Themen in der Automobilindustrie erfahren.

Ich möchte an dieser Stelle meinem Sohn Adrian danken. Er hat engagiert mitgeholfen, die neue Auflage termingerecht zu aktualisieren.

Weitere interessante Themen und Ergänzungen zu diesem Buch und zum Thema „Lernen und Lehren" finden Sie in der Homepage www.lernen-lehren.de. Sollten Sie darüber hinaus spezielle Wünsche haben, so bitte ich Sie, mit uns direkt Kontakt aufzunehmen (info@zuerl.com). Wir helfen gerne.

Frühjahr 2005 *Karl-Heinz Zürl*

Contents

Vorwort (Preface) 5

Contents 6

Glossary of Acronyms 10

1 The Motor Vehicle Market 15

1.1 Reliable sources 15
1.2 Import and export trade 23
1.3 The German market 25
1.4 The European market 32
    1.4.1 Trading and cheats in the car market? *37*
    1.4.2 What happens in Italy? *38*
1.5 The Asia-Pacific market 39
    1.5.1 What happens in China? *39*
    1.5.2 What happens in South Korea? *42*
    1.5.3 What happens in Japan? *43*
1.6 The U.S. market 44

2 Enterprise Marketing Strategies and Policies 48

2.1 Carmaker's focus: "Green" image 48
2.2 DaimlerChrysler's focus: The small car sector 49
2.3 Audi's focus: Aluminium 49
2.4 Ford's focus: Non-polluting and efficient 50
2.5 General Motors' focus: Saab's Turbo 51
2.6 VW's focus: Marketing to the under-30 group 52

3 Strategical Operational Planning 54

3.1 New technology challenges automotive managers 54
3.2 Reduction of Leadtime 54
3.3 Making changes happen 57
3.4 How should suppliers be dealt with? 58
3.5 How should proper quality be achieved? 60
    3.5.1 Quality of parts *60*
    3.5.2 Product Quality Planning *61*

4 Carmakers' Portfolio 65

4.1 Audi's TT 65
4.2 VW Concept D1 68
4.3 Opel's G90 concept 70

5 Styling 73

6 Advanced Engineering 79

6.1 A second generation H(hip)-point doll 79
6.2 Silver Vision SLR concept car 80
6.3 The 3 litre barrier and its relation with mass 83
6.4 Saving space by introducing flat wires 87
6.5 Introduction of a new network for car safety systems 88
6.6 Do telematics make an intelligent car? 89
6.7 Do you like joysticks? 94
6.8 New CVTs with ball bearing systems 100
6.9 New plastic rear seating system was a world first 101
6.10 The smog-eating radiator 101
6.11 Metals drive back plastics 102
      6.11.1 *Why does the mass of cars increase?* *102*
      6.11.2 *Magnesium fever everywhere* *103*
      6.11.3 *Aluminium advantages and disadvantages* *107*
      6.11.4 *All about steel design* *109*
      6.11.5 *Plastic development* *112*
      6.11.6 *Last but not least: Copper, brass and zinc* *115*
6.12 Lightmass design is pulling the fat from body panels 115
6.13 Heat-shrinkable tubing 118
6.14 How to get cleaner diesels 119

7 Alternative Propulsion 120

7.1 Electric Cars 120
      7.1.1 *How far is the next charging station?* *120*
      7.1.2 *Electric delivery vehicle* *121*
7.2 Fuel Cell Technology 123
      7.2.1 *GM's fuel cell secrets* *123*
      7.2.2 *Renault's fuel cell concept* *127*
7.3 Natural Gas Vehicles 127

8 Product Engineering 130

8.1 Body, Interior 130
      8.1.1 *How to cure door rattles* *130*
      8.1.2 *Space saving by a new interior padding system* *130*
      8.1.3 *Low cost electric window motor* *131*
      8.1.4 *Liquid HVAC systems avoid goose pimples* *132*
      8.1.5 *Active seats* *134*
8.2 Powertrain 136
      8.2.1 *A golden area for diesels* *136*
      8.2.2 *Neural networking manages engine combustion* *139*
      8.2.3 *New catalytic converters* *140*
      8.2.4 *Ford Transit's 16-valve diesel was a world first* *142*
      8.2.5 *Variable valve timing is a key technology* *142*
      8.2.6 *The next generation spark ignition engines* *145*
      8.2.7 *Diesel direct injection* *149*
8.3 Chassis 153

    8.3.1 New seal design for suspension systems on Formula One cars. 153
    8.3.2 The magic triangle of tyre development 154
    8.3.3 Use of plastics for fuel systems 158
    8.3.5 Brakes for motor racing 161
    8.3.6 All-in-one exhaust system for small cars 162
    8.3.7 Switching from metal to plastic pedal assembly 164
    8.3.8 Air suspension system 165
    8.3.9 Porsche's new SUV needs stability management in 2002 167
8.4 Electric / Electronic 170
    8.4.1 A car battery revolution 170
    8.4.2 ASIC controls for airbags and seat belt systems 170
    8.4.3 Low cost fluid level sensor 171
    8.4.4 Cheaper and lighter lighting systems 171
8.5 Laboratory Tests 172
    8.5.1 Aluminium-magnesium superalloy 172
    8.5.2 Surface structures at atomic level 173
    8.5.3 Cold-rolled ultra-high-strength steel 174
    8.5.4 Low sulphur diesel fuel 174
8.6 Noise, Vibration and Harshness (NVH) 177
    8.6.1 The science of silence 177
    8.6.2 Noise and vibration irritate drivers 182
8.7 Heating, ventilation, air condition 186
    8.7.1 Gel improves thermal conductivity 186
    8.7.2 Parking Heaters 186

9 Manufacturing Engineering 190

9.1 Automotive painting technologies 190
9.2 New glass forming process 193
9.3 "Smart" core structures eclipse foam 194
9.4 Advanced castings for low volume markets 196
9.5 New type of heat shields from lateral thinking 197
9.6 Modern coil and leaf spring manufacturing 198
9.7 New injection moulding processes 200
9.8 Sports car chassis manufactured with aluminium 203
9.9 Manufacturing processes and techniques 205
    9.9.1 Component fabrication 205
    9.9.2 Assembly processes 210
9.10 Cost and mass reduction modelling for manufacturing processes 216

10 Information Technology Services 219

10.1 Hybrid software allows 3D working 219
10.2 Fluid flow modelling 219
10.3 Limitations of Virtual Reality modelling 220
10.4 Thermofluid analysis 221

11 Finance 223

11.1 The U.S. steelmarket 223
11.2 Product costs and investment are important 224

11.3 Carmakers' fight against recycling commission 225
12 Plants **228**

12.1 New Plant in Germany 228
12.2 General Motors' new plant 229

13 Sales, Logistics and Distribution **232**

13.1 Tax credits support sales 232
13.2 How to trim logistics costs 233

14 Aftersales and Service **234**

14.1 General 234
14.2 The interior 235
    14.2.1 Instrument panel 235
    14.2.2 Lighting 237
    14.2.3 Seats 238
    14.2.4 Load compartment 238
    14.2.5 Airbags 241
14.3 Chassis equipment 243
    14.3.1 Brakes 243
    14.3.2 Wheels and tyres 245
    14.3.3 Special safety features 246
    14.3.4 Handling with caravans and trailers 247
    14.3.5 Steering 248
14.4 Heating, Ventilation, Air Conditioning 249
14.5 Optional equipment, accessories 251
14.6 Engine, attaching parts 252
14.7 Exhaust systems 255
14.8 Clutch, transmission 255
14.9 Electrical equipment, instruments 256
14.10 Body parts 257

Appendix **259**

Vocabulary German – English 259
Vocabulary English – German 311
Pictures and Sources 358
Bibliography 359

Glossary of Acronyms

Abbreviation	Meaning
A&D	Assembly and Disassembly
A/C	air conditioning
AAA	Australia Automobile Association, Canberra
AAM	Automobil Association of Malaysia
AAMA	American Automobile Manufacturers Association, Detroit
AASA	Automobil Association of South Africa
AASM	Association of American Steel Manufacturers
AAV	all activity vehicle
ABS	Anti Block System
	acrylonitrile-butadiene-styrene-polymer
AC	Alternating current
	Automobile Club
ACAP	Association of Portugese Motor Vehicle Traders, Lisbon
ACI	Automobil Club d'Italia
ADEFA	Asociation de Fabricas de Automotores, Buenos Aires
AFR	air/fuel ratio
AG	German type public limited company; stock corporation
AIA	The Thai Automotive Industry Association
AIAM	Association of Indian Automobile Manufacturers, Bombay
AICC	autonomous intelligent cruise control
Al_2O_3	Aluminium Oxide
AMIA	Association of the Mexican Motor Industry, Mexico
AMVIR	Association of Motor Vehicle Importers, Athens
ANFAC	Asociación Espanola de Fabricantes de Automóviles y Camiones, Madrid
	Association of the Spanish Motor Industry, Madrid
ANFAVEA	Associado Nacional dos Fabricantes de Veiculos Automotores, Sao Paulo
ANFIA	Association of the Italian Motor Industry, Torino
ANSI	American National Standards Institute
APAA	Automotive Parts and Accessories Association
APIA	Association of Automotive Manufacturers and Importers, Bucarest (Romania)
ASIC	Application-Specifc Integrated Circuit
ASME	American Society of Mechanical Engineers
ASPECT	Automotive Seat and Package Evaluation and Comparison Tool
BASE	British Aerospace Systems & Equipment
BBW	Brake by Wire
BIL	Association of the Swedish Motor Industry, Stockholm
Bn	Billion (1,000 millions)
BNB	Institut National de la Statistique, Bruxelles
CAAM	China Association of Automobile Manufacturers, Beijing
CAD	Canadian Dollar
	Computer Aided Design
CAFE	U.S. Corporate Average Fuel Economy
CAM	Computer Aided Manufacturing
CAN	Controller Area Network
CARB	California Air Registration Board
CART	Championship Auto Racing Teams, Inc.
CAS	Computer Aided Styling

CATRC	China Automotive Technology and Research Center	
CBS	Netherlands Central Bureau of Statistics, Heerlen	
CCFA	Comité Des Constructeurs Francais d'Automobiles	
CCV	Concept Coupe Vehicle	
	Composite Concept Vehicle	
CD	Compact Disc	
CdA	Drag Coefficient * Area exposed to the wind	
CDI	Common Rail Direct Injection	
	condenser-discharge ignition	
CEO	Chief Executive Officer/ Corporate Executive Officer	
CFD	Computational Fluid Dynamics	
CH_3OH	Methanol	
CMVSS	Canadian Motor Vehicle Safety Standards	
CNG	Compressed Natural Gas	
CNY	Renminbi Yuan	
CO	Carbon Monoxide	
CO_2	Carbon Dioxide	
COE	cab-over-engine (US)	
COMAND	Cockpit Management and Data System	
CP	communications processor	
CPG	clock-pulse generator	
CPM	cylinder pressure management	
CRS	Common Rail System	
CV	Continuously variable	
	Centre Valve	
	Constant value	
CVT	Continously Variable Transmission	
DAB	Digital Audio Broadcasting	
dB	Decibel	
DBW	Drive by Wire	
DC	Direct Current	
DDM	Dimensional Data Measurement	
DEM	Deutsche Mark	
DFA	Design for Assembly	
DFD	Design for Disassembly	
DFM	Design for Manufacturability/ Design for Manufacture	
DFMEA	Design Failure Mode and Effects Analysis	
DIN	German Industrial Standard	
DPF	Diesel Particulate Filter	
DSA	Dynamic Safety	
DTB	data transfer bus	
DTL	diode transistor logic	
ECM	electronic clutch management	
	electrochemical machining	
	electronic control module	
	engine control module	
EDC	Electronic Diesel Control System	
EDS	Electronic Data Systems Corporation	
EEC	European Economic Community	
EHBS	Electrohydraulic Brake System	
ELV	End of Life vehicle	
e-Mail	Electronic Mail	
EPA	Environmental Protection Agency	

EPAS	Electrically operated power-assisted steering
EPDM	Ethylene Propylene Diene Monomer
EPS	electric power steering/system
	electrostatic powder spraying
EQ	equaliser
ESP	Electronic Stability Program
ETBE	Ethanol
ETRTO	The European Tyre and Rim Technical Organization
ETS	engine test stand
ETW	emission test weight
EU	European Union
EV	experimental/electric vehicle
	exhaust valve
EVA	electromagnetic valve actuator
EVOH	Ethylene Vinyl Alcohol
FAU	Federation Automobile d'Ukraine, Kiew
FCAI	Federal Chamber of Automotive Industries, Canberra
FEBIAC	Fédération Belge des Industries de l'Automobile et du Cycle, Brussels
	Association of the Belgian Motor Industry, Brussels
FEM	Finite Element Modelling
FEVER	Fuel Cell Electric Vehicle with Extended Range (Project)
FFÖ	Association of the Austrian Vehicle Industry, Vienna
FMEA	Failure Mode and Effects Analysis
FMVSS	Federal Motor Vehicle Safety Standards (USA)
GAIKINDO	Association of Indonesian Motor Vehicle Manufacturers, Jakarta Pusat
GAPC	Global Alternative Propulsion Center
GCI	gray cast iron
GDH	gas-discharge headlamp/headlight
GDI	gasoline-direct-injection-engine
GM	General Motors
GMTG	General Motors Truck Group
GPS	Global Positioning System
GRF	Government of Russia
H_2	Hydrogen
H_2O	Water
HC	Hydrocarbon
HDPE	High Density Polyethylene (e.g. BASF: Lupolen)
HID	High Intensity Discharge
HNO_3	Nitrate
H-Point	Hip point
HR foam	High Resilience foam
HS	Harmonised System
HSLA	High Strength Low Alloy
HV	high voltage
HVAC	Heating, Ventilation, Air-Conditioning
IAP	Industry Advisory Panel
IBRD	International Bank for Reconstruction and Development, Washington
IC	Internal Combustion
IGES	CAD dataexchange format
IMPACT	Integrated Manufacturing Precison Assembly Cellular Technology
IMSA	International Motor Sport Association
IP	Instrument Panel
IRF	International Road Federation, Geneva

ISO	International Standards Organization
JAMA	Japan Automobile Manufacturers Assocation, Tokyo
JMIF	Japan Motor Industrial Federation, Inc.
JPL	Jet Propulsion Laboratory
JV	Joint Venture
KAMA	Korea Automobile Manufacturers Association, Seoul
KHF	Krupp Hösch Federn
LCF	Lost Core Film
LD-SRIM	Low Density Structural Reaction Injection Moulding
LEDS	Light Emitting Diodes
LF	low frequency
LFI	Long Fibre Injection (process)
LG	low gear
	level gauge
LHD	left hand drive
LI	load index
MAD	manifold air density
MCI	malleable cast iron
MCM	multichip module
MCPS	megacycle per second
MCVT	Milner Continously Variable Transmission
MD	managing director
	medium duty
MDP	Magnetodynamic Positioning System
ME	mid-engine
MIA	Motor Industry Association, Wellington (New Zealand)
MIG	metal-inert-gas
MLT	Multi Layer Tube
Mn	Million
MOSFET	Metal Oxide Semiconductor Field Effect Transistors
MPM	Metal-Plastic-Metal
MPVS	Multi-Purpose Vehicles
MTBE	Methyl-t-Butyl Ether
MVMA	Motor Vehicles Manufacturer's Association, Toronto
MY	Model Year
N_2	Nitrogen
NAAMSA	National Assocation of Automobile Manufacturers of South Africa, Pretoria
Nd:YAG	Neodym (solid substance) share within a yttrium-aluminium-granat-crystal
NGV	Natural Gas Vehicle
NHTSA	National Highway Traffic Safety Administration
NO_x	Nitrogen Oxides
NVH	Noise, Vibration and Harshness
O_2	Oxygen
OCATD	Occupant Classification Anthropomorphic Test Device
OECD	Organization for Economic Cooperation and Development
OEM	Orignal Equipment Manufacturer
OHV	Overhead Valves
OICA	Organisation Internationale des Constructeurs d'Automobiles, Paris
OSD	Association of the Turkish Motor Industry, Istanbul
PASS	Philips Automatic Section Switch
PC	Personal Computer
PFMEA	Process Failure Mode and Effects Analysis
PLANET	Philips Lite Automotive NETwork

PP	Polypropylene
PSM	Stability Management System
PU	Polyurethane
PVDF	Polyvinyldeneflouride
QA	Quality Assurance
QS	Quality Standard
R&D	Research & Development
RAI	Association of the Dutch Motor Industry, Amsterdam
RAMSIS	CAD-3D ergonomic tool for development of vehicles and cockpits (Abk. für Rechnergestütztes Anthropologisch-Mathematisches System zur Insassen-Simulation)
RASIC	Responsible/Approve/Support/Inform/Consult
Ref.	Reference
Rev.	Revision
RHD	Right Hand Drive
SAE	U.S. Society of Automobile Engineers, Inc.
SAFEWORK	CAD-3D ergonomic tool
SAP	Automotive Industry Assocation, Prague
SAT (ACIS)	CAD-3D ergonomic tool
SBR	Styrene-Butadiene
SBW	Steer by Wire
SCooSR	Slovakian Statistical Office, Bratislava
SITC	Standard International Trade Classification
SMC	Sheet Moulding Composite
SMMT	The Society of Motor Vehicle Manufacturers and Traders Ltd., London
SQ	Supplier Quality
SUV	Sport Utility Van
t	Ton, Tonne (unit of mass)
TCS	Top Climate System
TDI	Turbo Direct Injection
TPES	Thermoplastic Elastomers
TTVMA	Taiwan Transportation Vehicle Manufacturer Association, Taipei
UG	Unigraphics
UHS	Ultra-High-Strength Steel
UIS	Unit Injector System
UK	United Kingdom
ULEV	Ultra Low Emission Vehicle
ULSAB	Ultra Light Steel Auto Body (Project)
ULSAC	Ultra Light Steel Auto Closures (Project)
USD	US Dollar
UV	Ultraviolet
VDA	Association of the German Automotive Industry
VDP	Vehicle Development Process
VE foam	Viscoelastic foam
VVT	Variable Valve Timing
VW	Volkswagen
WIFO	Central Statistical Office of Austria, Vienna
WTO	World Trade Organization
WTT	wind tunnel test
XPS	X-Ray Photoelectron Spectrometer
YS	yield strength/stress
ZAP	Automotive Industry Association of the Slovak Republic, Banovce
ZPDVJ	Association of the Motor Industry of Yugoslavia, Belgrado

1 The Motor Vehicle Market

1.1 Reliable sources

The German Association of the Motor Industry (VDA) is a wonderful association! All data is available in cooperation with a large number of organizations, official institutions and other associations of *motor industry*[1] around the world to prepare an annually statistical *compendium*[2]. In the following structurized figures of various countries of the world will be found. It is guaranted that *unreliable*[3] sources have been neglected, so the overall *comparability*[4] of the data on the structure can be trusted.

Commodities[5] are listed in a so-called Harmonised System of definitions and codifications (HS). There road tractors will be found, which are often used in Australia, as well as buses, passenger cars, trucks and special-purpose motor vehicles. German Standard DIN 70010 (which can be bought at Beuth Publisher GmbH, 10772 Berlin) contains naming and definitions of all kinds of vehicles (see Figure 1.1.2)

Figure 1.1.1: Passenger car Opel Astra (Source: Adam Opel AG, Rüsselsheim)

Passenger cars and buses are differentiated according to the cylinder capacities of their engines (e.g. 1.0 litre up to 2.5 litre engines) and their type of engines (e.g. diesel- or semi-diesel engines, *spark*[6]- or *compression*[7] -*ignition*[8] *internal combustion piston engines*[9]). *Trucks*[10] (goods vehicles) are *subheaded*[11] into *dumpers*[12] or into vehicles with different *gross vehicle mass*[13] (e.g. from sizes smaller than 5 tonnes to those not larger than 20 tonnes). Special vehicles can be crane lorries, *mobile drilling derricks*[14], *fire fighting vehicles*[15], *concrete-mixer lorries*[16], or others.

Type of vehicles	Definition (according to DIN 70 010)
Road vehicle	Power driven vehicles or towed vehicles
Power driven vehicles[17]	Power driven road vehicles (motor vehicles or power driven cycles); vehicles may also tow a *trailer*[18]
Motor vehicles[19]	Power driven vehicles with four or more wheels (passenger cars or commercial vehicles)
Power driven cycles[20]	Two-wheeled power-driven vehicles; can be combined with a sidecar.
Motor cycle[21]	Power driven cycle with rigid parts (e.g. fuel tank, engine) in the knee area
Scooter[22]	Power driven cycle without rigid parts in the knee area; the feet rest on the floor panel
Moped[23]	Power driven cycle that shows the usage characteristics of a bicycle, e.g. pedal crank
Passenger car[24]	A motor vehicle for carrying persons and their luggage or goods (max. 9 seats)
Saloon[25] (US: Sedan)	Passenger car with closed body, fixed roof, four or more seats in at least 2 rows, and a luggage compartment lid
Mini van	There are 6 or more seats in at least 3 rows
Convertible[26] (roadster, spider)	Passenger car with open body, and a roof with a closed (mounting rigid roof parts) or removed position (flexible roof).
Coupé	Passenger car with closed body and usually limited rear volume.
Station wagon[27]	Passenger car with rear shape which is designed to give a larger interior volume compared to the saloon (sedan)
Truck station wagon[28]	A passenger car derived from a commercial vehicle: 4 or more seats in at least 2 rows; the R point (see ISO 6549) of the driver's seat shall be at least 750mm above the surface, at curb mass.
Special passenger cars	Passenger cars with special equipment, e.g. emergency ambulance, motor vehicle for transportation of the disabled, motorhome
Commercial vehicles[29]	A motor vehicle which is dedicated to conveying persons or/and goods, like all kinds of buses: minibus, *urban bus*[30], *interurban coach*[31], *long distance coach*[32], *articulated bus*[33], *trolley bus*[34] and special bus; all kinds of *lorries*[35]: *general purpose goods vehicle*[36], special commercial vehicle; all kinds of *towing vehicles*[37]: *trailer towing vehicle* (draw-bar tractor)[38], *semi-trailer towing vehicle* (five-wheeled tractor)[39], *tractor*[40]
Special commercial vehicle	Tanker; fire-fighting vehicle; *breakdown lorry* (*wrecker truck*)[41]; passenger-car transportation vehicle; ambulance; funeral vehicle; refuse collection lorry (*garbage truck*)[42]; road cleaning vehicle; *salt, grit and sand spreader (gritting truck)*[43]; *sewer cleaning vehicle*[44]; lorry for special containers
Towed vehicle[45]	A non-power driven road vehicle, like *drawbar trailer*[46] (at least one steered axle), *rigid drawbar trailer*[47], *semi-trailer*[48], *goods trailer*[49], *bus trailer*[50], *caravan*[51] or special trailer (e.g. low bed trailer, air compressor trailer)
Combination of vehicles	e.g. car/trailer combination, road train (lorry and one or more drawbar trailers), *drawbar tractor combination*[52], *articulated vehicle*[53], *double road train*[54], *platform road train*[55]

Figure 1.1.2: Kinds of vehicles and their definition

Figure 1.1.3: Audi A6 3.0 DTI quattro, seen at Geneva Motor Show in spring 2004 (Source: Alexander Voos, Rüsselsheim)

Which manufacturers of passenger cars (including station wagons) do you know? In which countries do they have their headquarters and main production? Which companies produce *commercial vehicles*[56] (including trucks and buses)? The country mentioned means main production exists, but there is also some production in other countries.

Company	Car manufacturer	Commercial vehicle manufacturer	Country
Agrale		X	Brazil
Alfa Romeo (100 % Fiat Auto)	X		Italy
Ashok Leyland		X	India
Asia	X	X	South Korea
Astra		X	Italy
Audi	X		Germany
Autoalliance (Mazda)	X		USA
Autobianchi	X		Italy
Autoeuropa	X		Portugal
AvtoVAZ (41.5 % GM)	X		Russia
B.M.C. (Leyland, DAF, Volvo)		X	Turkey
Bajaj Tempo (including 3-wheeler Tempo)		X	India
Beijing Auto Group	X	X	China
Bertone	X		Italy
BMW (incl. Mini, Rolls Royce)	X		Germany
Bugatti (100 % VW)	X		Italy
CAMI (Canadian Automotive Manufacturing Inc.)	X	X	Canada
Changan Auto (JV with Suzuki)	X	X	China
Changhe Aircraft Industry		X	China
Chin Chun		X	Taiwan
China Motors (100 % Mitsubishi)	X	X	Taiwan

Continuation:

Company	Car manufacturer	Commercial vehicle manufacturer	Country
China NHDTG		X	China
Chinese Auto	X		Taiwan
Chrysler (100% JV DaimlerChrysler)	X	X	USA
Citroen	X		France
Dacia (100 % Renault)	X (including pick-ups)		Romania
Daewoo AVIA		X	Czech Republic
Daewoo Group (Daewoo & Ssangyong); GM Daewoo Auto & Technology Co. (44.6% GM)	X	X	South Korea
Daewoo/FSC Lublin	X	X	Poland
Daewoo/FSO	X		Poland
DAF		X	Netherlands
Daihatsu Motors (51.1% Toyota)	X	X	Japan
Daimler Chrysler	X	X	Germany
De Tomaso	X		Italy
Delta Motors (corresponding to Bedford, Isuzu & Suzuki)		X	South Africa
Delta Motors (corresponding to Opel)	X		South Africa
Diesel Nacional		X	Mexico
Dongfeng Motor		X	China
Dongfeng-Citroen Automobile	X		China
ERF		X	United Kingdom
Eurostar	X		Austria
FASA-Renault	X	X	Spain
FAW (China First Auto Group)	X	X	China
FAW-VW Automotive	X		China
Ferrari (100% Fiat Holding)	X		Italy
Fiat Auto: Alfa Romeo, Lancia (20% General Motors GM)	X		Italy
Fiat Group (Fiat & Iveco)		X	Italy
Ford Motor Company (Aston Martin, Ford, Jaguar, Land Rover, Lincoln, Mazda, Mercury, Volvo)	X	X	USA
Freightliner (belongs to DaimlerChrysler)		X	USA
FSO		X	Poland
Fuji Heavy Industry (Subaru; 4.1% Nissan Motors; 20% GM)	X	X	Japan
GAZ	X	X	Russia

Continuation:

Company	Car manufacturer	Commercial vehicle manufacturer	Country
General Motors GM (20% Fiat): Adam Opel AG, Buick, Cadillac, Chevrolet, GMC, Holdens, Hummer, Oldsmobile, Pontiac-Saab, Saturn, Vauxhall	X	X	USA
Guangzhou (JV with Peugeot/Honda)	X		China
Guangzhou Auto		X	China
Guizhou Aviation (JV with Subaru)	X		China
Harbin Hafei		X	China
Hindustan Motors	X		India
Hino Motors (20% Toyota)		X	Japan
Holden	X	X	Australia
Honda Motor (5.7% Mitsubishi Trust)	X	X	Japan
Hyundai Group = Hyundai & Kia (5% Mitsubishi)	X	X	South Korea
IBC	X		United Kingdom
Ind Auto	X		India
Isuzu Motors (12% General Motors)	X		Japan
IVECO Magirus		X	Germany
IVECO-Pegaso		X	Spain
IzhMash-Auto		X	Russia
Jaguar (100% Ford)	X		United Kingdom
Jiangling Motor		X	China
Jinbei GM Automative Company Ltd. (50% GM)	X		China
KamAZ	X	X	Russia
Kenworth		X	Canada
Kia	X		Korea
KrAZ		X	Ukraine
Kuozui Hua Tung (Toyota)	X	X	Taiwan
Lada	X		Russia
Lamborghini (100% VW/Audi)	X		Italy
Lancia (100% Fiat Auto)	X		Italy
LDV		X	United Kingdom
Leyland Trucks		X	United Kingdom
Lio Ho (Ford/Mazda)	X	X	Taiwan
Liuzhou-Wuling Auto		X	China
Lotus	X		United Kingdom
Mack		X	USA
Mahindra	X		India
MAN		X	Germany
Maruti Udyog (Suzuki Maruti)	X		India

Continuation:

Company	Car manufacturer	Commercial vehicle manufacturer	Country
Maserati (50% Ferrari, 50% Fiat)	X		Italy
Mazda Motor (33.3% Ford)	X	X	Japan
Mercedes		X	Germany
Mitsubishi Motors MMC (23.8% Mitsubishi Heavy, 33.4% DaimlerChrysler)	X		Japan
Mitsubishi Heavy (19.9% Volvo)		X	Indonesia, Japan
Morgan	X		United Kingdom
Moskvich	X		Russia
Multicar		X	Germany
Navistar		X	Mexico, USA
Nissan Motor (36.8% Renault)	X	X	Japan
Nissan Diesel		X	Japan
Nissan-Motor Iberica		X	Spain
NUMMI (GM & Toyota)	X		USA
NUMMI (Toyota)		X	USA
ÖAF-Gräf & Stift		X	Austria
Opel (100% GM)	X		Germany
Otosan (Ford)	X		Turkey
Otosan (Ford, IVECO-Ford)		X	Turkey
Otoyol (IVECO-Ford)		X	Turkey
Oyak-Renault	X		Turkey
PanAsia Technical Automotive Center Co. Ltd. (50% GM)	X		China
Perodua		X	Malaysia
Peugeot	X		France
Piaggio		X	Italy
Porsche	X		Germany
Premier Auto	X		India
Prince Motor	X		Taiwan
PSA (JV Citroen & Peugeot)	X	X	France
Qingling Motor		X	China
Renault	X	X	France
Revoz (Renault)	X		Slovenia
Rolls Royce (100% BMW)	X		United Kingdom
Roman		X	Romania
Rover Group	X	X	United Kingdom
Saab-Automobile (100% GM)	X		Sweden
Saab-Valmet	X		Finland
Samsung	X		South Korea
Samsung Heavy		X	South Korea
San Yang (Honda)	X		Taiwan
Santana-Motor		X	Spain
Scania (34% VW)		X	Sweden

Continuation:

Company	Car manufacturer	Commercial vehicle manufacturer	Country
Seat	X		Spain
Seat/VW	X	X	Spain
SeAz	X		Russia
Sevel (JV Fiat & PSA)		X	France
SFT (Steyr-Daimler-Puch-Fahrzeugtechnik AG & Co KG)	X	X	Austria
Shanghai VW Automotive	X		China
SIA	X		USA
SIA (Subaru/Isuzu)		X	USA
Sisu		X	Finland
Skoda Auto (100% VW)	X	X	Czech Republic
Skoda/VW Poznan	X		Poland
Smart	X		France
SNF (Steyr Nutzfahrzeuge AG)		X	Austria
Sangyong	X		Korea
Subaru (4.1-20% GM; rest of shares for Fuji Heavy)	X		Japan
Suzuki Motor (9.9% General Motors)	X	X	Japan
Ta Ching (Subaru)	X		Taiwan
Taiwan Isuzu		X	Taiwan
Tatra		X	Czech Republic
TELCO	X	X	India
Temsa (Mitsubishi)		X	Turkey
Tianjin Auto Industry (JV with Daihatsu)	X	X	China
Tofas (Fiat)	X		Turkey
Toyota Motor (5.2% Toyota Automatic)	X	X	Japan
TVR	X		United Kingdom
UAZ	X	X	Russia
UralAZ		X	Russia
Vauxhall	X		United Kingdom
Vauxhall/Bedford		X	United Kingdom
VAZ (Lada)	X		Russia
Volkswagen	X	X	Germany
Volvo (100% Ford)	X	X	Sweden
Western-Star		X	Canada
Yuejin Auto		X	China
Yulon (Nissan)	X		Taiwan
Zastava	X	X	Serbia/Montenegro
ZIL		X	Russia

Figure 1.1.4: Car and commercial vehicle manufacturers in the world (Source: VDI, JAMA)

Saab-Valmet in Finland *assembles*[58] more than 30,000 passenger cars for Saab, Porsche and EuroSamara. In Italy, neither Bertone (since 1995), Bugatti (since 1996), nor Autobianchi (since 1997) have produced any vehicle with their own *brand name*[59]. Daihatsu has belonged to the Toyota Group since 1998.

It is also worth noting *Joint Ventures*[60] (e.g. DaimlerChrylser as JV between Mercedes and Chrysler, PSA as JV of Citroen and Peugeot, Sevel as JV of Fiat & PSA and of Fiat & Lancia, Autoeuropa as JV between Volkswagen and Ford, CAMI as JV of GM and Suzuki, IBC as JV of GM and Isuzu, NUMMI as JV of GM and Toyota, SIA as JV of Subaru and Isuzu, FAW-VW Automotive as JV of Volkswagen, Audi and FAW, Shanghai VW Automotive as JV of SAIC Shanghai Automotive Industry Corp. and Volkswagen). In China, for instance, most manufacturers have JV with local companies. In Hungary, Subaru and Suzuki as JV are the car manufacturers which produce the most cars together (88,446 in 2003).

[1] Kraftfahrzeugindustrie	[2] Zusammenfassung, Handbuch	[3] (of information) nicht glaubwürdig.
[4] Vergleichbarkeit	[5] Waren, Artikel, Gebrauchsgüter	[6] Funke
[7] Verdichtung	[8] Zündung	[9] Hubkolbenmotor mit Innenverbrennung (Abk. ICE/IC)
[10] Lastkraftwagen, Lkw (US); GB: lorry, motor lorry	[11] subheading = Untertitel	[12] Muldenkipper (Schwerst-Lkw)
[13] Zulässiges Gesamtgewicht ZGG	[14] fahrbare Bohrtürme	[15] Feuerwehr-, Lösch-Fahrzeug
[16] Betonmischer-Lkw, Transportbetonmischer	[17] Kraftfahrzeug	[18] Anhänger
[19] Kraftwagen	[20] Kraftrad	[21] Motorrad
[22] Motorroller	[23] Farhrrad mit Hilfsmotor	[24] Personenkraftwagen
[25] Limousine	[26] Kabriolett	[27] Pkw-Kombi, Kombi
[28] Nutzkraftwagen-Kombi (Nkw-Kombi)	[29] Nutzkraftwagen (Nkw)	[30] Linienbus
[31] Überlandlinienbus	[32] Reisebus	[33] Gelenkbus
[34] Oberleitungsbus (O-Bus)	[35] US: trucks: Lastkraftwagen (LKW)	[36] Vielzwecklastkraftwagen
[37] Zugmaschine	[38] Anhänger-Zugmaschine	[39] Sattelzugmaschine
[40] Traktor	[41] Abschleppfahrzeug	[42] Müllwagen
[43] Streu-Lastwagen	[44] Kanalreinigungsfahrzeug	[45] Anhängefahrzeug
[46] Gelenk-Deichselanhänger	[47] Starr-Deichselanhänger	[48] Sattelanhänger
[49] Lastanhänger	[50] Busanhänger	[51] Caravan
[52] Zugmaschinenzug	[53] Sattelkraftfahrzeug	[54] Sattelzug
[55] Brückenzug	[56] Nutzfahrzeuge	[58] baut zusammen
[59] Markenname, Markenbezeichnung	[60] Gemeinschaftsunternehmen	

Figure 1.1.5: Golf GTI 2004 (Source: Volkswagen AG, Wolfsburg)

1.2 Import and export trade

Despite trade with passenger cars, road tractors, buses, trucks and special vehicles, commodities could also be assemblies of a vehicle, e.g.
- *chassis*[1] fitted with *engines*[2] for *tractors*[3] and motor vehicles
- *bodies*[4] for passenger cars and other motor vehicles
- *truck trailers*[5] and semi-trailers for transport of goods
- *caravans*[6] for housing or camping
- tanker trailers
- parts and *accessories*[7] and their assortments

Figure 1.2.1: Opel Movano (Source: Adam Opel AG, Rüsselsheim)

The countries which export most of the road tractors, passenger cars, buses, trucks, special purpose vehicles, chassis, bodies, truck trailers, semi-trailers, parts and accessories and other products are:

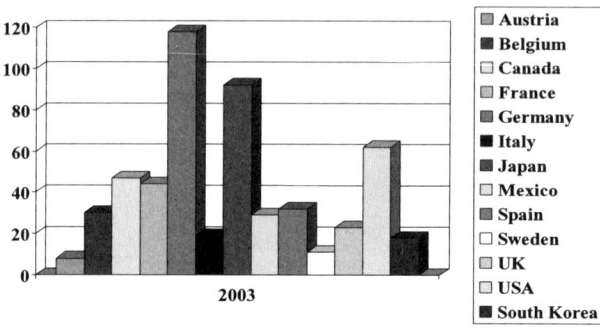

Figure 1.2.2: Export 2003 (Source: VDA)

The countries which import most of the road tractors, passenger cars, buses, trucks, special purpose vehicles, chassis, bodies, truck trailers, semi-trailers, parts and accessories and other products are:

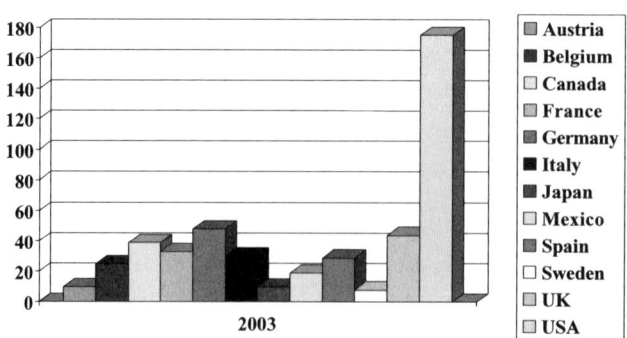

Figure 1.2.3: Import 2003 (Source: VDA)

[1] Fahrwerk	[2] Motoren	[3] Traktoren
[4] Karosserien	[5] LKW-Anhänger	[6] Wohnwagen
[7] Zubehör		

Figure 1.2.4: Audi A4 Cabriolet 2.0 (Source: Audi AG, Ingolstadt)

1.3 The German market

What kind of German and foreign types of cars do we find in Germany? Which companies do these cars belong to?

Figure 1.3.1: Opel Tigra Twin-Top (Source: Adam Opel AG, Rüsselsheim)

The most important German brand names on the road (for more information see appropriate internet address):

Audi (audi.de)	80, 100, A2, A3, A4, A6, A8, Cabriolet, Quattro, Roadster, RS4, RS6, S3, S4, S6, S8, TT
Bayerische Motoren Werke (bmw.de, mini.de)	1 Series (116i, 118d, 120i, 120d), 316-328; 330xi, M3; 518-540; M5; 6 series Coupe, 728-750; 760i, 730i, 850, Mini; X3, X5 ("Sport Active Vehicle"), Z1, Z3, Z4, Z8

Ford (ford.de)	Courier; Escort; Fiesta; Focus; Galaxy; Ka; Maverick; Mondeo; Puma; Scorpio; Streetka, Sierra, Sportka, Transit; Tourneo
Mercedes-Benz (mercedes.de; smart.de)	A140-170; Actros (truck), CLK 200-300; C180-280, C30, C36 AMG; CL600, E190-500; E36 AMG; E400 CDI, E50 AMG; G230-350; Maybach, MB100; S280-600; ML 320, ML350, S350 4matic, SL 280-600; SLA, SLK 200-230; SLR, Smart, Smart Roadster, Smart forfour, Sprinter 208-414; V series, Vario (light truck), Vito
Opel (opel.com)	Agila, Ascona, Astra; Calibra; Combo; Corsa; Frontera; Manta, Meriva, Monterey; Movano, Omega; Opel Coupe, Opel GT, Record, Senator, Signum, Sintra; Speedster, Tigra; Tigra Twin Top, Vectra, Vivaro Zafira
Porsche (porsche.com)	356, 911 series, 944 Targa, 956, 993, Boxster series, GT series, Carrera GT, Turbo Cabrio, Cayenne
Volkswagen (volkswagen. de)	Beetle, Bora, Caddy; Caravelle; Golf II, III, IV, V, Käfer, LT; Lupo; Multivan; Passat; Phaeton, Polo; Sharan; Transporter; Touareg, Touran, Vento

Figure 1.3.2: MB A-Class (Source: DaimlerChrysler)

Figure 1.3.3: Opel Signum (Source: Adam Opel AG, Rüsselsheim)

The most important French brand names on German roads are:

Citroen (citroen.de)	Cars: 2CV; AX; Berlingo; C2, C3, C3 Pluriel, C4, C5, C8, Evasion; Jumpy; Saxo; Xantia; Xsara (u. a. Picasso); XM; ZM Light trucks: Berlingo, Jumper, Jumpy
Peugeot (peugeot.de)	Cars: 106; 205; 206; 306; 307; 309; 405; 406; 407; 605; 607; 806 Light trucks: Boxter; Expert; Partner
Renault (renault.de)	Clio; Espace; F40 Rapid; Kangoo; Koleos; Laguna; Megane, Scenic (Midi van); R5; R19; Safrane; Trafic; Twingo, Modus, Vel Satis

The most important British brand names on German roads are:

Aston Martin (astonmartin.com)	DB series (Coupe, Heritage, Volante); V8 series (Coupe, Heritage, Le Mans, Vantage, Volante), Vanquish
Bentley (bentleymotors.com)	Arnage (Red Label); Azure; Continental R; Continental RC, Continental T, Continental GT, Mulliner Bentleys
Jaguar (jaguar.de)	EV12 Coupe; SJR; Sovereign; S-Typ V6; XK8; XJ8, XJ Type, X Type
Landrover (landrover.de)	Freelander
Lotus (webpti.com)	340R, Elise, Emme Lotus 422T, Esprit Sport 350, Esprit GT3, Esprit V8, GT1, M250, Omega
Rolls Royce (rolls-royce.co.uk)	Corniche; Park Ward; Silver Seraph, Saloon
Rover (mgrover.de)	25; 45; 75; Austin; MG; MGZR, MGZT 260/385, MGSV, Defendu

The most important Italian brand names on German roads are:

Bugatti (bugatti-cars.de)	EB110, EB118, Type 10 (MY1910)-251(MY1955), Veyron
Fiat (fiat.de; lancia.de)	Alfa Romeo (145, 146; 147, 147GTA/GTV/Spider, Alfa 155; 156, 164, 166, Alfa Spider, Sportwagon, Sprint), GTV; Berlinetta; Borchetta; Bravo, Brava; Cinquecento; Coupe; Ducato; Lancia (Cosmopolitan, Dedra, Delta, Elefantino, Kappa, KSW, Lybra, SW, Thesis, Y10, Zeta), Stilo Multiwagon, Y-Fire; Marea; Multipla; Multipla Hybrid Power, Panda; Punto; Tempra; Tipo; Ulysse; UNO; Scudo; Lancia Zeta
Ferrari (ferrari-deutschland.de)	Enzo (F60), F355 Spider, , F360, F40, F50; Modena
Iveco	Campcar; Daily, Dormobile; Turb Daily (transporter)
Maserati	3200GT; Barchetta; Quattroporte Evoluzione; Shamal
Lamborghini (lamborghini.de)	Baby Diablo; Countach; Diablo, L140 Coupé, Gallardo, Murciélago

Swedish brand names on German roads are:

Volvo (volvocars.de)	440; 460; 480; 745; 850; 944, 945, 964; LS, S40, S60, S80 (sedan), V40, V50; V70 (wagon), XC90
Saab (saab.de)	9-3 Aero/Cabrio, 9-5; 900, 900 Coupe, 900 Convertible; 9000 CS/CSE/CD/CDE/Aero/Griffin

Spanish brand names on German roads are:

Seat (seat.de)	Alhambra; Arosa; Cordoba; Ibiza, Ibiza Cupra, Inca; Leon; Marbella; Salsa; Toledo, Altea

The most important Japanese brand names on German roads are:

Daihatsu (daihatsu.de)	Applause; Charade; Cuore; Feroza; Granmove; Move; Terios
Subaru (subaru.de)	E12; Forester; Impreza; KAD/Justy; Legacy; Legacy Outback
Honda (honda.de)	Accord; Acura, Civic, CRX, CR-V; HR-V; Integra; Insight (Hybrid); Legend; Logo; NSX; Prelude; Shuttle (Van); S2000; Type R; Type R
Isuzu	Trooper (off-road vehicle)
Mazda (mazda.de)	121; 323; 626; Demio; Mazda 2, Mazda 3, Mazda 5, Mazda 6, MPV; MX-3; MX-5; Premacy (van); RX-6, RX-7, RX-8, Xedos 6; Xedos 9; Tribute

Mitsubishi (mitsubishi-motors.de)	Airtrack, Carisma; Colt, Lancer; Lancer Evo series, L200 Magnum; Eclipse; Galant; L300; L400, Space Gear; Pajero; Sigma; Space Runner; Space Wagon; Z car
Nissan (nissan.de)	200 SX, 200 ZX; 350 Z, Almera, Altima, Bluebird; B13, Infinity, Maxima QX; Micra; Patrol; Prairie; Primera; Serena, Vanette; Sunny; S13; S14; Terrano; Topic; Urvan, X-Trail
Suzuki (suzuki-auto.de)	Alto; Baleno; Cabrio; Grand Vitara, Ignis Sport, Swift; Vitara, X-90; Wagon R; Samurai
Toyota (toyota.de)	Avensis, Camry; Carina; Celica; Corolla; Hiace; Highlander; Jaris Cabrio; Landcruiser; Lexus (RX300, LS430); Paseo; Picnic; Previa (van); Prius, RAV4 (off-road vehicle); 4 Runner; Starlet, Yaris Verso

The most important South Korean brand names on German roads are:

Asia Motor	Rocsta Softtop (off-road vehicle)
Daewoo (daewoo-auto.de)	Espero; Evanda, Lanos; Kalos, Leganza; Matiz, Nexia; Nubira
Hyundai (hyundai.de)	Elantra, Getz, Lantra; Pony, Accent; S-Coupe; Sonata, Ascente, Confiro, XG 35
KIA Motor (kia.de)	Clarus, Credos; Magentis, Minicar, Opirus, Pride; Sephia; Shuma, Sportage, Sorento
Ssangyong	Korando; Musso (both off-road vehicles)

The most important American brand names on German roads are:

Chrysler (chrysler.de)	Cars: Cirrus; Concorde; Crossfire Coupé/Cabrio, 300M; LHS; Plymouth (Breeze; Prowler), Dodge (Intepid; Neon, Stratus; Viper; Sebring), PT Cruiser Light trucks: Town & Country, Plymouth Voyager, Dodge (Caravan, Dakota, Durango, Ram); Jeep (Cherokee series, Wrangler series, Grand Cherokee); Grand Voyager
General Motors (gm.com)	Cars: Buick (Century, Regal, Riviera, Park Avenue Ultra, Park Avenue, Roadmaster; Roadmaster Estate Wagon, Le Sabre, Skylark); Cadillac (CTS, Eldorado, Seville, DeVille, Fleedwood, Opera); Chevrolet (Cavalier, Camaro, Impala SS, Caprice Classic, Corsica, Beretta, Malibu, Monte Carlo, Corvette, Prizm); Oldsmobile (Achieva, Alero, Aurora, Cutlass Subreme, LSS, Intrique, Eighty Eight, Ninety Eight, Ciera); Pontiac (Bonneville, Firebird, Grand Am, Grand Prix, Montana, Sunfire,); Geo (Prizm, Metro); Saturn (SL, SL1, SL2, SC1, SC2, SW1, SW2) Light trucks/ SUVs: Cadillac (Escalade); Chevrolet (Astro, Beauville, Lumina, C/K Regular/Extended-Cab Pickups, S-Series Pickup, Tahoe, Venture, Medium, P-model, Siverado, S10, Blazer, Express, Suburban); Geo (Tracker); Hummer, Hummer H2; Oldsmobile (Bravada, Silhouette); Pontiac (Montana, Trans Sport); GMC (Yukon, Medium, P-model, Sonoma, Jimmy, Safari, Suburban, Savana, Rally/Vandura)
Ford Motor Company (fordvehicles. com; ford.de)	Cars: Contour; Crown Victoria; Escort; Focus; Grand Marquis; Lincoln; Mercury; Mustang; Mystique; Sable; Taurus; Tracer; Windstar; ZX2 Light trucks/ SUVs: Escape, Explorer, Expedition, Excursion, Econoline, Super Duty; F series, Ranger; Landrover (Defender)

Finally, the Eastern European brand names on German roads are:

AZNP-Skoda (skoda.de)	Fabia, Favorit, Forman, Felicia, Octavia, Superb
VAZ Lada	Nova, 2107, Samara, Forma, Lada, Aleko

Figure 1.3.4: Brand names on German Roads (Source: VDA 2004)

Figure 1.3.5: Mc Laren BMW on 24-hour race in Le Mans (Source: Continental Teves, Frankfurt)

What happens in Germany?

At the two three Frankfurt Auto Shows it was possible to see a large glass tower containing 16 brightly coloured "Smart" cars the size of an electric golf cart.

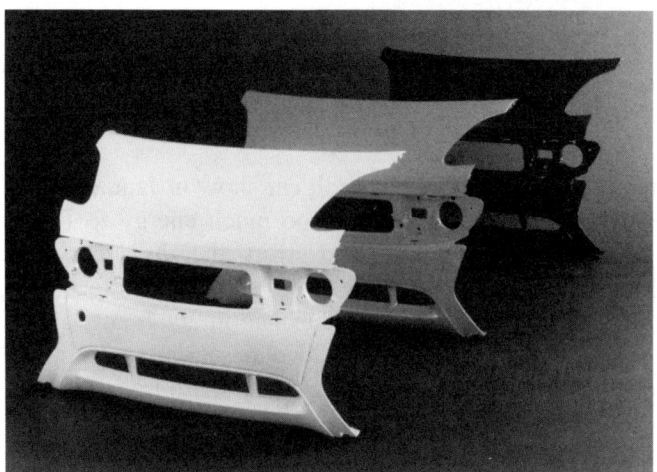

Figure 1.3.6: Brightly coloured "Smart" frontends (Source: Krauss Maffei, München)

This car is produced in Eastern France by DaimlerChrysler from a concept developed by the Swiss SMH company. DaimlerChrylser has already introduced its compact A-series car. Both cars had their problems just after the start of production by a so called "elk test".

Opel, which celebrated its 100 year anniversary in 1999, was founded by Adam Opel in 1862 in Rüsselsheim, at first produced sewing machines and bicycles. The production of the 1.5-litre, 3.5hp Opel Patent-Motorwagen System

Lutzmann begun in 1899. One year after the introduction of a new small all-steel bodied "Laubfrosch" in 1924, Opel became Germany's largest carmaker with a 37.5 percent market share. In March 1929 General Motors acquired 80% percent of Opel's shares by paying only $26 million, and Opel was sold completely in 1931. Over the years, Opel has developed into a fully-fledged German carmaker with a US background. A constant battle with Volkswagen for the position of No.1 selling brand in Europe is proof of the brand's competitiveness.

In order to retain its leading position, Volkswagen emphasizes technological *prowess*[1] in safety, economy, resistance to theft, performance and comfort.

Figure 1.3.7: New Beetle 1.8T (Source: Volkswagen AG, Wolfsburg)

BMW's lack of a cutting-edge model at the Detroit car show in January 2000 belongs to the past. The German carmaker devoted too much energy to Rover and its troubled British operation into a turnaround effort, thereby *hampered*[2] development of its own luxury sedans. Now, BMW is back on the market. Press the start button in a car of the new BMW 1 Series, launched in 2004, engage the transmission and feel the pure strength of the engine. Two diesel variants and one petrol model provide power for driving pleasure. Amazingly sharp transmissions and *unique*[3] rear-wheel drive see to it that this energy is transformed into forward motion with absolute efficiency. Whether you decide for the high-*torque*[4] 120i with Valvetronic or a BMW 118d diesel with common-rail technology, only one thing will interest you behind the wheel: when does it start?

In the following chart important data can be seen relating to the production of motor vehicles (figures in 1000 units), devided into passenger cars, trucks and buses. From 1998 until 2003, production of passenger cars reached more than 5 million units.

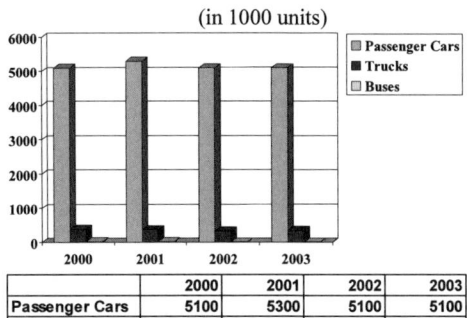

Germany
Production of Motor Vehicles
(in 1000 units)

Figure 1.3.8: Production of Motor Vehicles (Source VDA)

	2000	2001	2002	2003
Passenger Cars	5100	5300	5100	5100
Trucks	380	370	330	350
Buses	14	12	10	10

Passenger Cars
(in 1000 units)

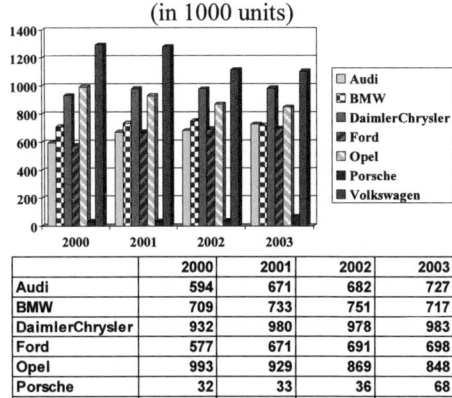

Figure 1.3.9: Production of passenger cars (Source VDA)

	2000	2001	2002	2003
Audi	594	671	682	727
BMW	709	733	751	717
DaimlerChrysler	932	980	978	983
Ford	577	671	691	698
Opel	993	929	869	848
Porsche	32	33	36	68
Volkswagen	1294	1283	1116	1104

Buses
(in 1000 units)

Figure 1.3.10: Production of buses (Source VDA)

	2000	2001	2002	2003
EvoBus	6,14	5,41	4,39	5,15
MAN	5,03	4,61	3,84	4,26
Neoplan	2	1,77	1,52	1,02

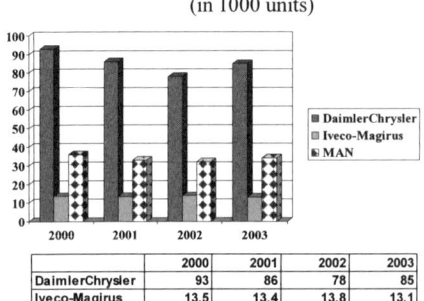

Trucks (more than 6t)
(in 1000 units)

Figure 1.3.11: Production of trucks (Source VDA)

	2000	2001	2002	2003
DaimlerChrysler	93	86	78	85
Iveco-Magirus	13,5	13,4	13,8	13,1
MAN	36	33	32	34

Figure 1.3.12: MB M-Class (Source: Webasto AG, Stockdorf)

[1] Tüchtigkeit	[2] verhindern	[3] einzigartig einmalig
[4] Drehmoment		

1.4 The European market

The auto industry accounts for about 3 percent of western Europe's economic output and 7.5 percent of its manufacturing base. So *buoyant*[1] car sales can be important economic drivers. Registrations also reflect consumer confidence in a broader European economy now battling joblessness and tepid growth.

Europe-built luxury brands are most affected by the weak dollar. The US is often their largest market. European automakers and suppliers are shifting production and are *hedging*[2] currencies *to cope with*[3] the US dollar's sharp decline against the euro. Volkswagen, Mercedes-Benz and BMW – already building vehicles in North America – are expanding capacity or considering it.

More selling days, generous buyer incentives and fresh models helped new car registrations in western Europe. For example, November 2004 had two more selling days in some countries and one extra day in major markets Germany,

France, Spain and Italy. Another powerful showing by German luxury automaker BMW and strong gains by Korean carmakers Hyundai and Kia led the rally, while Italy's hard-pressed Fiat had a *dismal*[4] month again. Brussels-based carmakers' group ACEA said November registrations of 1.14 million units brought the total number of cars sold in the first 11 months to just under 13.5 million - a rise of 1.7 percent from the same period of 2003. The ACEA data include registrations in the 15 legacy EU members plus Norway, Switzerland and Iceland.

Registrations in **Germany** rose 11.1 percent thanks to new models and discount wars as manufacturers offered margin-eroding incentives to boost sales in Europe's biggest car market by far. BMW, *basking*[5] in the biggest model offensive in its history, saw registrations gain 18.3 percent to 57,576 cars, helped by its new 1-series premium compact and the urban-chic Mini brand. Volkswagen, Europe's biggest carmaker, also profited from the boom on its German home market. Registrations rose 12.5 percent to 219,652 cars *amid*[6] strong VW and Audi brand sales. Its market share rose to 19.2 percent from 18.7 percent. *Rejuvenated*[7] A-class and C-class models helped DaimlerChrysler registrations swell 12 percent.

Figure 1.4.1: The new Passat (Source: Volkswagen AG)

In Europe's largest independent comparison test, organized by the magazine "Firmenauto", 120 fleet managers from various industries, tested and evaluated compact and mid-size models with regard to handling characteristics, functionality, comfort, design and price. In the end in the lowest price category (up to 20,000 euro) the new Golf achieved first place and is the "Company Car of the Year 2004". The Škoda Superb was rated the best import vehicle in the category up to 40,000 euro, while the Audi A6 won the overall rating. Volkswagen attaches great importance to fleet sales, which make up approximately one third of its new car sales.

After a record result in 2002, **French** automakers lost market share in western Europe in 2004. CCFA, the French carmakers association, blamed a weak home market and a pause in new model launches. French manufacturers PSA Peugeot

Citroen and Renault both had *gains*[8] but *trailed*[9] market growth. PSA, Europe's second-biggest carmaker, boosted registrations 6.9 percent but saw its market share ease to 13.3 percent. Faced with tough comparisons, Renault registrations rose 7.1 percent in November 2004, bumping its market share down to 11.3 percent.

In **Spain,** 1.7 million cars were registered in 2003, a slight increase since 1999 (1.4 million). The market leader is Renault, followed by Opel and VW's *subsidiary*[10] Seat.

Japanese manufacturer Honda *cranked out*[11] 30 percent growth, and struggling Mitsubishi saw registrations rise 31.5 percent, but Mazda registrations fell 10 percent and Nissan's weak *showing*[12] continued with a 6.8-percent drop. Toyota's market share dipped fractionally to 4.8 percent as registrations rose 7.6 percent, but its year-to-date share edged up to 5 percent from 4.8 percent. The Toyota Prius hybrid car has been voted the European Car of the Year for 2005. The Prius is the world's first mass produced hybrid vehicle and is propelled by the combination of an electric motor and a petrol engine. There were seven candidates for the award. Other *contestants*[13] for the award included the BMW 1-Series, Renault Modus, Citroen C4, Ford Focus, Opel Astra and Peugeot 407.

Korean carmakers continued to surf a wave of demand from *wary*[14] customers seeking fuel-efficient, well-built cars at a competitive price. Kia boasted boosting sales 128.3 percent to just over 16,000 units and doubling its market share to 1.4 percent. Registration growth for Kia's parent Hyundai accelerated to 34.1 percent after slowing in October 2004 to 4.2 percent. It grabbed 2.0 percent of the European market.

Figure 1.4.2: Opel Astra (Source: Adam Opel AG, Rüsselsheim)

General Motors' registrations advanced 12.3 percent as more than 100,000 Opel/Vauxhall models were signed up, while Ford registrations rose only 8.9 percent. Opel sold more than 1.4 Million cars in Western and Central Europe. Opel stays in the fast lane: Deutsche Telekom ordered 259 Opel Astra CNG (Compressed Natural Gas) in 2004 to enhance its natural-gas-powered fleet.

The cars will be used in customer service across Germany. In the German motoring magazine "Auto Bild" the Opel Astra 1.6 topped a comparison test against nine competitors, and the Opel Astra 1.9 CDTI station wagon wins a comparison test against rivals Renault Mégane Grandtour 1.9 dCi and Toyota Corolla Combi 2.0 D-40. All manufacturers are rated in seven categories: an inquiry among 25,000 car drivers, recalls, result of seven million reports from the German Technical Inspection Agency (TÜV), "Auto Bild" endurance tests, complaints readers reported to the magazine, dealership and service test and warranty conditions. The agile handling, in combination with the precise steering and the optional IDS Plus chassis, gave an impressive performance. In addition, the magazine praised the good breaks and the low interior noise level. The magazine also praised the overall quality appearance of the interior and the firm and well-contoured seats. It also emphasized the spacious luggage compartment and the comprehensive safety equipment. Thanks to the fair price, the two-year warranty, the ecological engine and the low insurance classification, the Astra was able to win crucial points against the Octavia and Golf in this category.

Figure 1.4.2: Interior of the Opel Zafira Snowtrekker (Source: Adam Opel AG, Rüsselsheim)

Also at "Auto Bild" quality survey: Opel is best European car manufacturer. Opel ranked on seventh place and was thus the best European car manufacturer. The "Auto Bild Quality Report" is conducted annually and is considered to be the most comprehensive study on the subject. It rates the long term quality, reliability and customer satisfaction of the 20 most important car brands in Germany. Opel achieved good results in the area of TÜV reports and reader complaints, and an excellent one in the endurance test.

Opel and General Motors exercised their options to buy the remaining 50% of Saab Automobile AB from the Swedish holding company Investor AB and took full control of the Swedish car maker in February 2000. They seek to expand in the sector of BMW and Mercedes Benz and improve the line of luxury cars. Saab sold 128,000 vehicles in 1999 and 74,400 in 2003. Future Saab cars are going to be built on Opel platforms. Opel staff should get the benefit of security technology and knowhow of *turbocharging*[15].

In **Portugal**, the Opel Astra has been elected "Car Of The Year" by the readers of "Auto Foco", one of the country's leading motoring magazines and a sister publication of the German magazine "Auto Bild". Auto Bild's "Auto1" is one of the most prestigious automotive awards in Europe, as it sums up the votes of readers, editors, racing drivers and engineers from a total of 21 European countries.

The trend of car manufacturers is towards leisure time. For example, the Zafira "Snowtrekker" with four-wheel drive, integrated roofbox and panorama roof (see Figure 1.4.2).

Below five countries can be seen which produce the most vehicles in Europe. Figures are available for 2003 in millions (except figures in italics).

Variable	Germany	France	Italy	Spain	United Kingdom
Production of passenger cars	5.14	3.22	1.32	2.40	1.66
Production of commercial vehicles (including buses and trucks; more than 6 tons)	0.16	0.05	0.04	0.06	0.02
Export of passenger cars, buses and trucks (in Europe only)	2.78	3.19	0.64	2.34	0.91
Export of motor vehicles (total world)	3.67	2.70	0.70	2.50	1.25
Passenger cars in use	45.0	29.6	34.3	19.3	29.0
A cars average annual distance travelled (km per year)	0.011	0.014	0.010	0.012	0.017
Road network (motorways, main or national roads, regional roads and others) in km (without municipal roads)	0.23	0.89	0.48	0.68	0.37
Cars per 1,000 inh.	546	495	597	461	486
Density of road network (km/sq.km)	1.81	1.62	1.59	0.31	1.62
Average consumption of petrol per car (tons per year)	0.6	0.4	0.4	0.4	0.7

Figure 1.4.3: Comparison Europe (Source VDA)

[1] steigend, lebhaft	[2] Vorrat halten	[3] fertig werden mit
[4] trübe, trist	[5] sich sonnen	[6] mitten unter; mitten
[7] verjüngen	[8] Gewinn	[9] im Rückstand sein, nachhinken
[10] Tochterunternehmen	[11] ankurbeln	[12] Vorstellung
[13] Bewerber, Mitbewerber	[14] vorsichtig	[15] Turboantrieb

1.4.1 Trading and cheats in the car market?

Only few people know the cost of a BMW convertible in Osaka, Frankfurt and in Sheerness, on the English south coast. The author was told, "There is a ridiculous difference of up to £10,000 ($15,900) between the continental and Japanese prices and what you pay for some models in the UK."

Since 1985, carmakers in the EU have been able to sell cars and set prices through *captive*[1] distributors, effectively enabling them to regulate market prices in different countries.

The UK's first public *inquiry*[2] (a US-style public hearing), started in 1999, was boycotted by car makers into *alleged*[3] price-fixing and manipulation of the car market. They were unwilling to answer questions about their pricing policy and avoided being accused of an *offence*[4] in public. This was an *insult*[5] to the comission. The Consumers' Association is also seeking further relaxation of the UK's grey import rules, which *limit*[6] *import quotas*[7] for independent dealers buying non-EU cars.

The Competition Commission complainted "that *distortions*[8] in the £24bn -a-year market for new cars in the UK led to consumers paying up to 40 per cent more for vehicles than in other parts of the world".

Carmakers insist that they were worried about having to *divulge*[9] commercially sensitive information. For example, Rover, the UK carmaker and former loss-making *subsidiary*[10] of BMW of Germany, instead suggested that they wish to fully cooperate with the commission on a private basis.

Figure 1.4.1.1: Interior of the BMW Mini with automatic transmission (Source:Alexander Voos, Rüsselsheim)

BMW had its own way and claimed that it *pursues*[11] common prices across the European Union. Operators and dealers may soon find it *uneconomic*[12] to import the *upmarket*[13] German cars. BMW is the first to have gone further than its European rivals. The company BMW *denies*[14] that this price move is the result of consumer pressure. BMW insists its strategy is a by-product of the single market, rather than the result of *mounting*[15] pressure from consumer groups.

^{1} zum Unternehmen gehörend	^{2} Untersuchung	^{3} Allegation = Anschuldigung
^{4} Vergehen	^{5} Beleidigung	^{6} begrenzen
^{7} Importkontingent	^{8} Verzerrung	^{9} ausplaudern, preisgeben
^{10} Tochtergesellschaft	^{11} hier: weiterführen	^{12} unwirtschaftlich, unrentabel
^{13} für höhere Ansprüche	^{14} leugnen, dementieren, abstreiten	^{15} steigend, wachsend

1.4.2 What happens in Italy?

First, we should briefly investigate the past. In their *heyday*[4], *cutting-edge*[5] technology and racetrack glories put cars, like Maserati, Lamborghini and Ferrari, at the top of 'car lovers' wish lists around the world.

Maserati and Lamborghini, as well as motorcycle companies Ducati Motor and Moto Guzzi, are certain they can *resurrect*[7] celebrated brand names in the world's highly competitive luxury markets. What can they do? Firstly *unveil*[8] new models, *overhaul*[9] *aging*[10] plants, and cultivate their images through *merchandising*[11] and museums.

Figure 1.4.2.1: The new Alfa Romeo Bc Competition, seen at Geneva Motor Show in spring 2004 (Source: Alexander Voos, Rüsselsheim)

Consequently, Fiat wants the company to work the same magic on Maserati, also a subsidiary. In 1997, Fiat sold a 50% stake in Maserati to Ferrari. Since then, Ferrari has poured a lot of money into *revamping*[12] Maserati's factory in Modena.

A similar renaissance took place in nearby Bologna, where Lamborghini found a German rescuer. Volkswagen's Audi luxury carmaking unit purchased Lamborghini in July 1997 for an estimated $110 million and already has new models in the pipeline.

Fiat Auto's market share in Italy slightly rose in 2004 in comparison to last year. That was a particularly positive year for the Italian car market, especially of Fiat, Lancia and Alfa Romeo. Fiat Auto increased its market *penetration*[13], confirmation of the positive trend of the Group's Brands. Top of the latest Italian sales rankings were the Fiat Punto, the Fiat Panda (voted 2004 as "Car of the Year"), and the Lancia Ypsilon. Others sellers in the luxury range are the Fiat Ulysse and the Lancia Phedra. In the premium market, Alfa Romeo moved up.

Luca Cordero di Montezemolo, who is both chairman of Fiat and president of its sports car unit Ferrari, has attained *celebrity*[14] status by reaching the very top of Italy's business elite. In 2004, he was named the president of the powerful Association of Italian Industrialists, or Confindustria. Three days after his appointment, Fiat chose Montezemolo as its own chairman following the death of Umberto Agnelli, the brother of company's founder. The 56-year-old Montezemolo was named Ferrari's sporting director at the age 26 by Gianni Agnelli, the *late*[15] family patriarch. Since then, Montezemolo has led Ferrari down a successful path in sales and F1 racing. But despite its strong track record, Ferrari has seen its operating profit decline recently because high restructuring costs and a strong euro, which has cut into its exports.

[4] Blütezeit	[5] riskant, Schneidekante	[7] wieder aufleben lassen
[8] enthüllen	[9] überholen, instand setzen	[10] alternde
[11] Handel	[12] aufmöbeln	[13] Durchdringung; Durchschlagskraft
[14] Berühmtheit	[15] verstorben	

1.5 The Asia-Pacific market

1.5.1 What happens in China?

Market

No country in the world has seen greater expansion in its automotive industry over the past 20 years than China. International operating vehicle manufacturers and suppliers are working with local affiliates to support the development of China's automotive industry. China contains one of the oldest civilizations in the world, and has a history of industry and invention.

China has about 130 local automotive companies, but only 16 of them produce cars. There is *widespread*[1] agreement about what the Chinese market will look like when the dust settles: China will have 140 million vehicles on its roads by 2020. China is on track to become the biggest new-vehicle market in the world. *Lured*[2] by growth that the country will become the world's second biggest auto market after the United States by 2015, every major automakers from around the world have *scrambled*[3] to set up shop in China.

Low price in a low-income country and acceptable quality: The formula has worked well in other developing countries. Analysts say that foreign automakers with a presence in China shouldn't *dismiss* [4] the upcoming challenges. China has issued the draft of a new auto-industry policy that appears to *curtail*[5] sharply the ability of foreign automakers and suppliers operating here to *safeguard*[6] their *proprietary*[7] technology and intellectual property.

Figure 1.5.1.1: VW Bora, seen in China (Source: Volkswagen AG, Wolfsburg)

Chinese Companies

First Auto Works (FAW), China's oldest carmaker, was developed in the 1950s with Russian help in the northeastern city of Changchun. FAW manufacture cars named "Redflag". Together with Volkswagen and Audi they produce Audi (A6, A4), Bora and Jetta there.

China's Shanghai Automotive Industry Corp. (SAIC), the joint venture partner of both General Motors and Volkswagen AG, is *on the verge*[8] of signing a final agreement to acquire South Korea's fourth largest automaker, Ssangyong Motor Co. SAIC aims to be one of the world's top six auto manufacturers by 2020. Together with Volkswagen, SAIC produces Passat BS and Polo. Together with GM, they launched Buicks.

Foreign companies

China is the world's most profitable market for **Volkswagen AG**. With a market share of >30%, it is the dominant automaker in that country. And China has become a major export base for **Honda**, which plans to export a China-made car to Europe. Also **Ford Motor Co.**'s plan to source $1 billion worth of parts from China every year. But it does not mark the beginning of a flood of China-produced components onto world markets. Ford Motor Co. will import the Lincoln Navigator luxury SUV to China in 2005, industry sources say. The first vehicles may arrive in April or May 2005.

They may be rivals, but German automakers are cooperating on logistics in China. Volkswagen AG, Audi AG, DaimlerChrysler AG (Cherckee at Beijing) and BMW AG (3 & 5 series at Shenyang) have formed a joint logistics partnership to support their rapidly expanding production in China and other developing markets.

The first **Chrysler** 300 and 300C sedans have arrived in China, and sources say DaimlerChrysler will begin assembling the vehicles there in 2005.

General Motors has about 10,000 employees in China and operates six joint ventures and two wholly owned foreign enterprises. GM has participated in investment of over $2 billion in China. Boasting a combined manufacturing capacity of 530,000 vehicles, which are sold under the Buick, Chevrolet and Wuling nameplates, GM and its joint ventures offer the widest portfolio of products among foreign manufacturers in China. GM and Shanghai Automotive Industry Corp. will jointly operate a demonstration fuel cell vehicle in China. The agreement is GM's latest move in the battle between foreign automakers over whose fuel cell technology should become standard in China.

Suppliers

Higher costs, lower volumes make investing in China a gamble. The question of whether or not to export is just one of the issues facing suppliers in China. Conventional wisdom holds that China's suppliers can produce any part more cheaply than rivals in any other region. That's a *myth*[9], say auto executives who do business there. Costly raw materials, high transportation costs and a lack of domestic Chinese suppliers with modern manufacturing skills *offset*[10] the benefit of cheap labour.

As sales slow in China, how do suppliers stay ahead of the competition? With the latest technology, especially in areas the Chinese government is emphasizing such as safety and emissions, suppliers say.

Figure 1.5.1.2: VW Passat, seen in China (Source: Volkswagen AG, Wolfsburg)

[1] weit verbreitet	[2] geködert, angelockt	[3] drängen, hetzen, raufen
[4] abweisen, zurückweisen	[5] drosseln	[6] schützen
[7] Marke	[8] am Rande; nahe	[9] Märchen
[10] kompensieren, ausgleichen		

1.5.2 What happens in South Korea?

Ford Motor Co. and General Motors took over (in 2002) the nearly *insolvent*[1] Daewoo Motor Co with 44,6% interest equity. Other carmakers are also *sniffing*[2] around for *tie-ups*[3] or *acquisitions*[4] of Hyundai Motors Co. (the country's largest), Kia Motors Co. (which was taken over by Hyundai when it collapsed in 1997), Daewoo, Sangyong Motor Co and Samsung Motors Inc.

Why is there a sudden interest in a group of auto companies long well known for *headstrong*[5] management, *shoddy*[6] quality and *combative*[7] unions? South Korea, at the *doorstep*[8] of China and Japan, seems to be a new frontier for expansion in a recovering Asia.

With such take-over activities, the global reputation of Korean cars is improving, and exports are booming. In the tough U.S. market, Korean car sales *soared*[9] in 2003 to 734,000 units. The export capability of Korean carmakers is *formidable*[10], shipping abroad 1.72 million vehicles a year (2003).

Hyundai Motor Co. raised their reputation by packaging their vehicles with more extras to give the consumer better value. Furthermore, Hyundai offered an *unprecedented*[11] 10-year warranty on its engines and transmissions to *underscore*[12] their quality *gains*[13].

Figure 1.5.2.1: Hyundai Concept Car E-Cubed, seen at the Genf Motor Show in 2004 (Source: Alexander Voos, Rüsselsheim)

[1] zahlungsunfähig	[2] schnüffeln	[3] Zusammenarbeit
[4] Erwerb	[5] eigenwillig	[6] schäbig, minderwertig
[7] kämpferisch	[8.] Schwelle; Fig: (very close) vor der Tür.	[9] in die Höhe schnellen
[10] gewaltig	[11] beispiellos; noch nie dagewesen	[12] unterstreichen
[13] Vorteile		

1.5.3 What happens in Japan?

It is rumoured, that 40% of the cars made in Japan may have mixed *pedigrees*[1]. Although Japan's domestic auto market grew, most car makers are still having a hard time. The stronger yen plus rising production in Japanese factories in Southeast Asia and North America will prevent exports directly from Japan and leave carmakers with overcapacities.

The *mighty*[2] Toyota Motor Corp. is not as *vulnerable*[3] as the others. The company itself is *on the prowl*[4] for an acquisition in Europe, not for *small fries*[5], but for major companies, such as Italy's Fiat or France's Peugeot.

Figure 1.5.3.1:Mitsubishi CZ3 Concept, seen at the Geneve Motor Show in 2004 (Source: Alexander Voos, Rüsselsheim)

The table below shows five countries which produce the most vehicles in the Asian and Pacific area. Figures are available for 2003 in millions (except figures in italics)

Variable	China	India	Japan	Russia	South Korea
Production of passenger cars	2.02	0.71	8.48	1.00	2.77
Production of commercial vehicles (including buses and trucks)	2.42	0.45	1.81	0.27	0.41
Export of passenger cars, buses and trucks (to Europe only)	–	–	1.15	–	0.58
Export of passenger cars (total world)	–	–	4.08	–	1.72
Passenger cars in use (including small number of buses)	6.79	6.67	55.2	23.38	10.28
Car's average annual distance travelled (km per year)	0.05	–	0.010	–	–

Road network (motorways, main or national roads, regional roads and others) in km (percentage paved)	1.91 (–)	3.38 (52)	1.17 (77)	0.54 (68)	0.10 (77)
Cars per 1,000 inh.	5.3	6.3	433	161	210
Density of road network (km/sq.km)	0.20	0.75	3.10	0.33	0.90
Average consumption of petrol per car (t per year)	5.2	–	0.8	0.7	0.8

Figure 1.5.3: Comparison Asia & Pacific (Source VDA)

[1] Stammbaum; Herkunft	[2] mächtig	[3] anfällig
[4] to be on the prowl herumschleichen	[5] kleine Fische	

1.6 The U.S. market

Japan's Toyota has overtaken Ford as the biggest seller of passenger vehicles in the US. All US carmakers lost ground. Total sales, meanwhile, helping the automotive industry register one of its best ever years. What comes next? Forecasters are *skittish*[1] about making predictions for the coming next years, but analysts were optimistic that the buying trend will continue, driven by low interest rates, improving job and stock markets, and new models.

On the one hand, a strong economy will encourage spending on big, option-loaded cars and trucks that fatten the industry and carmakers plan plenty of attractive new models and segment-crossing hybrids to *whet*[2] consumers' appetites. On the other hand, steeper interest rates on lease or finance plans could dampen sales, and rising gas prices could *curb*[3] buyers' enthusiasm for *pickups*[4], one of the industry's fastest-growing and most lucrative segments.

Carmakers have had a difficult couple of years as slowing economic growth and a slump in the stock market have dented demand. Many of the companies are trying to tempt consumers with interest-free loans, further hitting their profitability. With increasing evidence of a global economic rebound and surging stock markets, many analysts are predicting better times ahead.

American automakers dominated the finalists for the 2005 North American Car of the Year awards:
Car of the Year: Cadillac XLR
Sports Car of the Year (Most Sex Appeal): Cadillac XLR
Luxury Car of the Year (Most Respected): Jaguar XJ
Sedan of the Year (Most Dependable): BMW 5-Series
Entry-Level Car of the Year (Most Spirited): Dodge SRT-4
Minivan of the Year (Most Compatible): Nissan Quest

Crossover/Sport Wagon of the Year (Most Versatile): Chrysler Pacifica
Classic Car of the Year (Most Memorable): Chevrolet SSR
SUV of the Year (Most Likely to Survive Anything): Volkswagen Touareg

Europe's largest carmaker **Volkswagen** has suffered as demand declined, the euro surged against the dollar. Volkswagen reported also an 8% drop in US sales in 2004, as did its luxury Audi brand, after profit dropped already in 2003. Volkswagen's profit in the U.S. is directly connected with the success of the New Beetle. The *whimsical*[5] mobile just keeps picking up *speed*[6] of success and the rest of the VW *lineup*[7] is going along for the *ride*[8]. "*Groovy*[9].

Figure 1.6.1: New Beetle Cabrio (Source: Volkswagen AG, Wolfsburg)

Also **General Motors (GM)**, the world's largest automaker, lost ground. Sales fell 5% in October 2004 to 338,826 vehicles. However its Cadillac and sports utility ranges provided positive news. GM will reduce its fourth-quarter 2004 US production targets, by 10,000 to 1.27 million vehicles. GM's global automotive strategy is characterized by a regional presence where the company can *contribute*[10] to local economies. In many cases this involves local partners, joint ventures or other *affiliates*[11]. Outside of North America there are over 160 such entities (e.g. China, Japan, Russia, South Korea).

Also **Ford**, the second-biggest US car company, reported weaker results with a 5.3% drop to 249,484 vehicles.

The drop in sales at US motor giants Ford and GM has been to the fact that there were fewer *incentives*[12] for customers to buy their products. Various "sweeteners" have been a key element recently in generating sales. Both GM and Ford offered interest-free loans for terms of up to six years. However, it may have *stifled*[13] demand after the deals ended.

Mercedes-Benz USA, on the back of record demand for the E-Class, C- and SL-Class vehicles, the company sold 122,100 passenger cars in the United States through July 2004. This figure is slightly two percent lower than the record result posted during the same period in 2003. Also sales at **Chrysler**, the US arm of DaimlerChrylser, rose 2%.

Japanese carmakers increased their market share in the US in 2004. **Toyota** saw its US sales rise by 13% in October to 170,815. **Nissan's** American sales soared 27.3% to 86,599 vehicles, while **Honda** put on a 10.2% increase 110,502 vehicles.

Another firm doing well in the US was German luxury carmaker **BMW**, which saw sales of its BMW brand cars up by 15%. Mini brand car sales rose about 3%.

Figure 1.6.2: Chevrolet Trailblazer LT (Source: Adam Opel AG, Rüsselsheim)

The US automobile *aftercare*[14] and *accessories*[15] market increased 4% to US$123.5 billion in 2003 from US$118.7 billion in 2002. The largest sector of the aftercare and accessories market is the replacement parts segment.

The automobile aftercare and accessories market is fragmented with the top five players:

Delphi's net *revenues*[16] increased 2.4% to reach a value of US$28.1 billion in 2003 from US$27.4 billion during 2002.

Johnson Controls' revenues grew 12.6% to reach a value of US$22.6 billion in 2003, up from US$20.1 billion in 2002.

However, **Visteon's** revenues decreased 4% to US$17.6 billion during 2003, from US$18.4 billion in 2002

Lear's revenues increased 9.2% to US$15.7 billion in 2003, up from US$14.4 billion in 2002.

Magna International had revenues of US$15.3 billion in 2003, representing a 3.1% growth from 2002 figures.

The table below shows five countries which produce the most vehicles. Figures are available for 2003 in millions (except figures in italics).

Variable	Argentina	Brazil	Canada	Mexico	USA
Production of passenger cars	0.16	1.58	2.52	1.52	11.83
Production of commercial vehicles (including buses and trucks);	0.10	0.10	0.03	0.55	0.26
Export of passenger cars, buses and trucks (in Europe only);	–	–	–	–	0.23
Export of passenger cars (total world)	–	–	1.83	–	1.28
Passenger cars in use	5.4	16.7	17.8	13.6	131.6
Car's average annual distance travelled (km per year)	–	–	–	–	0.019
Road network (motorways, main or national roads, regional roads and others) in km (percentage paved)	0.22 (30)	1.73 (6)	1.41 (–)	0.34 (33)	6.41 (59)
Cars per 1,000 inh.	139	93	561	132	452
Density of road network (km/sq.km)	0.08	0.20	0.10	0.17	0.65
Average consumption of petrol per car (t per year)	0.9	–	2.3	1.6	–

Figure 1.6.3: Comparison America (Source VDA)

[1] nervös	[2] anregen	[3] in Zaum halten
[4] Leichtlastwagen mit Pritsche	[5] hier: schrullig	[6] beschleunigen
[7] Gruppierungen; Angebot	[8] spazieren fahren; davon profitieren	[9] toll
[10] beitragen, beisteuern	[11] Konzerngesellschaften; angeschlossene Firmen; affiliated companies: Tochtergesellschaften	[12] Anreiz, Ansporn
[13] ersticken	[14] Nachbehandlung	[15] Zubehör
[16] Einnahmen, Ertrag		

2 Enterprise Marketing Strategies and Policies

2.1 Carmaker's focus: "Green" image

How green is your car? Environmental *ratings*[1] of cars can cause *boardroom*[2] pains, the car manufacturer Volvo told costumers in a recently published environmental product declaration of a *cradle-to-grave*[3] look at pollution generated by manufacturing, use and eventual *dismantling*[4] of its S80 luxury sedan, produced in Torslanda, Sweden.

Figure 2.1.1.: Ready-to-install hoses (Source: Continental Teves, Frankfurt)

It is not surprising, then, that when the Council on Economic Priorities, a nonprofit making research institution in New York that *advocates*[5] responsible behaviour, rated 56 US auto plants, there was an *outcry*[6] from the carmakers that had been rated poorly.

The top scorer in the massed ratings was DaimlerChrysler AG followed, in *descending*[7] order, by General Motors Corp., Bayerische Motoren Werke AG, Ford, Nissan Motor Co. and Toyota Motor Corp.

Not surprisingly, DaimlerChrysler's mood was *sanguine*[8]: "The result is a positive acknowledgment that we've been pro-active in dealing with plant environmental issues", DaimlerChrysler said.

[1] Bewertungen	[2] Sitzungsraum	[3] "Wiege zu Grabe tragen"
[4] auseinander nehmen, zerlegen	[5] befürworten	[6] (lautstarker) Protest
[7] absteigend	[8] (of temperament) heiter; zuversichtlich	

2.2 DaimlerChrysler's focus: The small car sector

DaimlerChrysler, the German-US carmaker, launched its innovative two-seater vehicle Smart (fortwo roadster) in the UK and Japan in 2001, as part as an aggressive marketing campaign to bolster sales. This action signals an attempt by DaimlerChrysler to *bury*[1] speculation that it may *abandon*[2] the Smart car after disappointing sales in the first years. See Figure 8.3.6.2 or www.smart.com.

In the meanwhile, fortwo roadster coupe, fortwo cabrio, crossblade, roadster, roadster-coupé, forfour, edition starblue, fortwo i-move, fortfour cdi blackbasic, MTV roadster, and BRABUS series is available on international markets.

[1] begraben	[2] verlassen, aufgeben	

2.3 Audi's focus: Aluminium

The A2 has become a production reality.

Figure 2.3.1: An aluminium brake disc weighs only 1.97 kg. A comparable steel disc, on the other hand, weighs 4.94 kg. (Source: Continental Teves, Frankfurt)

Initially, the car was presented with three-cylinder direct-injection diesel and gasoline engines. In the future, an ultra fuel-efficient version of the A2 is expected to be capable of 3.0 l/100 km (78 mpg) combined fuel consumption. Audi said it has paid particular attention to routine maintenance of the engine by incorporating a "service module". This *constitutes*[1] a folding *flap*[2] with *a high-gloss*[3] *finish*[4] that takes the place of a conventional radiator *grille*[5]. Positioned behind it are the engine oil *dipstick*[6], and filler flaps for *windshield*[7] washer fluid. The hood is to be lifted only by workshop personnel when the car is serviced. ABS is standard, *allied*[8] to electronic brake force distribution (EBD) and an electronic stability program (ESP). Driver and front passenger get front and side airbags, while sideguard head airbags will be an option as will an enormous opening glass roof.

Figure 2.3.2: The glass roof of the Audi A2, seen at Geneva Motor Show in spring 2000 (Source: Alexander Voos, Rüsselsheim)

[1] darstellen	[2] Blende, Klappe	[3] Hochglanz
[4] Ausführung	[5] Kühlergrill	[6] Messstab
[7] Windschutzscheibe	[8] verbunden	

2.4 Ford's focus: Non-polluting and efficient

The Ford Motor world's first family-size *fuel-cell*[1] research car, P2000 HFC, uses a third-generation fuel-cell *stack*[2] and an advanced electric-drive system. It is currently being driven by compressed *hydrogen*[3] gas power on an own *dynamometer*[4] laboratory and other testing sites on Dearborn, Michigan, engineering campus, but a switch to liquid hydrogen is expected.

The prototype (*reflecting*[5] a $5 to $10 million *price tag*[6]) rides on a stretched Ford Contour platform. Its 1515-kg *curb mass*[7] includes an all-aluminium *body*[8] and *chassis*[9] as well as a 91-kg electric motor. Packaging changes would improve the four-door car's present 169 to 483 km (100 to 300 mi) *range*[10].

Ford is trying to explore any promising path which is non-pulluting and efficient at the same time. Therefore, research and development work focuses on hydrogen and fuel-cell power as well as elements to power *internal-combustion engines*[11]. New *catalysts*[12] had to be developed that allowed the reformation process to begin at much lower temperatures.

A hydrogen internal combustion engine would achieve 25-30% better fuel efficiency than a conventional internal combustion engine while producing no *hydrocarbons*[13], no *carbon monoxide*[14], and no *carbon dioxide*[15] emissions, while the *nitrogen oxide*[16] emissions would meet proposed *federal standards*[17].

Hydrogen application will reach the market much sooner than a fuel cell. A fuel cell, however, is capable of much better *fuel efficiency*[18] and less NOx.

Ford, as well as Shell, Texaco, and DaimlerChrysler will deliver these kind of cars to California in a *validation*[19] project, where 45 vehicles, including buses, will be road tested.

[1] Brennstoff-Zelle	[2] Stapel	[3] Wasserstoff
[4] Leistungsprüfstand	[5] wiederspiegeln	[6] Preisschild
[7] Leergewicht (GB: kerb mass)	[8] Karosserie	[9] Fahrwerk
[10] Reichweite	[11] Motor mit Innenverbrennung	[12] Katalysatoren (GB: catalysers)
[13] Kohlenwasserstoffe	[14] Kohlenmonoxid	[15] Kohlendioxid
[16] Stickstoffoxid (NOx)	[17] Bundesvorschriften/-normen	[18] kraftstoffsparend
[19] Gültigkeitserklärung; Validierung		

2.5 General Motors' focus: Saab's Turbo

Saab Automobile AB became a 50-50 *joint venture*[1] on March 15, 1990, with the GM group holding half of the *shares*[2], and Saab-Scania AB owning the other half. Saab-Scania was *acquired*[3] in 1991 by Investor AB.

By the end of January 2000, General Motors Corp (GM) exercised the *option*[4] to buy the remaining 50 percent of Saab Automobile AB from Investor AB, the Swedish industrial *holding company*[5], with which the GM group has shared ownership for the last decade. So, with this deal, GM group takes full ownership of Saab.

Saab has a strong product lineup, *unique*[6] *brand*[7] *equity capital*[8], and has an important position in GM's automotive portfolio.

GM expect that to take full ownership will be to move ahead even faster in developing new innovative Saab products, *contributing*[9] even more to a global portfolio of resources, *expertise*[10] and products. This expectation is important, as Saab is known as a particularly focused brand and has unique expertise in developing turbo applications. The last mentioned is an important *asset*[11] to GM on a global research and development as well as sales basis.

¹ Gemeinschaftsunternehmen	² Aktien	³ erwerben
⁴ Ausübung des Prämienrechts; Optionsausübung	⁵ Holdinggesellschaft; Dachgesellschaft	⁶ einzigartig
⁷ Marke	⁸ Eigenkapital (hier: Wert)	⁹ beitragen, beisteuern
¹⁰ Sach-, Fachkenntnis	¹¹ Vorteil; Plus	

2.6 VW's focus: Marketing to the under-30 group

Firms that specialize in youth research say, carmakers are always chasing after younger customers. In recent years, however, marketing to the under-30s has become trickier, because the twentysomethings are tired of being targeted. They have been marketed to so heavily in the past years that advertising rarely *engages*¹ them. Car advertisers made mistakes:

Firstly they were using flashy commercials with a look of fast-moving shots and *hip*² muscles. These kind of ads were already outdated. This group wants information and *honesty*³. Secondly, they talked to them using colloquial or slang vocabulary, using the words "extreme", "cool" or "radical".

Figure 2.6.1: The new Volkswagen 1-Litre Car (Source: Volkswagen AG, Wolfsburg)

If the under-30 were asked to name their favourite commercials in any category, only one car commerical surfaced. It was Volkswagen of America's Jetta spot. VW tried to keep its advertising simple but somehow intellectual. It took people watching the Jetta spot a few times to figure out the music rhythmically matched the background events. Watchers felt clever when they did *figure it out*⁴.

The carmaker's research of consumers between ages 18 and 30 *revealed*⁵ they hate *blatant*⁶ commercialization. VW markets to a young-at-heart attitude rather than an age group. The Jetta and Golf are popular with college students although the median age of owners of those two cars is 31.

Figure 2.6.2: Two of the competitors of Jetta and Golf in 2005, the BMW Mini Works and the Fiat Idea 5 Terra (Source: Alexander Voos, Rüsselsheim)

| [1] beschäftigen, mit befassen | [2] Hüfte | [3] Ehrlichkeit |
| [4] bocken, etwas zu tun | [5] enthüllen, verraten | [6] eklatant, himmelschreiend |

3 Strategical Operational Planning

3.1 New technology challenges automotive managers

Global expansion and increasing competition in the automotive industry are affecting management.

What does this mean? For example, a developing country like China needs a *durable*[1], inexpensive vehicle with minimal *maintenance*[2]. These objectives can be achieved by research and development in materials, manufacturing processes, and vehicle suspension systems. Suppliers, as important partners in vehicle design and development, can deliver required technology to *capture*[3] value for the customer through new or improved products.

This view also is reflected in *surveys*[4]. These issues are increasingly important for *seamless*[5] innovation processes, skills and knowledge advantages, and worldwide R&D management.

There is, however, another level of change *occurring*[6]. Many firms are transferring R&D responsibilities to strategic business units (SBUs). This further increases the pressure for R&D to produce results, because SBUs are *rated on*[7] profit/loss results.

[1] haltbar, (of material) strapazierfähig	[2] Wartung	[3] erobern, gewinnen
[4] Untersuchung	[5] nahtlos	[6] vorkommenn
[7] gemessen an		

3.2 Reduction of Leadtime

Why do automotive industries need to change? They can only gain a customer's enthusiasm and maintain their good *reputation*[1] through continuous improvements on the way to future global programs. The shortening of the vehicle development process is of *vital*[2] interest to all automobile manufacturers.

Comprehensive[3] planning data has to be generated by detailed component *development plans*[4] which will be the line to be taken through *carline*[5] projects. Staff have to contribute their *expertise*[6] and best practise approach in the generation of these plans. An intensive lesson learning process is required for the successful execution of this.

According to A.T. Kearney and Deloitte & Touche, as seen below (see Figure 3.2.2), competitive *lead times*[7] and improvement *targets*[8] are the key. What are the main advantages of lead time reduction?

 − Carmakers are allowed to realize the latest technologies
 − A guarantee of the most up-to-date styling *features*[9]

*Figure 3.2.1: CAD
(Source: Continental
Teves, Frankfurt)*

Competitive Lead Times

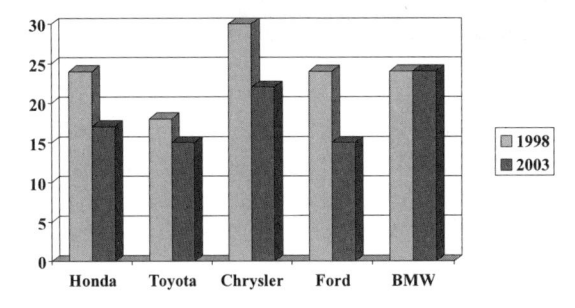

*Figure 3.2.2: Competitive
Lead Times*

What is needed to gain these goals is:
- More modern software is needed to create virtual models (e.g. *digital mockup*[10] DMU), instead of time and money 'spent' on hardware vehicles, components and building tools?
- More creativity, process and communication knowledge of research and development engineers is needed to *match*[11] their working results against following or neighbour working areas.
- More development time is needed to achieve *validated*[12] quality before building *prototype vehicles*[13].
- *Decoupling*[14] of component and subsystem programs with a separate budget is needed to have components readily developed and produced just-in-time before vehicles are build (except styling related components and subsystems).

- Results in clearly defined *milestones*[15] (beginning with "*architecture*[16] agreement" and finishing with "start of production") should be checked against timing, quality and financial figures to gain the best customer and efficiency oriented results .

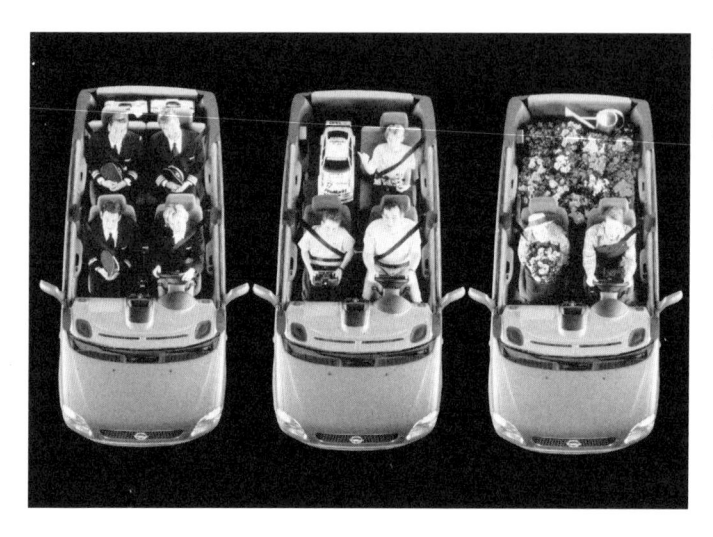

Figure 3.2.3: Passenger compartment of Opel Agila (Source: Adam Opel AG, Rüsselsheim)

How does a reduced lead time process work? Assume that a new vehicle development process for new vehicle models, which as they do now is *style*[17] driven. This means, *exterior*[18] and *interior*[19] shape should be developed first.

One can assume there is a lot of *interaction*[20] within such a complex project management of a vehicle:
- What do markets and customers need?
- Does the carmaker have the manpower to manage this task (*research*[21], development, manufacturing, plants)?
- Is the equipment[22], floor space[23] or assembly line[24] sufficient?
- Are all financial figures available to calculate "*return of investment*[25]"?
- Can the car performance requirement be fulfilled?
- Can the design *constraints*[26] be accepted?
- Is the process adequately and *leanly*[27] defined? Are all voices along the processing chain considered? Are they able to meet regularly in milestone meetings, so-called "quality gates", to accept timing, quality and costs?
- Are all system suppliers *involved*[28], selected and *nominated*[29] just-in-time by *purchasing*[30] areas? Do they have close contact during the development phases? Are the *interfaces*[31] well defined? Are the contracts accepted?

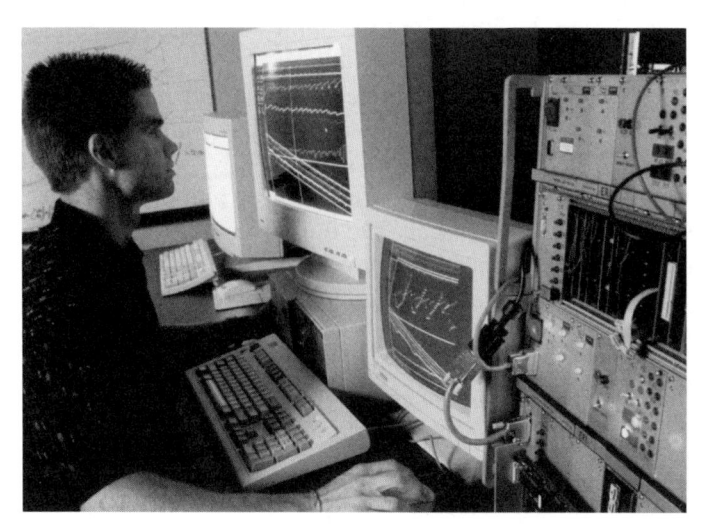

Figure 3.2.4: Analysis of braking performance at a system stimulation lab.(Source: Continental Teves, Frankfurt)

[1] Ruf	[2] lebenswichtig	[3] umfassend
[4] Komponentenentwicklungspläne	[5] Fahrzeuglinien; hier: Automodelle	[6] Erfahrung
[7] Entwicklungszeiten; Vorlaufzeiten	[8] Ziele	[9] Austattung, Ausrüstungn
[10] Digitales Modell, Attrappe	[11] abstimmen; abgleichen	[12] anerkennen
[13] Prototypenfahrzeuge	[14] entkoppeln	[15] Meilensteine; Projektkontrollen
[16] Aufbau; Architektur	[17] Stilistik, Formgebung, Gestaltung	[18] Außenform
[19] Fahrzeuggastraum, Fahrzeuginnenraum; Interieur	[20] Wechselwirkungen	[21] Forschung
[22] Ausstattung	[23] Bodenfläche	[24] Montagestraße, Fließband
[25] Rückkehrzeitpunkt der getätigten Investitionen	[26] Zwänge	[27] schlank
[28] eingebunden	[29] (offiziell) ernannt	[30] Einkauf
[31] Schnittstellen		

3.3 Making changes happen

Any challenges facing the engineering and R&D[1] communities must be addressed to the staff affected, otherwise they are not involved with making changes happen.

Collectively, employees sometimes find it difficult to imagine what they really want and don't allow themselves to make new changes. Relying on the force of *personality*[2] to determine the direction in which the organization should go, however, will not work. Where does one find the ability to make something new happen? Three solutions:

First, a shared vision is gathered by using the collective intelligence and *inspiration*[3] of the team. Make sure, that management understand how *staff*[4] think and work, so cooperation can take place across boundaries.

Secondly, system thinking is necessary to discover the deep and often hidden dynamics of cause and effect, action and reaction, and initiative and *backlash*[5].

Third, senior management must support the development of competencies with clear messages (e.g. *persuasive*[6] communication, participation, *expectancy*[7], role modelling, structural *rearrangement*[8], *coercion*[9]).

These competencies are not difficult to develop and use, if attention is paid to them, otherwise wrong, foolish or *inadequate*[10] things will be choosen, or something new ends *prematurely*[11] or is actively *opposed*[12] or sabotaged.

[1] Forschung und Entwicklung	[2] Persönlichkeit	[3] Eingebung
[4] Personal	[5] starke Gegenreaktion	[6] überzeugend
[7] Erwartung	[8] Umordnung, Neuordnung	[8] Zwang
[10] ungenügend	[11] frühzeitig	[12] abgeneigt

Figure 3.3.1: CAD-made drawing of braking system.(Source: Continental Teves, Frankfurt)

3.4 How should suppliers be dealt with?

Suppliers will be selected by car manufacturers to get the best quality out of a minimum of production costs. How will this be done? Many evaluation questions have been asked after project completion and should be answered with yes to achieve a next contract offer. Answers are noted into a *efficiency analysis*[1] for each supplier.

Questions of the category "most important" can be:

- Does the supplier maintain awareness of new technology and develop world-class technology?
- Is the supplier able to provide sample parts at short notice?
- Does the supplier have required and well maintained testing equipment available?
- Is the supplier able to provide expert support for problem resolution for complete product life?

Figure 3.4.1: Quality check: Dimensional check of valve blocks (Source: Continental Teves, Frankfurt)

Questions of the category "more important" can be:
- Does the supplier meet prototype schedules?
Does the supplier *comply*[2] with requirements on drawings and specifications?
- Does the supplier provide *samples*[3] and prototypes produced in line with production standards?
- Is the test equipment *calibrated*[4] to national standards?
- Does the supplier have *compatible*[5] CAD/CAM systems?

Questions of the category "important" can be:
- Does the supplier have the required language skills?
- Does the supplier perform designs for mass reduction?
- Does the supplier conduct formal design reviews?

Figure 3.4.2: Automatic loading at assembly lines (Source: Continental Teves, Frankfurt)

Questions of the category "less important" can be:
- Does the supplier perform analysis (e.g. *stress analysis*[6], kinematics, dynamics)?
- Does the supplier use designs for the use of recycled materials?

[1] Nutzwertanalyse	[2] (einer Bitte) nachkommen	[3] Muster
[4] geeicht	[5] gut zusammen passend	[6] Spannungsanalysen

3.5 How should proper quality be achieved?

3.5.1 Quality of parts

Quality critera is based on quality definition and requirements for non-sheet metal, *sheet metal*[1] and *vendor*[2] parts in stages of before and during production.

Quality criteria at the *pilot*[3] stage (before production) of sheet metal parts:
- Parts should come from original *production dies*[4]
- Original material should be used
- They should be dimensionally accurate according to checking *fixtures*[5]
- They should run on *try out presses*[6]
- Matching results should be *incorporated*[7]
- Surface optimization should be achieved.

Quality criteria at production stage of sheet metal parts:
- Parts should run on original production press lines
- Parts should be completely (dimensions and *surfaces*[8]) satisfactory.

On the other hand, at vendor parts, there are some different quality definitions. Quality criteria at pilot stage (before production):
- Parts should come from original *tool*[9]
- Parts should be dimensionally satisfactory according to checked fixtures
- Safety of parts at laboratory should be sufficient
- Parts should be matched and 100% perfect
- Parts should run on original equipment.

Quality critera at production stage:
- *Run at rate*[10]
- Parts *grained*[11]
- Part colours acceptable.

[1] Blech	[2] Verkäufer	[3] Modell; Pilot
[4] Formwerkzeuge	[5] Vorrichtungen	[6] Versuchspressen
[7] eingearbeitet	[8] Oberflächen	[9] Werkzeug
[10] Lauf mit gewünschter Stückzahl	[11] Teile mit Körnung	

3.5.2 Product Quality Planning

The term "product" is meant as either product or service (e.g warehousing, transportation). In the past, Chrysler, Ford and General Motors each had their own guidelines and formats for ensuring supplier (the term "supplier" is also used for subcontactors) *compliance*[1]. Differences between these guidelines and formats had resulted in additional demands on supplier sources before a common structured method was prepared to describe how to handle a typical program, consists of up-front planning and act of implementation. The never-ending *pursuit*[2] of continual improvement can only be achieved by taking the experience in one program and applying it to the next program.

A disciplined problem solving method is recommended in difficult situations, and analytical techniques should be used. Effective status reporting supports program *monitoring*[3] with a focus on identifying items that require special attention.

Figure 3.5.2.1: Opel Vivaro (Source: Adam Opel AG, Rüsselsheim)

Timing of product quality is divided into several steps, according to product development process, starting from concept initiation, program approval, prototype build, pilot and product launch:
- Planning of design, *reliability*[4] and quality goals, as well as preparing a preliminary process flow chart. The voices of customers, business plans and marketing strategies are needed, as well as product benchmark data being necessary.
- Product design and development of DFMEA, DFM, DFA, design verification, design reviews, prototype build, control plan, engineering drawings (incl. Math data), engineering and *material specifications*[5], drawing and specification changes.
- Process design and development of packaging standards, product/process quality system review, process *flow chart*[6], floor plan layout, characteristics matrix, process failure mode and effects analysis (PFMEA), pre-launch control plan, process instructions, measurement system analysis plan, preliminary process capability study plan, packaging specifications and management *support*[7].
- Product and process validation by *production trial run*[8], *measurement systems evaluation*[9], preliminary process *capability*[10] study, production part approval, production validation testing, packaging evaluation, *production control*[11] plan, quality planning sign-off and management support.

An important phase of the process for quality planning is the development of a Control Plan, which is a written description of the systems for controlling parts and processes. As a living document it reflects the current methods of control and measurement systems.

Figure 3.5.2.2: Plastic Injection Moulding Machine (Source: Krauss Maffei, München)

There are many control plans available:
1. For *set-up*[12] dominant and stable processes. For example: Automobile *grills*[13] are producted on *plastic injection moulding machines*[14]. After setting up the *mould*[15], the machine must be adjusted to produce a dimensionally correct part, which must be free of *blemishes*[16], *flow lines*[17] and *sink*[18] marks on the surface. The *moulding machines*[19] have computer controlled parameters. A set-up card provides specifications for setting all controls on the machine.
2. For machine dominant processes, machine setting parameters are variable according to process output. For example: On *circuit boards*[20] electronic components are *soldered*[21]. These soldered connections are the major product characteristics. Process characteristics for *wave solder machines*[22] are solder level and *flux*[23] concentration, which have to be controlled, *sampled*[24] and tested.
3. For *fixture*[25]/*pallet*[26] dominant processes. For example: *Metal castings*[27] are loaded on a *rotary machine*[28] with several fixtures. Each part has a machined surface on which *perpendicularity*[29] and depth of cut are critical. The *cutting tool*[30] and proper adjustment of the fixtures can affect the product characteristics.
4. For tooling dominant processes, life and design characteristics affect process outputs. For example: A *sheet metal*[31] *stamping die*[32] is used to form a steel *bracket*[33] which has *several angles*[34] and *pierced holes*[35]. Tools have parts (e.g. punches) which can break. Tools can be repaired incorrectly.
5. For operator dominant processes, which system is dependent upon operator knowledge and control. For example: *headlamp aiming*[36] is one of

the final operations during car and truck assembly. The operator adjusts the headlamps by turning *aiming screws*[37] until the *bubble*[38] centre in the *level*[39]. The product characteristic is measured by shining the headlamps on an aim board which measures *beam pattern*[40].

6. For material dominant processes, if characteristics of material or components affect the process output. For example: An automobile *hood*[41] is made of a material which is a temperature sensitive *moulding compound*[42]. The parts can become *brittle*[43] when the material is *improperly*[44] mixed, handled or rotated. Control charts, lab reports or error proofing tests are necessary to control the specifications.

7. For a climate dominant process, e.g. temperature, *humidity*[45], noise and vibration affects the function of a plastic injection moulding machine. Plastic material absorbs *dampness*[46] from the air, causing defects in the moulding parts. Material dryers have to be installed. Periodic visual product examinations are necessary.

[1] Übereinstimmung; Einhaltung	[2] Verfolgung	[3] hier: Überwachung
[4] Zuverlässigkeit	[5] Leistungsbeschreibungen	[6] Ablaufplan
[7] Unterstützung	[8] Fertigungslosgröße für Versuch, Erprobung	[9] Bewertung des Vermessungssystems
[10] Tauglichkeit	[11] Fertigungssteuerung	[12] einrichten
[13] Kühlergrill/-Gitter	[14] Kunststoffspritzgussmaschinen	[15] Form; Formwerkzeug
[16] Schönheitsfehler	[17] Strömungslinien	[18] Senke
[19] Formpress-/Spritzguss-Maschine	[20] Leiterplatten; gedruckte Schaltungen	[21] gelötet
[22] Frequenzlötmaschinen	[23] Lötmittel	[24] bemustert; stichprobenweise überprüft
[25] Befestigung, Aufnahme	[26] Palette	[27] Metallgussteile
[28] Drehmachine	[29] Rechtwinkeligkeit	[30] Schneidwerkzeug
[31] Blech	[32] Stanzwerkzeug	[33] Halter
[34] Winkel	[35] durchgestochene Löcher	[36] Scheinwerfereinstellung
[37] Einstellschrauben	[38] Luftblase	[39] Wasserwaage
[40] Straßenausleuchtung	[41] Motorhaube	[42] Gemisch
[43] spröde	[44] falsch	[45] Luftfeuchtigkeit
[46] Feuchtigkeit		

4 Carmakers' Portfolio

4.1 Audi's TT

Audi *revealed*[1] its individualistic TT Coupe and TT Roadster concept cars in 1995. Many thought the *likelihood*[2] of one of them reaching production to be questionable and both as next to impossible. But Audi *confounded*[3] the *sceptics*[4] by producing the TT Coupe in 1998. Due to the car's popularity, there was manufacturing pressure on the Coupe lines (assembly in Germany; *powertrain*[5] from Audi's factory at Gyor, Hungary). The TT Roadster is currently also in production.

Figure 4.1.1: Audi TT Coupe (Source: Audi AG, Ingolstadt)

The Roadster's body stiffness

Great attention has been paid to making the Roadster's *structure*[6] torsionally *rigid*[7]. Audi quotes 10,000 Nm/°, which is excellent for an open-top car. Natural body *frequency*[8] is 22 Hz. Compared to the Coupe, mass increases with every 40 kg. A mass increase of around 100 kg might have been expected for its stiffening program. The Roadster has a "massive portal frame structure" behind the seats. A link between *floor assembly*[9] and *side panels*[10] *constitutes*[11] "extreme torsional stiffness*[12].*" A *rectangular*[13] aluminium *crossmember*[14] makes a *flexurally stiff mounting*[15] for the car's *twin*[16] *rollover bars*[17]. The rollover bars can *bear*[18] *impact loads*[19] of up to 3.2 t on the structure without any noticeable *deformation*[20]. Rollover protection also comes from *interlocking*[21], high-strength *steel*[22], *tubular A-pillar reinforcements*[23], *anchored*[24] at the *door sill*[25], plus connecting points in the *front-end structure*[26].

Compared to the Coupe, the Roadster's *instrument-panel*[27] *module support*[28] has been further developed as an effective body-stiffening *member*[29]. It is integrated into the structure via a number of robust *screw connections*[30].

The front-end structure is stiffened by a *rigidly*[31] mounted *subframe*[32] with *diagonal*[33] support against the side member and door sill structure.

Already used on the Coupe, *spring-strut*[34] *mounting*[35] and tubular reinforcements at the front of the *side members*[36], support the stiffness.

Large-profile door sills are also carry-over parts from the Coupe but are *reinforced*[37] by thicker material and the use of *gusset plates*[38] at the connection points.

Audi states that by using targeted optimization measures, together with experience gained in aluminium technology for production applications, engineers were able to undercut the theoretical figure by 60%. Body stiffness is a contributor to primary and secondary safety. Other safety aspects of the Roadster include *seatbelt tensioners*[39] with reinforce limiters and four airbags. The side airbags are integrated into the *seat backs*[40].

Figure 4.1.2: Body structure of Audi TT Roadster (Source: Audi AG, Ingolstadt)

Aerodynamics

Great attention has been paid to the shape of the *folding roof*[41] to ensure that it contributes to the car's overall Cd (0.36) and helps keep noise levels down. A quarter-scale model of the TT Roadster was subjected to water tank tests, and a prototype was tested in Audi's new wind tunnel, resulting in design work that helped reduce turbulence around the car's wheels. A rear spoiler is fitted to the underbody. A *toughened*[42]-glass, *powered*[43] *windbreak*[44] can be raised between the roll bars to give effective protection from *buffeting*[45] at speed.

Handling of the roof

The *folding roof*[46] of the TT is available with manual or powered operation. In powered form, a single *handle*[47] needs to be turned manually to release the roof from the *windshield header rail*[48] before it is *lowered*[49]. Closing the roof calls for a final sharp pull and *twist*[50] movement to *secure*[51] it.

The roof folds into a *recess*[52] and can be hidden by a hard cover made of *composite material*[53]. This fits neatly into the trunk when not in use and in theory it is a clever design element.

The roof must be unclipped and removed before the *hood*[54] can be raised, which in the event of a sudden rainstorm is likely to dampen more than the *occu-*

pants[55], spirits. Also, the contents of the *trunk*[56] must be removed to stow the cover, which is hardly ideal. It is suspected that most owners will not use the cover if there is any question about weather stability. Questioned as to why a *hinged*[57] cover part of the *bodywork*[58] could not have been used, Audi designers explained that this would have necessitated a *shut line*[59] being imposed on *the rear fender*[60], which was regarded as aesthetically unacceptable.

Figure 4.1.3: Audi TT Roadster (Source: Audi AG, Ingolstadt)

Powertrain and chassis

The TT Roadster is available with a choice of power units, both *turbocharged*[61] and of 1.8-l capacity, producing 132 kW (available with front-wheel drive or quattro all-wheel drive) or 165 kW (available only as a quattro). Performance figures for the 165-kW car include a 0- 100 km time of 6.7 s, with a top speed of 237 km/ h. The *unladen mass*[62] without a driver is 1475 kg. At the front, both versions use McPherson *struts*[63], but at the rear, the quattro has a *trailing arm*[64] and two *wishbones*[65] on each side, with separate spring and *shock absorber mountings*[66].

Figure 4.1.4: McPherson front axle (Source: ATZ, 3/2000)

[1] enthüllen	[2] Wahrscheinlichkeit	[3] (den Gegner usw.) verwirren
[4] Skeptiker	[5] Antriebsstrang (Motor + Getriebe)	[6] Struktur, Aufbau; Gerippe
[7] verwindungssteif, verdrehsteif	[8] Frequenz, Häufigkeit	[9] Bodengruppe
[10] Seitenwände	[11] darstellen, ausmachen	[12] Verdrehsteifigkeit, Verwindungssteifigkeit
[13] rechtwinklig, rechteckig	[14] Querträger	[15] biegesteifer Einbau
[16] zwei, doppelt	[17] Überrollbügel	[18] aushalten, tragen
[19] Aufprallbelastung, Stoßbelastung	[20] Verformung	[21] Verriegelung; Sperren, Verblockung
[22] hochfester Stahl (HSS)	[23] rohrförmige Verstärkung in der A-Säule	[24] verankert
[25] Türschweller; Einstiegsschweller	[26] Vorbaustruktur	[27] Armaturentafel, Instrumentenbrett
[28] Halterung, Träger, Stütze	[29] Träger; Holm	[30] Schraubverbindungen
[31] starr	[32] Hilfsrahmen, Fahrschemel	[33] Quer-, Diagonal-, Schräg-
[34] Federbein	[35] Lagerung	[36] Längsträger, Rahmenlängsträger
[37] verstärkt	[38] Winkelbleche, Knotenbleche	[39] Gurtstraffer; Gurtstrammer
[40] Sitzlehne, Rückenlehne	[41] Faltdach	[42] widerstandsfähig
[43] angetrieben	[44] Windschutz, Windschott	[45] Turbulenzen, Luftwirbel
[46] Faltdach	[47] Griff	[48] oberer Windschutzscheibenrahmen; vorderer Dachquerträger
[49] abgesenkt	[50] verdrehen	[51] sichern
[52] Mulde; Vertiefung	[53] Verbundwerkstoff	[54] Verdeck; Klappverdeck; Faltdach
[55] Insassen	[56] Kofferraum, Gepäckraum (GB: boot)	[57] schwenkbar; klappbar
[58] Karosserie; Aufbau	[59] Fuge; Spalt; Schließlinie	[60] hinterer Kotflügel; hinterer Schutzblech
[61] mit Abgasturbolader	[62] Leergewicht	[63] Federbeine
[64] Längslenker; Zugstrebe	[65] Querlenker	[66] Stoßdämpferhalterungen

4.2 VW Concept D1

Concept D was a very long way from the original concept of a "people's car", but it was the pointer towards VW's plans for a future luxury model. The V10-engined *direct-injection*[1] diesel was *unveiled*[2] at the Frankfurt Motor Show in 1999 and was described as a "four-door coupe". It represented a "first taste" of the luxury *sedan*[3] Phaeton which has been built in Dresden since 2002. In 2003, only 6,000 cars were sold, and in 2004, again only 15,000 cars were sold.

The choice of a diesel engine was significant and indicates this type of engine is gaining acceptance at the upper end of the market in Europe.

Figure 4.2.1: VW Phaeton (Source: Volkswagen AG, Wolfsburg)

The power unit has a volume of about 5.0 l and incorporate twin turbochargers, *charge air cooling*[4], and *electrical charge pressure control*[5]. Power output is quoted at 230 kW, with 750 Nm of torque at only 2000 rpm.

Figure 4.2.2: Transparent Factory at Dresden: Running gear installation for the new Phaeton (Source: Volkswagen AG, Wolfsburg)

It will *incorporate*[6] a *balance shaft*[7]. The Phaeton has *all-wheel-drive*[8] and an automatic plus Tiptronic (manual selection) *gearbox*[9]. The car is 4995 mm long. Lighting systems include double Xenon headlights and *indicators*[10] behind *tapered*[11] clear glass covers. *Turn indicators*[12] are in the door mirrors. The car has a luxury interior using walnut and leather, materials with which Bentley, also in the VW Group, has great experience applying to an upmarket sporting car's interior.

Figure 4.2.3: V10 engine (Source: Volkswagen AG, Wolfsburg)

[1] Direkteinspritzung; Zylindereinspritzung	[2] enthüllt	[3] Limousine; geschlossener Pkw
[4] Ladeluftkühlung	[5] elektrische Ladungsdruckkontrolle/-steuerung	[6] einbinden; integrieren
[7] Ausgleichswelle	[8] Allrad-Antrieb	[9] Getriebe; Getriebegehäuse
[10] Blinker; Fahrtrichtungsanzeiger	[11] kegelförmig; konisch	[12] Blinker

4.3 Opel's G90 concept

The aim was to design a car that could perform an emission figure of 90 g of CO_2 per km. Therefore, when Opel achieved its goal, it simply called the new vehicle G90, and unveiled it at the Frankfurt Motor Show in 1999.

Due to the use of aluminium, magnesium and other lightmass materials, engineers were able to achieve a *curb mass*[1] of just 750 kg. "This is a four seat car in the Astra size category," said Hans Demant, a member of the Opel *Management Board*[2], when unveiling the car. The G90 is powered by a three-cylinder gasoline engine with an output of 60 hp (45 kW) and a *displacement*[3] of 1.0-l.

Figure 4.3.1: The Opel concept car G90 (Source: Adam Opel AG, Rüsselsheim)

He also said the combination of lightmass construction and good aerodynamics (0.22 Cd) enabled the car to record a fuel consumption of 3.88 l/100 km. "This puts us about one third below the fleet average pollution value of 140 grams per km that is planned for the European Union in the year 2008," he said. Herr Demant added that the figures demonstrated that independent of the powertrain, and without having to resort to exotic materials or *detract from*[4] passenger comfort, it was possible to make "a reasonably priced car" with fuel consumption in the region of 3.0 l/100 km." The G90 is said to be capable of 180 km/h (112 mph).

It was decided that the engine should be a direct-injection gasoline unit from the Opel production program, because this technology had a lot of potential. In the G90, it drives through a *five-speed*[5] *sequential-shift*[6] *transmission*[7] with manual or automatic operation. The G90 has a drop shape for good aerodynamics, which has *necessitated*[8] a narrower *rear track*[9] than that at the front – by 92mm. The car has two individual rear seats instead of a bench. Its exhaust system is integrated into the body as a further aid to aerodynamics. The most significant contribution to aerodynamics efficiency in the *underbody*[10] area, however, was to *slope*[11] the rear floor upward at an angle of 6°. This result in a "*diffuser*[12] effect". Together, the rearward sloping roofline and the *low trailing edge*[13] of the *tailgate*[14] combine to reduce rear surface area. The airflow above and below the car passes the body faster, resulting in less turbulence and reduced *drag*[15].

The use of lightmass materials for the car's construction allowed additional savings in *brake*[16] mass and other components such as *steering knuckles*[17]. Aluminium *suspension struts*[18] are also used. The car's *exhaust system*[19] has a mass of about 13kg – some 6kg less than a conventional system. It has five *mounts*[20].

As you may know, Opel's G90 concept has never been set into production. The reason of this decision by Opel's management was a bad "return of investment" (ROI). Also its predecessor, named MAXX, seen at Geneva already in 1995 was never built for sales. The latest concept was shown in Geneva in 2004, it is called TRIXX.

Opel's TRIXX concept took top honors in the concept car category at the Autocar awards due to its ingenuity and stylish looks. With its inflatable rear seat and pantograph doors, TRIXX convinced the judges from the prestigious weekly magazine who praised its clever packaging and originality, saying it was "*bursting*[21] with innovation."

This innovation is evident in many more ways, including the incorporation of a foldaway front passenger's seat and a luggage rack at the rear that pulls out like a drawer to carry heavy items or sports clothing which is too dirty to travel inside.

Figure 4.3.2: The Opel concept car MAXX2 (Source: Adam Opel AG, Rüsselsheim)

[1] Leergewicht	[2] Vorstand; Vorstandsgremium	[3] Hubraum; Zylinderinhalt
[4] to detract from sth.: etwas beeinträchtigen	[5] fünfstufig	[6] sequentielle Gangschaltung
[7] Antrieb; Getriebe	[8] (etwas) notwendig machen; fordern.	[9] hintere Radspur, hintere Spurweite
[10] Unterboden	[11] abfallen; ansteigen	[12] Zerstäuber
[13] Hinterkante	[14] Heckklappe	[15] Luftwiderstand; Strömungswiderstand
[16] Bremsen	[17] Achsschenkel	[18] Federbeine; Radaufhängungsbeine
[19] Abgassystem; Auspuffsystem	[20] Lager; Stützlager; Halter, Halterungen	[21] platzen

5 Styling

Tatsuhide Hoshi is 29, he has cash, and he is a Toyota designer. But he doesn't like any car in Toyota's line up enough to buy one. He believes old Chevrolets have more style. He drives a 1961 Corvette.

Normally, the idea of Toyota employees admitting to a Corvette obsession would *have seemed like*[1] *treason*[2]. But Hoshi's boss recruited him to join a team of young designers in Tokyo's trendy Sangenjaya district precisely because Hoshi doesn't like Toyotas. Some day soon, he will style entire cars for young customers of the company brand.

By spending big *bucks*[3] on creating a new image, Toyota, Honda and Nissan are overhauling styling procedures by hiring foreign designers. The Japanese car industry is playing a high-risk game to create a *daring*[4] design that will give carmakers an edge in a hyper-competitive arena. They are now trying to make their models a hit.

Can it be imagined why the Japanese are so intent on creating new designs? Japanese cars are top sellers in America and Japan, for example Honda Accord, Toyota Camry, or Corolla compact. Why *tinker*[5] with success? The reason is that success, even for Japan's best, can be *fleeting*[6]. Auto executives already see a disturbing trend: the traditional sedan is *fading*[7], but it is the *backbone*[8] of the market, old favorites, such as Toyota's *stodgy*[9] Mark II, that just aren't selling anymore. It is unfortunate that the Japanese recession is making it *imperative*[10] to come out with breakthrough products. By the end of 1999, 7 of Japan's 11 carmakers were in the red, with only Toyota and Honda showing real strength.

What happened in Japan could eventually also affect Camrys and Accords in the U.S. There, *pickup trucks*[11], *sport-utility vehicles*[12], and *minivans*[13] have been competing on sedans for a decade.

The Japanese face an even bigger challenge in Europe, in competition with Volkswagen and Fiat in the market for compact cars. The Japanese see new design as the only way out.

Before styling was the most important point for selling cars, the choice of engine or suspension were questioned. People now are paying attention to the *distinctiveness*[14] of the design. Competitors say in that area the Japanese have a long way to go. If the brandname is removed from a Japanese car, the customer is unaware if it is a Mitsubishi, a Toyota, or a Honda. Is this statement *exaggerated*[15] or is it true?

The Japanese don't need to think of an answer, since they have thought ahead. In the first instance, a tremendous *diversification*[16] in the lineup has been necessary.

Honda, for example, had only sedans, such as the Accord and Civic. It is now *churning out*[17] a whole range of minivans and sport-utilities, and a convertible roadster is yet to come.

Toyota also thought of the $16,000 Toyota RAv4, which introduced a *bubbly*[18], *playful*[19] body of the sport-utility category and became a hit.

Japanese carmakers recently unveiled numerous new models. The efforts fall into several categories.

Firstly the development of a new category of "*crossover*[20]" vehicles has come about that merges the attributes of sport-utes, vans and cars. The *cross-breed*[21] vehicles offer a good view of the new approach. The idea is to build sport-utility vans on car platforms for easier handling and then *jazz up*[22] the styling. These car-truck *crossings*[23] should soon be the fastest-growing segments of the car markets in both Japan and North America. At the top of this list is Toyota's $24,600 LEXUS RX300, known as the Harrier in Japan. This is also leading Lexus sales in the U.S. and Japan. It is competing with Mercedes' M-Class with looks that are sporty but *sleek*[24] enough to be parked in front of the best hotels.

Another move is to add nicely styled alternatives to such old standbys as the Corolla.

A third tactic of Japanese carmakers is to revolutionize car interiors to make maximum use of every cubic cm, and so they are rewriting the rules for interiors.

Yet another concerns the look of Japan's mini cars. Younger Japanese buyers see their vehicles as an extension of their living room, yet they also want small vehicles to navigate Japan's narrow, crowded roads. *That's a tall order*[25]. Tiny vehicles make up 25% of light vehicle sales in Japan.

Figure 5.1: Tail of Mazda RX8 (Source: Alexander Voos, Rüsselsheim)

The space revolution extends to the exterior styling in minicars and compacts, with the Japanese devising a boxy look that adds headroom and *departs*[26] radically from rounded aerodynamic forms. Nissan has *racked*[27] up sales with the

$9,000 car. It has a superhigh roof for such a tiny car and sports an *offbeat*[28], cubish profile. In the same *vein*[29], designers of the $15,000 Honda s-mx, for example, envisioned a '*barn*[30]' on wheels that could carry a young couple's bicycles and surfboards but that would also feel as comfortable in front as a sofa.

Figure 5.2: Clay model of Opel Speedster (Source: Adam Opel AG, Rüsselsheim)

How can Japanese cars be sold in Europe?

At Toyota's European Design Center in Brussels, designers are styling cars that can replace Toyota's traditional rounded, *sober*[31] look and compete with the broad-shouldered German design of the Volkswagen Passat, the Opel Astra, and the Audi A4. The Brussels-designed Yaris, is the inspiration for the subcompact Toyota. The Yaris has a *stubby*[32], *snub-nosed*[33] look that has nothing in common with the Camry. If it works, the Yaris may revolutionize the look of Toyota subcompacts everywhere.

Nissan is looking abroad, too. In the U. S., Nissan's 50 designer studio will have design authority over 85% of the vehicles *rolled out*[34] in North America.

Will the mainstream sedans look different in future, too? The answer is: yes. While the Accord, Camry, and Nissan Altima will not start sporting varied outlooks in the next year or so, they may look quite different in the next three years, because the present design of the Camry is too soft. A taste of things to come arrived with the 2000 launch of Toyota's $16,300 Nadia. Its sharply lined doors, short overhang in front, and rounded *hatchback*[35] lined with special designed rear lamps give the car a futuristic look.

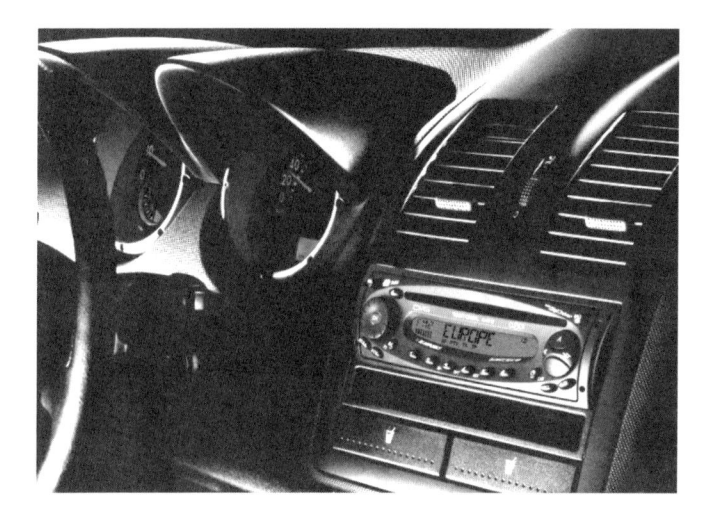

Figure 5.3: New car radio generation Fun Line form. Blaupunkt has adopted stylistic elements of modern cars which harmonise with the interior character of trend-setting vehicles (Source: Robert Bosch GmbH, Stuttgart)

Figure 5.4: Opel Speedster passenger compartment (Source: Adam Opel AG, Rüsselsheim)

Meanwhile, the designers are getting stranger, too. They have even consulted architects and *artisans*[36] of traditional crafts, such as *lacquerware*[37], to improve Toyota interiors. The new art of automotive design could raise car styling to new heights.

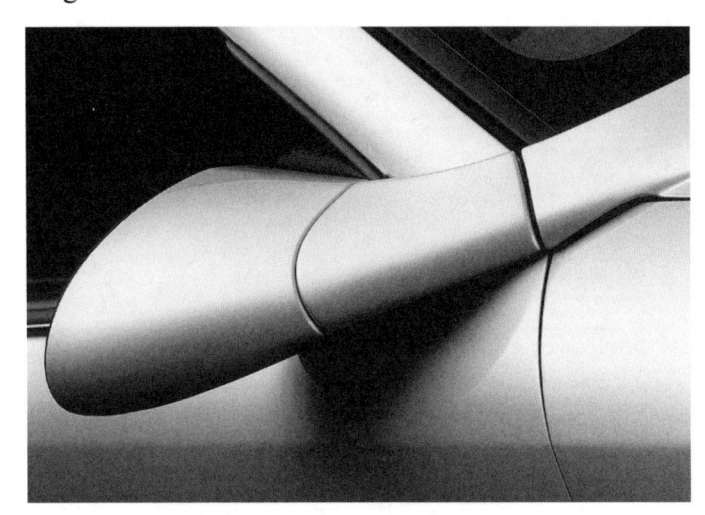

Figure 5.5: Outside rearview mirror of Opel Vectra (Source: Adam Opel AG, Rüsselsheim)

Figure 5.6: Lamella Roof (Source: Webasto AG, Stockdorf)

Figure 5.7: Rear spoiler Porsche Boxster (Source: Webasto AG, Stockdorf)

[1] kommt vor wie/ erscheint wie...	[2] Landesverrat	[3] N.Am: Dollar
[4] gewagt, verwegen	[5] herumpfuschen	[6] verflüchtigen
[7] verblassen	[8] Rückgrat	[9] schwer verdaulich; schwerfällig
[10] dringend (notwendig), unerläßlich	[11] Leichtlastwagen mit Pritsche	[12] Freizeitfahrzeuge
[13] Großraumlimousine; Großraumfahrzeug	[14] Unverwechselbarkeit; Deutlichkeit	[15] übertrieben
[16] Diversifizierung; Verschiedenartigkeit	[17] to churn out sth: etwas am laufenden Band produzieren	[18] to churn out sth: etwas am laufenden Band produzieren
[19] zum Spielen aufgelegt; (wild) ausgelassen; verspielt	[20] Übergang	[21] Kreuzung
[22] (ein Stück) verjazzen	[23] Kreuzungen	[24] schnittig
[25] that's a tall order! das ist ein bißchen viel verlangt!	[26] abweichen	[27] foltern
[28] ausgefallen	[29] Stimmung	[30] Scheune
[31] nüchtern, sachlich	[32] kurz und dick	[33] snub-nose: Stupsnase
[34] erste Gehversuche unternehmen	[35] Ladeklappe; Kombi-Hecktüre	[36] Handwerker
[37] Lackware		

6 Advanced Engineering

6.1 A second generation H(hip)-point doll

The automotive industry sponsored a program to develop a new set of tools for designing and measuring vehicle seats and interiors, called "Automotive Seat and Package Evaluation and Comparison Tools" (ASPECT). It was sponsored by 11 manufacturers and interior systems suppliers, including Daimler-Chrysler, BMW, Ford Motor Company, General Motors, Johnson Controls, Lear, Magna, PSA Peugeot-Citreon, Toyota, Volkswagen of America and Volvo.

Representatives from each of the companies formed an Industry *Advisory Panel*[1] (IAP) that was actively involved with the research team, ensuring the project addressed current and future needs of vehicle packaging engineers and seat designers.

Biomechanic researchers of Universities *collaborated*[2] to develop new tools for measurement, design and evaluation of vehicle interiors and seats.

The IAP-member companies have a new set of tools for designing and measuring vehicle seats and interiors since completion of ASPECT in July 1999. The *primary*[3] *objective*[4] of the program was the development of a three-dimensional massed doll to replace the SAE J826 hip-point doll developed in the 1960s.

The new doll, called "manikin" by experts, represents a midsize U.S. male by body size and mass to provide measurement continuity with the current doll and *anthropometric consistency*[5] with the standard midsize-male Hybrid III crash-test dummy. The new ASPECT manikin will offer a more consistent and useful representation of human *posture*[6] and positioning than the current H-point manikin. The ASPECT manikin has an *articulating*[7] lumbar *spine*[8] that allows the *torso*[9] of the manikin to conform to seats with *prominent*[10] lumbar *supports*[11]. Revised seat interface contours provide a more realistic pressure distribution on the seat. The manikin is easier to use and provides more ways of measuring the seat and vehicle geometry. The ASPECT manikin measures *seatback angle*[12], lumbar support prominence, *seat cushion*[13] angle and *seat defection*[14]. It also provides reference points to define a large number of additional seat and vehicle dimensions. Lightmass legs and a foot reference tool can be attached to the manikin to measure vehicle interior geometry and legroom.

[1] Beratungspodium	[2] zusammenarbeiten	[3] Haupt-
[4] Ziel	[5] anthropometrische Beständigkeit	[6] Stellung; Haltung; Position
[7] gelenkig	[8] Lendenwirbelsäule	[9] Rumpf; Oberkörper

[10] vorstehend	[11] Lendenwirbelstütze; Lordosenstütze	[12] Sitzlehnenneigungswinkel
[13] Sitzkissen	[14] Sitzfehler	

6.2 Silver Vision SLR concept car

DaimlerChrysler's extraordinary new Vision SLR concept car, the first time seen at the Frankfurt Motor Show in 1999 and launched as Mercedes Benz SLR in end of 2003, took its design *cues*[1] from a broad spectrum. The styling, inside and out, the 410 kW power output, and its advanced technology, including an electrohydraulic brake system with ceramic *brake discs*[2], and *swivelling headlights*[3], may seem a touch *fanciful*[4]. This car's *arrow-shaped*[5] nose shows the way to future products. Mechanical and styling elements of the car will appear in future production Mercedes models including the *forthcoming*[6] SL replacement. But there is one piece of technology that is missing from the Mercedes Benz SLR: a folding hardtop. However, it does have a great deal of highlights, including elements of design which *hark back to*[7] the 1950s, the time of the gull wing door 300SL sportscar and the sports-racing 300SLR with direct gasoline injection. Instead of true gull-wing openings, its doors *pivot*[8] forward vertically through 75° in the manner of the Renault Sport Spider.

Figure 6.2.1: The new Mercedes Benz SLR (Source: DaimlerChrysler, Stuttgart)

In recent years, Mercedes has demonstrated an increasing willingness to expand its range to *embrace*[9] both relative conservative models such as the C-class and E-class and more avant-garde designs including the SLK, A-class, and M-class. The Mercedes Benz SLR takes that philosophy a big step forward. The car's styling, with its arrow-shaped nose and twin spoilers, borrows elements of the F1 racecar in which Mikka Häkkinen won the 1999 World Championship, but to balance this, the car has the *quadruple*[10] headlamps of the E-class and CLK.

Beneath the Mercedes Benz SLR's *striking*[11] surface lies a *plethora*[12] of advanced technology. As with the four-cylinder SLK 230 compressor, Mercedes has *opted*[13] to use a *supercharger*[14] to extract more power from the car's 5.5 l V8 power unit. This engine is a development of that already being used for the new S-class. Its 410 kW is produced at 6500 rpm with maximum torque of 720 N.m at 4000 rpm. Along with the supercharger, Mercedes uses a water *intercooler*[15] with a separate cooling circuit. In line with the energy saving philosophy of the S-class, which considers cylinder deactivation under part-load conditions for the V12 powered cars, the SLR's supercharged engine has a similar system. Interesting detail elements of the engine include *staggered*[16]-*phase*[17] *dual ignition*[18], which aids fuel consumption and efficiency of exhaust gas *recirculation*[19]. Mass saving in the engine is a priority and Mercedes uses aluminium and magnesium *die castings*[20]. Performance figures include a 0-100 km/h time of 4.2 s and a 0-200 km/h time of 11.3 s with an electronically controlled top speed of 320 km/h. The supercharged engine is likely to be seen in S-class and other models.

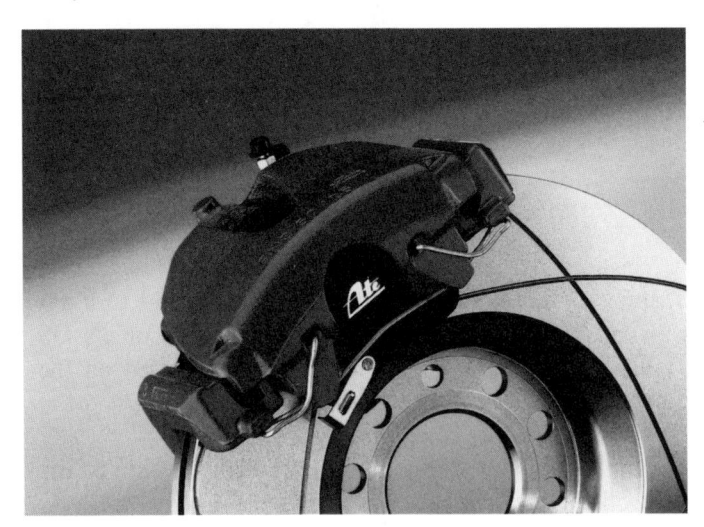

Figure 6.2.2: The PowerDisc and colour painted brake caliper from ATE Bremsen (Source: Continental Teves, Frankfurt)

The campaign to reduce mass is rigorous in the Mercedes Benz SLR. Mercedes claims the body of the car to be some 40% lighter than that of a conventional sports coupe. Its chassis uses *carbon fibre*[21] and *aluminium*[22]. The deformable crumple zone at the front of the vehicle is made of aluminium; the passenger cell includes *fibre-reinforced*[23] materials. The *doorsills*[24] have a foam core to absorb energy. Aluminium is an increasingly accepted material for suspension systems and the Mercedes Benz SLR uses it for wheel guide elements, integral carrier for the front axle and its *control arms*[25], plus some components for the rear axle. Mass is also saved by the use of fibre-reinforced ceramics for brake discs, quoted as being 67% lighter than *gray cast iron*[26] and having heat resistance to a maximum of 1600°C, about twice that for *cast iron*[27].

Data from the ABS speed sensor and *steering angle*[28] inputs and *lateral accelerometers*[29] are correlated to operate wheel-pressure *modulators*[30] that are combined into a hydraulic unit. Mercedes says the system not only provides individual wheel braking but also builds pressure more quickly and will compensate for brake *fade*[31] by boosting pressure. The company explains that the core of the electrohydraulic brake system is a central hydraulic unit linked to the master brake cylinder, the *pedal travel*[32] simulator, the disc brakes, and EHBS (electrohydraulic brake system) computer, replacing the regular servo unit. An electric pump and high-pressure reservoir are part of the system.

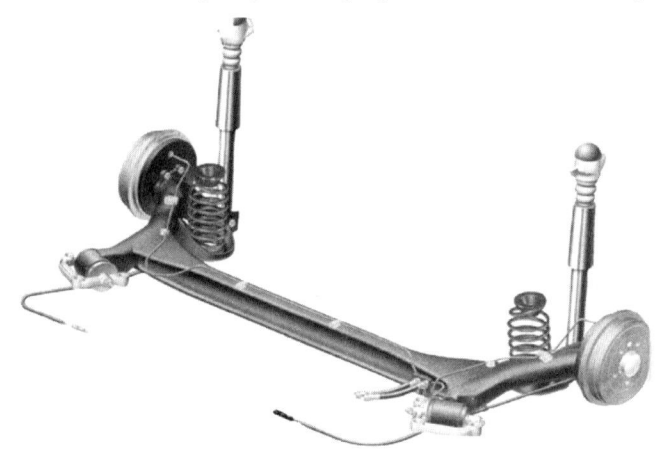

Figure 6.2.3: Twist beam rear axle[33]
(Source: ATZ, 3/2000)

Another interesting feature of the car is its use of cornering- and turning-beam headlights, which swivel by 5°. Citroen had a similar system on its DS models in the 1960s. High-performance light emitting diodes (LEDS) on the car's flanks are activated by a steering angle on winding *secondary roads*[34] or at *junctions*[35].

The *shift lever*[36] for transmission is positioned on the right hand side of the steering wheel. Carbon is used for the seat structure. Seats have some *backrest adjustment*[37] and use individually adjustable *cushions*[38] instead of a one-piece covering. The mass saving achieved by the seats is said to be about 25% compared to conventional designs. The Mercedes Benz SLR is an image-maker, a technology demonstrator, and a clear indicator of the company's belief in the continuing potential of the road-going supercar.

[1] Anhaltspunkte	[2] Bremsscheiben	[3] Kurvenscheinwerfer; Kurvenleuchten
[4] fantasiereich; phantastisch	[5] pfeilförmig	[6] bevorstehend; in Kürze erscheinend

[7] to hark back to sth.: auf etwas zurückgreifen	[8] drehen	[9] umfassen
[10] vierfach	[11] imponierend, eindrucksvoll	[12] Überfülle
[13] sich entschieden	[14] Auflader; Verdichter; Kompressor	[15] Zwischenkühler
[16] versetzt angeordnet	[17] Takt	[18] Doppelzündung
[19] Rückführung	[20] Druckguss	[21] Kohlenstofffaser
[22] Aluminium	[23] faserverstärkt	[24] Türschweller
[25] Querlenker; Führungslenker	[26] Grauguss	[27] Gusseisen
[28] Lenkeinschlag; Radeinschlag; Lenkwinkel	[29] Querbeschleunigungsaufnehmer, -sensoren	[30] Regler
[31] Wirkungsverlust; Schwund; Nachlassen der Wirkung	[32] Pedalweg	[33] Verbundlenker-Hinterachse
[34] Nebenstraßen	[35] Kreuzungen	[36] Schalthebel; Einrückhebel
[37] Sitzlehnenverstellung; Rückenlehnenverstellung	[38] Kissen; Polster	

6.3 The 3 litre barrier and its relation with mass

Overshadowed by the extravagance of the blue Bugatti concept car and its 18-cylinder engine on the opposite corner of the Volkswagen stands at the last Paris Salons and Frankfurt Motor Shows, the "three-litre" Lupo was virtually overlooked. Technically it is a far more interesting car.

Figure 6.3.1: The blue Bugatti EB118 with W18 engine and 408 kW power (Source: Adrian Zürl, Nauheim)

Rather than[1] starting from scratch to develop an all-new car, Volkswagen's design team has taken an existing, proven vehicle – the Lupo – and extensively re-engineered it to meet the challenge.

First and foremost[2] among new technologies employed in the "three-litre" Lupo has been extensive use of lightmass materials so that at 800kg it is some 180kg lighter than the car it is based on. The Volkswagen group has a long history of using what were once called exotic metals - the original Beetle with a magnesium *gearbox casing*[3] and, of course, the Audi A8, which became the world's first all-aluminium bodied car. In the Lupo, VW combined materials that were once thought incompatible into one product.

If the sale price of less than 27,000 DM is at all accurate, then the three-litre Lupo - like the Audi A8 - is being heavily *subsidised*[4].

Body and interior

Although the steel *superstructure*[5] remains in place, *aluminium*[6] now replaces the *wings*[7], door inners and outers, the *outer skin*[8] of the *rear hatch*[9] and *seat frames*[10].

VW worked together with a number of German technical institutions and *adhesives*[11] producers to succeed in *bonding*[12] a magnesium inner frame to the rear hatch's aluminium outer skin. An adhesive/*sealant*[13] material is used and the two elements are rolled together.

VW claims that in safety issues, the aluminium version exceeds in side impact areas to the steel version. The all-aluminium door structures, despite being lighter than steel, improve side-impact protection, absorbing the energy and *dissipating*[14] it through the *body structure*[15].

Thinner glass is also used to save mass.

Figure 6.3.2: Lupo 3L TDI (Source: Volkswagen AG, Wolfsburg)

Chassis

Pedals are made of aluminium. The suspension system also contains a large proportion of light-mass components including an aluminium *sub-frame*[16], front *struts*[17], *forged*[18] *wishbones*[19] and *brake callipers*[20] (front and rear). The rear *beam axle*[21] is manufactured from hardened, thinner steel as are the *trailing arms*[22]. The supplier source Mannesman Fichtel & Sachs provides the lightmass aluminium-bodied *shock absorbers*[23] and *cold drawn*[24] wire is used for the *coil springs*[25] which, at the rear, are separated from the shock absorbers to provide improved interior packaging.

Expensive magnesium is also extensively used, for example, for a magnesium steering wheel inner. No wonder, since it is supplied by VW's joint-venture at the Dead Sea.

On the subject of tyres, lightmass Bridgestone tyres reduce mass by 150g per tyre by using *aramid fibres*[26] instead of steel wires.

Powertrain

The all-aluminium direct-injection three-cylinder diesel engine produces 45kW at 4000 rpm and 140 Nm between 1800 and 2400 rpm. Direct injection is achieved using *camshaft*[27]-driven *injectors*[28] with individual pumps that pressurise fuel up to 2000 bar. A turbo, with a *variable turbine*[29] and blowing at up to 2 bar, provides *boost*[30] while a *sump*[31]-mounted *counterbalance shaft*[32] reduces *imbalances*[33].

Figure 6.3.3: The brake booster, master cylinder and ABS from one unit. The ABS system "ABS Compact", has been specially developed for compact/small cars (Source: Continental Teves, Frankfurt)

A *cut-out*[34] switches off the engine when the vehicle has been stationary for more than 3 seconds with the brake pedal depressed, starting again when the *throttle*[35] is activated.

Figure 6.3.4: Lupo Colour Concept (Source: Volkswagen AG, Wolfsburg)

The natural corrosive *incompatibility*[36] of aluminium and magnesium has been overcome by production engineering techniques. Therefore, VW is able to offer the same 12-year body *warranty*[37] on this car as in the rest of its *product range*[38].

The CdA has also been reduced from 0.62 to 0.57 qm due to the need to reduce the size of cooling *intakes*[39], adding a *flat under body*[40] to reduce *drag*[41], *profiled*[42] *bumper covers*[43] and providing a new *lip*[44] on the *tailgate*[45].

[1] Lieber als	[2] Zuallererst	[3] Getriebegehäuse
[4] subventioniert, bezuschusst	[5] Oberbau; Aufbau	[6] Aluminium (US: aluminum)
[7] Kotflügel; Schutzbleche	[8] Außenhaut	[9] Heckklappe
[10] Sitzrahmen; Sitzgestelle	[11] Klebstoff; Klebemittel	[12] kleben; festkleben, einkleben
[13] Dichtmaterial; Dichtungsmasse	[14] ableiten; abführen	[15] Karosserierohbau; Rohbau
[16] Fahrschemel; Unterrahmen	[17] Lenker; Beine, Streben	[18] geschmiedet
[19] Querlenker	[20] Bremssattel	[21] Starrachse
[22] Längslenker; Zugstange	[23] Stoßdämpfer	[24] kaltgezogen
[25] Schraubenfeder	[26] Aramidfaser; AFK-Faser	[27] Nockenwellen
[28] Einspritzdüsen	[29] Einspritzdüsen	[30] Verstärkung
[31] Ölwanne	[32] Ausgleichswelle	[33] Ausgleichswelle
[34] Abschalter	[35] Drosselventil; Drosselklappe	[36] Unverträglichkeit
[37] Garantie	[38] Produktsortiment; Produktprogramm	[39] Zylindereinlass
[40] flacher/ebener Unterboden	[41] Strömungswiderstand	[42] formgefräst; profilgefräst
[43] Stoßfänger-Abdeckung	[44] Lippe; Falz	[45] Ladeklappe; Heckklappe

6.4 Saving space by introducing flat wires

Flat ribbon cables[1], with directly *surface-mounted*[2] electronic components, can be used as *multi-conductors*[3]. An example is a super-integrated instrument panel where flat ribbon wires are used.

An *instrument panel*[4] (IP) that is lighter, takes up much less space and is more easily switchable between left-hand and right-hand-drive models, will be seen on European and North American cars in 2001. It was developed by Visteon in less than a year and has 35 patented *features*[5] with a further 250 *disclosures*[6] under *review*[7] by patent authorities.

With these connectors, *glove boxes*[8] become "interior trunks" and, now there is space for it, the HVAC system moves to the centre of the IP. Electrically and electronically, this system is extremely flexible, a feature that could not be better timed given the explosion in on-board communications with plug-and-play modules proving *instant*[9] *upgrades*[10].

Figure 6.4.1: Flat wires (Source: Adam Opel AG, Rüsselsheim)

A magnesium support structure incorporating both mechanical and electrical component mountings, *heat sinking*[11] and air bags housing, is the core of such a super-integrated cockpit.

In a *shielded*[12] environment come all the electrical and electronic functions together. A flexible interface is used to eliminate connectors. All the electronics can be mounted directly on the soft flat wiring.

Mass and cost reduction are the major benefits of the flat wire system. Flat wiring is much lighter, but by *populating*[13] the electronics directly onto the flex, also eliminating the housings of electronic modules is possible. Doing away with connectors saves mass again. In all there is up to a 30 per cent mass reduction, depending on content.

Cost reduction of 10 to 20 per cent along with "hidden" savings for the customer such as those provided by ease of access to the electronics. Remove a panel and everything is exposed to the mechanic for easy *serviceability*[14]. This feature reduces access time by 50 per cent.

In developing the cockpit prototype, some Visteon systems areas, like chassis, *climate control*[15], electronics and interiors, are closely integrated. They are currently able to feature an integrated steering column and *ducts*[16] for greater air flow and the centre-position HVAC system which greatly simplifies the engineering involved in providing right- hand-drive and left-hand- drive options.

Is using flat wires in a cockpit the only area within a car? No, since there are advantages also in the rear and on seats.

The *rear package tray*[17] incorporates interior trim, audio and electrical and electronic capabilities and features into a complete unit. Distributed electronics improve the rear package, offering more styling flexibility and eliminating *redundant*[18] *circuits*[19] and "box-in-a-box" packaging.

[1] Flachbandkabel	[2] oberflächenmontiert	[3] Mehrfachpol; Vielpol
[4] Armaturenbrett; Instrumententafel	[5] Merkmale; Eigenschaften	[6] enthüllen; Bekanntgabe
[7] unter Überprüfung	[8] Handschuhkasten	[9] sofort; unverzüglich
[10] Aufwertung	[11] Kühlbleche; Kühlkörper	[12] abgeschirmt; entstört
[13] bestücken	[14] Servicefreundlichkeit	[15] Fahrzeugklimaregelung
[16] Kanäle	[17] Hutablage; Heckablage; Kofferraumbrücke	[18] überflüssig
[19] Schaltkreise		

6.5 Introduction of a new network for car safety systems

Neither *short circuits*[1] nor broken wires don't matter to a new network designed for car systems. Why is this new network unusually tolerant of *faults*[2]?

Despite its capabilities, the Philips Lite Automotive NETwork (PLANET) uses only two wires to carry power, data and synchronising *clock signals*[3]. Modern systems may include seat *buckle*[4] switches, passenger mass sensors, *child seat recognition*[5] sensors and seat and passenger position sensors.

In the PLANET system power and data are transmitted together as an AC[6] signal. Positive *wave crests*[7] deliver the power but the corresponding negative voltage swings are sometimes *permitted*[8] and sometimes *suppressed*[9]. When the negative voltage swings are allowed to occur, they deliver a 1-bit and when they are suppressed, they register as 0. The negative data phase is turned on and off by one of the *data nodes*[10], momentarily connecting the data bus wires together. A diode ensures that this can only happen during negative data swings and not during power giving positive swings.The regular positive peaks also provide clock synchronisation.

In a crash situation, it is quite possible that one wire will be *shorted to ground*[11] or battery. This situation can be improved by isolating both wires from the ground. In this situation, it is of no consequence if the body work of the car becomes part of the circuit on one side or the other. Should it become part of the circuit on both sides, shorting the wires together, there is a bigger problem. To cope with this, there has to be a system which disconnects the faulty part of the circuit, without shutting down the whole thing. This is *accomplished*[12] by a Philips Automatic Section Switch (PASS). The PASS permanently senses the voltage on the bus sections on either side of it. When a fault is detected, the PASS automatically opens the switch for disconnecting the faulty section.

For each door *branch*[13], one PASS has to be used, since the wires in the door are the most likely ones to be damaged during a crash.

If a *twisted cable*[14] is used, the system produces very low radio frequency emissions. Test comparisons between a 150kHz PLANET bus and a 40kHz CANbus showed that the PLANET produced a maximum of 12dBµV while the CANbus produced up to 35dBµV.

PLANET therefore shows great promise as a means of improving reliability and, consequently, safety in cars equipped with modern air bag and seat pretension devices as well as for general automotive databus use.

[1] Kurzschlüsse	[2] Fehler; Störungen	[3] Taktsignale
[4] Auswölbung	[5] Kindersitzerkennung	[6] Wechselstrom
[7] Wellenspitzen	[8] zulässig; genehmigt	[9] unterdrückt; gedämpft
[10] Datenknotenpunkte	[11] Massenschluss, Erdschluss	[12] vollendet
[13] Bereich	[14] verdrehte, verdrillte	

6.6 Do telematics make an intelligent car?

What technology is possible and desirable to deliver intelligent cars for the 21st century?

Telematics[1] used to be a word which meant nothing except to a group of specialists.

In former times, at the end of the last millenium, the pan-European programme Prometheus was set up to explore various possibilities and examine potential. The result has come up with some fascinating working hardware. The strategy of Prometheus, knowing where you are, where you want to go, and how best to get there safely and economically, seems to be simple.

Knowing where you are

Knowing where you are is a matter of checking with a few GPS satellites and, where necessary, *refining*[2] that knowledge with further software. GPS is already the standard position-finding technology for all current automotive-navigation systems and will soon be routinely used for auto-emergency systems in cars: if you crash, the same sensor which *inflates*[3] your airbag will switch on a communicator to *alert*[4] the *emergency services*[5].

Figure 6.6.1: Videosensorics in motor vehicles. One important use is the Traffic Signal Assistant, which by means of visual or audible signals draws attention to traffic regulations, such as speed limits (Source: Robert Bosch GmbH, Stuttgart)

Figure 6.6.2: Combination instruments made by Bosch. Display systems for the cockpit are continuously becoming more efficient, even in lower-priced cars. Electronic displays provide the driver with still more data from a combination instrument (Source: Robert Bosch GmbH, Stuttgart)

Renault has begun offering an extension of the technology with the simplest interface possible. You hit a red button for emergency (with auto-activation following a major impact), a yellow button if you need *breakdown*[6] assistance, and a green button if you are simply lost, or need to know how to find the nearest *filling station*[7] open. Communication via a telephone channel is automatic once a button has been pushed. The cost is a charge for installation of the system and a monthly *subscriber*[8] fee. That will cover the cost of the network of stations to provide 24-hour *monitoring*[9] and advice, and *presumably*[10] also a profit margin.

Figure 6.6.3: Electronic driver information system Comand. In 1998, Bosch developed the electronic driver information system Comand (Cockpit Management and Data System). It includes a dynamic navigation system which changes the selected route to take traffic conditions into account (Source: Robert Bosch GmbH, Stuttgart)

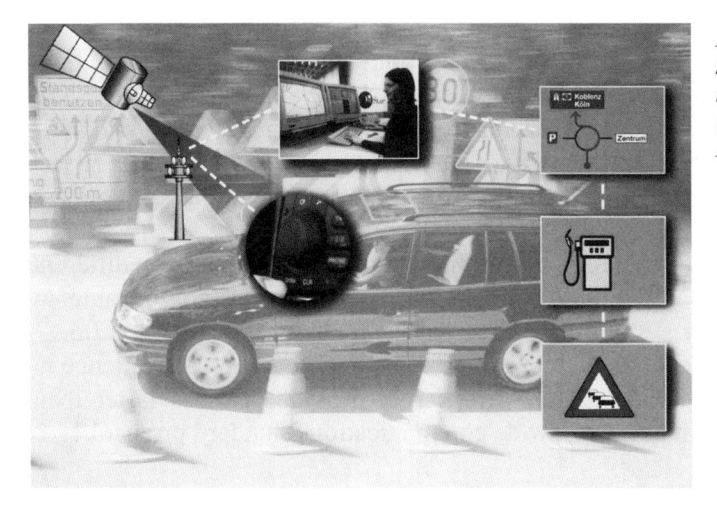

Figure 6.6.4: On-star system with GPS satellite navigation system (Source: Adam Opel AG, Rüsselsheim)

This desirable objective is likely to be achieved in stages, starting with the auto-navigation systems which are already becoming more familiar, and adding *congestion*[11] data.

Opinions vary as to how many vehicles would need to be telematic-equipped before they began to *exert*[12] a significant smoothing effect, but some estimates are as low as 10 per cent. A *predictive system*[13] would prevent, or at least delay, the appearance of *traffic jams*[14]. Telematics, after all, is about allowing maximum productive use to be made of existing road space.

Figure 6.6.5: Workplace of an On-star advisor (Source: Adam Opel AG, Rüsselsheim)

Email and television

We should bear in mind that passengers and drivers will have basic telematics requirements, plus an e-mail download, a conventional audio channel, and a television channel for those in the back seat. This kind of challenge has already attracted some of the larger players in industry of *wiring harnesses*[15] and connectors. Companies have bought themselves high-level electronic expertise in fast developing *optical channels*[16] as the most realistic way of handling such a mass of data.

Mobile telephones can be made to work to two different standards on different sides of the Atlantic; why should vehicle telematic systems not be able to function with whichever system is in force wherever they happen to be? *Thus*[17] the argument runs, and, even though there is a considerable technical challenge in achieving this kind of *versatility*[18], it will surely provide answers faster than waiting for the agreement of a worldwide communications standard protocol.

Figure 6.6.6: Digital Audio Broadcasting, the radio of the future. In the area of communication technology, Bosch is developing the radio of the future. In addition to first-class tone, pictures, for example street maps, can be broadcast using new Digital Audio Broadcasting (DAB) standard (Source: Robert Bosch GmbH, Stuttgart)

Is telematics processed in the vehicle or *remoted*[19]? It is interesting that two of the giants in this field, Delphi and Visteon, seem to represent opposing views on this philosophical discussion, with Visteon on the side of performing tasks mainly in the vehicle and Delphi looking to *exploit*[20] communications. Again, there seems no reason why either approach should *reign*[21] *supreme*[22].

Where is the filling station that is still open?

Inside the car, there is the driver interface, which data can't be transparent. The driver needs to be able to input his (or her) own needs, primarily destination points but also requests for specific information (e.g. that filling station that is still open). This is an area where no fully satisfactory solution has been achieved. Most current systems use *switches*[23] - up/down .and left/right - to move a cursor around a screen, and a third switch to select. It works, but it is slow, it is not intuitive, and it cannot really be done on the move by a driver. A passenger's help is necessary.

Voice recognition

The latest technology in this area is voice recognition. In theory, it is the ideal solution: there is no need to scroll through a series of menus, simply to speak into a microphone. In this case the main problem is that the technology is not yet sufficient for the task. The Jaguar S- Type offers *voice activation*[24], but only for a limited number of functions - telephone number selection, *audio system*[25] selection and climate control - and then only using a strictly limited and carefully defined vocabulary which the user has to learn. Workers in this field insist the day will come when the system is able to give understandable commands.

Indeed, Delphi sees this future capability as one of the *justifications*[26] for its "central processing base" route, arguing that if you need super-computer power for high level activities like advanced voice recognition, then there is no place for it on the car. Voice recognition may still have some way to go, but verbal navigation instructions work surprisingly well in the best systems available on the market.

[1] Telematik	[2] verfeinern; veredeln	[3] aufblasen
[4] alarmieren	[5] Notdienst	[6] Autopanne
[7] Tankstelle	[8] Abonnent (in)	[9] Überwachung, Kontrolle
[10] vermutlich	[11] Verstopfung	[12] (eine Kraft, einen Einfluß) ausüben
[13] Vorhersagesystem	[14] Verkehrsstau	[15] Kabelsätze, Kabelstränge
[16] optische Kanäle	[17] folglich; auf diese Weise	[18] Vielseitigkeit; Wandelbarkeit
[19] ausgelagert	[20] entwickeln, erschließen	[21] regieren
[22] höchst; unschlagbar	[23] Schalter	[24] Sprachsteuerung; Sprachbedienung
[25] Soundsystem; Audioanlage	[26] Rechtfertigungen	

6.7 Do you like joysticks?

Will electronic driving controls with the possibility of joystick-controlled steering, *throttle*[1] and braking be rolled out before the new millennium is 10 years old?

History

At the beginning of automation, there was a steering wheel, three pedals, a *gear lever*[2] and a handbrake. Some time later, with electricity the car become more comfortable and convenient: there were added switches for the lamps and wipers. Eventually, a *plethora*[3] of extra switches served the needs of *direction indicators*[4], heated rear window and so on. Afterwards, automatic transmission did away with one pedal but, in all other respects, things continued unchanged until very recently.

Today

Today controls still use mechanical linkages while most of what came later in history use electrical signalling, if only in the binary sense of an on/off switch. An interesting *diversion*[5] was provided by the heating and ventilation system, which began life as a hybrid system (mechanical linkages to the *valves*[6], an electric switch for the *fan*[7]). Most modern HVAC systems have now moved to electrical signalling for all purposes, with *vacuum servo*[8] or *stepper motor*[9] control of the valves. The greatest advantages of electrical *actuation*[10] are the other things you can do with it, if the need and budget exists, e.g. automatic thermostatic control of cabin heating or continued fan operation when parked.

Future

Similar strategies are now being aggressively developed by other control system engineers, the ones responsible for accelerator, brake and steering. Electric drive-by-wire *accelerator*[11] linkages are becoming more commonplace and they no longer raise eyebrows. Brake-by wire demonstration vehicles exist, and are very convincing. Steer-by-wire is the hardest concept to sell because, even more than with the braking system, the *layman*[12] is inclined to ask what happens if the signalling link goes *short-circuit*[13] or *open-circuit*[14]? Does this mean that they are safe enough? This is almost the only argument which now stands in the way of *wholesale*[15] *adoption*[16].

Drive-by-wire (DBW)

Look at how drive-by-wire has helped those who have *adopted*[17] it:

How does one set a maximum safe *rev*[18] limit? Simply arrange for the control signal to be levelled when it is reached. There is no need to interfere with the ignition or begin *chopping*[19] fuel injection pulses.

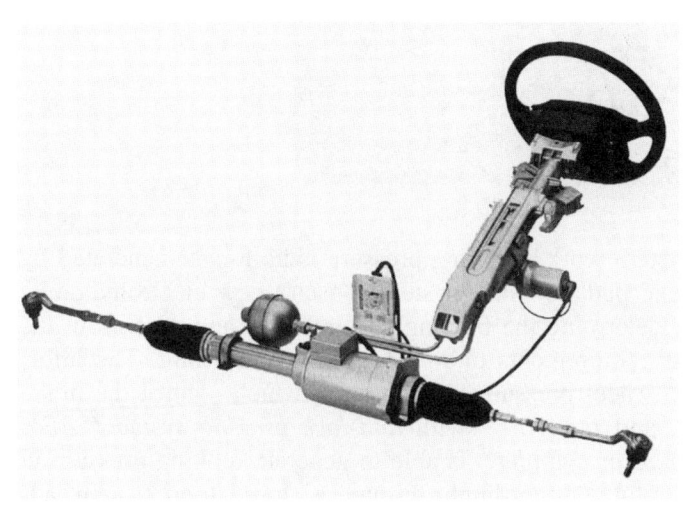

Figure 6.7.1: Steering by wire (Source: ZF Friedrichshafen AG, Schwäbisch Gmünd)

Do you want cruise control? Do you want to cut back power output as part of your *traction control*[20] or *stability enhancement*[21] strategy? Do you want to be able to interface your automatic transmission with engine management to trim the *torque*[22] to smooth shifting? Do you need to smooth out (that is, prevent the driver from executing) one particular *transient*[23] condition which is putting a *blip*[24] into your emissions curve? Everything is much easier with DBW. Simply take a signal from a speed sensor or other sensors and use it to modulate the DBW signal.

Brake-by-wire (BBW)
BBW would permit the optimised braking of each wheel in all circumstances, a situation with which today's ABS systems are only just coming to grips and this only with electronic assistance. The use of individual wheel braking for stability enhancement would be a lot easier. This means that *brake intervention*[25] would be part of an intelligent cruise control. The hand (or parking) brake could become a switch.

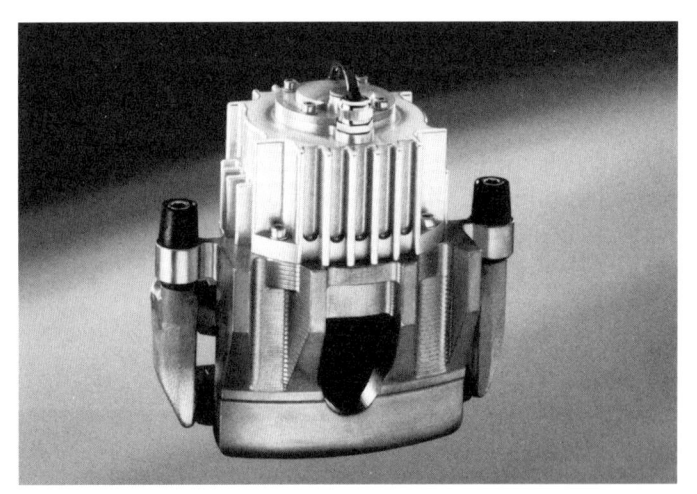

Figure 6.7.2: Electro-mechanic Brake by wire-system. Series start-up projected for around the year 2005 (Source: Continental Teves, Frankfurt)

How does a BBW system work? Braking pressure is no longer generated by foot pressure on the brake pedal. A new system, Bosch's new electrohydraulic brake (EHB), is able to determine the braking requirements and sensors in the pedal communicate these requirements to an electronic control unit. The information is then passed to wheel pressure *modulators*[26], which control the brake pressure in each wheel, and *integrate*[27] with *anti-lock braking systems*[28]. For safety reasons, a *brake master cylinder*[29] is able to generate braking pressure in the event of a systems failure. Accordingly through a closed loop system, adjusting system pressures offers enhanced driver comfort.

What other advantages can be *turned to account*[30]?
– EHB reduces the component count in a braking system.
– Allowing designers the flexibility to integrate the feature with other safety systems.

Other safety systems are in the future, for example, driver assistance systems, like *braking intervention*[31] systems.

Steer-by-wire (SBW)

The doubts about BBW are small compared with those *surrounding*[32] steer by wire (SBW).

Instinct suggests that steering is a more *subtle*[33] process than braking. We can understand how an electric brake signalling system might be split in a way analogous to a hydraulic system split, so that a single system failure leaves two or three brakes still operating. However, a steering system cannot be split.

Again, brakes are either on or off, but you can never say the steering is either left, right, or straight ahead. The signal has to reflect the whole range of possibilities. Nor is there an easy-to-engineer back-up system, other than to retain the option of "manual reversion".

That is the *essence*[34] of the argument against it, but the engineers who have looked deeply into the subject say it can be *overcome*[35]. Pure electrical power supply *integrity*[36] is not an issue: signal paths can be duplicated. Ensuring continued operation in the event of a single open or short circuit is not difficult. In any case such failures would be rare by comparison with loss of car control through mechanical failure. Signal processing need not be duplicated (though in aerospace applications it is often triplicated and more). Modern control programs continuously self-check and drop into a safe *mode*[37] if they detect an anomaly.

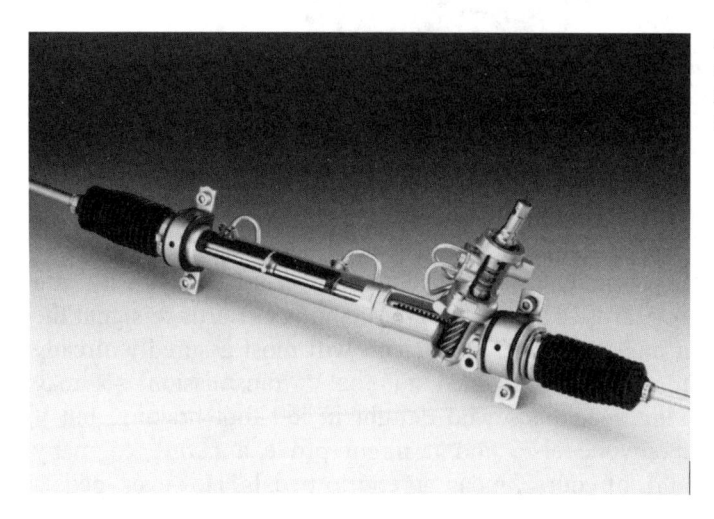

Figure 6.7.3: The steering mechanism (Source: ZF Friedrichshafen AG, Schwäbisch Gmünd)

Eventually these arguments, and continued demonstrations of reliability, will win the day, because the benefits are so great. With SBW, stability enhancement systems can intervene directly in the steering instead of indirectly via the brakes.

Automatic lane-tracking systems can do likewise. Such a system *can head off*[38] steering inputs, allowing *maximum-rate cornering*[39] without risk.

Nevertheless, from the engineer's point of view, one of the biggest advantages would be not having to *thread*[40] a mechanical column through the engine compartment.

As an illustration of the original thinking *provoked*[41] by the approach, Delphi engineers reckon the optimum SBW system would have separate *actuators*[42] for the two front wheels, with no mechanical link between them (doing away with another installation headache). What is more, signal processing could *take account of the fact*[43] that the correct *"Ackermann" geometry*[44] changes according to speed and *cornering force*[45].

Figure 6.7.4: Engine compartment of the Opel Corsa 1.0 12V (Source: Adam Opel AG, Rüsselsheim)

A joystick is sufficient and has many advantages

With SBW, a wheel would not be strictly necessary. A "joystick" would be sufficient. Moreover, once you have a joystick, there is no reason why you should not also move it forwards to signal the DBW and backwards to signal the BBW (remembering that once you have SBW, you will most assuredly already have the other two and, it is *presumed*[46], automatic transmission). It may *confound*[47] the rally-driving specialists who delight in left-foot braking, but it would not greatly upset anyone else, and it might prove a *boon*[48] to many *disabled drivers*[49]. It would, of course, mean an end to pedals. However, pedals are becoming a headache anyway, with safety specialists increasingly worried about driver foot and *lower leg injuries*[50]: It thus seems reasonable to take away the pedals and safety-optimise the *footwell structure*[51]. Without the wheel, you can standardise the same airbag on both sides of the car, and the driver has a clear view of instrument panel displays.

Voice activation is an additional help
The key technology here is voice activation, which is near the stage where it can be used for any on/off function. *Rain detectors*[52] will operate the wipers automatically, and headlamps according to *ambient light level*[53]. *Slaving*[54] the *demist function*[55] and the heated rear window to *cabin temperature*[56] and *humidity*[57] ought to be easy.

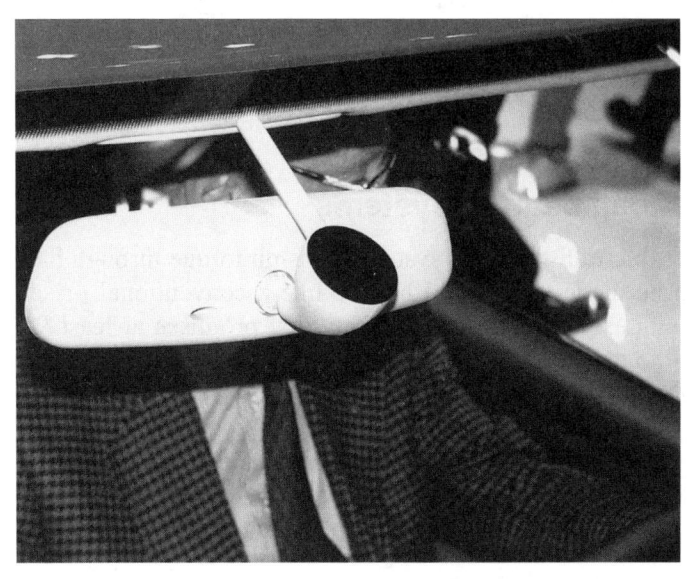

Figure 6.7.5: A rain detector, seen on the VW Polo (Source: Alexander Voos, Rüsselsheim)

[1] drosseln	[2] Schalthebel; Schaltknüppel	[3] Überfülle
[4] Fahrtrichtungsanzeiger; Blinker	[5] Umleitung; Ablenkung	[6] Ventile
[7] Gebläse	[8] Unterdruckunterstützung	[9] Schrittmotor
[10] Bedienung; Steuerung, Betätigung	[11] Gaspedal	[12] Laie
[13] Kurzschluss	[14] offener Stromkreis	[15] Großhandel
[16] Annahme; Übernahme	[17] übernehmen, annehmen	[18] hoch beschleunigen, hoch fahren (Motor)
[19] zerhacken	[20] Schlupfregelung, automatische Schlupfregelung	[21] Stabilitätsverbesserung
[22] Drehmoment	[23] vorübergehend; vergänglich	[24] leuchtender Punkt (auf dem Bildschirm)
[25] Bremseneingriff	[26] Regler	[27] integrieren, einbeziehen
[28] Bremsanlagen mit Antiblockiersystem	[29] Hauptbremszylinder	[30] sich etwas zunutze machen; aus etwas Vorteil ziehen
[31] Bremseingriff	[32] umgebend; einfassend	[33] subtil, raffiniert
[34] das Wichtigste; die Hauptsache	[35] überwinden	[36] Vollständigkeit
[37] Betriebsart; Modus	[38] ablenken	[39] Kurvenfahrten mit Höchstwerten

[40] schrauben, winden	[41] provozieren; hervorrufen	[42] Stellglieder
[43] der Tatsache Rechnung tragen	[44] Spurdifferenzgeometrie, Lenkdifferenzgeometrie der Lenkanlage	[45] Seitenführungskräfte
[46] vermuten	[47] verwecheln, durcheinander bringen	[48] Segen
[49] behinderte Autofahrer	[50] Unterschenkelverletzungen	[51] Fußraumkonstruktion
[52] Regen-Erkenner/Aufspürer	[53] umgebendes Lichtniveau	[54] hier: zwingen
[55] Beschlagentfernungs-funktion; Entfeuchtungsfunktion	[56] Innenraum-, Fahrgastraum-Temperatur	[57] Luftfeuchtigkeit

6.8 New CVTs with ball bearing systems

CVT (continously variable transmission) systems transmit torque through ball bearings, but it can also be made to feel and behave like a conventional or sequential gearbox. A continously variable transmission that promises at least 95 per cent efficiency could do away with conventional *clutches*[1] and has the potential of being cheaper, lighter and more compact than rival CVT technology.

After analysing the good and bad points of existing CVT technology and concentrating on the problems of efficient CVTs, Mr. Milner has designed a system which contains almost all the advantages and none of the disadvantages of rival CVTs.

How does it work?

Unlike other CVTs, the Milner system relies on frictional properties between ball bearing-like spheres, *races*[2] and *roller followers*[3] in contact with them to transmit the power from the input to the output *shaft*[4]. Power from the input shaft is taken up by a pair of race halves that are attached to the input shaft. Opposite them is a pair of outer race halves, mounted on a *collar*[5]. One is fixed to the collar and its opposite number is secured by a conventional or ball-type *thread*[6], while the collar is keyed to the outer casing to prevent it from rotating. Sandwiched between the two race pairs are a trio of free bearing balls, separated by three roller followers, mounted on a *carrier*[7] linked to the output shaft.

The ball bearings are squeezed by the action of the inner thread driving the inner race halves towards each other with a force proportional to the input torque. By varying the amount of "squeeze" there is sufficient friction, or rolling traction, to support the balls and races so that the balls are driven round the races without *slipping*[8].With the balls acting like *gears*[9] they are able to deliver power to the carrier and the output shaft, simply by pushing the *followers*[10] round.

Outlook

Milner is realistic about the prospects for his invention, believing it could take up to eight years for the technology to be developed fully enough for automotive applications.

^{1} Kupplungen	^{2} Laufringe	^{3} Rollenstößel
^{4} Welle	^{5} Bund, Flansch	^{6} Gewinde
^{7} Träger; Halterung	^{8} rutschen, gleiten	^{9} Zahnräder
^{10} Nachfolgenden		

6.9 New plastic rear seating system was a world first

The Mercedes-Benz V-Class minivan is the first car using a metal/plastics rear seating system. The seat back is moulded in Bayer's Durethan nylon 6 and the *seat pan*^{1} is in NovodurABS. Development of the seat was a collaborative effort between Mercedes Benz, Bayer and the seat manufacturer, Grupo Antolin Irausa SA, Spain. The *moulder*^{2} is Simoldes Plasticos, Portugal.

Objectives were comfort, integral seat belts and variability of use. The seat may be turned round and the design meets the specifications under which a seat may be driven backwards. The seat may also be folded to save space, or converted to a flat table with *tray*^{3}.

Weighing about 36 kg, the seat is 30 to 50 per cent lighter than traditional automotive seats and cost-savings may be *of the order of*^{4} 10 to 20 per cent.

The seat back (normally comprising 20 to 30 parts) is a single moulding with frame-*stiffening ribs*^{5}. It also has an integrated *headrest*^{6} and *belt housing*^{7}. The mechanism's metal frame is married to the plastic on the side where the belt is directly attached at shoulder height, instead of to other parts of the car.

^{1} Sitzschale	^{2} Formmaschine; hier: Formhersteller	^{3} Fach, Ablage
^{4} in der Größenordnung von	^{5} Versteifungsrippen	^{6} Kopfstütze
^{7} Gurtgehäuse		

6.10 The smog-eating radiator

In 1999, Volvo started selling its new S80 saloon in California and became the first manufacturer to fit a car with Engelhard's smog-eating PremAir radiator. Eventually, the Swedish company also intends to install the PremAir system in all its cars. It seems to be a shift in the *paradigm*^{1} for the OEMs: instead of them being *perceived*^{2} as selling vehicles which pollute the atmosphere, they are selling ones which help to clean the air.

How does a smog-eating system work?

As air passes through the *radiator*[3], the PremAir system converts ozone molecules into oxygen. Theoretically such a system could be developed to destroy other *pollutants*[4]. It is merely a question of chemistry, temperature and thermodynamics. *Ozone*[5] is the easiest thing to destroy, so for Engelhard it is a good place to start. PremAir is just the first step in radiator *catalyst*[6] technology.

What about cost-effectiveness?

After following a nine-month field trial with Ford, the US manufacturer dampened enthusiasm by saying its was not as cost-effective as initially thought. The original technology was based on platinum and would have added more than $ 1,000 to the price of a new car. Engelhard's latest version uses base metals and will eventually add only $50 to the price of a medium-sized car.

Although *it is not possible to elaborate*[7], the next step, would include systems development with OEMs - and not just for engine or radiator catalysts.

[1] Musterbeispiel	[2] wahrnehmen	[3] Luftkühler; Wasserkühler
[4] Verschmutzer	[5] Ozon	[6] Katalysator
[7] nicht ausführlicher sein können		

6.11 Metals drive back plastics

6.11.1 Why does the mass of cars increase?

There was an increase of 15-20% in the mass of cars over the past 15 years. This resulted in an increase in fuel consumption ranging from 6 to 10% while maintaining comparable car performance. This trend toward heavier cars will continue to meet consumers' continuously growing demands and increasingly stricter standards.

Summarizing, the reasons for increase in mass have been:
- the addition of new features
- improved safety and security
- improved acoustical/vibrational comfort
- compliance with the latest standards (e.g. external noise, exhaust emissions, passive safety)
- improved reliability.

All carmakers have initiated mass reduction programs in which structure, manufacturing, material, functions, and others have had to be considered.

The purpose of mass reduction is not merely reduced consumption, emissions and improved vehicle performance, but also the reduction of *fatigue*[1] assembly line workers in the handling of items, and the lowering of the cost of individual components.

Customer demand and these driving forces have moved to a critical look at vehicle mass, more efficient *powerplants*[2], more slippery shapes, electronics, and materials. Life cycle (e.g., recyclability, manufacturability, environmental issues) and engineering needs are major factors, but costs are probably the most critical long-term strategic consideration in selection of materials.

[1] Ermüdung	[2] Motor-Getriebe-Einheiten; Antriebsgruppe	

6.11.2 Magnesium fever everywhere

Figure 6.11.2.1: Manual transmission housing of F23 transmission of Opel Vectra (Source: Adam Opel AG, Rüsselsheim)

In the early 1990s, magnesium was used for more automotive products in the U.S. than in Europe or Japan. Among the applications were clutch and manual transmission housings, steering column components, brackets, some covers, and automatic transmission parts. By the year 2000, this list will add such things as seat frames, *steering wheel cores*[1], IPs, wheels, oil pump housings, oil pans, and door handles.

Car manufacuturers and their suppliers have experience in applying magnesium components on their vehicles. Fiat Auto, for example, presently uses instrument panel (IP) crossbeam, steering wheel frame, seat frame, and steering column support for its new cars, like the Alfa Romeo 156. A mass reduction as well as better performance in terms of stiffness, dimensional precision, and noise reduction was achieved.

Figure 6.11.2.2: New instrument panel (IP) crossbeam made of magnesium, used in Opel Vectra (Source: Adam Opel AG, Rüsselsheim)

Cost impact

The cost of the basic metal is not stable for magnesium. However, it is possible to obtain assemblies without increasing costs by integrating subcomponents and eliminating operations. As far as the process is concerned, the main variables affecting the results are:
- percentage of mass *discarded*[2]
- percentage of *scrap*[3] reused
- economic penalties for recovery of discards and scrap
- plant productivity
- need for additional processing of the component.

Consider the full cost C to be the sum of: $C = C_m + C_t + q = C_v + q$

where *Cm* is the cost of material, *Ct* the cost of transformation, *q* the rate of *depreciation*[4], and *Cv* the variable cost.

The *transformation cost*[5] maybe expressed as: *Ct* = *Cs* + *Ce* + *Cw* + *Cl*
where *Cs* is the cost of scraps and discards, *Ce* is the cost of energy necessary for transformation, *Cw* is the *cost of labour*[6], and *Cl* is the logistical cost.

By taking these values into account, Fiat engineers estimate that $\Delta C/\Delta mass$ will result in a saving of about 4700 lire/kg saved (ca. $2.70/kg).

Increasing demands for design engineers' ability

Parameters such as *demity*[7], *Young's modulus*[8], *yield strength*[9], *ultimate*[10] *tensile strength*[11], *elongation at fracture*[12], *draft angle*[13], resistance to corrosion, *weldability*[14] and *resistance to creepage*[15] are *inherent*[16] characteristics of a specific magnesium alloy. For a given alloy, therefore, they can only be modified to a very *minor*[17] extent, for example, *sintered*[18] surface protections are applied to reduce the tendency for corrosion.

Among all these parameters, the most important is the Young's modulus. The value of Young's modulus for Mg is valid for use at temperatures up to 90 °C. A low value, in many cases, influences the minimum thickness of components made of magnesium when it is necessary to obtain the same *rigidity*[19] as steel components.

Selecting assemblies allows design engineers to integrate functions and reduce the number of parts, as well as create design solutions that reduce negative characteristics to a minimum, such as the large draft angle.

Finally, design engineers have to take care of defining the cost of energy consumption, processing scrap, ways to reuse scrap and penalties for misuse.

With regard to the *recyclability*[20] of the items used on cars, there is no doubt that the necessary procedures must be performed.

The thickness of magnesium is in relation to the wall thickness and height of possible *ribbings*[21]. One must increase number and/or thickness, if ribbings cannot be lengthened enough. Thus further mass is *penalized*[22].

The current value of the minimum technological thickness of *die cast magnesium*[23] makes it impossible to reduce the mass according to its potential. If the component's mass is already penalized by the dimensioning, components with large dimensions are further penalized by the impossibility of obtaining smaller castings thicknesses than below 2mm. This thickness is the minimum value now obtainable using the *cold chamber process*[24] on such parts as *IP crossbeams*[25], *steering wheel frames*[26] or *seat frames*[27]. Difficulties of *die*[28] filling increase with the distance from the *gate*[29] and the risk of creating *internal stresses*[30] during *solidification*[31]. For example, a steel sheet thickness of 0.7 mm needs a 1.2-mm-thick magnesium wall to maintain rigidity, but it is impossible to obtain a 1.2-mm thickness with the present state of technology. To raise the thickness to 2 mm is a considerable waste of material, cost and a greatly overdimensioned strength and rigidity.

In this way, when the *excess cost*[32] has dropped to acceptable levels, magnesium is used whenever it is most convenient.

It is expected, most automobile growth to be in castings such as *cylinder head covers*[33], *intake manifolds*[34], steering columns, instrument panel frames and seats. Later applications may be in *engine hoods*[35], *engine blocks*[36], oil pans, *grille reinforcements*[37], wheels, *roof panels*[38], *rear deck lids*[39] and structural supports.

Advantages and disadvantages:

According to a US magnesium *die casting*[40] producer, modern *magnesium alloys*[41] are of *high purity*[42], made in a closely controlled process, with a *corrosion-resistance*[43] *superior to*[44] most common aluminium alloys.

However, it has been slow to take off because of its *reputation*[45] for *inflammability*[46], *proneness*[47] to corrosion, and the price. It looks as if solutions have now been found for these classic objections to magnesium. Although pure magnesium can ignite easily in air, machining the alloy does not present a fire risk as long as appropriate cutting conditions are maintained. Magnesium costs twice as much as aluminium.

An *instrument panel support*[48] is a complex assembly and can challenge plastics, steel and magnesium. By redesigning for die cast magnesium, the total mass can be reduced by at least 15 per cent. The number of parts can also be reduced. Moreover, several components can be combined in one and (like engineering thermoplastics) parts can be snapped together. However, there is no die casting machine specifically designed for magnesium alloys. An optimised machine could reduce die casting costs by a further 20 per cent.

[1] Lenkrad-Kerne/Innenringe	[2] entsorgen	[3] Schrott
[4] Wertminderung; Wertverlust	[5] Umformungskosten	[6] Arbeitskosten
[7] Beschlag; Befeuchtung	[8] Elastizitätsmodul	[9] Formänderungsfestigkeit; Fließgrenze, Streckgrenze
[10] äußerste	[11] Zerreißfestigkeit, Zugfestigkeit	[12] Bruchdehnung, Reißdehnung
[13] Ziehwinkel	[14] Schweißbarkeit	[15] Kriechstrombeständigkeit
[16] Eigen- [19] Steifigkeit	[17] geringfügig [20] Wiederaufbereitungsfähigkeit	[18] gesintert [21] Verrippungen
[22] bestrafen	[23] Magnesium-Druckguss	[24] Kältekammerverfahren
[25] Instrumententafel-Querträger	[26] Lenkradgerüst; Lenkradgestelle	[27] Sitzgestelle
[28] Gussform; Giesform	[29] Bordwand, Seitenwand	[30] Eigenspannungen; innere Spannungen
[31] Verfestigen, Erstarren	[32] Zuschlagskosten	[33] Zylinderkopfdeckel
[34] Einlasskrümmer; Ansaugkrümmer	[35] Motorhaube; Kühlerhaube	[36] Motorblöcke

37 Kühlerverstärkungen	38 Dachhaut	39 Kofferraumdeckel
40 Druckguss	41 Magnesiumlegierungen	42 höchste Reinheit
43 Korrosionsbeständigkeit	44 herausragend, überragend	45 Ruf
46 Zündfähigkeit	47 Neigung (zu etwas neigen)	48 Instrumententräger; Armaturenbretthalter

6.11.3 Aluminium advantages and disadvantages

As manufacturers try to meet official environmental standards and customer fuel economy, usage is expected to rise from 39.5kg/car to 114.5kg/car.

HVAC advantages:
Thermal conductivity[1] of aluminium makes it particularly effective for air conditioning systems.

Chassis advantages:
Reducing mass in one component can also have a benefit on other parts, for example, a lighter engine block uses a lighter engine *cradle*[2]. The thermal conductivity of aluminium makes it particularly effective for radiators and oil coolers.

Body advantages:
Corrosion resistance[3] of aluminium is ideal for *bumpers*[4] and other body parts.

Figure 6.11.3.1: Bonnets (US: hoods) of Opel Vectras are made of aluminium (Source: Adam Opel AG, Rüsselsheim)

During daily use of vehicles, small objects such as stones and hail hit outer parts of the car and may result in visible *dents*[5]; this is called dynamic denting. There are aluminium materials that have an equivalent or better *dent resistance*[6] than comparable panels made of steel.

Audi, for example, uses a frame structure in which all surface elements, including outer panels, are an integral part of the load-bearing structure. It is called the "Space Frame" concept. Extruded aluminium skeleton frame and *bonded*[7] aluminium body panels are used (bonded extruded aluminium space pioneered by Lotus for the Elise). Extruded sections (straight and curved) are connected by complex *die castings*[8] (*nodes*[9]) at the *highly-stressed*[10] corner points and *joints*[11]. For the sheet metal, extrusions and castings, special alloys were created and new fastening methods were developed.

At the painting process, aluminium metal is set to its design strength by the "baked through" process. The behaviour of aluminium panels is like *thermosets*[12]. They are processed in a softer and more easily deformable state.

Body disadvantages:

No manufacturer has attempted production of an all-aluminium body. However, Ford is now working on an all-aluminium body using a *monocoque design*[13].

Aluminium is not as malleable as steel. The production process of a part should, therefore, be optimized to aluminium. The most critical deformation of aluminium takes place during the *hemming process*[14], which brings outer and inner parts together. Aluminium should be optimized for hemming, too, resulting in a hem quality similar to that for steel. Extensive computer calculations have to be used. The hemming process is basically a two-step operation. In the first operation, the 45° hem is made, and after that the final hem is formed. A result of such simulation for an optimized hemming process is an optimized aluminium material: it is possible to produce a flat hem without cracks even after 10% *prestrain*[15]. Finally, a special *hot ribbing*[16] (where a small rib is pressed in the material using a hot die) and *subsequent*[17] conventional cold hem flanging process (leads to sharp flanges, with radii well below 2 mm) has been developed and is now state-of-the-art in automotive industry.

Aiming to improve the surface treatment of aluminium so that its paintability and spot welding performance are similar to those *of zinc-coated steel*[18] is another goal of other research projects. A recent development is the introduction of Electron Beam Texturing. This type of texture has a high *roughness*[19] for better lubrication, which is beneficial for forming as well as for paint appearance.

For optimal mass reduction of aluminium hang-on parts, the hood and tailgate are a combination of outer and aluminium inner panels. One of the differences between aluminium and steel is the lower *Young's modulus*[20] and thus lower *stiffness*[21]. To meet the stiffness demands of the automotive industry, the design of an aluminium hood (inner) has to be optimized for aluminium.

A completely new development is alumimum foam structures (pioneered by Karmann and the Fraunhofer Institute in Germany). These structures are even lighter than solid aluminium parts.

It might take 25 years *to get round to*^{22}, but the takeover of car body production by aluminium is "almost *inevitable*^{23}."

^{1} Wärmeleitfähigkeit	^{2} Gestell, Träger	^{3} Korrosionsbeständigkeit
^{4} Stoßdämpfer; Stoßstangen	^{5} Dellen	^{6} Einzelwiderstand
^{7} geklebt	^{8} Druckguss	^{9} Knotenpunkte
^{10} hoch beansprucht	^{11} Fügeverbindungen, Gelenke	^{12} duroplastische Kunststoffe
^{13} Einschalenbauweise, Monocoque-Bauweise	^{14} Umbördeln um 180 Grad	^{15} Vorspannung
^{16} warm verrippt, warm versickt	^{17} nachfolgend	^{18} Stahl mit Zinkschicht
^{19} Rauhigkeit	^{20} Elastizitätsmodul	^{21} Steifigkeit
^{22} dazu kommen	^{23} unvermeidlich	

6.11.4 All about steel design

Finite element analyses and stereolithography have produced more optimal designs for *steel castings*[1]. Therefore, cars' steel content may have decreased in volume, but has simultaneously improved in technological content. Tailored blanks, hydroforming, various metallurgical improvements, and increased use of high strength low alloy (HSLA) steel has contributed to maintaining material leadership. There are no defined boundaries to the product and process improvements possible via the *ingenuity*[2] of the technologists and designers from all producers.

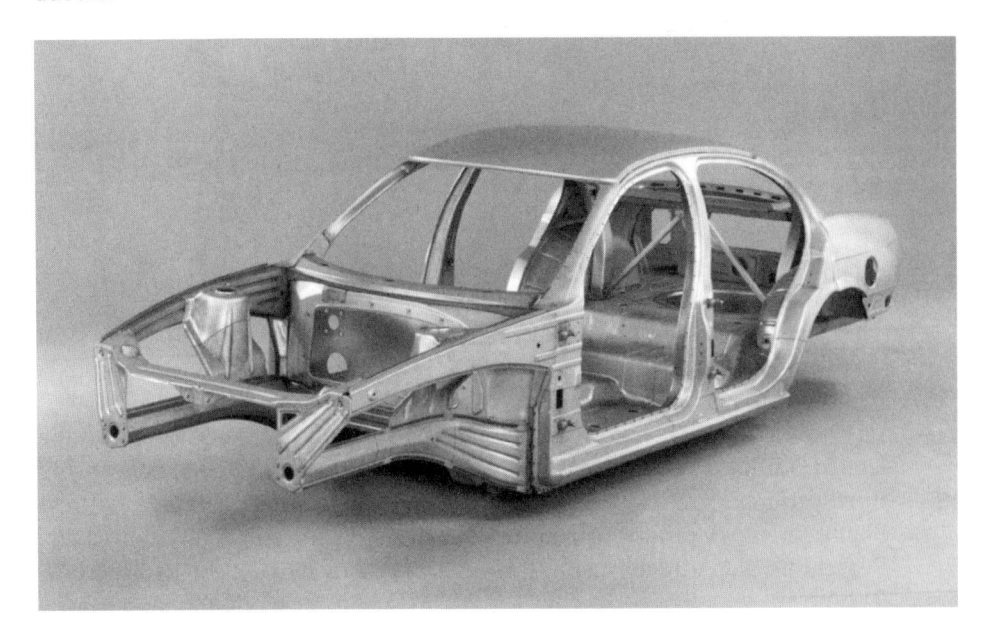

Figure 6.11.4.1: ULSAB (Source: Thyssen Krupp Stahl AG, Duisburg)

Vehicle manufacturers have an *intimate*[3] knowledge of steel. This is still the key advantage of steel. Nevertheless, the steel industry is not going to watch more than millions of automobile bodies being taken away.

An Ultra Light Steel Auto Body project (ULSAB), led by Porsche's North American-based engineering *consultancy*[4] and a group of steel companies including Bethlehem Steel, Nippon Steel, Krupp Hoesch and British Steel, developed new technology and an integrated approach to design. The first *tangible*[5] result of this $22 million project was shown at the 1998 Geneva Motor Show. A BMW 5-Series-sized body shell weighs 203kg, which is 25 per cent lighter than the average comparable shell in production today.

A new integrated design, new manufacturing techniques, thinner *gauge*[6], but stronger material (high-strength steel comprised 90 per cent of the body) and reduction in the number of individual parts (from about 200 to 158) led to savings of 80 per cent and a 52 per cent improvement in torsion and *bending stiffness*[7]. Virtual crash testing showed it comfortably exceeded 56km/h frontal, side and rollover requirements.

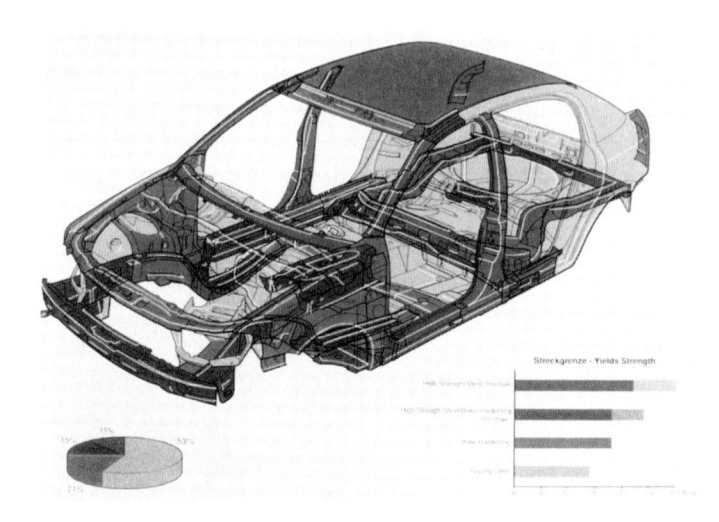

Figure 6.11.4.2: Yield strength of steel (Source: Adam Opel AG, Rüsselsheim)

But this was not enough. What comes next?
- Thin sheets bonded to a plastic *composite*[8] *honeycomb*[9] (called steel sandwich). With steel sandwich panels, body mass is reduced by 25% compared to a similar car produced today.
- Laser-welded tailored pressform *blanks*[10]. The one-piece body sides of the latest Cadillac Seville are pressed from a single tailored blank, comprising three different grades and gauges of steel. The Ford Focus uses tailored blanks in its B pillars to achieve the desired side impact performance. Porsche is also already using this technology in its Boxster and the new 911.
- Selective continuous *laser welding*[11]

– *Stainless steel*[12] could be used in *bodywork*[13], but more proof of the claims will be needed.

All these new techniques contribute to strength and lightness, mass-savings, increased strength and lower costs.

Figure 6.11.4.3: Ford Focus (Ford AG; Köln)

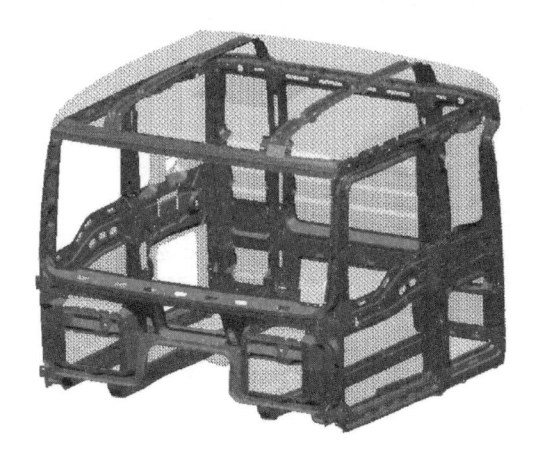

Figure 6.11.4.4: Safety concept: Driver's cab structure of trucks (Source: MAN, München)

Preliminary calculations show a total mass saving of about 35% compared to the body of comparable cars produced today.

There is a new cold-rolled ultra-high-strength steel (called Docol UHS) on the market with a minimum tensile strength of between 1000 and 1400Mpa. That means this sort of steel is particularly suitable in vehicle *crumple zones*[14] because of its high energy absorbing properties. This steel is hardened before leaving the factory, so industries using them do not need to invest in warm-up plant and *hardening furnaces*[15].They are delivered with a bright cold-rolled surface which has not *oxidized*[16] and is therefore suited to continuous manufacturing processes.

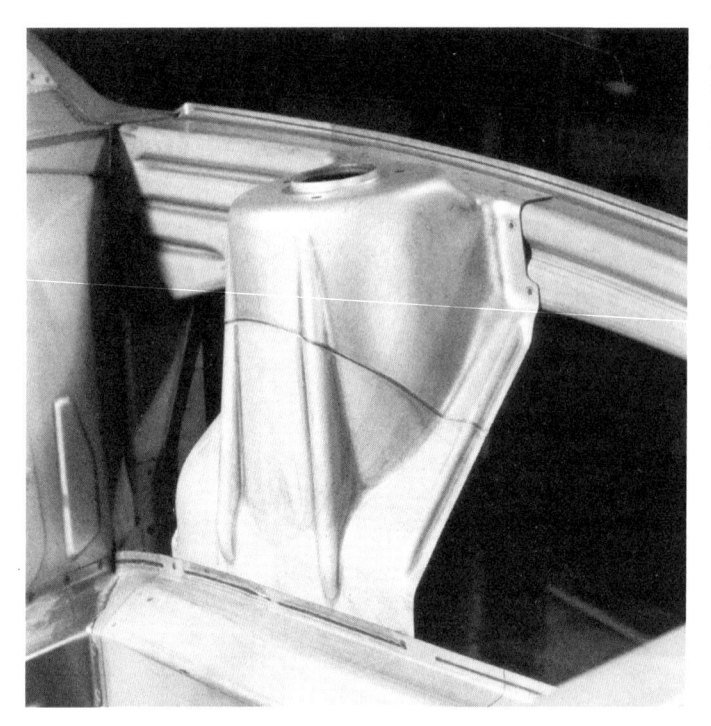

Figure 6.11.4.5: ULSAB's dome technique (Source: Thyssen Krupp Stahl AG, Duisburg)

¹ Stahlguss	² Erfindungsgabe; Einfallsreichtum	³ vertraut
⁴ technische Beratung; Beratung	⁵ greifbar, konkret	⁶ Blechdicke
⁷ Biegesteifigkeit	⁸ Verbundwerkstoff	⁹ Bienenwabe; Wabenkörper
¹⁰ Bienenwabe; Wabenkörper	¹¹ Laserstrahlschweißen	¹² Edelstahl; rostfreier Stahl
¹³ Karosserie	¹⁴ Knautschzonen	¹⁵ Härteöfen
¹⁶ oxidiert		

6.11.5 Plastic development

Not surprisingly, plastics manufacturers are also developing products. In two former plastics key areas, however *bodywork*[1], *underbonnet*[2] components and metals are coming back. The advance of plastics has been slow and irregular over the past two decades, mostly because no-one in the industry has revised their opinion.

Metals are now using exactly the same claims and slogans as plastics did before: light mass, lower investment, easy processing, thin-walls, parts integration, easy assembly and even *snap-fits*[3]. If it is only mass-saving that some plastic parts can offer, they will not be able to compete anymore in future. Magnesium, for example, offers low mass with mechanical properties that can *outperform*[4] plastics.

However, plastics body panels are accepted by OE manufacturers. These are glass-reinforced composites such as polyester *Sheet Moulding Compound*[5]. Within the last few years there has been a marked shift towards thermoplastics. These can be *injection moulded*[6] in realistic quantities.

Figure 6.11.5.1: Plastic Injection Moulding Machines (Source: Krauss Maffei, München)

Are there any disadvantages of plastic usage then? Yes. Poor *heat resistance*[7] generally limits their use in conventional *paint processes*[8], while their high *thermal expansion*[9] presents problems of *joining*[10], *fixing*[11] and *gap*[12] control. Therefore, new *paint lines*[13] with new technologies are necessary (such as *powder coating systems*[14], which will operate at significantly lower temperatures) to replace conventional paint processes.

Do we have some plastic parts already being produced in the automotive industry? Yes, the thermoplastic front fenders of the latest Renault Clio model, at over 400,000 cars a year (the highest volume of plastic fenders). Mass was reduced by 30-50 per cent over steel. It works, because the supplier GE Plastics has switched its attention to *conductive formulations*[15] while continuing to raise heat stability. It already has a conductive grade of the polyamide/polyphenylene ether blend Noryl GTX which will withstand 170°C (under development 190°C). It allows fenders to be painted throughout the whole process, including the heat-intensive *curing process*[16].

VW uses another GTX grade for fenders on the newly-launched Beetle without sacrificing impact performance.

Chrysler is working with glass fibre-reinforced polyester (PEl) for the *concept coupe vehicle*[17] (CCV), reducing the shell to just four *massive*[18] *injection mouldings*[19].

The first self-coloured interchangeable plastics body panel system was introduced by the launch of the MCC "Smart" car. This uses a PC/PDT alloy (Xenoy) which is painted with a *powder clearcoat*[20], offering outstanding *UV stability*[21], unique *brightness*[22] and depth of colour. The need for a coloured *basecoat*[23] is eliminated. Important benefits are a plunge in cost and *environmental loading*[24].

The most spectacular application is the *air intake manifold*[25], where engineering thermoplastics (particularly glass-reinforced nylon) offers significant savings in mass and cost against aluminium. According to forecasts, moulded components will lead to a market *penetration*[26] in the under-bonnet area rising to 70 per cent by the year 2001.

Plastics suppliers are pressing ahead fast. The driving force is parts integration and also integration of processes, such as injection and *blow mouldings*[27], as is already done in the packaging industry.

Systems under the bonnet don't demand an absolute dimensioned accuracy, e.g. components joined to *hollow sections*[28], like *ducting*[29]. Against die castings in new metal alloys, this could prove a powerful defensive position for plastics.

Still to be reckoned with is the new *polystyrene*[30], developed in Japan and going into commercial production in Europe in 2001. Melting at a high temperature of 270°C, *low viscosity*[31], low *specific gravity*[32] and *moisture*[33] and chemicals resistance are the latest performance details. Good flow properties suggest thin-walled parts. The *heat resistance*[34] is the highest of any product based on a polystyrene. *Grades*[35] at present are reinforced with glass fibre and tailored to electronics and automotive applications (e.g. *coolant systems*[36], *headlamp reflectors*[37] and electrical/electronic *connectors*[38]).

[1] Karosserie	[2] Motorraum-; motornah	[3] Einschnapp-Passung/-Sitz
[4] übertreffen	[5] Verbundbauteil, Blech/Kunststoff-Formteil	[6] spritzgegossen
[7] Wärmebeständigkeit	[8] Lackierprozess	[9] Wärmeausdehnung
[10] Fügen	[11] Befestigung	[12] Spalt
[13] Lackierbandstraßen	[14] Pulverbeschichtung; Pulverlackierung	[15] leitfähige Mischungen/ Ansätze
[16] Aushärteprozess	[17] Coupe Styling Studie	[18] wuchtig
[19] Spritzgussteile	[20] Pulverklarlackschicht	[21] UV-Beständigkeit
[22] Glanz	[23] Grundlackschicht	[24] Umweltbelastung
[25] Einlasskrümmer; Ansaugkrümmer	[26] Durchdringung	[27] Spritzgussteile; Blasformteile
[28] Hohlprofile	[29] Kanalauslegung; Führung	[30] Polystyrol (PS)
[31] Dünnflüssigkeit	[32] spezifisches Gewicht; Raumgewicht	[33] Feuchtigkeit
[34] Hitzebeständigkeit	[35] Sorten	[36] Kühlmittelsysteme
[37] Scheinwerferspiegel	[38] Verbindungstücke	

6.11.6 Last but not least: Copper, brass and zinc

The use of *copper*[1] and *brass*[2] in cars over the last 20 years has risen from about 16 kg per vehicle to 20-kg and has remained at the same level to the present. Seemingly, this relatively small increase must be related to the increasing amounts of electrical and electronic *gears*[3] in cars.

One of the major influences on the use of zinc in the automotive industry may be efforts in this area by the Ultra Light Steel Auto Body (ULSAB). The steel used for the ULSAB is 100% coated, with 65 g/m^2 per side. This could represent a steady application for this metal.

The object is to obtain coating that will combine reduced mass and improved corrosion protection performance. Therefore, a new zinc coating especially to protect auto underbody parts (e.g., *engine cradles*[4], *trailing arms*[5], *transverse links*[6], and *bracketry*[7]) against *stone chipping*[8] and corrosion has to be developed.

The percentage of zinc-coated steel sheet in the bodies-in-white of Western Europe's OEMs has increased almost linearly from about 10% in 1980 to a little more than 60% in 1995. By 2005, it is projected to reach nearly 80%.

[1] Kupfer	[2] Messing	[3] Mechanismus, Mechanik
[4] Motorträger; Motorhilfsrahmen	[5] Längsträger, Zugstangen	[6] Querlenker
[7] Lagerungen	[8] Steinschlagschaden	

6.12 Lightmass design is pulling the fat from body panels

Sandwich material

Fuel economy demands the lowering of the mass of today's vehicles. Doors, *hoods*[1], *deck lids*[2] and *hatch backs*[3] account for 6% of a typical vehicle's mass. Especially for such hang-on panels, sandwich material is the mass reduction champion.

Such a typical sandwich material measures 1.2 mm of its total outer panel. It is composed of two 0.2-mm aluminium outer skins and a 0.8-mm polypropylene inner filling. It is lighter than both steel (65% mass savings), and aluminium (30% mass savings).

What are the disadvantages of such lightmass aluminium sandwich sheets? Apart from being about 15% more costly than aluminium on a material basis, there are none. A considerable advantage is that companies are able to use the same presses as steel and need not invest in completely new equipment. If one wishes to use plastics to save mass, one needs expensive process changes. Aluminium sandwiches have shown a *Class A surface finish*[4] and dent resistance, too.

Automakers often *perceive*[5] *reluctances*[6] to *overcome*[7] questions of quality, functionality, and manufacturing process compatibility by suppliers. The aluminium sandwich answers each of those questions, but in the automobile world remains a limited-production solution and is currently not a market share threat. For instance, Volkswagen's 3-litre-Lupo is produced with an aluminium sandwich hood, and the French-made Aixam Mega microcar contains three floor panels of this type of material, but for both cars the vehicle volume is low.

Sheet Moulding Composites

Volume production application is under way for three *Sheet Moulding Composite (SMC)*[8] technologies that will debut in the next few model years. The Budd Company (providing inner panel roof) and Cambridge (which provides all other panels) hold about an 80% share of the SMC automotive market in the U.S.

- Low-density SMC (specific gravity of 1.3, due to the addition of hollow glass *beads*[9] to the material), roof inner panels (debuting on the 1999 Chevrolet Corvette), and others in doors, hoods, *liftgates*[10], *tonneau cover*[11] are produced from low-density SMC. When compared to steel, low-density SMC provides a 45% component mass saving, because of panel-thickness differences. Low-density SMC can be used on outer panels because, if *sanded*[12], the beads may break.
- Lite SMC (specific gravity of 1.6) appear as body panel applications, such as the hood of the Dodge Viper. Lite SMC reduces its mass by 35% as compared to a conventional steel hood. Lite SMC is used for outer panels because of its different type of calcium carbonate.
- Low-pressure SMC appears in low-volume, heavy-truck applications. Up to now, it does not have a Class A surface finish.

Figure 6.12.1: The Chrysler Dodge Viper, seen at the Frankfurt Motor Show in 1999 (Source: Adrian Zürl, Nauheim)

Thermoplastics popularity

It is *anticipated*[13] that a trademarked thermoplastic, called "Surlyn Reflection Series", made by DuPont Automotive, will appear as front and rear *fascias*[14] lower rocker panels on cars, and Surlyn as a *moulded-in-colour*[15], scratch-resistant alloy with a sharp exterior finish and a smooth, *glossy*[16] look.

Thermoplastics offers part integration possibilities for impressive cost savings, e.g. for hybrid electrics, fuel cell-powered cars or other future low-emission vehicles.

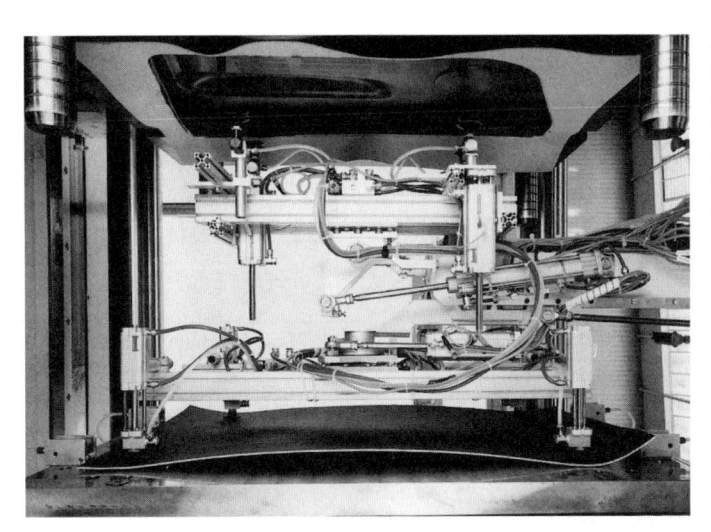

Figure 6.12.2: Taking off and insertion of thermoplastic components at the same time. Performed by an handling device, made by Krauss Maffei (Source: Krauss Maffei, München)

Aluminium

Vehicle areas with the greatest aluminium growth potential are bodies-in-white and body panels. *Closure panels*[17] are *prime zones*[18] for lightmassing. The 1998 Ford Ranger pickup has the lightest-gauge, lightest-mass hood closure of any vehicle in the world. In general, a steel hood closure has a mass of about 17-23 kg, against 10-11.4 kg for an aluminium hood. The Chrylser Concorde (1999 model year) has an aluminium hood of 10.6 kg, which is 6.9 kg lighter than that of a steel hood.

The present leader in aluminium vehicle volume production is the Ford Motor Company. Aluminium is part of its very serious *pursuit*[19] of significant fuel- economy improvements. Reasons why automakers are using aluminium, especially aluminium sheets, are that it can match steel processes and save vehicle mass.

Steel usage

Even *amid*[20] heavy competition, steel maintains its *reign*[21] as body panel usage champion. Galvanized mild, high-strength, and ultra-high-strength steel still account for 98% of the body panel market share in the U.S. The other 2% are plastic composites and aluminium. There is an increased use of aluminium, but it is mostly engines and castings that are truly replacing iron. To attack the other 2% market share, the U.S. steel industry recently released lightmassing design concepts for automotive doors, hoods, deck lids, and hatchbacks via the Ultra-Light Steel Auto Closures (ULSAC) study. The ULSAC concept features thin-gauge, high- and ultra-high strength steels, steel sandwich panels, as well as tailored blanking and hydroforming technologies. The closure panels can be fabricated via current steel manufacturing processes, but weighs 10% less than best-in-class parts.

[1] Motorhauben	[2] Kofferraumdeckel	[3] Ladeklappen; Kombi-Heckdüren
[4] Oberflächenbeschaffenheit mit 1A Qualität	[5] wahrnehmen	[6] Widerwille, Abneigung
[7] überwinden	[8] Blech/Kunststoff-Formteil, Verbundbauteil	[9] Kügelchen; Perlen
[10] Ladeklappen; oben/unten angeschlagene Heckklappen	[11] Fahrgastraumabdeckung; Verdeckhülle	[12] abgeschliffen
[13] voraussehen	[14] Verkleidung; Aussenverkleidung	[15] durchgefärbt
[16] glänzend	[17] Deckbleche, Abschlussbleche	[18] Hauptbereiche
[19] Verfolgung	[20] mitten in/unter	[21] Herrschaft

6.13 Heat-shrinkable tubing

A new *heat-shrinkable tubing*[1] has been *formulated*[2] to protect automotive pipes and *hoses*[3]. It is *adhesive lined*[4] and *thin-walled*[5]. It is also useful for pre-positioning hose bundles prior to installation and keeping them secure during their service life.

Some figures: The material's operating temperature range is -55 to 125°C. Shrink temperature is 120°C. Shrink ratio is 2:1.

Some advantages: tubing is *flame retardant*[6] and meets the surface *flame spread*[7] requirements of FMVSS302. This material provides a barrier against chemical attack and will not split on installation or in service. It is called DURAS 2OOGP, made by Canusa Systems.

[1] Warmschrumpfschlauch; Aufschrumpfschlauch	[2] konzipiert	[3] Schläuche
[4] klebstoffbeschichtet	[5] dünnwandig	[6] schwer entflammbar, feuerhemmend
[7] Flammenausbreitung		

6.14 How to get cleaner diesels

A challenge that has been occupying automotive engineers and chemists for many years is the development of efficient techniques for dealing with passenger car diesel *exhaust*[1] *particulates*[2]. A new Electrocat Diesel Particulate Filter (DPF), made by AEA Technology in the UK, should help. It operates at low exhaust temperatures, is self-cleaning, does not require *fuel additives*[3], and is unaffected by *sulphur content*[4] in fuel. Its plasma filters remove all types of *carboniferous*[5] particulates, including *ultrafines*[6] and *gaseous*[7] *hydrocarbons*[8], including *suspected*[9] *carcinogenic*[10] *polyaromatic hydrocarbons*[11].

The next generation will be Electrocat technology, which employs a gas plasma. If an *electrical current*[12] passes through this filter, the plasma gas will be at least partially *ionized*[13] and then chemically reactive because of the electrons and free radicals it contains. Chemical reactivity under low-temperature conditions (non-thermal plasmas), in which reactivity would not normally be expected, will be the next goal of engineers and chemists. This property makes plasma particularly suitable for the environmental treatment of gases. For example, an *organic*[14] *contaminant*[15] can be removed from a gaseous waste stream, such as an engine's exhaust, without the need for thermal or catalytic oxidation. Plasma technology will play a vital role in future automotive *aftertreatment systems*[16].

For initial applications, the Electrocat technology package includes a dual-voltage *alternator*[17] in readiness for 42-V systems.

A problem will be the *sealing*[18] of plasma-based aftertreatment systems for *onboard*[19] usage. This problem can be solved by allowing the DPF to double as an *exhaust muffler*[20].

DPF has the potential to deliver a fuel efficiency benefit.

[1] Auslass; Auspuff	[2] Teilchen; Körnchen	[3] Kraftstoffzusätze
[4] Schwefelgehalt	[5] kohleführend	[6] hochfeine
[7] gasförmig	[8] Kohlenwasserstoffverbindungen	[9] verdächtig
[10] krebserregend	[11] polyaromatische Kohlenwasserstoffe	[12] Elektrischer Strom
[13] ionisiert	[14] organisch	[15] Schadstoff
[16] Nachbehandlungssysteme	[17] Drehstromgenerator	[18] abdichten
[19] Einbau	[20] Abgasschalldämpfer; Auspufftopf	

7 Alternative Propulsion

7.1 Electric Cars

7.1.1 How far is the next charging station?

Nissan has introduced a revolutionary electric car, a new kind of all-electric, two-seat *commuter*[1] vehicle with a new type of battery. They stepped boldly into the future with the launch of its Hypermini, the latest *contestant*[2] in a motor industry game. To understand why Nissan is pressing ahead with the Hypermini, it helps to understand the cultural context. Until recently, a job for life was given in Japan. Performance-related bonuses were a western idea. *Perseverance*[3] and not talent led to promotion. Innovation in engineering and design was not necessary and customers' needs were irrelevant.

Nissan's alliance with Renault has changed all that. Under the campaign name "**Renaissan**ce", the two carmakers are bringing their restructuring plan to the people.

The Hypermini electric car programme looks like good public relations, demonstrating that innovation and engineering remain important to Nissan despite the company's *wholesale*[4] restructuring. It is *strikingly*[5] modern and its *appealing looks*[6] are a rarity among cars wearing the Nissan logo. But there's another reason. Japan still has real pollution problems: nitrogen dioxide, *soot*[7] and a *benzene*[8] level rise. Zero- emission electric cars, then, remain a good idea.

The problem is an *inherent*[9] and so far unavoidable paradox in their design. The only way to increase range and performance is to add batteries. Adding batteries, however, means adding mass, and losing *range*[10] and performance.

Of course, there are a lot of *appealing*[11] *justifications*[12] about a modern electric vehicle:
– Electric motors drive without the need for a gearbox, so the power is engendered quickly.
– Never having to visit a petrol station could be a *seductive*[13] idea.
– Pollution-free motoring.

But there are some disadvantages:
– You may need no petrol station. The only problem is, forgetting to plug it in at night after getting home.
– Pollution free driving, ignoring the fact that electricity is generated at a *power station*[14] in the first place. Power stations, however, are less efficient at burning *fossil fuels*[15] than *internal combustion engines*[16].
– Electric vehicles are limited in their usefulness and in their impact.

Every electric car programme is a help to advancing the art of zero-emission. Even the Hypermini is not perfect. But what is new about this car?

- The Lithium-ion battery retains a greater amount of charge than older ones. Drivers are capable of travelling about 70 miles on a four-hour charge. A new design has been developed in cooperation with Sony. These sort of batteries are quicker to charge up and significantly lighter than traditional batteries.
- Low battery mass in conjunction with an aluminium frame and plastic panels makes for a *nippy*[17] car (as long as the car's air-conditioning is kept switched off).
- The *fashionably*[18] modern half-tone *finish*[19] is good to look at.

Due to the high *list price*[20] (Y4m = £23,000, including the recharging apparatus; twice the price of Nissan's Micra and as much as a small Mercedes in Japan) it is unlikely to set the market on fire, even with sales efforts concentrated around urban areas and with a government environmental rebate.

Nissan is instead planning to sell the cars into local government or commercial *car-sharing*[21] schemes. The first of these, near Yokohama, opened for business in January 2000. *Subscribers*[22] are able to book a Hyper mini online, then access the car at an *unmanned*[23] base station via a smart card.

[1] Pendler; Berufspendler	[2] Bewerber; Wettbewerber	[3] Ausdauer; Durchhaltevermögen
[4] Großhandel	[5] imponierend, eindrucksvoll	[6] zum Schauen auffordern
[7] Ruß	[8] Benzol	[9] eigen
[10] Reichweite; Aktionsradius	[11] reizen; Anziehungskraft ausüben	[12] Daseinsberechtigungen; raison d'etre
[13] verführerisch	[14] Kraftwerk	[15] fossile Brennstoffe
[16] Kraftmaschine mit Innenverbrennung	[17] schnell; wendig	[18] modern, modisch
[19] Endlackierung	[20] Listenpreis	[21] gemeinsame Fahrzeugbenutzung
[22] Abonnent(in)	[23] unbemannt	

7.1.2 Electric delivery vehicle

The electrically-driven *tow-tractor*[1] maker John Bradshaw (UK) has moved into the delivery market with the first purpose-built vehicle at a price which is competitive, with a high cube-shaped van having diesel propulsion. The base model is £11,800 for a *chassis-cab*[2] with *platform body*[3].

Converted vans and *light goods vehicles*[4] are well-known but the tailored delivery vehicle is rare with battery power, even with an *IC-engine*[5]. The batteries are lightmass units which can propel the vehicle with 680 kg *payload*[6] at up to 50 km/h. The vehicle has an 8 hour or 80 km operating range. Performance is a relatively modest 16s for 0-40 km/h. The vehicle is unusually styled, using a cab with few *double-curvature*[7] panels. However, the company can supply a high cube *integral variant*[8] with streamlined *front end*[9] for the relative *low-density*[10] city delivery products with which the vehicle is involved.

Figure 7.1.2.1: Computerized streamlined front end for better aerodynamics (Source: ATZ, 3/2000)

The vehicle has a *CV-standard*[11] *track-width*[12] and standard automotive components, mostly US Ford, are used for the *drive line*[13] and *running gear*[14]. The 21 kW motor is made by General Electric of America, and it can speed the response for sudden power demand. The battery pack comprises twelve 6-volt *lead-acid batteries*[15], *series-connected*[16] to give 72 V, and a *DC-DC*[17] converter reduces a portion of this to 12V for running the vehicle's *accessories*[18]. For the vehicle-mounted *charger*[19], a nine hour period is required to charge the battery from a 13A *mains supply*[20].

[1] Abschleppfahrzeug (US: tow truck)	[2] Fahrgestell mit Fahrerhaus	[3] Pritschenaufbau
[4] Leichte Nutzfahrzeuge	[5] Motor mit innerer Verbrennung	[6] Zuladung
[7] doppelt gekrümmt/gerundet	[8] integrierte Variante	[9] Stirnseite; Vorderseite
[10] niedrige Dichte	[11] Nutzfahrzeug-Standard	[12] Fahrspurbreite
[13] Antrieb; Antriebsstrang	[14] Fahrgestell; Fahrwerk	[15] Blei-Säure Batterien
[16] in Reihe/Serie geschaltet	[17] Gleichstrom-Gleichstrom	[18] Nebenverbraucher
[19] Ladegerät	[20] Stromversorgung	

7.2 Fuel Cell Technology

7.2.1 GM's fuel cell secrets

Do you know that fuel cells are already in use? There are many applications in the world including lights for river *buoys*[1], traffic signs, a power station in the Netherlands, and some video cameras. Researchers into Solar Energy Systems have also developed a miniature fuel cell that can power a notebook computer for up to 10 h.

Figure 7.2.1.1
Opel Zafira with fuel cell technology (Source: Adam Opel AG, Rüsselsheim)

Also for the automotive industry, fuel cell technology comes closer to reality. It is only with advances in electronic controls, software systems, and process engineering that the motor industry may be on the *threshold*[2] of change greater than anything seen for decades. Sufficient *momentum*[3] has been gained in research departments to make their production *viable*[4].

Most of the world's major automotive companies have fuel cell programs in place, but each of those companies is cautious about giving out details or even secrets of the technology. However, General Motors Europe (GME), which includes Opel and Vauxhall, has announced that it will have a fuel-cell-powered car ready for the market by the year 2004. GM has established a Global Alternative Propulsion Center (GAPC) in the U.S. and Germany to develop fuel cell technology in cooperation with Exxon/Esso.

At a development stage, GAPC is running a fuel-cell-powered Opel-Vauxhall Zafira, a small multipurpose vehicle or *compact van*[5]. The system concentrated on is fueled by *methanol*[6] or *synthetic gasoline*[7]. *Hydrogen*[8] produced with the aid of solar energy as an input is also *conceivable*[9].

Advantages and disadvantages
Fuel cell technology has some advantages which have been known for years:
- The efficiency[10] of the fuel cell (over 60%) is the highest in electric power generation[11].
- Fuel cell drive systems have significantly low pollutant emissions.
- Carbon dioxide (CO_2) is produced during the reformation of methanol to obtain hydrogen, but the amount is about half that of an internal combustion (IC) engine. If pure hydrogen were used and reformation avoided, exhaust gas emissions would be completely eliminated.

Currently there are some disadvantages:
- Methanol gas has to be carried safely.
- *Replenishment*[12] of gas remains impracticable for production cars. The time taken to *replenish*[13] energy is measured in hours compared with minutes for an IC car.
- The fuel cell system which drives a 50 kW *AC*[14]-electric motor, fitted to the Zafira, is still too large and takes up much of the rear of the car. This effect in early development hits every carmaker and major miniaturization efforts are underway to reduce size.
- Compromises in terms of performance, range, mass and cost are still *militating against*[15] production usage: driving with fun.

GM's *multiphase plan*[16] for the introduction of fuel cell vehicles shows a range of models including a small car, large executive cars and tailor-made vehicle concepts. It is regarded as essential by GME to meet commercially viable price levels. In 2004, the first fuel cell car needs to be seen as a *straightforward*[17], practical piece of transport and not a limited-volume, niche-type freak.

Up to now, electric cars have still had major problems and show their *inability*[18] to match the *convenience*[19] of an IC vehicle. To compare pluses with minuses, the fuel cell solution looks good, although massive investment in manufacturing systems, processes and a changed infrastructure of fuel supply is needed.

GME's Zafira demonstrates how components could be arranged for easy access and the ability to exchange components quickly:
- Fuel cell, fuel preparation system, and methanol tank at the rear.
- To control the system, the electric motor, battery, and electronic components positioned under the hood.

How does a fuel cell work?
The *electric current*[20] produced by a fuel cell is called a "cold combustion" process. It occurs when *hydrogen*[21] and *oxygen*[22] react at 80° - 90° C to form water. The output of a single cell is typically 0.6-0.8V, but when many cells are

combined into a block, or stack, there is sufficient energy to power a 50 kW three-phases *assynchronous motor*[23], driving the front wheels. Each cell *comprises*[24] three parts: the fuel electrode (anode), the *electrolyte*[25], and the oxygen electrode (cathode). Supply the anode with hydrogen and it releases electrons. The positive ions (protons) migrate via the electrolyte toward the cathode, where they combine with negatively charged oxygen ions to form water. It is this migration process that produces an electric current. It is a silent process and it produces no exhaust gases.

Hydrogen occurs naturally only in combination with other substances: for fuel cell technology it is needed in elemental form. Transportation and storage requirements for pure hydrogen are expensive, involving either compression of the gas or storage as a liquid. The containers available today have thick walls due to the high pressure under which liquid hydrogen is stored, and are therefore extremely heavy. A better and mass-saving solution to this is that hydrogen can be obtained continuously from a fossil *regenerative*[26] energy carrier source in a process that takes place on board the vehicle and *entails*[27] the use of a *reformer system*[28]. *Sulphur-free gasoline*[29], a synthetic fuel, is the only suitable quality which is just sufficient to meet the requirements of the fuel cell for production of electric energy. Synthetic fuel is made from natural gas and methanol. Methanol (CH_3OH) is used due to its high hydrogen (H_2) and low carbon content, and the lack of any need for special safety requirements for its handling.

To get oxygen is easier: the oxygen required for the reaction is taken from the atmosphere and fed into the system by a compressor.

Companies fuel cell goals

The company's goal is a family car based on the Zafira with CO_2 emissions of 90g/km. That is equivalent to gasoline consumption of 3.0l/ 100km. Conversely, customers will expect the vehicle to meet the same standards of day-to-day practice as its modern gasoline or diesel-powered counterparts:
- Therefore components that take up load space and part of the passenger area must be *tucked away*[30].
- With regard to performance, when the driver presses the accelerator, power should be available immediately to provide a two-second start-up cycle. To achieve this, it is necessary to *hasten*[31] the production of hydrogen in the reformer and electric current in the fuel cell.
- The system needs *to cope with*[32] temperatures as low as −30°C and in conditions of extreme humidity.
- The *narrow band hum*[33] of the fuel cell system and driveline, frequencies generated by auxiliaries, aerodynamic and tire noises have to be insulated.
- New designs for power-steering, air-conditioning compressor, and water pumps, need to be powered electrically to compensate for the lack of a conventional *belt drive*[34].
- With the change of power unit, crashworthiness must be considered again.

A company introducing such radically different technology will need to ensure that it convinces potential buyers *from the outset*[35]: major problems through underdevelopment would have commercially *disastrous consequences*[36].

Suitable fuel of the right type seems to be crucial to the fuel cell car project. It is either natural gas, methanol (which is produced from natural gas), or liquid *hydrocarbons*[37] (produced from petroleum or natural gas). The result of performance of the vehicle/fuel system, emission efficiency, start- up time, and responsive is different in each choice. Consideration must also be given to production and distribution of fuel.

Refineries[38], tankers, pipelines, and countless service stations serve 700 million vehicles across the world. They have built practicable gasoline and diesel fuel infrastructures. Drivers of fuel cell vehicles expect appropriate fuel at an easy reachable filling station. Although *segregated*[39] storage tanks and pumps would be required if the fuel cell required a fuel substantially different in composition from today's gasoline or diesel, liquid hydrocarbon fuels would take advantage of the existing infrastructure. On the other hand, methanol can also be made compatible with *retail*[40] facilities with minor investments. They would, however, have to be segregated from HC fuels in transport and storage svstems.

In order to find acceptance, fuel cell technology has to have a view on running costs and effects on the environment, fuel source and fuel infrastructure. Individual companies *pursue*[41] their solutions, but overall compatibility in the automotive industry is necessary.

[1] Bojen	[2] Schwelle	[3] Schwung; Impuls
[4] lebensfähig	[5] kompakte Großraumlimousine	[6] Methylalkohol
[7] synthetisches Benzin	[8] Wasserstoff	[9] denkbar
[10] Wirkungsgrad	[11] Energieerzeugung	[12] Nachfüllen (des Tanks/ der Zellen)
[13] wieder auffüllen	[14] Wechselstrom	[15] dagegenwirken
[16] Mehrstufenplan	[17] unkompliziert	[18] Unfähigkeit
[19] Bequemlichkeit	[20] elektrischer Strom	[21] Wasserstoff
[22] Sauerstoff	[23] Asynchronmotor; Induktionsmotor	[24] aus etw. bestehen; bestehen aus
[25] Elektrolyt; Säure	[26] nachwachsend	[27] nachwachsend
[28] Reformeranlage	[29] schwefelfreies Benzin	[30] wegstecken, verstecken
[31] beschleunigen	[32] fertigwerden mit	[33] Schmalbandbrummen
[34] Riemenantrieb	[35] vom Anfang an	[36] vom Anfang an
[37] Kohlenwasserstoff- verbindungen	[38] Ölraffinerien	[39] abgetrennt
[40] Einzelhandel	[41] verfolgen	

7.2.2 Renault's fuel cell concept

Limited production of a fuel-cell-powered Renault Laguna, *commencing*[1] in 2005, is planned by Renault and its five European Partners. Renault and De Nora (Italy), Ansaldo (Italy), Volvo TD (Sweden), Ecole des Mines engineering school (France), and Air Liquide (France) have taken part in the FEVER (Fuel-cell Electric Vehicle with Extended Range) project. The result is a fuel-cell-powered Renault Laguna.

What are the *highlights*[2] of this car?
- A range of 400 km.
- The carriage of 8 kg of hydrogen in liquid form, *cryogenically*[3] stored at a temperature of $-253°C$.
- An output of 30 kW at 90 V.
- An inverter (such as that on an electric car) changing the output from DC to AC. A transformer increasing output voltage to 250 V to supply a synchronous electric motor driving through a fixed-ratio transmission.
- An electric control unit undertaking operation and systems control.
- A group of nickel/metal-hydride batteries *housed*[4] at the front of the vehicle providing start-up power for the fuel cell auxiliary systems and boosting power for hill climbing and maximum acceleration.
- The employment of *regenerative braking*[5].

Whole-cycle CO_2 output shows a reduction of 50% compared to a gasoline engine if the hydrogen fuel is made using electricity produced in France. A possible alternative employs an onboard reformer, *deriving*[6] hydrogen from conventional and practical fuels (HCs and methanol). In this configuration, with a fuel cell and reformer, a vehicle of a similar specification would emit about 15% less CO_2 than with the best "conventional" technology in the form of the DTI (direct injection turbodiesel), with the additional advantage of lower emissions of CO and HC, and the total absence of NOx.

[1] anfangen	[2] Höhepunkte; Glanzlichter	[3] tieftemperaturmäßig
[4] untergebracht	[5] Bremsung mit Energierückgewinnung	[6] ableiten; herleiten

7.3 Natural Gas Vehicles

Ford Research Laboratory has developed an ultra-efficient catalyst system and engine control strategy which enables natural gas versions of Ford's pickup trucks and vans to be among the cleanest internal-combustion-powered trucks available in the United States. These vehicles are the first to be certified to California's Super Ultra Low Emission Vehicle standards, as they *emit*[1] 85% fewer smog-forming emissions than required.

In comparison to gasoline, clean-burning alternative fuels such as methanol and natural gas produce higher concentrations of hydrogen molecules in the exhaust gases. Downstream in the catalytic converter, the hydrogen molecules react with oxygen to form harmless water.

What about costs?
- Natural gas costs 15% to 50% less than gasoline,
- It is a clean-burning fuel which reduces vehicle maintenance.

What are the other advantages of natural gas?
- Natural gas is the cleanest-burning alternative fuel. NGVs emit significantly less *greenhouse gas*[2] than do gasoline vehicles. Compared to gasoline-powered vehicles, natural gas vehicles (NGVs) can reduce exhaust emissions of *carbon monoxide*[3] by approximately 69%, *oxides of nitrogen*[4] by 87%, and carbon dioxide by almost 20%.
- NGVs have little or no *evaporative emissions*[5] during *refueling*[6]. In gasoline vehicles, evaporative and fueling emissions account for at least 50% of a vehicle's total hydrocarbon emissions.
- Natural gas engines produce only tiny amounts of fine particulate matter[7]. This feature could become more significant in the future as diesel exhaust is currently under review as a *hazardous*[8] air pollutant.
- Due to the higher octane rating of natural gas, NGVs have the potential to provide greater power and efficiency than gasoline-powered vehicles.
- Natural gas is neither toxic nor corrosive and will not *contaminate*[9] groundwater.
- Combustion produces no significant *aldehydes*[10] or other air toxins, which are a concern with gasoline and some other alternative fuels.
- CNG *dissipates*[11] into the atmosphere in the event of an accident. Gasoline, on the other hand, *pools*[12] on the ground, creating a *fire hazard*[13].
- Tax incentives encourage the use of natural gas vehicles.

Disadvantages?
- Compressed natural gas (CNG) fuel cylinders have to be much thicker and *sturdier*[14] than gasoline tanks, with respect to safety.
- NGVs require fueling stations and infrastructure construction. In the U.S., currently only 1200 natural gas refueling stations operate in 46 states. Only half of these are open to the public, but many oil companies and utilities have plans to develop more public fueling stations.

What about the latest infrastructure plans?
In theory, NGVs can be refueled by a *dispenser*[15] directly connected to a home's natural gas line, because natural gas for cooking and home heating has already been available for more than 100 years.

[1] ausstoßen, emittieren	[2] Treibhausgas	[3] Kohlenmonoxide
[4] Stickstoffoxide	[5] Kraftstoffverdunstung	[6] Nachtanken; Auftanken
[7] Feststoffe; Partikel, Ruß	[8] gefährlich	[9] verschmutzen, verunreinigen
[10] Aldehyde	[11] verteilen; zerstreuen	[12] Pfütze/Lache verursachen
[13] Brandgefahr	[14] robuster	[15] Spender; Dosierbehälter

8 Product Engineering

8.1 Body, Interior

8.1.1 How to cure door rattles

Major carmakers received complaints from their customers that the doors of their cars were *rattling*[1]. Nylon *clips*[2], which were being used to hang *the door panels*[3], were found to be the problem, since they did not *fit as snugly*[4] as they should have done. This causes tolerance gaps, which again cause vibration and rattling. To cure this problem, these gaps have to be filled with a liquid vinyl compound made by ND Plastisol.

By *applying*[5] heat, this liquid vinyl *compound*[6] is *fused*[7] directly to *fasteners*[8]. Liquid vinyl is designed to *seal*[9] against air, water and dirt while *absorbing*[10] noise and vibration.

What other advantages does this liquid vinyl compound have?
– It remains flexible even at very low temperatures.
– The material has *dielectric*[11] strength
– It has good *resistance*[12] to fire, chemical attack, *abrasion*[13], UV and ozone.

[1] klappern	[2] Schellen, Halter	[3] Türbleche, Türblätter
[4] wie angegossen passen	[5] einsetzen	[6] Verbindung, Mischung
[7] verschmolzen	[8] Verbindungselemente	[9] versiegeln, konservieren
[10] aufnehmen, schlucken	[11] nichtleitend	[12] Widerstand
[13] Abnutzung, Verschleiß, Erosion		

8.1.2 Space saving by a new interior padding system

If you combine polyurethane (PU) and aluminium *honeycomb*[1], a new *padding*[2] system is developed. As well as offering improved performance it also doesn't *encroache*[3] much on interior space, at least much less than traditional materials do. This new material can reduce padding thickness by up to 50 per cent. Reduced *invasion*[4] of interior space is important to designers.

What other qualities does the combination of two materials have?

Foam has acoustic and superior *impact-absorbing*[5] qualities. Aside from being ideal for absorbing low energy impacts, it has the advantage of being soft. However, to absorb higher energy levels it needs to be thicker. Thickness, however, compromises on the interior volume of the vehicle.

On the other hand, honeycomb, with its *structural integrity*[6], has excellent high energy impact properties, but is not helpful for light impacts or acoustical problems in car interiors.

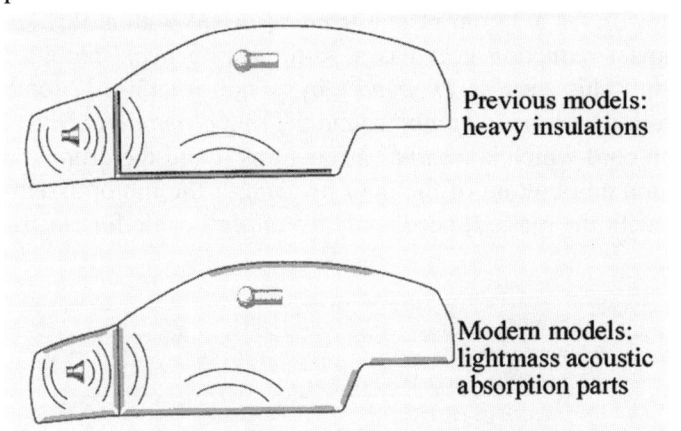

Previous models: heavy insulations

Modern models: lightmass acoustic absorption parts

Figure 8.1.2.1: New insulation material (Source: ATZ, 3/2000)

New regulations will come into force in the United States in 2001 regarding head injuries. Just-in-time, the development of honeycomb/foam combinations *keep pace with*[7] regulations.

In the past, *rigid*[8] foams were used due to the manufacturing method involved. Two materials were pushed together in such a way that the honeycomb cut into the foam. With a new approach, holes in the side walls of the honeycomb cells materials allows *foaming PU*[9] to flow efficiently into the structure, ensuring a total fill.

What other advantages does this method have?
– The surface skin is impregnated, producing a truly *monolithic structure*[10].
– Engineers are able to control the rate of collapse of the honeycomb structure with the holes in the side walls of the honeycomb cells.
– With these holes, the new hybrid materials can be tuned to absorb different energy levels and, therefore, applications.

What other applications are possible? Development objectives are crash helmets and body *fairings*[11] for motorcycles.

[1] Wabenkörper	[2] Polsterung; Aufpolsterung	[3] übergreifen
[4] Eindringen; Eingriff	[5] Stoß aufnehmend	[6] Strukturintegrität
[7] mit etwas Schritt halten	[8] fest, formstabil, steif	[9] schäumendes Polyurethan
[10] Wabenkörper-Struktur	[11] Verkleidungen, Verschalungen	

8.1.3 Low cost electric window motor

How does a *novel*[1] electric window winder mechanism cut costs? It eliminates the usual *cranks*[2], *levers*[3] and *links*[4] and assembly requirements and thus causes less *frictional losses*[5] and mass. This window winder was developed in Argentina.

The mechanism has a small high speed motor fixed to the *bottom edge*[6] of the window glass. This motor drives a 38mm plastic *winding drum*[7] with a 38:1 *reduction gear*[8]. The compact reduction gear has a 38-tooth ring *gear*[9] moulded inside the winding drum. This gear is *engaged*[10] by a non-rotating 37-tooth plastic *spur gear*[11] that follows an *orbital path*[12] round the ring *circumference*[13].

Together with a nylon cord which is *wound*[14] a few turns round the drum and *stretched*[15] between the top and bottom of the door *pressing*[16], the motor assembly moves up and down with the glass. It needs only a *trailing*[17] cable for electrical connection.

[1] neu	[2] Drehkurbel	[3] Hebel
[4] Gelenke	[5] Reibungsverluste; mechanische Verluste	[6] Unterkante
[7] Aufwickeltrommel	[8] Untersetzungsgetriebe; Zwischengetriebe	[9] Zahnrad
[10] steht in Eingriff mit	[11] Zahnrad mit Geradverzahnung; Stirnrad	[12] Ring; Umgehung
[13] Umfang	[14] gewickelt	[15] gespannt
[16] Pressteil; Ziehteil	[17] auf Zug beansprucht	

8.1.4 Liquid HVAC systems avoid goose pimples

The owners of cars left under a burning sun for hours had to either open the doors for hours (because if the seats were leather trimmed and you are wearing shorts, one dared not sit down), or turn on the air-conditioning (icy air blasts from the *vents*[1] caused *goose pimples*[2]).

Moreover, what solution could be found for those mornings with frost on both sides of the windscreen, icy leather seats and a foggy, cold interior for 10 minutes before it was safe and comfortable to drive away?

Sophisticated[3] *HVAC systems*[4] do not need to rely on *blasts*[5] of hot or cold air to regulate temperature. New, liquid-based systems will do it differently. Such an all-enveloping heating and ventilation system has been developed by Fiat's research centre and is described as a Top Climate System (TCS), a so-called "non-aggressive climate system". That new technology should be in production in the next generation of Lancia Kappa, in the year 2002.

Current systems use relatively small *outlets*[6] and high air speed. On the other hand, TCS is a less aggressive climate control system which makes use of *radiant heat*[7] exchange through the surfaces of the car's interior. For example, the seats (developed with the aid of Lear Corp.) and roof create micro-climates, one for each passenger. Fiat's system works on the same principle as a *domestic*[8] heater: hot or cold water and a glycol solution are carried through the climate-controlled areas by hoses and heat exchangers to heat or cool the air which is pushed out by *fans*[9]. *Trimming*[10] seats and *roof lining*[11] with cloth means it is possible to *diffuse*[12] the air over a big surface area through *micropores*[13] in the material. It is possible to generate air flow into the cabin through the breathable cloth surface by maintaining sufficient pressure in each *cavity*[14], which could be *concealed*[15] in *plenum chambers*[16] on each side of the *dashboard*[17].

Figure 8.1.4.1: Ice scrapping (Source: Adam Opel AG, Rüsselsheim)

A Webasto-developed *solar panel*[18] is also incorporated into the system of Fiat. It is located where the sunroof is normally fitted. This solar panel drives a fan which cools the interior when the car is parked in high temperatures. To reflect excessive sun loads, the windscreen has a layer of *conductive foil*[19] and the windows are double-*glazed*[20].

The TCS is controlled by conventional dials and switches. In addition, each passenger has a small joystick located in the door which can be used to adjust temperatures and increase or decrease ventilation within their own micro-climate.

In this way, the TCS stabilises the passenger compartment temperature within a time period similar to that of a normal system.

Fiat intends to develop and introduce the technology step by step. Meanwhile, steering wheels and seats can be warmed or cooled using liquid-to-air heat pipes. The advantage is, that heat pipes require no external power source, other than the heat to be transferred. Heat pipes are *sealed*[21] devices that transfer heat by evaporation and condensation of a working fluid. It is planned to install heat pipes in the steering wheel rim for heating it in the winter and cooling in the summer. This system is under development in the USA by Thermacore of Lancaster, Pennsylvania. Heat pipes already have potential applications in US military tanks and throughout the transport industry for engine cooling, air-conditioning, oil and fuel coolers. They are able to reduce heat loads in the passenger compartment.

They could also be used for cooling down batteries in electric vehicles which would increase efficiency and improve their range. To absorb *excess*[22] body heat taken from *back rest*[23] and seat surface and transfer it to thermoelectric modules, is another complex task using flexible heat pipes.

The thermoelectric coolers are *solid state*[24] pumps (operating by means of the Peltier effect) that absorb heat at a low temperature and pump it to a higher temperature. This additional heat evaporates some of the working fluid and raises the local *vapour pressure*[25]. The increased pressure moves the vapour down the pipe. A low pressure and temperature area is created. This leads to condensed vapour, giving up its heat. The condensed fluid is then returned back to the heat input zone either by capillary action in a suitable *wick*[26] or by gravity.

Do you know what a "Peltier effect" is? At the cold *junction*[27], as electrons pass from one *semi-conductor*[28] to another, heat is *absorbed*[29]; electrons move from the cold junction to the hot junction by electrical power which provides the energy. At the hot junction, an air-cooled heat exchanger *expels*[30] the heat to *ambient air*[31]. Within this system, the only moving part is a fan used to circulate air through the heat exchanger. The prototype seat system is both reliable and quiet. A lot of companies are interested in purchasing it.

[1] Belüftungen, Lüfter	[2] Gänsehaut	[3] hochentwickelt; raffiniert
[4] Heizungs-, Lüftungs- und Klimatisierungssysteme	[5] Windstöße, Böen	[6] Ausgänge
[7] Strahlungswärme	[8] heimisch	[9] Gebläse
[10] hier: garnieren	[11] Dachhimmel; Dachverkleidung	[12] zerstreuen; zerstäuben
[13] Mikroporen	[14] Hohlraum	[15] verborgen
[16] Luftkästen; Luftspeicher	[17] Armaturenanlage	[18] Sonnenkollektor
[19] Leiterfolie	[20] verglast	[21] abgedichtet; eingeschweißt; versiegelt
[22] übermäßig	[23] Sitzlehne	[24] Festkörper
[25] Dampfdruck	[26] Dampfdruck	[27] Zonenübergang; Sperrschicht
[28] Halbleiter	[29] aufgenommen; geschluckt	[30] ausstoßen
[31] Umgebungsluft; Außenluft		

8.1.5 Active seats

Active seats are a luxury feature with which BMW and Mercedes-Benz are planning to capture an extra market share. Both carmakers use different technologies but claim similar benefits for their seats. BMW's "Active region" uses hydraulics and Mercedes Benz uses pneumatics. Both improve blood circulation and help to avoid *tenseness*[1], *fatigue*[2] and *backache*[3].

BMW's *seat base*[4] contains two hollow containers filled with a liquid similar to that used in water beds. A raising and lowering of the right and left sides of the seat is caused by chambers which are alternately filled and emptied. A 60s cycle gently (almost *imperceptibly*[5]) *rocks*[6] the *pelvis*[7] and *lumbar vertebra*[8]. These kind of seats are just becoming available in conjunction with the Comfort Seat on 7 Series models.

Mercedes-Benz S-class seats have a dynamic contour *backrest*[9] (three individually adjustable air chambers in the back of the seat and another two at shoulder level) which cause a massage effect. The air chambers slowly *deflate*[10] and *inflate*[11] under electronic control, *alternating*[12] between *firm*[13] and soft. The effects for the *spinal column*[14] are amazing (it encourages the driver to keep changing position effectively), even though the gentle rocking is barely perceptible. Once activated the cycle runs for five minutes before automatically switching off, but drivers may repeat the program as often as they wish.

Figure 8.1.5.1: BMW Z8 (Source: Adrian Zürl, Nauheim)

[1] Gespanntheit; Verspannung	[2] Ermüdung	[3] Rückenschmerzen
[4] Sitzaufnahme; Sitzträger	[5] unmerklich; verschwindend gering	[6] schaukeln
[7] Becken (menschl.)	[8] Lendenwirbel	[9] Rückenlehne; Sitzlehne
[10] zusammenfallen, entleeren	[11] aufblasen; aufblähen	[12] wechselnd; hin- und hergehend
[13] fest; hart	[14] Wirbelsäule; Rückgrat	

8.2 Powertrain

8.2.1 A golden area for diesels

Figure 8.2.1.1: Production of diesel injectors[1] for the high-pressure accumulator injection system[2] CRS (Common Rail System) at Bosch's Bamberg plant (Source: Robert Bosch GmbH, Stuttgart)

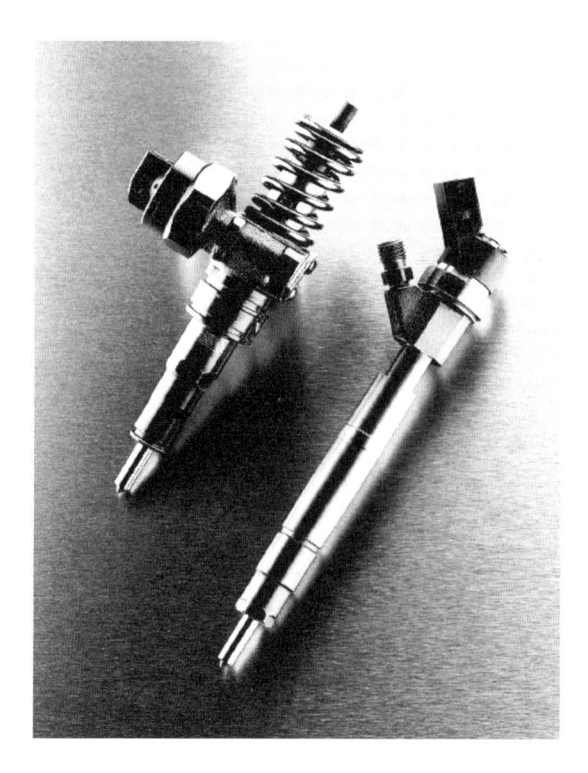

Figure 8.2.1.2: Innovative technology from Bosch for direct-injection diesel engines: injectors of the new high-pressure injection systems Unit Injector System UIS (left) and Common Rail System CRS (right) (Source: Robert Bosch GmbH, Stuttgart)

EU expects five litre/100 km over the period 2005 to 2110. This will *spur*³ a new growth in diesel sales.

To the astonishment of Diesel doubters, Audi has just launched a turbocharged, 24-valve V6 2.5-litre direct injection diesel which is able of propelling the A8. It is an important engine for Audi, because the German company wishes to be one of the best luxury makers. In *creating*⁴ the world's first high performance V6 TDI, Audi has *erected*⁵ another milestone. The new four-valve concept with variable turbocharger and ultra-high pressure fuel injection represents the next stage of TDI development.

Figure 8.2.1.3: In 1996 Bosch introduced high-pressure injection systems for direct-injection diesel engines. Shown here is the production of Common Rail injectors in the Bamberg plant.
(Source: Robert Bosch GmbH, Stuttgart)

What about other carmakers? General Motors and Isuzu have made a JV for developing V6 diesel engines. Perkins Technology, part of the merged Lucas-Varity group, *showcased*⁶ an impressive 3-litre V6 high speed direct injection engine in Detroit which debuts in Renault's new Safran executive car. It should have the best-in-class figures for noise, vibration and harshness (NVH). Mercedes-Benz and BMW are not far behind. Multi-valve, turbocharged engines and V- configurations open up a new market for luxury cars.

Admittedly, the *soundproofing*⁷ is *awe-inspiring*⁸ and effective. Padding is used to such a degree that you cannot even see the engine *wrapped*⁹ and sealed under the bonnet, the reason being that good acoustic behaviour, with a soft impact of the combustion process, was also a major development target.

To establish favourable combustion conditions for the main quantity of fuel, a small amount of fuel is pre-injected and mixed by a *preliminary stroke*[10] of 0.03mm.

Instead, the main focus should be on the ecological advantages of such engines:

Figure 8.2.1.4: Cutaway of Diesel 2.0 DI 16V Ecotec of Opel (Source: Adam Opel AG, Rüsselsheim)

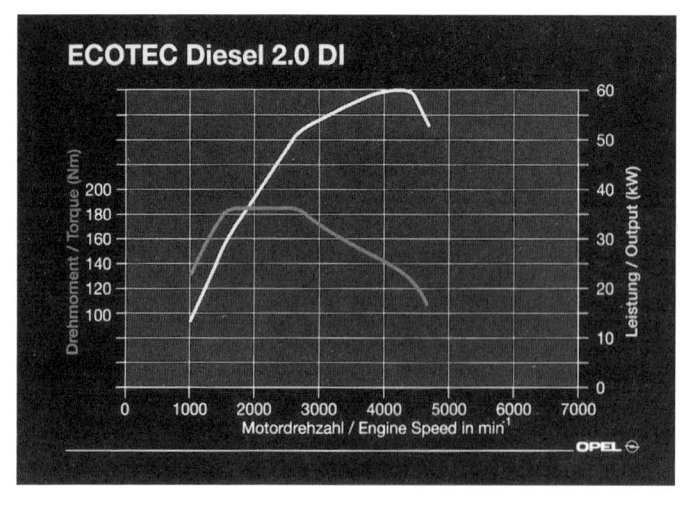

Figure 8.2.1.5: Pulling power: the new 60 kW (82hp) 2.0-litre diesel engine from Opel develops impressively high torque at low rpm. The maximum 185 Newton meters is available at just 1800 rpm and remains at this strong level until 2500 rpm. This engine is offered in the Vectra 2.0 DI (Source: Adam Opel AG, Rüsselsheim)

It undercuts all current emissions legislation by 30 to 50 per cent. Particle emissions are also down by 25 to 30 per cent.

How can this happen?

The four-valve technology features two *intake ports*[11], one taking the form of a *swirl*[12] and one tangential port for high cylinder filling. A vertical, central *nozzle*[13] position guarantees even distribution of the fuel which is a vital condition of good mixture preparation and low *soot emissions*[14].

These engines have a central *piston relief*[15] for good air swirl with a *low-low*[16] *charge cycle*[17] and they also feature high utilisation of the combustion air at full load, coupled with high performance and low emissions across the entire speed range. The two *exhaust passages*[18] share the same *port*[19]. The fuel injection system is based on a *radial piston distributor injection pump*[20], optimised in a *lengthy*[21] development process to fulfill the high demands of the engine. For high boost pressure at low engine speeds Audi has used a *variable turbocharger*[22]. This simulates a small turbo at low engine speeds and a large one at high speed. Adjustable *vanes*[23] regulate *boost pressure*[24]. In conjunction with four-valve technology and the high pressure fuel injection system, the result is a thermodynamically ideal balance of torque, power output and fuel consumption.

To get a fast return on investment, the engine makers are seeking customers. North America could be a surprise market for sport utility models, pick-up trucks and minivans.

[1] anspornen	[2] Einspritzdüsen	[3] Speichereinspritzsystem
[4] Entstehen	[5] errichten	[6] ausgestellt
[7] Schalldämmung	[8] Ehrfurcht gebietend	[9] ummantelt; umhüllt
[10] Vorhub	[11] Einlaufkanäle; Saugkanäle	[12] Strudel; Wirbel
[13] Düse; Mundstück	[14] Rußausstoß	[15] Kolbenmulde; Ventiltasche
[16] im unteren Drehzahlbereich	[17] Ladungswechsel	[18] Auslasskanäle
[19] Kanal; Anschluss	[20] Radialkolben-Verteilereinspritzpumpe	[21] übermäßig lang
[22] verstellbarer Turbolader	[23] Flügel; Schaufel	[24] Ladedruck; Ladeluftdruck

8.2.2 Neural networking manages engine combustion

Neural systems can process large volumes of information simultaneously. In vehicle applications, artificial neural networks have three tasks: to diagnose problems such as engine *misfires*[1], monitoring of engine combustion, and to control the engine to optimise fuel economy and emissions. This neural chip will lead to reduced fuel consumption. The neural system is the biggest breakthrough in vehicle computers.

The Jet Propulsion Laboratories (JPL) at NASA and Ford have already designed a powerful neural processor that can be mass-produced in the next few years in a highly cost-effective way and does not *envisage*[2] additional cost to the customers. This processor consists of a highly complex neural network software code in dedicated hardware logic. This will bring a tremendous boost in computational ability, enabling real-time onboard diagnostics for the first time. Furthermore, the system should have an error rate of only less than one in a million by observing and diagnosing engine firing events. This error rate could be *accomplished*[3] by "learning" diagnostic tasks during the vehicle's development process.

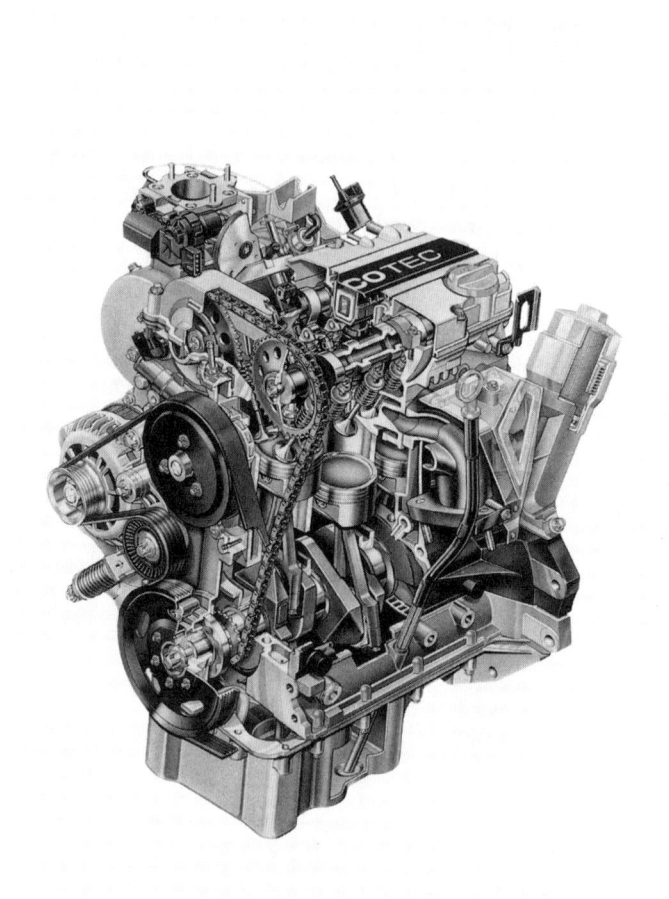

Figure 8.2.2.1: Ecotec Compact 1.0 12V engine of Opel. This four-stroke engine[4] has three cylinders and four valves per cylinder. The short-stroke engine[5] has a displacement of 973 ccm, a bore[6] diameter of 72.5 mm, a maximum power of 43kW @ 5600rpm and a maximum torque of 85Nm @ 3800rpm. Compression ratio is 10.1:1. (Source: Adam Opel AG, Rüsselsheim)

The neural network chip, designed to carry out parallel neuron computations efficiently, overcomes current computational limitations. It is too early to speculate, but neural networks could also be integrated into active ride and handling technologies as well as braking systems and transmissions.

[1] Fehlzündungen; Aussetzer	[2] voraussehen	[3] vollendet
[4] Viertaktmotor	[5] kurzhubiger Motor	[6] Bohrung

8.2.3 New catalytic converters

Eco-friendly cars need efficient working catalytic converters. By utilising a special crystalline material (already known by the refining of petrochemicals as a common application), new catalysts for all petrol (gasoline) fuelled vehicles are set to *surpass*[1] European targets as well as the U.S. ULEV (Ultra Low Emissions Vehicle) standards. Developed by Delphi Automotive Systems with Allied Signal Environmental Catalysts, they are ready for production in the year 2000.

The new technology, called Adcat, enables complete catalytic operation even at start-up phase. What technology makes this performance? It is a Zeolite-coated honeycomb *brick*[2]. Zeolite is a crystalline material with an open, three-dimensional crystal structure and very precise micropore size. Its size can be *adjusted*[3] by varying its *composition*[4]. Therefore, Zeolite can absorb molecules of suitable sizes and is used for separating mixtures by selective absorption and are therefore often called molecular *sieves*[5].

Only when *light-off temperature*[6] has been reached are *trapped*[7] cold (low energy) hydrocarbons released into the catalytic converter. They then are dealt with in the usual manner of a *three-way catalytic converter*[8]. The honeycomb has only a minor impact on *exhaust back pressure*[9].

What about car manufacturers' developments?

Toyota's new direct injection petrol engine needs a *complement*[10] to absorb and control NOx emissions released in the engine's *lean burn concept*[11]. During these oxygen rich cycles it is impossible for conventional three-way catalytic converters to eliminate NOx. Therefore, Toyota have switched to a *reduction catalytic converter*[12] which is able to store NOx.

How does such a reduction catalytic converter work? When the engine is running on mixtures *leaner*[13] than the *stoichiometric air-fuel ratio*[14], platinum catalyses NO and O_2 into NO_2, which is stored *temporarily*[15]. The next time the engine runs at the stoichiometric ratio, the NO_2 is released to mix with HC and CO to form N_2, H_2O, and CO_2, and other harmless compounds. If there are times when the engine runs in lean burn mode for extended periods, this will create a storage problem in the catalyst due to its capacity of about 2 minutes. When capacity is reached, a *rich*[16] mixture is sent through the system which ignites and converts the gases. Once cleared, the catalyst *reverts*[17] to its storage condition.

This idea works perfectly in Japan where the sulphur content of fuel is approximately 50ppm, but there is a drawback to this *novel*[18] idea for usage in Europe. There, the levels of sulphur are typically up around the 300 to 500ppm mark. At these levels this catalyst will not work effectively. This problem needs to be addressed by the petrochemical industry.

[1] übertreffen	[2] Ziegel; Stein	[3] eingestellt; justiert
[4] Zusammensetzung	[5] Siebe	[6] Anspringtemperatur; Ansprechtemperatur
[7] gefangen	[8] Dreiwege-Katalysator; Katalysator mit Lambda-Sonde; Selektivkatalysator	[9] Abgasgegendruck; Abgasstaudruck
[10] Ergänzung	[11] Magerkonzept (mit magerer Verbrennung)	[12] Reduktionskatalysator

[13] magerer	[14] stöchiometrisches Kraftstoff-Luft-Verhältnis (ideales Verhältnis; Lambda=1)	[15] vorübergehend, zeitweise
[16] fett	[17] zurückkehren	[18] neu

8.2.4 Ford Transit's 16-valve diesel was a world first

Ford developed a medium commercial vehicle diesel engine by using four valves per cylinder. It is a world-first for this class after start of production in 2000. What are the main features?
– Iron block and aluminium cylinder configuration with *ladder frame*[1] construction.
– Structural *sump*[2] for improved NVH.
– By forcing air through the *inlet ports*[3] at high speed with diesel mist being injected under high pressure, optimum ratio fuel/air mix results in a clean burn.
– Specially developed *concave-pistons*[4] further increase turbulence in the combustion chamber.
– Fuel economy is achieved by combination with a automatic transmission, called the AutoShift gearbox.

In comparison to a manual transmission, Ford's AutoShift gearbox offers a 15 per cent improvement in fuel economy. The electro-hydraulic system, which does away with both clutch and gear lever, is operated by up and down buttons on the steering wheel or switched into a fully automatic mode that changes gears for maximum fuel efficiency.

[1] Leiterrahmen	[2] Ölwanne	[3] Eingangskanäle
[4] Hohlkolben		

8.2.5 Variable valve timing is a key technology

Improving fuel economy and exhaust emissions also needs to improve specific power and driveability of engines.

Fixed valve timing always represents a compromise between low-speed driveability and high-speed power output. Current systems use a *helical actuator*[1], turning a linear input (created by hydraulic pressure on a piston) into a rotary output. A cut-out in the *plunger shaft*[2] is then translated into rotation by the *opposing movement*[3] of *followers*[4].

Variable valve timing (VVT) will be a key technology in future engines, despite its additional cost and complexity. Benefits are gained by altering the timing of both inlet and exhaust valves. Research and Development departments wish to find acceptable solutions to variable *valve timing*[5].

Mechadyne, an UK research company, offers five approaches to the application of VVT (see below). The most appropriate solution according to each engineering need can be chosen. Thinking into the *actuator mechanism*[6] could be one solution in particular. After *surveying*[7] the whole field of engine technology, the company has built up an extensive database relating to existing and *expired*[8] patents in this field of VVT.

- *Phase shifting*[9] technology: rotating the *camshaft*[10] in order to achieve earlier or later *valve operation*[11] (without *altering*[12] *valve lift*[13] or opening *duration*[14]).

Figure 8.2.5.1: 1.6l-16V-engine, 77kW (Source: Volkswagen AG, Wolfsburg)

- Profile switching: valve operation between two camshafts with different profiles can be switched to enable valve timing, lift and opening duration to be changed from one *state*[15] to another.
- Variable valve lift: the use of a mechanism to vary the amount of valve lift, usually in conjunction with speed changing.
- Hydraulic systems: offering of complete, or at least highly flexible, control of valve operation.
- Variable speed changing: the *cyclic*[16] modification of camshaft speed, *altering*[17] the valve opening duration, possibly in conjunction with phase shifting. This system is based on separating the torsional and bending loads in the camshaft. The *torsional force*[18] is provided by a *quill shaft*[19] which runs through the centre of a hollowed camshaft. This camshaft is divided into single-cylinder sections, which are driven by the *drive shaft*[20]. Each camshaft section bears the *bending load*[21]. Variable speed timing is then achieved by moving the drive shaft *laterally*[22], creating an *eccentric*[23] effect in the drive to the *cams*[24]. Moving the drive shaft inevi-

tably[25] also involves moving the camshaft *drive sprocket*[26], but it is said there is no problem as long as the geometry is correct.

Figure 8.2.5.2: Test engines with gasoline direct-injection on the <u>test stand</u>[27]. In gasoline direct injection (BDE) a high-pressure pump supplies the high-injection valves via a common fuel rail. A fast-switching <u>solenoid valve</u>[28] and an open selection of injection pressures up to 120 bar guarantees precise fuel quantities and precise injection timing. This future-oriented technology enables a reduction in fuel consumption of up to 15%. (Source: Robert Bosch GmbH, Stuttgart)

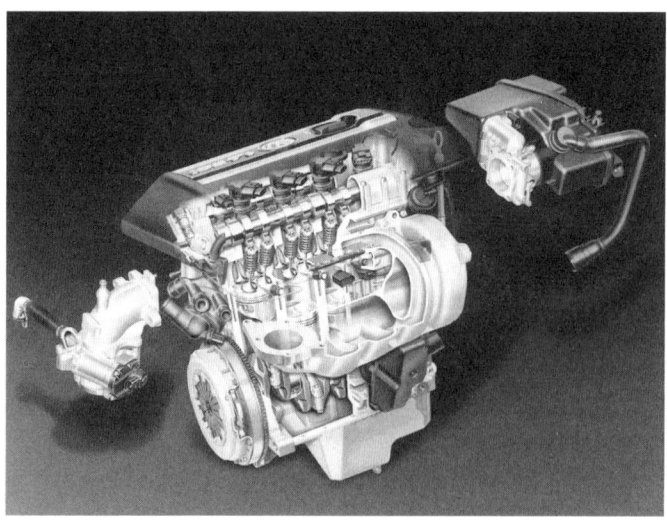

Figure 8.2.5.3: 1.4l-FSI-engine (Source: Volkswagen AG, Wolfsburg)

In high speed operation, gas flow through an engine is improved if VVT is used to increase overlap (the inlet valve opening before the exhaust valve closes), whereas in low speed operation, VVT can reduce overlap to avoid *poor*[29] *idling characteristics*[30] and *throttle response*[31].

In recent years, VVT has been increasingly applied to gasoline engine inlet valve operation, helped by powerful and flexible electronic engine management systems to provide the control output. The OHV^{32} engine with a single camshaft between the cylinder banks offers compactness and has had success in automotive industry. Engineers are now encouraged to use a new VVT-equipped engine to deal with *twin overhead camshafts*[33].

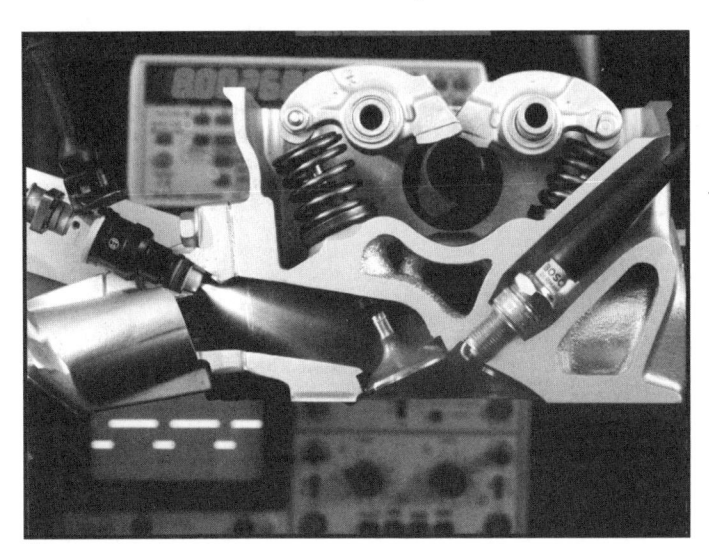

Figure 8.2.5.4: Electronic gasoline injection systems ensure optimal fuel air mixture. The electronic gasoline injection system from Bosch ensures an optimal mixture of fuel and air and minimizes damaging exhaust gases. The picture shows a cross-section of a cylinder head. The finely atomized fuel is directly injected into the intake valve (Source: Robert Bosch GmbH, Stuttgart).

[1] schneckenförmiges Stellglied	[2] Kolbenwelle	[3] Gegenbewegung
[4] Nockenstößel	[5] Ventilsteuerzeiten	[6] Stellwerk
[7] untersuchen; beobachten	[8] abgelaufen; verfallen	[9] Phasenverschiebung
[10] Nockenwelle	[11] Ventilsteuerung	[12] verändern
[13] Ventilhub	[14] Öffnungsdauer	[15] Zustand
[16] zyklisch, periodisch	[17] verändern	[18] Torsionskraft
[19] Hohlwelle	[20] Achswelle; Antriebswelle	[21] Biegebeanspruchung, Biegelast
[22] seitlich	[23] exzentrisch	[24] Nockenwellen
[25] unvermeidlich; zwangsläufig	[26] Kettenantriebsrad	[27] Teststand, Prüfstand
[28] elektromagnetisches Ventil	[29] hier: niedrig	[30] Leerlaufkennkurven
[31] Ansprechverhalten des Motors (auf Drosselklappenbefehle)	[32] (Motor) mit oben hängenden Ventilen	[33] zwei oben liegende Nockenwellen

8.2.6 The next generation spark ignition engines

In addition to safety and economics, environmental compatibility is the primary development goal of the European automobile industry and its suppliers. The industry has made a voluntary commitment to lawmakers to reduce average carbon dioxide (CO_2) emissions of newly registered cars and station wagons by 25 percent by 2008. The reduction of CO_2 will be proportional to the reduction in fuel consumption in vehicles.

In concrete terms this means reducing CO_2 emissions from an average of 186 grams per kilometer in 1995 to 140 grams (4.9 *ounces*[1]) by 2008. This is equivalent to average gasoline consumption of 5.8 litre (6 fluid *quarts*[2]) for every 100 kilometers (62 miles).

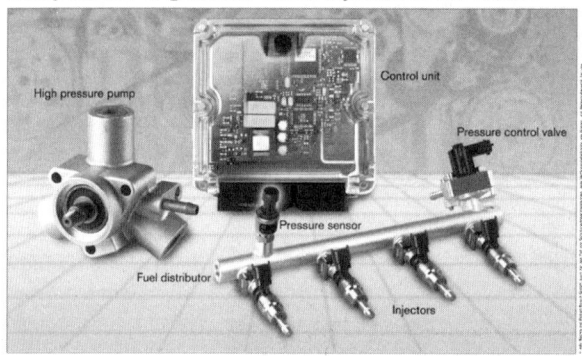

Figure 8.2.6.1: Components of a gasoline injection system (Source: Robert Bosch GmbH, Stuttgart).

From indirect to direct injection

High-pressure direct injection has helped the diesel engine gain a new image - from the comfortable, thrifty diesel engine with an undeniably harsh combustion noise, to a powerful, even thriftier engine with a noise level acceptable for even luxury class automobiles.

Bosch also uses the expertise of its engineers for high-pressure direct injection technology in spark ignition engines.

Only in recent years have engineers created the technological and technical prerequisites in order to benefit from the fuel consumption advantages of this process while simultaneously achieving good emission values. Like diesel technology, direct injection is leading to compact, high-power gasoline engines with dynamic response behaviour.

The main components of Motronic MED7

The expertise of Bosch is also reflected in the high-pressure injectors of the Motronic MED7 (electronic engine control unit). Compared to the traditional manifold injection system, the entire fuel amount must be injected in full-load operation in a quarter of the time.

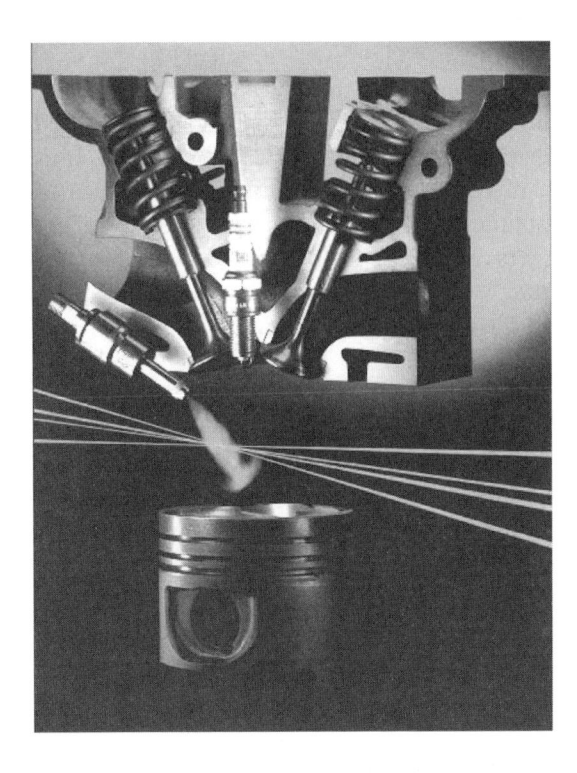

Figure 8.2.6.2: Injection technology for gasoline engines on the verge³ of a major breakthrough. Bosch's new system for gasoline direct injection offers the potential for further reducing fuel consumption. Developers use a laser measuring technique to analyze mixture formation⁴ in cylinders. (Source: Robert Bosch GmbH, Stuttgart)

The available time is significantly shorter during stratified charge operation in part-load. Especially when idle injection times of less than 0.5 milliseconds are required due to the lower fuel. This is only one-fifth of the available time for manifold injection. Still the fuel consumption must be atomized very finely in order to create an optimal mixture in the brief moment between injection and ignition. The fuel *droplets*[5] for direct injection are on average smaller than 20 µm. This is only one-fifth of the droplet size reached with the traditional manifold injection and one-third of the diameter of a human hair. More important than fine atomization is even fuel distribution in the injection beam to achieve fast and uniform combustion. These demands to the injectors can only be fulfilled with the latest, extremely precise manufacturing technology.

Transition into homogenous operation at higher load

With increasing engine load and therefore increasing injection quantities, the *stratified charge*[6] cloud becomes even richer and emissions characteristics even worse. Like diesel engine combustion, *soot*[7] may form. In order to prevent this, the Motronic MED7 engine control converts to a homogenous cylinder charge starting with a defined engine load. The system is injected very early during the intake process in order to achieve a good mixture of fuel and air at a ratio of Lambda = 1.

Complex control tasks for engine management

In stratified charge operation the nitrogen oxide (NOx) segments in the very lean exhaust cannot be reduced by the conventional, three-way catalytic converter, which is very effective with a homogenous mixture. The NOx can be reduced by approximately 70 percent through exhaust returns before the catalytic converter. This is not, however, enough to fulfill the ambitious threshold values of the future. Therefore, emissions containing NOx must undergo special subsequent treatment. Today, engine designers are use an additional NOx accumulator catalytic converter in the exhaust system to deposit the nitrogen oxide in the form of nitrates (HNO_3) on its surface with the oxygen still contained in the lean exhaust.

The starting points for better efficiency

According to the laws of thermo-dynamics, experts calculated the overall efficiency of prior spark ignition engines in the European test cycle at 13 percent. In other words, only about an eighth of the energy applied with gasoline can be converted into useable motion energy. In order to minimize these losses, the Bosch designers have addressed three issues:
– About five percent can be gained with a large operating segment stratified charge operation at Lambda values greater than 1.
– Another five percent of losses can be avoided from "non-ideal combustion and wall heat losses".
– Through frequent unthrottled operation, an additional five percent of losses can be reduced.

The improvement in efficiency from gasoline direct injection resulting in fuel savings or higher power have been known for a long time. Until very recently, however, this could not be used for spark ignition engines because of limited engine power with stratified charge operation and the nitrogen oxide emissions from a lean exhaust.

These hurdles were overcome with Bosch's Motronic MED7 and an accumulator catalytic converter. After the production of the first European vehicles with Bosch Motronic MED7 at Volkswagen, the new technology is expected to be used broadly within the medium range for spark ignition engines, due to interest among the European automobile industry.

[1] Unzen	[2] Quarts	[3] Rand; Grenze
[4] Gemischbildung; Kraftstoffaufbereitung	[5] Tropfen; Tröpfchen	[6] Schichtladung
[7] Ruß		

8.2.7 Diesel direct injection

Figure 8.2.7.1: Taking measurements of a diesel engine. In the test room of the Bosch plant in Stuttgart-Feuerbach injection components are tested under actual engine operating conditions (Source: Robert Bosch GmbH, Stuttgart)

The Diesel injection technology division of Bosch

Figure 8.2.7.2: Measurement of the injection jet for diesel injection systems. Bosch researchers are working on improving diesel injection systems. The photo shows measuring of an injection beam[1] using special laser techniques (Source: Robert Bosch GmbH, Stuttgart)

Injection Technology Division had sales of seven billion DM in 1998. This corresponds to 22 percent of total sales of the Automotive Equipment Division, which was 31.8 billion DM in 1998. In the prior year, the division spent 500 million DM on the development of diesel injection systems – seven percent of sales. Moreover, about 800 million DM was invested last year in machinery and building. The sales structure of the division is changing.

Figure 8.2.7.3: Flow tests and nozzle[2] models. The flow behaviour inside a diesel injection nozzle[3] is tested on a large model. The flow is visible thanks to the electrolyte gas bubble[4] marking and laser technology (Source: Robert Bosch GmbH, Stuttgart)

Distributor pumps still make up the largest segment. But in 1998, 18 percent of sales consisted of the new high-pressure direct injection systems for passenger and commercial vehicles. Additional important products are *inline pumps*[5], *nozzle holder*[6] combinations and sensors and starting systems.

Passenger vehicle diesel engines with Bosch injection systems are offered today in a broad range of vehicles, ranging from the three-cylinder 0.8 litre engine of the DaimlerChrysler "Smart" to the eight-cylinder 3.9-litre engine of BMW with 180 kW power and 560 Nm torque. However, the before mentioned engines do not mark the end of development work. Engines with a higher number of cylinders, more power and more torque are currently being developed for production readiness.

Emissions value and measures

If one considers the emission test values of passenger vehicles with DI (Direct Injection) diesel engines, one recognizes the significant tightening of requirements between the Euro II and Euro III (in effect starting in 2000), or the Euro IV (as proposed for 2005). Several vehicles are already coming close to fulfilling the Euro-IV requirement and one, the VW-Lupo 3L TDI, has already overcome this obstacle.

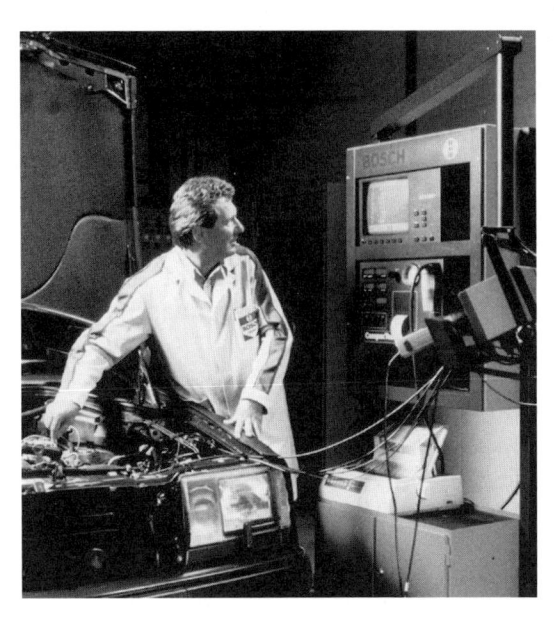

Figure 8.2.7.4: Customer service technician using testing equipment. State-of-the-art testing equipment means excellent customer service for all mechanical and electrical vehicle systems. Service employees are qualified as system technicians in Bosch customer service schools worldwide and kept up to date on the latest developments in automotive technology (Source: Robert Bosch GmbH, Stuttgart)

In this context, it is interesting that even when the emission values of different cars are carefully analyzed, there is no fundamental difference between the various injection systems. In other words, all high-pressure systems offered by Bosch offer the potential to undercut the Euro III and Euro IV exhaust *threshold values*[7], depending on vehicle weight, with or without subsequent treatment of the exhaust.

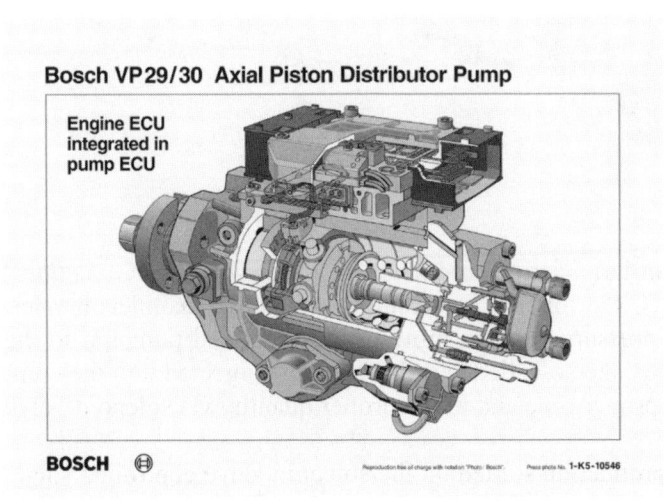

Figure 8.2.7.5: Axial piston distribution pump (Source: Robert Bosch GmbH, Stuttgart)

CO_2 emissions, which are considered co-responsible for the *greenhouse effect*[8], correlate directly to fuel consumption. According to a *pledge*[9] from the

European Union of Automakers, newly registered passenger cars in Europe must achieve average carbon dioxide emissions of less than 140 grams per kilometer. This threshold value can only be reached if fuel consumption is drastically reduced for a portion of the vehicles.

Leading the way in this direction is the VW Lupo 3L TDI with a Unit Injection System (UIS) from Bosch with CO_2 emissions of 90 grams per kilometer.

A wide range of technical work is required to permanently reduce CO_2 emissions: the reduction of average vehicle weight, the use of smaller, highly *stratified*[10] engines, new transmission technology and new methods of subsequent treatment of exhausts for a more consumption-favorable/performance-friendly design.

Bosch high-pressure systems for direct injection Diesel engines

Bosch has improved the *axial piston distributor pump*[11] VP 37, which is still being produced today in high quantities, by providing a version with *solenoid valve*[12] control. Another pump – the VP 30 – is used for direct injection engines of up to two litre swept volume at injection pressures up to 1400 bar.

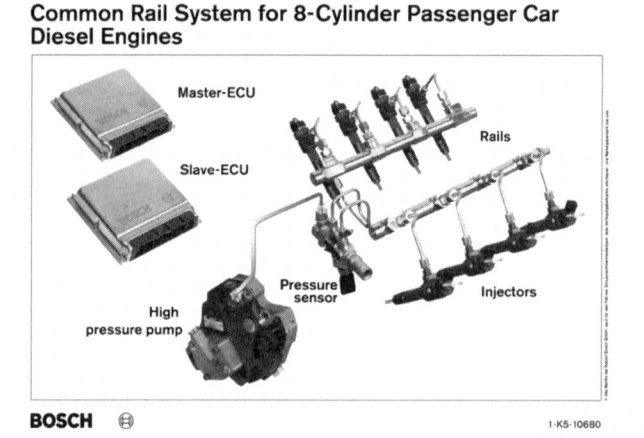

Figure 8.2.7.6: Common rail system for diesel engines (Source: Robert Bosch GmbH, Stuttgart)

In 1997, Bosch began large series production of the *accumulator injection*[13] *Common Rail*[14] System (CRS) for first applications at Fiat and DaimlerChrysler. For this system, a high-pressure pump compresses the fuel and pumps it to the high-pressure accumulator, the so-called "rail". The fuel is injected into the combustion chambers at the proper time and in the proper quantity via solenoid-valve controlled injectors.

At the end of 1998, production started on the solenoid valve controlled single cylinder system, the "Unit Injector System" (UIS), also called the pump-nozzle system. This system with maximum 2050 bar has the highest pressure potential of all injection systems. Pump and nozzle are combined in a module for the UIS;

there are only a few high-pressure parts. One module is used per cylinder, so that this system is equally good for any number of cylinders.

[1] Einspritzstrahl	[2] Düse	[3] Einspritzventil
[4] Blase	[5] Reiheneinspritzpumpen	[6] Düsenträger; Düsenhalter
[7] Schwellenwerte; Grenzwerte	[8] Treibhauseffekt	[9] Versprechen
[10] geschichtet	[11] Axialkolben-Verteilereinspritzpumpe	[12] elektromagnetisches Ventil
[13] Speichereinspritzung	[14] gemeinsame Versorgungsleitung	

8.3 Chassis

8.3.1 New seal design for suspension systems on Formula One cars.

A new design of *sealing*[1] within high performance *suspension systems*[2] is used to reduce running friction on *damper rods*[3] by up to 50 per cent on a Formula One car. With this in mind, Greene Tweed engineers examined the *separator piston*[4] (used to separate gas and oil), the *damper piston*[5] and the damper rod seals and *bearings*[6]. Careful redesigning was able to *enhance*[7] their performance significantly.

By changing the materials used in the construction of the separator piston, Greene Tweed has been able to offer an enhanced seal. The body of the piston is made from Arlon. Instead of the former "O"ring, a ring consisting of a high strength elastomer is used. This configuration offers many advantages over its *predecessor*[8]. Sealing efficiency is improved due to a more stable seal configuration and the seal is not *susceptible*[9] to movement. Arlon offers a reduced *coefficient of friction*[10] and the elastomer offers higher temperature capability. The removal of the "O"ring allows tighter *running clearances*[11] which reduce seal thickness. The overall mass of the separator piston has been halved, reducing hysteresis and system response times. The main purpose of the seal, in this case, is to prevent metal-to-metal contact.

Sealing efficiency is less important in the damper piston, ultra low *friction*[12] being the main goal. In replacing the piston material with thermoplastic, the piston had to be redesigned. The damper piston, also made from Arlon, promotes better dynamic properties and enhanced *tribological properties*[13]. Sealing efficiency can be improved with a reduced seal contact area without a friction compromise.

Damper rod seals and bearings also have to deal with *misalignment*[14]. Because the end of the damper rod is connected directly to the wheel, it must move as the wheel moves. The opposite end is connected to the damper piston. As the damper unit is often used in conjunction with a spring, this applies a *bending moment*[15] to the damper rod, so a bearing is required to *counteract*[16] side loading. Current solutions typically show a chrome-plated damper rod running through an aluminium bearing and seal housing, *cap seals*[17] made by *PTFE*[18], and *scrapers*[19]. Greene Tweed's solution instead replaces the cap seal with one seal, made from "MSE" material. The bearing is manufactured from Avalon and an "MSE" scraper is used.

To summarize the advantages of the new design by recent tests on a Formula One car:
- Reduction in breakout and running friction of 50 per cent compared with the existing solution.
- Leakage performance is equal.
- Sealing installation into the correct *groove*[20] geometry was quicker and easier than with the "O"ring-caps.

These redesigns offer benefits to suspension system designs and improves performance dramatically.

[1] Abdichten	[2] Radaufhängungssystem; Federungssystem	[3] Stoßdämpferstange
[4] Abscheiderkolben	[5] Stoßdämpferkolben; Arbeitskolben	[6] Lager
[7] verbessern	[8] Vorgänger; Vorläufermodell	[9] sensibel; anfällig
[10] sensibel; anfällig	[11] Laufspiel	[12] Reibung
[13] tribologische Eigenschaften	[14] Fluchtungsfehler; Achsversatz	[15] Biegemoment
[16] entgegenwirken	[17] Aufsteck-Dichtungen	[18] Teflon Polytetrafluorethylen)
[19] Abstreifer	[20] Nut; Fuge	

8.3.2 The magic triangle of tyre development

The *inflatable*[1] tyre was *envisaged*[2] over a century-and-a-half ago. Since then, there has been constant development. The construction brings together *layers*[3] of *fabric*[4] and reinforcement (*synthetic fibre*[5], glass fibre, steel wire) and different *rubber compounds*[6] to meet the specific requirements for the *tread*[7], sidewall, and inner *air-proof liner*[8].

There is a magic triangle between *wear*[9] (durability), wet *skidding*[10] (safety) and *resistance to rolling*[11] (fuel economy). It means, an improvement in one or two has demanded a sacrifice in the third. The *quest*[12] to reduce tyre manufacturing costs, while improving safety and durability, is a question of materials technology. With new materials and technology, there is a chance to get the balance of durability, safety and fuel economy right. There is a *trade-off*[13] between materials, costs and properties.

Safety

The trouble is that with tyres, the trade-off could be life-threatening. The contact area between the sole of a shoe and the road is about as large as a tyre and the road. Pedestrians do not need to carry a quarter of a ton mass on each sole. There is a tiny margin for safety. It demands extraordinary skills from the tyre manufacturer suppliers of the materials, reinforcements and chemical additives. It is still a risk driving a car, especially on a wet road. The tyre has to *sweep*[14] water away from the *gripping tread*[15] and provide stability and accuracy when cornering. But a contradiction arises, when fuel should be saved by reducing the rolling resistance of the tyre. The faster the tyre rolls, the greater is the volume of water that has to be removed. If the tyre fails, it will start aquaplaning. One of its main functions of *thread*[16] must always be to remove water from between the road surface and the *tyre's footprint*[17].

What about the possibility of using a *"run-flat" tyre*[18]?. The overall demand for replacement tyres is twice as high as the car-makers' requirement - and so the tyre industry is one of the few that has actually welcomed safety legislations.

Another main function of thread is to reduce noise. Therefore a *focal point*[19] is the development of thread patterns and optimum formulation of rubber compounds. A *minor*[20] function of thread is image.

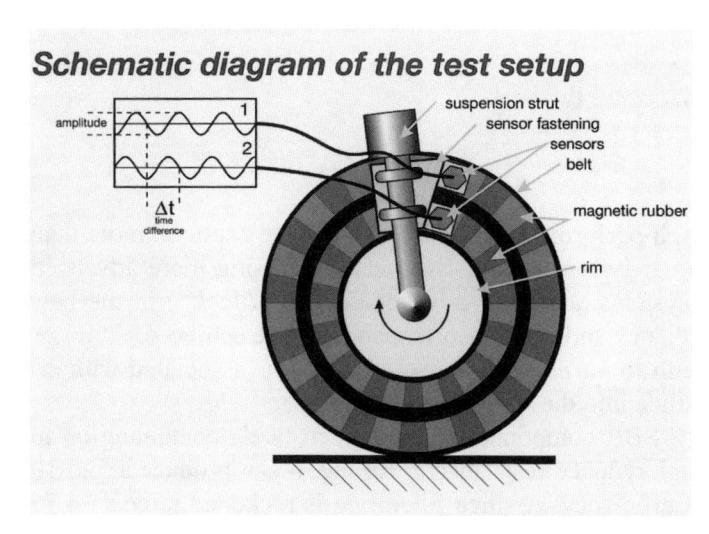

Figure 8.3.2.1: Sidewall torsion sensor. Schematic diagram of the test setup (Source: Continental Teves, Frankfurt)

Durability

Quite a lot of petrol is necessary to overcome the resistance of the tyres to rolling. With special rubber compounds, the tyre industry has been able to reduce rolling resistance of tyres by up to 35 per cent, which could account for up to 5 per cent in fuel-saving. A low-energy rubber *militates against*[21] good grip, but high tread *radii*[22] increase rolling resistance. We are back in the magic triangle. In the past, most *styrene-butadiene*[23] (SBR) tyres were produced by an *emulsion*[24] process. Today, the more environmentally-friendly *solution process*[25] (S-SBR), which is also extremely flexible and allows the production of tailor-made rubbers in terms of micro- and macro-structures, is increasingly being used in tyre treads. Shell was one of the first to balance the equation and develop rubber compounds giving improved rolling resistance without sacrificing wet grip.

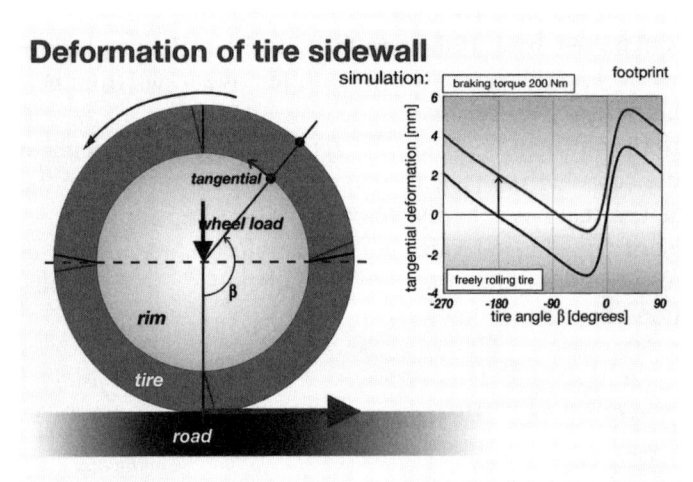

Figure 8.3.2.2: Sidewall torsion sensor. Deformation of tire sidewall (Source: Continental Teves, Frankfurt)

Fuel economy

Eco tyres, made of high-performance S-SBR grades, have captured more than a third of the European car tyre market in five years. By using more advanced fillers (such as *silica*[26] systems and more advanced *carbon black*[27]) in the new rubber, even greater efficiency and cost-performance could be achieved.

Silica has been difficult to *harness*[28] because of problems associated with effectively *bonding*[29] the silica into the *rubber compound*[30].

Bayer developed an S-SBR compound, called "green tyre", containing up to 20 per cent silica. Through reduced resistance to rolling, it can produce a 5 to 10 per cent increase in fuel efficiency. A silica-filled tyre is reckoned to cost $4.75 extra, $1 representing increased raw material cost, while the remainder is for the extra cost of equipment and processing.

Economical points of view

Economics of size and distribution are beginning to run out of benefits. Over the years, many routes to cost-reduction have been explored. As a product which is still essentially hand-made, tyre manufacturing is expensive and the prizes go to anyone who can reduce costs. One way was shown by major concentration such as the acquisition of Uniroyal and Goodrich by Michelin: As a result, 60 per cent of the market is now in the hands of just four groups.

Another way is through the reduction of manufacturing costs. There is no easy way, because the tyre combines different rubbers, chemicals, fabrics, fibres and steel wire. It is still the world's most advanced composite. Materials technology may provide an answer:
- High performance reinforcing fibres, such as aramids, are interesting. The function of the rubber is essentially to *resist*[31] sunlight, rain, moisture and wear. New types of rubber have already been introduced.
- Injection moulding a tyre might happen in the future. After all, fuel tanks are now moulded with six extruded layers and *insert moulding*[32] technology is merely *skimming over the surface*[33] of potential developments. For tyres however, it is still hard to imagine all these elements being combined into one production stage.
- Only one material is being developed to provide all these properties (maybe polyurethane, self- reinforcing elastomers, or flexible material to dissipate the heat)
- Accurate studies can now be made quickly and at low cost by a raw material manufacturer, using small *specimens*[34], instead of carrying out tests on finished tyres.

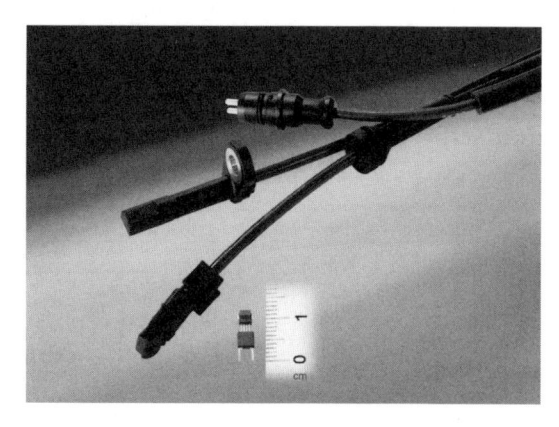

Figure 8.3.2.3: Active wheel speed sensors. On the left the pencil sensor for conventional assembly, on the right the clip-on sensor for innovative assemby. In the center the active sensor element (Source: Continental Teves, Frankfurt)

Goodyear is currently rated world Number Three, but *vows*[35] to *leap*[36] into first place with a manufacturing process which
- cuts production time by 70 per cent,
- boosts tyre-building productivity by 135 per cent,
- halves *inventories*[37] and
- cuts labour by 35 per cent.

Goodyear has developed radically new technology called Integrated Manufacturing Precision Assembly Cellular Technology (IMPACT).

It means this technology can be installed in existing plants. For making the *carcass*[38] of a tyre, the cutting and *splicing*[39] of many materials, e.g. fabrics and cords, will be eliminated. The company is being understandably *tight-lipped*[40] about the actual details.

Furthermore sufficient innovation should bring a *sustainable*[41] competitive advantage.
- The company is streamlining its product lines from 59 to 38.
- Ultra-tensile steel reinforcement gives an advantage in the market.
- They plan to extend the technology for "run-flat" tyres which give safe driving after a blow-out.

[1] aufblasbar	[2] vorausgesehen	[3] Schichten
[4] Gewebe	[5] Kunstfaser	[6] Gummimischungen; Kautschukmischungen
[7] Profil	[8] innerer, luftundurchlässiger Mantel	[9] Verschleiß, Abnutzung; Abrieb
[10] Verschleiß, Abnutzung; Abrieb	[11] Rollwiderstand	[12] Suche
[13] Kompromiss	[14] kehren	[15] haftende/klebende Lauffläche
[16] Gewinde; Schraubengang	[17] Reifenaufstandsfläche	[18] Reifen mit Notlaufeigenschaften
[19] Schwerpunkt	[20] klein; unbedeutend	[21] gegen etwas wirken
[22] Radien	[23] Styrol-Budadien	[24] Emulsion
[25] Auflösungsprozess	[26] Kieselerde; Quarz	[27] technischer Ruß
[28] bündeln	[29] kleben	[30] Gummimischung
[31] widerstehen	[32] Formpressen mit Einlegeteilen	[33] dicht über die Oberfläche dahingleiten
[34] Muster; Proben	[35] geloben	[36] springen
[37] Lagerbestände	[38] Karkasse, Unterbau	[39] Spleißung; Naht
[40] verschlossen	[41] lebenserhaltend	

8.3.3 Use of plastics for fuel systems

The days are gone when an auto manufacturer purchased a tank from one supplier and fuel lines from another and then put them together. The demand is to engineer the complete system, in line with the establishment of *Tier One suppliers*[1], which will bring together manufacturers of tanks, *fuel lines*[2] and components. The aim is the development of a safe automotive fuel system, with lowest-possible or even zero emissions.

Plastic tanks
Plastic tanks were pioneered by BASF in Europe. Produced by blow moulding in high molecular mass high density polyethylene, they offer several advantages:

- a seamless container
- good mechanical properties
- great flexibility in shape

To reduce *permeation*[3] by fuel and to meet the US CARB (California Air Registration Board) and European requirements, a special barrier layer and a good integral bond between structure and barrier layer must be introduced by *extrusion*[4]. A complex six-layer construction, made of Ethylene vinyl alcohol (EVOH) is growing in popularity.

Chrysler's 1995 Grand Cherokee jeep has the first six-layer tank. It is blow moulded in BASF's Lupolen HDPE with EVOH from Eval Co of America. *Re-grind*[5] from production *scrap*[6] made up about half of the 8kg mass of the tank.

The old method, post-treatment by *fluorination*[7] or *sulphonation*[8], which is able to meet the high emission standards, is too costly and involves pollutants. Furthermore, widely used Nylon requires special treatment to make it compatible with *HDPE*[9] when it comes to recycling. In comparison to plastic, a metal tank would have weighed 10-11kg and would not have given freedom of design.

Multi-layer blow moulding needs expensive tooling. In Europe, DuPont offers laminar technology in which a nylon-based barrier material is added to the HDPE. The company is working on an EVOH barrier which would give higher resistance. Laminar technology needs less expensive tooling.

Current trends in tank construction in Europe are:

Technology	Market share	Trend
All-metal	30%	Declining
Fluorination	48%	Steady
Laminar	14%	Growing
Sulphonation	1%	Declining
Coextrusion	2%	Growing
Untreated HDPE	5%	Declining

An integrated plastic fuel system

Belgian's chemical giant Solvay and its U.S. based subsidiary Solvay Automotive, with headquarters in Troy, Michigan, is the world's largest independent manufacturer of *blow-moulded*[10] automotive fuel tanks.

Solvay has developed an integrated plastic fuel system, which includes the fuel tank, *fuel-filler neck*[11], on-board *refueling vapour recovery system*[12], fuel pump, *fuel level sensor*[13] and *fuel lines*[14], aimed at helping U.S. car makers meet Federal Clean Air Act legislation. Since 1998 all American cars have had to meet the requirement which allows vehicles to *emit*[15] no more than 2g of hydrocarbon per day. Plastic fuel systems reduce hydrocarbon emission to less than 0.1 g per day. It is mostly manufactured from HDPE. The system has been closely studied

by European automotive experts with a view to transferring some of the lessons learned to their fuel system development:
- There are more advantages.
- The materials also allow design flexibility
- Light mass.
- *Coaxial*[16] fuel filler-pipe design improves crash performance.
- Its *corrugated*[17] form is designed to bend under stress rather than break.

The fuel and the tubes

US car manufacturers are still using a large amount of metal tubing under the car with rubber or plastic *jumpers*[18] at each end. Polyamide (PA) tubes meet higher specifications, are efficient, flexible and available at lower costs. To manufacture PA, *fuel lines*[19] have been developing multi-layer, coextruded constructions. These require *tied*[20] layers to give an efficient *long-lasting bond*[21].

Adding ethanol and methyl-t-butyl ether (ETBE and MTBE) to conventional hydrocarbon fuel gives higher combustion efficiency. However, the *permeability*[22] of the system is increased. Moreover, a 10°C increase in fuel temperature increases the permeability of a monolayer tube system by 50 - 100%.

To counteract build-up of static electricity, conductive lines are specified in the U.S. This can be met by the simple addition of *carbon black*[23] to the outer and inner layers, but this tends to *impair*[24] the mechanical properties. *Graphite*[25] is an alternative. Rover seems to be the only European manufacturer working to these specifications.

Monolayer against multilayer lines

In Europe, monolayer lines in PA are still being used widely. *Non-leaded*[26] fuels do not present any serious problem.

Elf Atochem warns that the layers can be separated by differential expansion and attachment to joints. Its Multi-layer Tube (MLT) concept offers three options, using Rilsan nylon with Kynar *PVDF*[27] and a tie-layer of modified polyamide, with the option of antistatic PA. HuLs, also a specialist in polyamides, do not require a tie layer to bond with nylon by using barrier layers of polybutylene terephthalate (PBT).

Efficiency calculation

Ultimately, the question of cost arises. High performance systems at low permeability can cost from 35 to 200% more than monolayer systems. Currently, European auto manufacturers are *opting*[28] for the cheaper lines. For the future, there is obviously a cost advantage in engineering the complete system. A monolayer system is not the favorite. Polyketone, already commercialised by Shell and in an advanced pilot stage with BP Chemicals, could be the answer. Polyketone is a family of thermoplastics with good resistance to high temperatures, good mechanical properties and excellent chemical resistance and barrier properties, particularly to automotive fuels. Tests show polyketones compare very favourably with HDPE and easily pass the requirements of the CARB test: but at a price of about DM 13.85/kg, some quite exclusive speciality niche is needed to justify the price.

The basic question that remains is concerning how how high the fuel emission specifications are to be in Europe. There is also evidence that realistic tests should cover a longer period of time. Many plastics absorb fuel during the initial stages of *exposure*[29] and give a low permeability figure: but over time, as plastics become saturated, permeation can rise sharply.

[1] Hauptzulieferer; Komplettsystemlieferant	[2] Kraftstoffleitung	[3] Durchdringung
[4] Fließpressen	[5] nachschleifen	[6] Schrott
[7] Fluorieren	[8] Schwefeln	[9] hochdichtes Polyethylen
[10] blasgeformt	[11] Kraftstoff-Einfüllstutzen	[12] Kraftstoffverdunstungsabsaugsystem; Gaspendelanlage
[13] Kraftstofffüllstandsgeber; Tankgeber	[14] Kraftstoffzuleitungen	[15] emittieren; ausstoßen
[16] rundlaufend; konzentrisch	[17] gewellt; gerieffelt	[18] Verbindungen
[19] Kraftstoffleitungen	[20] gebunden	[21] Langzeitverbindung
[22] Durchlässigkeit; Porosität	[23] technischer Ruß	[24] beeinträchtigen
[25] Graphit	[26] bleifrei	[27] Polyvinylidenfluorid
[28] sich entscheiden	[29] Aussetzung; Einwirkung	

8.3.5 Brakes for motor racing

Motor racing rules forbid carbon-fibre composites, but cast iron brake discs are heavy. However, permitted light alloy metal matrix composites (MMCs) combine the low mass of light alloy with the strength of ceramic reinforcement.

MMC, reinforced with 20% particulate SiC, is *sand-cast*[1] 2.0 mm oversize in all dimensions. The cast has then to be machined to a finished diameter of 278 mm with a tolerance of ± 0.1 mm and a good *surface finish*[2].

Up to now, conventional tooling, such as *tungsten*[3] *carbide*[4], has quickly worn out and could not hold tolerance for long. To overcome this, Metal Composite Technology, based at Silverstone, the home of British motor racing, uses De Beers SYNDITE to give the necessary machining accuracy, together with an acceptable tool life.

With this new tool material, the discs are machined on a *lathe*[5], using *round blanks*[6] at a cutting speed of 300 m/min and a *feed*[7] of 0.35 mm/rev. All machining is completed in a *single pass*[8] - *facing*[9] in around 2 minutes and turning in 12 seconds.

Finally, a 0.3 mm thick coating of Al_2O_3 is then applied and machined again, removing approximately 0.1 mm to give the required shape and size.

Figure 8.3.5.1: Brake components on the inertia dynamometer[10]. Safe driving starts with good brakes (Source: Continental Teves, Frankfurt)

[1] Sandguss	[2] Oberflächenbeschaffenheit; Oberflächengüte	[3] Wolfram
[4] Hartmetall	[5] Drehmaschine	[6] runde Rohlinge
[7] Vorschub	[8] in einem Durchgang	[9] Belag
[10] Schwungmassenprüfstand		

8.3.6 All-in-one exhaust system for small cars

Eberspächer's all-in-one *catalytic converter*[1], *exhaust pipe*[2] and *silencer*[3] is already in production at the Smart car. It represents the first system that places the complete system within a short *header pipe*[4] in close *proximity*[5] to the engine. This solution will become increasingly popular with the mass and space-conscious designers of small vehicles.

The new design reduces heat loss from exhaust gases and thereby significantly shortens the catalytic converter warm-up time.

What about package figures? The entire assembly measures around 83cm in length and 16cm diameter and has a total volumetric capacity of 8 litre. It is mounted *transversely*[6] at the rear. Silencers are placed both *upstream*[7] and downstream of the catalytic converter.

Figure 8.3.6.1: Opel Agila (Source: Adam Opel AG, Rüsselsheim)

How does this exhaust system work? Exhaust gases are directed onto the surface of the converter and flow through the palladium/rhodium-*coated*[8] *monolith*[9]. They can then "choose" between two routes: either through a *perforated*[10] *partition*[11] directly into the *baffle*[12] chamber of the silencer, or by a *circuitous route*[13] through the *resonator*[14] (located ahead of the catalytic converter and acoustically connected to the silencer *bypass*[15]). The monolith is mounted in expanding *mats*[16] filled with particles, which *absorb*[17] the *variations*[18] as the monolith expans.

Figure 8.3.6.2: The new two-seater Smart Roadster (Source: Adrian Zürl, Nauheim)

¹ Katalysator	² Auspuffrohrleitung	³ Abgasschalldämpfer
⁴ Krümmerrohr; Vorrohr	⁵ Nähe; Nachbarschaft	⁶ quer
⁷ stromaufwärts	⁸ beschichtet	⁹ Wabenkörper
¹⁰ durchlöchert	¹¹ Trennwand	¹² Prallblech; Blende
¹³ Umweg	¹⁴ Resonator; Reflexionsschalldämpfer	¹⁵ Umgehungsleitung
¹⁶ Matten	¹⁷ aufnehmen, schlucken	¹⁸ Streuungen; Schwankungen

8.3.7 Switching from metal to plastic pedal assembly

Switching from metal to plastic pedal assembly means that mass, strength, cost and performance of new parts has to be considerably improved. A new *methodology*[1] is being applied to both accelerator and clutch assemblies with automotive companies in North America, Europe, South America and Asia. A three-way partnership between Ford, Comcorp Technologies and AlliedSignal Plastics made the first plastic decision for the 1999 version of one of Ford's top selling models. This new plastic material and design reduces the assembly mass by 50% and the number of parts by 50%, resulting in cost savings of 10%.

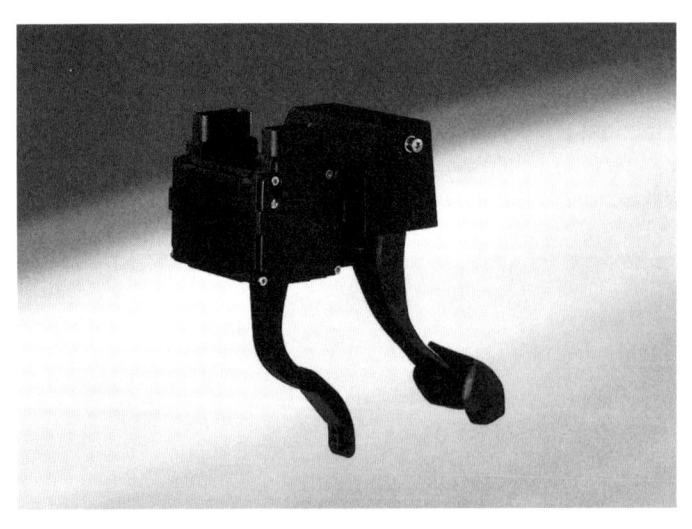

Figure 8.3.7.1: Final solution of the pedal module for the electro-mechanical brake (EMB). The use of brake fluid for transmitting pressure is dispensed with[2] completely (Source: Continental Teves, Frankfurt)

How has the engineering been done?
Allied Signal has turned to their *proprietary*[3] Structural Design Optimisation Process analysis (attempts to adapt the existing metal design wouldn't have worked). The result was an efficient accelerator pedal assembly with significant cost savings: a pedal with the open channel facing the passenger compartment, and a reinforcement rib pattern that shows angled parallel ribs crossed *intermittently*[4] with diagonal ribs.

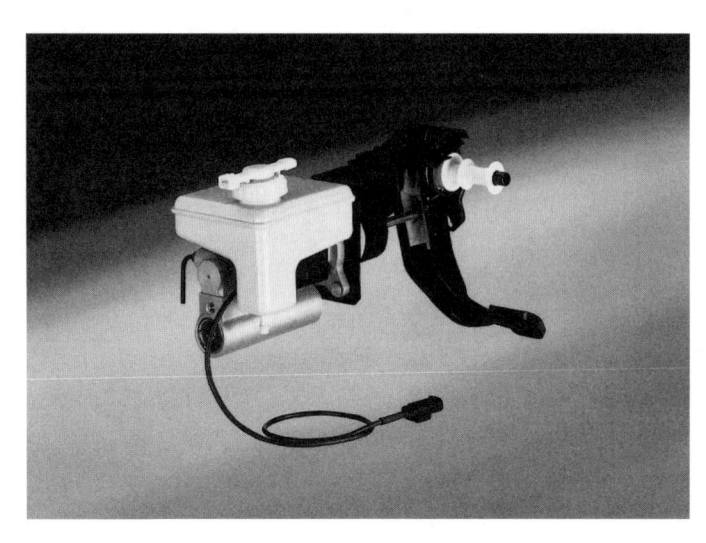

Figure 8.3.7.2: An interim solution[5] on the way to the completely fluid-free Brake by Wire: Pedal actuation unit[6] (Source: Continental Teves, Frankfurt)

A material has been found which has the desired combination of *strength[7], stiffness[8], impact resistance[9], processability[10]* and *dimensional stability[11]*: a 33% *glassfibre reinforced[12]* polyamide (nylon) called Capron 8233. Design exceeds the 113kg loading requirements at temperatures of -20°C to +70°C. *Fatigue tests[13]* included 2 million cycles at 18kg.

[1] Methodik	[2] verzichtet	[3] Marken; Eigentum
[4] absatzweise, periodisch auftretend	[5] Zwischenlösung	[6] Pedalbetätigungseinheit
[7] Festigkeit	[8] Steifigkeit	[9] Schlagfestigkeit
[10] Verarbeitbarkeit	[11] Maßhaltigkeit, Formbeständigkeit	[12] glasfaserverstärkt
[13] Dauerproben		

8.3.8 Air suspension system

Krupp Bilstein, as a partner of Mercedes-Benz, has developed the suspension system of the top-of-the-range Mercedes S-class model. The body of the S-class is cushioned pneumatically with an adaptive shock absorber system adjusted to driving conditions. The S-class model takes its inspiration from the 1960s with state-of-the-art electronics technology for the 21st century.

The specifications *stipulated[1]* a clear reduction in internal damper component friction. To do this, two bypass pistons are necessary, each plated on both sides, arranged together with the two required *solenoid valves[2]* in the *casing[3]* which is flange-mounted at the *lower end[4]* of the damper. Furthermore, gas pressure in the shock absorber has been halved by a "technical trick" about which Krupp Bilstein is saying no more. In conjunction with the internal air spring pressure, this results in an extremely *low pressure differential*[5] across the *piston rod seal*[6].

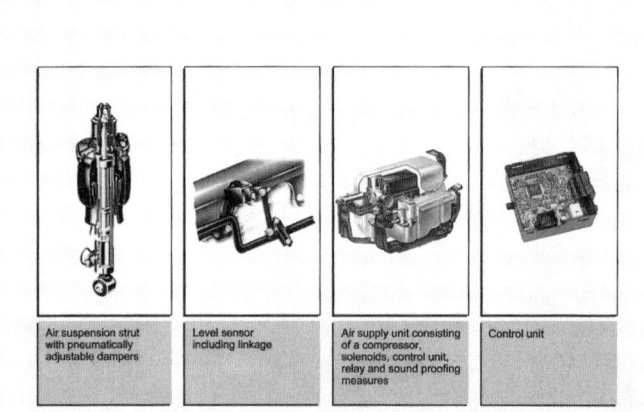

Figure 8.3.8.1: Air suspension system. Components of Rear-Levelling System[7] (Source: Continental Teves, Frankfurt)

[1] vorschreiben	[2] elektromagnetische Ventile	[3] Gehäuse
[4] Fuß; unteres Ende	[5] Niederdruckgefälle	[6] Kolbenstangendichtung
[7] Niveauregulierungsanlage		

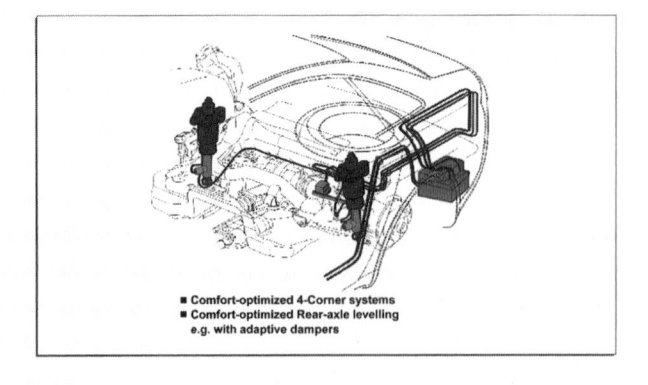

Figure 8.3.8.2: Comfort-optimized 4-corner systems. Comfort-optimized rear-axle levelling (Source: Continental Teves, Frankfurt)

8.3.9 Porsche's new SUV needs stability management in 2002

Porsche is investing DM 1 billion in the joint venture with Volkswagen and is the development leader of this new car, which is a *multi purpose vehicle*[1] (MPV) with off-road ability.

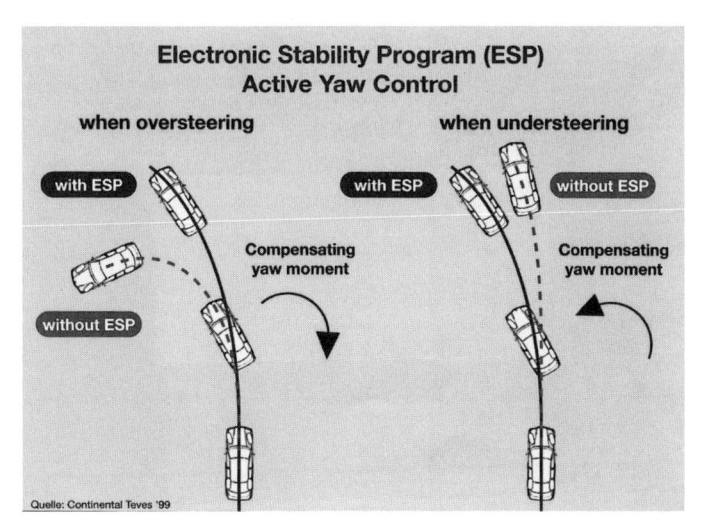

Figure 8.3.9.1: Electronic Stability Management[2] *(Source: Continental Teves, Frankfurt)*

Porsche's advanced 4 x 4 system for the new *SUV*[3] due to be launched in 2002, needs a *stability management system (PSM)*[4], which has already been *featured*[5] on the new Carrera 4. PSM hardware has been developed by Bosch, whereas the sophisticated 4 x 4 *algorithm*[6] has been developed by Porsche engineers.

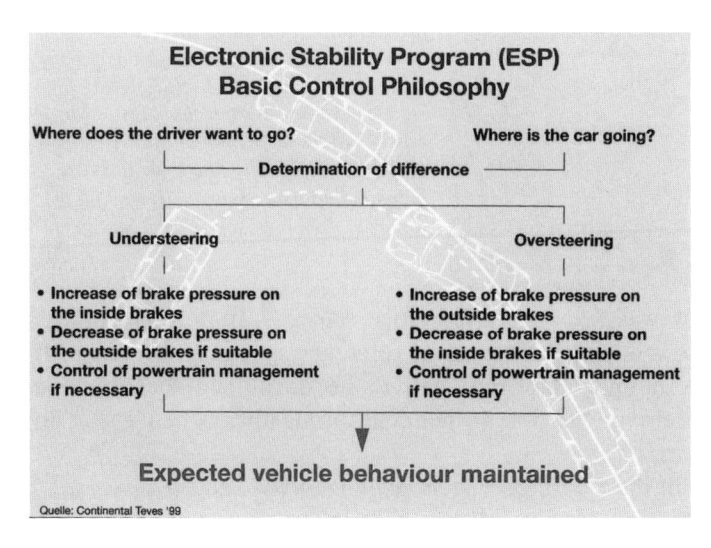

Figure 8.3.9.2: Basic control philosophy of the Electronic Stability Program (Source: Continental Teves, Frankfurt)

*Figure 8.3.9.3: Micromechanic yaw sensor[7]. The yaw sensor is the key component of the vehicle dynamics control ESP (Electronic Stability Program). In 1998, Bosch introduced a micromechanical version to the market. This new technology makes the sensor considerably smaller and lighter.
(Source: Robert Bosch GmbH, Stuttgart)*

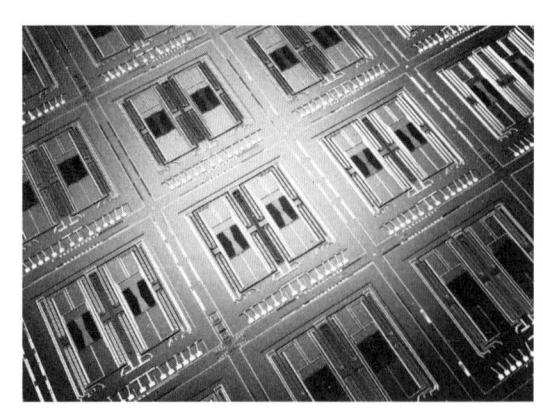

*Figure 8.3.9.4: Astronomical demand for the ESP (Electronic Stability Program) from Bosch has created several hundred new jobs in application development and production. At the same time, it has helped accelerate the latest generation of yaw sensors, the heart of ESP. Using state-of-the-art micro technology, a large number of these tiny finger nail size chips with microscopically fine structures are being manufactured on a carrying plate[8].
(Source: Robert Bosch GmbH, Stuttgart)*

The most difficult task was detecting a reference *velocity*[9]. In normal stability management systems this is not a problem as the reference speed can be taken off the undriven wheels. A unique algorithm had to be developed, because the Carrera 4 is a four-wheel drive with 5 to 40 per cent torque always being *fed*[10] to the front wheels.

PSM takes inputs from the steering, wheels, *yaw velocity*[11] and *transversal*[12] sensors to counteract *under and oversteer*[13]. Understeer is *countered*[14] by applying the brake on the inner rear wheel, whereas oversteering is countered by applying the outer front brake.

Figure 8.3.9.5: Electronic Stability Program (ESP): Yaw stability control[15] is made possible by several sophisticated sensors, with the most important module being the Yaw Rate Sensor[16] (Source: Continental Teves, Frankfurt)

PSM can also detect any *drift*[17] in the vehicle and *subtly*[18] counteract it by introducing the differential in speed between the inner and outer wheels together with the steering, *lateral*[19] and yaw sensors.

Figure 8.3.9.6: The vehicle on the right without the ESP which is concerning on the snow-covered circuit, loses control. No problems arise with ESP (Source: Continental Teves, Frankfurt)

[1] Mehrzweckfahrzeug	[2] Elektronisches Stabilitätsprogramm (ESP)	[3] Freizeitfahrzeug (sport utility vehicle)
[4] Fahrdynamikregelsystem	[5] beinhaltet	[6] Algorismus
[7] Gierwinkelsensor; Gierwinkelaufnehmer	[8] Trägerplatte	[9] Geschwindigkeit

[10] zugeführt; eingeleitet	[11] Gierwinkelgeschwindigkeit; Giergeschwindigkeit	[12] quer, transversal
[13] unter- und übersteuern	[14] entgegentreten, gekontert	[15] Giermomentenregelung
[16] Gierratensensor	[17] schieben, wegschieben	[18] fein
[19] seitlich, quer		

8.4 Electric/ Electronic

8.4.1 A car battery revolution

Advances in nickel-zinc batteries could lead to a battery revolution in the transportation sector. It may change the shape and performance of car batteries. The chemical compound is more energy-dense and less toxic than lead-acid. Unfortunately the batteries tend to *drain*[1] quickly and expire after being recharged just 50 to 100 times. IBM's Evercell, a special class of nickel zinc batteries, can be recharged 500 times, which is five times as often as such batteries today.

Special *MOS (metal oxide semiconductor)*[2] *FETs (field effect transistors)*[3] of power batteries are targeted primarily at automotive applications where *circuits*[4] are employed to limit the effects of *load dump*[5]. These lower voltage MOSFETs are optimised for significantly lower values of *resistance*[6] and higher efficiencies. An increase in power efficiency ultimately increases fuel efficiency. The new *devices*[7] result in extremely efficient and *rugged*[8] components and in reduction of costs by using less *silicon*[9] to perform the same task.

[1] entleeren, auslaufen	[2] Metalloxid-Halbleiter, MOS	[3] Feldeffect Transistoren, MOS Transistoren; MOSFETs
[4] Stromkreise; elektrische Schaltungen	[5] Lastabschaltung	[6] Widerstand
[7] Einrichtungen; Ausstattungen	[8] robust, stabil	[9] Silizium; Silicium

8.4.2 ASIC controls for airbags and seat belt systems

Four-*loop*[1] automotive air bags and seat belt systems need an *ASIC (application-specific integrated circuit)*[2], which provides the monitoring, diagnostic and control functions. Additionally, a password-protected 16-bit *serial interface*[3] for command and diagnostic status reporting is also offered.

There are four *current-controlled*[4] *drivers*[5] for the pyrotechnic *squibs*[6] included, which provide the air bag inflation and seat-belt *retention*[7] functions. Two additional drivers, which can operate as *high-side*[8] or *low-side*[9] drivers, are included for *bulb*[10] or *relay control*[11]. A further low-side driver is intended to *trigger*[12] an *alarm system*[13], such as a *chime*[14] module.

For diagnostic functions, an analogue multiplexer provides interfaces for *accelerometers*[15], *occupant detection sensors*[16] and other system components.

[1] Regelkreis, Regelschleife	[2] anwendungsspezifischer integrierter Schaltkreis	[3] serielle Schnittstelle
[4] stromgesteuert	[5] Mitnehmer	[6] Zündpille (für Airbags)
[7] Halt; Sicherung	[8] Hochdruck-Seite	[9] Saugdruck-Seite
[10] Lampe	[11] Relaissteuerung	[12] auslösen; zünden
[13] Alarmanlage	[14] Gong; Läutewerk	[15] Beschleunigungsmesser
[16] Belegungserkennung-Sensoren		

8.4.3 Low cost fluid level sensor

A new *push-fit*[1] fluid *level sensor*[2] (named IS CS-02) is designed for *low pressure*[3] applications such as windscreen washer tanks. It has an integral connector for fast installation at low cost. It is simply fitted into a pre-drilled or formed hole and horizontally mounted with a self-sealing *grommet*[4]. The sensor provides a maximum switch mode of 24V *DC*[5], 1A, 15W, a minimum *breakdown voltage*[6] of 100V DC and initial *contact resistance*[7] of 0.25 Ohms. The operating temperature is –30 to +600°C.

[1] Montieren durch Stoßen/Drücken	[2] Füllstandsfühler	[3] Niederdruck; druckarm
[4] Schutztülle; Abdichtstulpe	[5] Gleichstrom	[6] Überschlagspannung; Durchbruchspannung
[7] Kontaktwiderstand; Übergangswiderstand		

8.4.4 Cheaper and lighter lighting systems

Contemporary[1] lighting systems can't be used anymore due to styling restrictions *imposed*[2] on designers.

Two new headlamp technologies are influencing car headlight design, their developments having *emerged*[3] from OSRAM research teams. One exploits *novel*[4] lens technology while the other uses *electromagnetic forces*[5] to control the beam. These new technologies are claimed to be cheaper and lighter than conventional systems.

The first, called a zoned lens lamp, borrows technology from lighthouses, where light is projected through *fresnel spots*[6] which *feature*[7] a series of concentric rings. In the zoned lens lamp, circles are *moulded*[8] into the GE Plastics polycarbonate lens *carved*[9] areas for the light to pass through, working in conjunction with a reflector to create the *beam pattern*[10]. The new lamps are made entirely from plastic. Conventional projector systems use metal casings, and so plastic ones are half the mass of metal, as well as being 35 to 50 per cent smaller overall. Furthermore, despite using a smaller light source, a zoned lens lamp delivers a 10 per cent increase in *lumens*[11] over its closest competitors.

The second development describes a major breakthrough, combining *high intensity discharge (HID) lamps*[12] with a magnetodynamic positioning system (MDP). This technology allows the use of two-headlamp HID systems at one time: one light source and one headlamp on each side of the car for both *low beam*[13] and *high beam*[14] functions. Material and assembly costs have also been reduced. Magnetodynamic positioning works by using a magnetic field to *capture*[15], locate and move the *arc*[16] from one position to another inside the HID light. By way of comparison, conventional HID lamps create and maintain an arc between the two electrodes at either end of the quartz *capsule*[17].

Under some conditions the HID-MDP arc may come into contact with the top of the capsule wall but within the new technology it is stabilised by the magnetic field. This results in a straight horizontal arc on low beam, *enhancing*[18] the optical design and improving the colour of the light. By increasing the magnetic field which moves the arc towards the bottom of the capsule, a high beam is produced.

[1] zeitgenössisch	[2] aufbürden, auferlegen	[3] in Erscheinung getreten
[4] neu	[5] elektromagnetische Kräfte	[6] Fresnel Linsenscheinwerfer
[7] aufweisen, beinhalten	[8] formgepresst	[9] geschnitzt
[10] Lichtverteilung	[11] Lichtstrom	[12] Gasentladungs-Scheinwerfer
[13] Abblendlicht	[14] Fernlicht	[15] erfassen
[16] Bogen	[17] Steuerdose; Kapsel	[18] verbessern

8.5 Laboratory Tests

8.5.1 Aluminium-magnesium superalloy

Alloys with 10 per cent or more magnesium can be stronger than steel and one third of its mass. Originally *conceived*[1] for aerospace, Russian metallurgists have developed aluminium-magnesium superalloys also for use in motor vehicles.

The advantages expected are that:
- The superalloys are so called because they have very high strengths. *Ultimate*[2] *tensile strength*[3] is 380 to 400 MPa, and *yield strength*[4] is from 190 to 230 MPa.
- New processing techniques allow them to be stamp-formed from sheet and *extruded*[5].

- Superalloys are cost-effective for both cars and commercial vehicles. Cost is no more than 25 per cent more than for aluminium alloys with 6% magnesium.
- They have good mechanical properties. The key is in the *crystallising*[6] stage in their process *flow sheet*[7]. It is possible to process these alloys at a price the car industry will find attractive.
- After suitable processing, *elongation*[8] is 36 to 42 per cent, similar to that for steels.
- The new alloys are weldable and deep cold stampable.
- The density is 2.58 Mg/cbm.
- Ericsen test results are 9.5 to 12mm
- *Bendability*[9] $r = 0.5\ b$, so the superalloy is difficult to form and fabricate.
- Corrosion resistance is similar to that found in aluminium alloys with 6% magnesium.
- *Ingots*[10] have been made 300mm in diameter. Sheets with thicknesses from 1 to 4 mm have been tested at the Russian AVTOVAZ plant and were found to meet and exceed all the requirements for metal sheets. After having licensed the technology, developers have been able to supply small quantities for test purposes.

[1] ausgedacht	[2] äußerst; hier: maximal	[3] Zugfestigkeit
[4] Streckgrenze, Fließgrenze	[5] fließgepresst; stranggepresst	[6] Kornbildung; Kristallbildung
[7] Fließbild	[8] Dehnung; Verlängerung	[9] Biegevermögen
[10] Rohblöcke, Barren		

8.5.2 Surface structures at atomic level

A new *X-ray*[1] photoelectron spectrometer (XPS) will allow engineers and scientists to *probe*[2] surface structures at an atomic level over large areas. *Disc brake pads*[3], bearings, *pistons*[4], *gaskets*[5], *camshafts*[6] and powder metal components are *undergoing*[7] further development and are all expected to benefit from the capabilities of the XPS. The new equipment is also able to produce a *depth profile*[8] of the *sub-surface*[9] *chemistry*[10] by progressively analysing and removing layers a few atoms thick. In the development of *friction*[11] materials for disc brake pads, for example, the XPS is being used to investigate the thin layers which are formed by the friction materials on the surface of the brake disc during braking. The brake pad's interaction with the disc affects performance parameters like friction, *wear*[12], brake noise and *judder*[13], having a major controlling influence on the tribological mechanism of these thin layers. Due to this, the new data is already being used to develop disc brake pad materials. *Additives*[14] have to be selected to optimize the characteristics of the *film*[15].

[1] Röntgen	[2] sondieren; untersuchen	[3] Scheibenbremsen-Bremsbelag
[4] Kolben	[5] Dichtungen	[6] Nockenwellen

[7] erleben; sich unterziehen	[8] Tiefenprofil	[9] untere Fläche
[10] Chemie	[11] Reibung	[12] Verschleiß
[13] rattern; vibrieren	[14] Zusatzmittel; Wirkstoffe	[15] Beschichtung

8.5.3 Cold-rolled ultra-high-strength steel

Cold-rolled ultra-high-strength (UHS) steel is particularly suitable for components used in vehicle *crumple zones*[1] because of its high energy absorbing properties. UHS steel has minimum *tensile strength*[2] levels of between 1000 and 1400 Mpa. In the automotive industry it should contribute to the *quest*[3] to build lighter vehicles and allow new construction methods to be used. One example is laser welded tailored blanks. The steel is *hardened*[4] before leaving the factory, so industries using them do not need to invest in warm-up plant and *hardening furnaces*[5]. It is delivered with a bright cold-rolled surface which has not oxidised and is therefore suited to continuous manufacturing processes.

[1] Knautschzonen	[2] Zugfestigkeit	[3] Suche
[4] verhärtet	[5] Aushärteöfen	

8.5.4 Low sulphur diesel fuel

Low-sulphur diesel causes abnormal injection pump wear due to the *inferior lubricity*[1]. This phenomenon is well known in Europe and North America. However, few Asian countries, eg. Korea, Thailand, Taiwan, and Japan, have *adopted*[2] low-sulphur diesel fuels. Currently, little is known about the wear effects of low-sulphur diesel fuel in Asian conditions. Fuel lubricity *hinge on*[3] several factors, such as fuel composition, driving conditions, temperature and humidity, which can be slightly or entirely different from those in Western countries. Field tests in Asia show *injection pump*[4] *wear*[5] within normal limits only after 30,000 km.

In Japan low-sulphur diesel fuel was introduced in two steps. In 1992, the fuel had 0.2 wt% sulphur. Since October 1997, fuel contained 0.05 wt% sulphur. Despite early evaluation of Japan's 0.2 wt% sulphur fuels, the effets of sulphur reduction on lubricity are uncertain. Before introduction of 0.05 wt% sulphur fuel in Japan, high-frequency *reciprocating*[6] *rig*[7] wear data on 0.2 wt% sulphur fuels showed a trend toward high wear *scar*[8] diameters from 400 to greater than 500 μm. This test result indicates significant problems with lubricity. Catastrophic mechanical failure or unacceptable loss of pump performance could be the result of abnormal wear of *distributor pumps*[9], caused by severe *scuffing*[10] of the *rollers*[11] and *camplate*[12].

Pumps are an important aspect of engine performance. Japanese light-duty pick-up trucks are the basis of goods and passenger transportation within Asian countries, including Thailand. Uncontrolled injection pump *deterioration*[13] tends to *adversely*[14] affect the general population, which, in Thailand's case, often lacks the resources to replace the costly pumps that have historically been reliable.

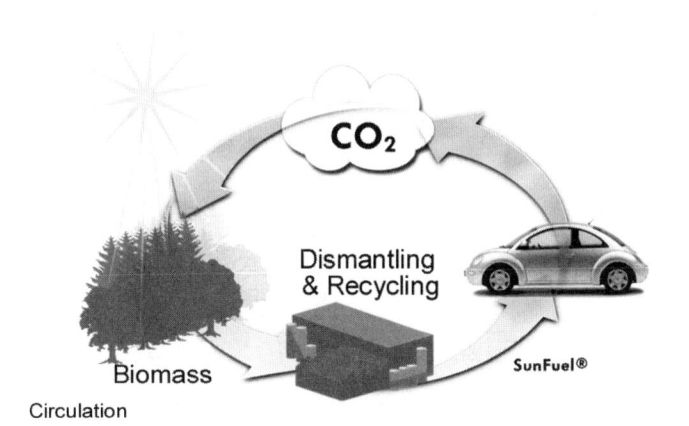

Figure 8.5.4.1: CO_2 circulation and CO_2 forecast (Source: Volkswagen AG, Wolfsburg)

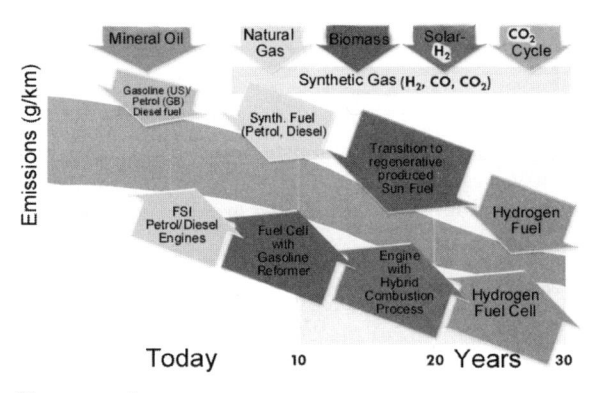

Circulation

Forecast

To determine the effects of low-sulphur diesel fuel on *rotary pump*[15] performance, typical test conditions were chosen that allowed vehicles to operate, including high-speed and stop-and-go driving. Imported and locally refined fuels, some without lubricity additiv or treated with them are used.

The following parts within the pump are used as indicators of a fuel's lubricity property, because of their *susceptibility*[16] to wear: *Flymass*[17], camplate, camplate roller and *torque control fulcrum*[18].

The assessment of normal wear after 30,000 km is especially interesting for fuels with its borderline value and lack of lubricity additives. This fuel was usually believed to cause a certain degree of abnormal wear. This was not the case here.

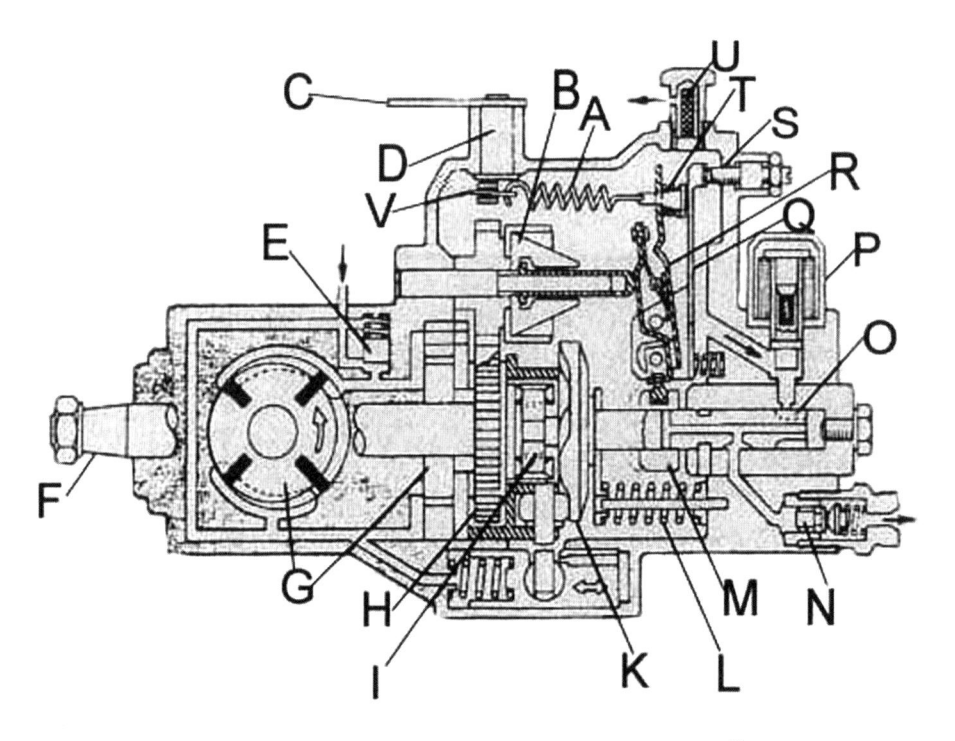

Figure 8.5.4.2: Draft of a VE-type injector pump. Note: Fuel-supply pump[19] (G) is shown from two aspects, one being a 90°-rotated view with the pump vanes and rotor in section and the other being a normal side view. Timing device[20] (J) is shown as turned around by 90°. (Source: Automotive Engineering International, 10/99)

A = governor spring[21]; B = Flymass[22]; C = Control lever[23]; D = Contol lever shaft[24]; E = Regulating valve[25]; F = Drive shaft[26]; H = Flymass drive gear[27]; I = Driving disc[28]; K = Cam plate[29]; L = Plunger spring[30]; M = Control sleeve[31]; N = Delivery valve[32]; O = Plunger[33]; P = Fuel-cutoff solenoid[34]; Q = Corrector lever[35]; R = Tensioning lever[36]; S = Full-load adjusting screw[37]; T = Idling spring[38]; U = Overflow valve[39].

[1] untergeordnete/niedrige Schmiereigenschaften	[2] übernommen	[3] von etwas abhängen
[4] Kraftstoffeinspritzpumpe	[5] Verschleiß; Abnutzung	[6] hin- und hergehend, wechselnd
[7] Prüfstand, Teststand	[8] Kratzer, Narbe	[9] Verteilereinspritzpumpen
[10] scheuern, reiben	[11] Rollkörper	[12] Hubscheibe
[13] Verschlechterung; Beschädigung; Zerstörung	[14] ungünstig; nachteilig	[15] Drehkolbenpumpe
[16] Empfindlichkeit	[17] Fliehgewicht	[18] Angleich-Drehpunkt, Angleichregler
[19] Kraftstoffförderpumpe	[20] Versteller	[21] Reglerfeder
[22] Schwungmasse; Fliehgewicht	[23] Steuerhebel; Einstellhebel	[24] Verstellhebelwelle

[25] Regelventil	[26] Antriebswelle	[27] Schwungmassenantriebsrad
[28] Mitnehmerscheibe; Antriebsscheibe	[29] Nockenscheibe; Kurvenscheibe	[30] Kolbenrückholfeder
[31] Verstellmuffe; Regelhülse	[32] Druckventil	[33] Kolben; Stempel
[34] Magnetventil für Kraftstoffabschaltung	[35] Korrekturhebel	[36] Spannhebel; Klemmhebel
[37] Einstellschraube für Vollbelastung	[38] Leerlauffeder	[39] Überströmventil

8.6 Noise, Vibration and Harshness (NVH)

8.6.1 The science of silence

Developments in both plastics and elastomers, combined with how noise is caused and transmitted, promise further improvements in the future. Therefore, an insight into the latest technologies of noise control is not an add-on extra. For example, the role of materials with decorative trim or carbets is *essential*[1].

Figure 8.6.1.1: New testing center at Boxberg (North-Württemberg). After two years of construction Bosch commenced[2] operation in June 1998 of the Boxberg (North-Württemberg) testing center with its many test tracks. The proving grounds[3], with an area of almost 95 hectares, in which Bosch invested about 100 million DM, are of great importance for the development and testing of new and visionary products in automotive technology (Source: Robert Bosch GmbH, Stuttgart)

The Engine, tyres, road surface and components inside the passenger compartment create noise, which is irritating. Noise is transmitted through the structure, via the *bodywork*[4], particularly the *floorpan*[5] and the *bulkhead*[6].

The frequency range of 100 to 1000 Hz is the main range of interest. As the frequency increases, the *noise level*[7] drops. A typical frequency spectrum of interior noise shows a broad *background-noise level*[8] with *discrete*[9] frequency bands *superimposed*[10]. Inside car noise range from simple interference with speech to actual the onset of driver *fatigue*[11].

To improve the situation, either noise at source is to be limited by improving the design of components, and using noise absorbing materials, or effective noise insulation is added. Each type of vehicle has its own distinctive noise signature. Each car model has to be treated individually. Therefore, *versatile*[12] methods of noise control are needed.

What is the best material?

Design engineers are faced with a *contradiction*[13] in providing excellent sound-deadening materials like plastics or *composites*[14]. On the one hand, there is pressure to reduce mass and improve fuel efficiency while, on the other, classical acoustic insulation for noise, vibration and *hardness*[15] calls for mass of the order of 5- 6kg/qm. The materials required should cover all the surfaces via which noise enters the *car interior*[16].

Formulations based on rubber heavily filled with *baryta*[17] have been shown to produce adequate *attenuation*[18] profiles at 5kg/qm x 1.7mm thickness, with *substrate*[19] of 0.8kg/qm x 15mm thick. *Operating temperatures*[20] are in the region of 110-120 °C. A further 20°C can be obtained with *chlorosulphonated polyethylene*[21]. Operating temperatures of 160°C and above can be met with an *ethylene acrylic elastomer*[22]. The *compounds*[23] can be formulated for application by *coating*[24] or supplied as sheets.

By incorporating up to 2500 parts particles of filler per 100 parts rubber, compounds are 80 to 85 per cent solid, which can be easily applied. For example, one compound can be used for moulded shapes for the engine compartment and for *backing*[25] the carpet and *interior trim*[26]. A gearbox coated with about 2mm of one of these compounds produced an improvement of about 2dB(A) at low frequencies.

Figure 8.6.1.2: Aluminium foam is used in Opel vehicles (Source: Adam Opel AG,Rüsselsheim)

Under the name Antiphon MPM (Metal-Plastic-Metal), comprising two metal facing sheets sandwiched by a viscoelastic core, a sound-damped steel is on the market. It has been developed by U.S. Coffins & Aikman Automotive Systems. A cold- rolled steel or any type of metal or alloy can be used. The sandwich can be formed and pressed. A dampened *structure-borne sound*[27] often allows a reduction in thickness.

By good choice and design of materials, components in the interior can make a major contribution to noise-reduction. Any noise reduction greater than two per cent is considered significant. Moulding of *air ducts*[28] in a special sound-deadening thermoplastic elastomer has produced reductions of up to three decibels (dB) of air noise, against ducts in EPDM (*ethylene propylene diene monomer*[29]), *epichlorohydrin*[30] and general purpose TPE (thermoplastic elastomer).

How much *oscillation*[31] energy is absorbed and *radiated*[32] again by each material has been shown by airborne noise testing. Studies suggest that the greatest absorption difference between different plastics parts *coincides with*[33] the range of human ear maximum *auditory sensation*[34], amounting to over 12dB at some frequencies. The high acoustic damping of polypropylene (PP) is particularly useful in interior components, and PP shows less tendency to *squeak*[35] when in contact with other plastic mouldings. The decision by Opel for its Vectra model, to use *talc*[36]-reinforced PP with a rigid substrate for foam-coated *door panel lining*[37] and *unlaminated*[38] *facing parts*[39], was a result of this work. Tests have shown a reduction of 7dB(A), compared with *ABS*[40].

Layers of thermoformable open-cell semi-rigid polyurethane foam sheets replace an expanded polystyrene laminate. This new material used for *headliners*[41] may be an example of useful sound insulation. It is sandwiched between two layers of glass mat and fabric and bonded by hot melt adhesive.

Polyurethane foams have come in for special attention for airborne noise attenuation as, dynamic modulus and *loss factor*[42] are the foam properties which play a positive role in acoustic attenuation. Dynamic modulus is the more critical, controlling the position of the *resonance frequency*[43].

Results for new High *Resilience*[44] (HR) foams show that increasing dynamic modulus improves the low frequency performance below 400 Hz, but reduces it above this level. A reduction in dynamic modulus improves higher frequency performance. Viscoelastic (VE) foam, by increasing the loss factor from 0.16 to 0.30, improves low frequency performance below 400 Hz against that obtained by the HR series.

Without compromising *flowability*[45] or *demould time*[46], it is possible to meet a particular vehicle noise input by careful selection of an appropriate foam dynamic modulus and loss factor.

Bayer has developed its Bayfit formulation which, in addition to being resilient, is able to dampen structure-borne noise. It has good internal damping properties and the *suppression*[47] of low-frequency vibrations (*humming noises*[48]) is particularly effective. However, there is a disadvantage: the improved properties tend to be reflected in a slower recovery after deformation.

Bayer's competitor Dow uses a heavy-layer *septum*[49] coupled with a viscoelastic foam (which absorbs higher frequencies). Dow has managed to maximise damping while also minimising the mass of the septum, by modifying the dynamic modulus of the foam directly related to its noise-reduction capability. The septum is applied by *knife-edge*[50] coating onto the back of the carpet.

What about mass?

Noise reduction without a high mass penalty is possible. Thermoplastics, like high-performance nylons and polyphthalamide, as materials for moulded components, offer good noise attenuation: advantages in acoustics as well as mass-saving. Application is done, for example, to engine components, like *timing belt covers*[51] and *air intake manifolds*[52]. Sound-deadening formulations of thermoplastic elastomers (TPES) are also highly effective noise insulators and offer easier moulding into more complex shapes. In areas where a rubber-like material is useful, for example fire-wall dash mats to inhibit engine noise from the car interior, in offering effective noise insulation.

Primary sound sources[53], generated by vibration from the cylinder head and transferred to the manifold, in combination with internal pressure vibrations cause the part to vibrate: secondary sound sources are thus generated. To prevent this effect, the desirable sound quality of a nylon/glass air intake manifold can be attained by the reduction of *surface velocity*[54]. Higher part-stiffness, higher material damping and an increase of mass are necessary. Furthermore, additional ribs and modified wall thickness at specific points have served to tune the air intake manifold to an acceptable noise level.

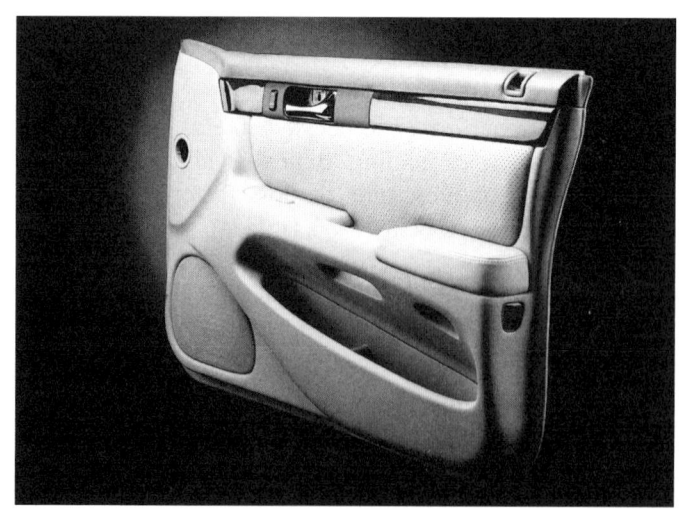

Figure 8.6.1.3: Foam backed door trim panel of A Class (Source: Krauss Maffei, München)

Solutions for car manufacturing

Airborne noise[55] can also be arrested simply by blocking the *apertures*[56] in any kind of structural *cavity*[57], such as *supporting members*[58], *sills*[59] and *door pillars*[60]. Solutions:
- For some applications polyurethane foam can be injected, or
- A new expanded sealing material (ESM) system, based on a polyethylene copolymer, in the form of preformed elements of a closed-cell (*impermeable*[61]) foam can be incorporated. It has an unexpanded density of 950kg/cbm, which can be expanded in certain *situations*[62] to 200kg/cbm. This sealing material is suitable for cavity diameters from 15 to 200mm.

These elements can be easily and quickly installed during body assembly before welding. They go with the body through chemical baths. Expansion is completed when the body is heated during the painting process.

[1] wichtig	[2] begonnen, gestartet, angefangen	[3] Testgelände; Versuchsgelände; Prüffelder
[4] Karosserie	[5] Bodenblech	[6] Schottwand; Querwand
[7] Geräuschpegel	[8] Hintergrundgeräuschpegel	[9] diskret; digital
[10] überlagert	[11] Ermüdung	[12] vielseitig
[13] Widerspruch	[14] Verbundwerkstoffe	[15] Härte
[16] Fahrzeuginnenraum	[17] Bariumoxid	[18] Geräuschdämpfung, Schalldämpfung
[19] Träger	[20] Betriebstemperatur	[21] chlorsulfoniertes Polyethylen
[22] Ethylen-Acryl-Elastomer	[23] Verbindung; Mischung; Zusammensetzung	[24] Beschichtung; Ummantelung
[25] Hinterspritzen; Verstärken; Hinterschäumung	[26] Innenverkleidung	[27] durch die Struktur übertragener Schall
[28] Luftkanäle	[29] Ethylen-Propylen-Dien Monomer	[30] Epichlorohydrin
[31] Schwingung	[32] abgestrahlt	[33] übereinstimmen mit
[34] Gehörgefühl	[35] quietschen, knarren, knarzen	[36] Talkum
[37] Türblechverkleidung	[38] ungeschichtet; unkaschiert	[39] Verkleidungsteile, Verblendungsteile
[40] Acrylnitril-Butadien-Styrol	[41] Dachhimmel	[42] Verlustfaktor
[43] Schwingungsfrequenz	[44] Nachgiebigkeit; Elastizität	[45] Fließvermögen
[46] Ausformzeit	[47] Schalldämpfung; Unterdrückung; Schwächung	[48] Summgeräusche, Brummtöne
[49] viskoelastische Schwerschicht	[50] hauchdünn	[51] Steuerriemenabdeckung
[52] Einlasskrümmer; Ansaugkrümmer	[53] Hauptschallquellen	[54] Oberflächengeschwindigkeit
[55] Luftschall; durch Luft übertragener Schall	[56] Öffnung; Ausschnitt	[57] Hohlraum
[58] tragende Bauteile; Stützglieder	[59] Einstiegsschweller, Türschweller	[60] Türholm, Türsäule
[61] undurchlässig	[62] Konstellationen	

8.6.2 Noise and vibration irritate drivers

NVH is one of the main areas vehicle development management is thinking about. It is as relevant as styling, performance and handling. To utilize cross-platform, laboratories work on all platforms simultaneously, in order to spread solutions throughout the product line-up. For example, Daimler-Chrysler has developed *spiral cut*[1] aerials to stop whistling noises and has installed it in Plymouth Neon, Dodge Neon and Chrysler Neon cars.

Figure 8.6.2.1: The knobbed belt[2] developed by ContiTech allows a positively-engaged[3], self-locating drive[4] and is not bound to direction of travel[5] (Source: Continental Teves, Frankfurt)

Nevertheless, there are some other measurements to be considered:
- To make engine operations quieter, a higher volume muffler and an exhaust *flex joint*[6] is used.
- To reduce steering wheel vibration at *idle speed*[7], a four-point *engine mount*[8] system is used.
- To minimize the resonance from powertrain vibrations, stiffer *suspension crossmembers*[9] and *control arms*[10] are used.
- To form a tight-fitting body noise barrier, glass *roll-up windows*[11] are replaced by full frame doors.
- To dampen road noise and support fuel economy, Neon's previous two-*ply*[12] tires are replaced by all-season single ply tires.
- To calm wind noise, the front windshield has been moved 76 mm further forward.
- To cause a further decrease in decibels, expandable foam *baffles*[13] are added inside the A, B, and C pillars as well as in the *frame rail*[14]. Typically, between six and 12 baffles, each expanding three to 20 times, essentially *impede*[15] noise, water and dust entrance.

In each of the real world acoustic simulation chambers in an automotive industry, a suite of *anechoic*[16] and *reverberant*[17] chambers are applied, including a material testings lab, a sound quality lab, an *adjoining*[18] jury evaluation room for playback of collected vehicle noise measurements, a computer room for design and analysis of acoustic, bonding, and sealing applications, a quiet room with a *bed- plate*[19] for analysis and other structural testing, a full-size body-in-white baking oven for the simulation of production baking processes, and carbon monoxide *extraction*[20] equipment.

Figure 8.6.2.2: Information on noise emissions of a vehicle alternator[21]. Lowering vehicle noise is a major concern of automotive manufacturers. Bosch uses a test stand to measure the noise emissions of individual components such as the alternator. Ten hemispherical[22] microphones register the noise. The noise is then analyzed and designs developed for noise reduction (Source: Robert Bosch GmbH, Stuttgart)

OEM suppliers are expected to have a dedicated NVH laboratory, to manage fit and function as well as NVH. Freudenberg opened a new noise and vibration testing center in Plymouth, Michigan, U.S., spending $7 million to become a global supplier with leading-edge technology of a broad portfolio, including *body mounts*[23], *cradle mounts*[24], *engine mounts*[25], *torsional vibration*[26] dampers, *jounce bumpers*[27], *suspension bushings*[28], and *spring isolators*[29]. Freudenberg knows, their products are unfortunately sources of unwanted NVH in chassis and powertrain.

Advanced *microfibre*[30] technology has created a composite of polyester and polyolefin, called Thinsulate Acoustic Insulation technology. Application areas for this material include *headliners*[31], door panels, door pillars, instrument panels, *under carpet*[32] and under hood.

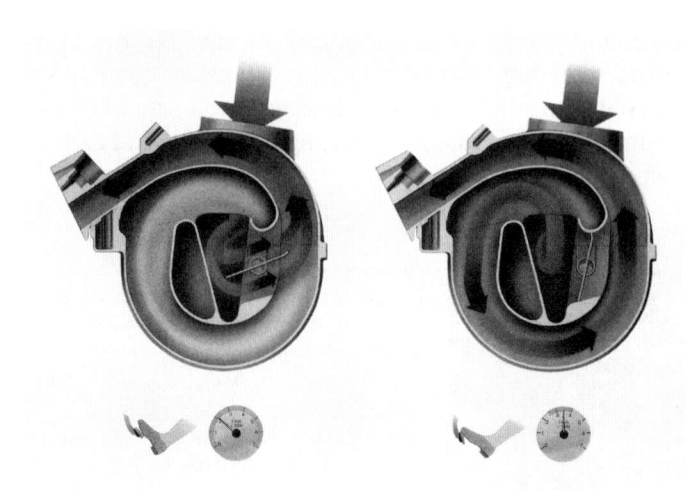

Figure 8.6.2.3: Intake manifold technology of 1.8 16V engines at Opel. Left: Intake of short channels at lower than 2.500 rpm. Right: Intake of long channels between 2.500 and 3.900 rpm (Source: Adam Opel AG, Rüsselsheim)

DuPont Automotive has also opened a NVH lab in Troy, Michigan, U.S. In-house testing equipment includes a holographic acoustic microphone system, scanning laser *vibrometer*[33], *white noise*[34] box, and an *anechoic*[35] chamber. DuPont's first application at its test site was to modify an *air intake manifold*[36] which had been producing an unwanted high frequency *hissing noise*[37]. For example, a cast aluminium intake manifold *masks*[38] a hiss sound. Changes of *the throttle body*[39], and *idle air bypass valve*[40] were necessary. The investigations show that the noise source normally involves more than one component.

Figure 8.6.2.4: Chassis (e.g. steering mechanism, stabilizer and engine mounts) of the Opel Corsa (Source: Adam Opel AG, Rüsselsheim)

NVH performance is traditionally *at odds with*[41] mass reduction. Usage of lightmass materials needs *crucial*[42] precision engineering for components, because mass is proportional to the attenuation of sound and vibration.

Seats are a primary focal point, because seats have the most potential for improved interior noise control, although other interior zones such as instrument panels, headliners and carpets possess *untapped*[43] noise absorption possibilities. Due to knee bolsters, airbags, and other structural concerns, not much is yet being done with instrument panels as noise absorbers.

Figure 8.6.2.5: Ecotec engine for the Opel Tigra (Source: Adam Opel AG, Rüsselsheim)

[1] spiralverzahnt, bogenverzahnt	[2] Noppenriemen	[3] formschlüssig
[4] selbstführender Antrieb	[5] Laufrichtung	[6] elastische Verbindung
[7] Leerlaufdrehzahl	[8] Motorlager	[9] Aufhängungsquerträger
[10] Querlenker	[11] Kurbelfenster; Hebefenster	[12] Lage, Schicht
[13] Leitbleche, Ablenkbleche; Abweiser	[14] Rahmenlängsträger	[15] verhindern
[16] schalltot; nicht reflektierend	[17] nachhallend, reflektierend	[18] angrenzend
[19] Montageplatte	[20] Absaugung; Entlüftung	[21] Drehstrom-Lichtmaschine
[22] halbkugelförmig	[23] Karosserietraglager	[24] Träger-/Sattelbefestigung
[25] Motoraufhängungen	[26] Drehschwingungs-	[27] Einfederungsanschläge
[28] Radaufhängungslager; Fahrwerkslager	[29] Federisolierung; Blattfeder-Zwischenlagen	[30] Mikrofaser
[31] Dachhimmel	[32] Teppichrückseite; Teppichunterseite	[33] Schwingungsmessgerät
[34] Weißrauschen; weißes Rauschen	[35] schalltot	[36] Einlasskrümmer; Ansaugrohr
[37] Zischgeräusch	[38] verdecken	[39] Drosselklappengehäuse
[40] Leerlauf-Umleitventil	[41] to be at o. with s.o.: mit j-m uneins sein	[42] entscheidend
[43] nicht angezapft/angebohrt		

8.7 Heating, ventilation, air condition

8.7.1 Gel improves thermal conductivity

A new family of *thermally conductive*[1] *gels*[2] have significantly improved *thermal conductivity*[3] of *sensitive*[4] components in automotive electronic systems.

Gel thicknesses range from 0.25 to 15mm. Thinner variants are delivered on *woven*[5] *fibreglass*[6] or open-cell carriers while thicker products are cast into sheet or *custom*[7] profiles.

Known as HeathPath, the gel provides excellent thermal conductivity with much lower thermal resistance and more than five times the *compressibility*[8] of conventional elastomers. They can *outperform*[9] silicone grease and adhesives in thermal management design. The gel fills the gaps completely between components and *heat sinks*[10] with minimal pressure, thus avoiding damage to *delicate*[11] components: In this way, device *junction temperatures*[12] are significantly reduced.

[1] wärmeleitend	[2] Gels	[3] Wärmeleitvermögen
[4] empfindlich, feinfühlig	[5] gewebt	[6] Glasfaser
[7] maßgeschneidert	[8] Zusammendrückbarkeit	[9] übertreffen
[10] Kühlplatten, Kühlbleche	[11] empfindlich	[12] Sperrschicht/ Zonenübergang-Temperaturen

8.7.2 Parking Heaters

Parking heaters[1] keep things fresh in summer. Webasto, the parking heater specialist at Munich/Stockdorf, says it is more than just hot air, and independent ventilation in summer is possible.

The long lasting winters convinced many drivers – and not just those with on-street parking – of the benefits of a parking heater. What's more, a pre-heated engine suffers less *wear*[2] and *tear*[3] and is less harmful to the environment.

Optional parking ventilation is available for all the Thermo Top models, converting them from seasonal accessories to all-year-round products. In summer the *control unit*[4] can be used to activate the ventilator in the vehicle at a pre-programmed time or by a radio signal from the *remote control*[5], so that warm air is removed from the interior of the vehicle. This prevents heat build-up and a pleasant temperature inside the car is thereby achieved. An opened sunroof further increases this effect.

Figure 8.7.2.1: Auxiliary heating[6] installation (Source: Webasto AG, Stockdorf)

Aftermarket Thermo Top parking heaters can be retrofitted at Webasto installation workshops, Bosch service centres and other automobile dealers. For a few vehicles from Mercedes-Benz, BMW and Audi, Webasto parking heaters can be installed at the factory.

With a total of seven models in the Thermo Top range, Webasto is able to offer an ideal heating solution for any vehicle, from compact class to vans.

Figure 8.7.2.2: Air Top 3500/5000 (Source: Webasto AG, Stockdorf)

The basic mode of function is similar in every model. The heaters are integrated into the *coolant circuit*[7] and combust fuel in a *combustion chamber*[8]. The Thermo Top E and C take the fuel directly out of the vehicle's fuel tank via a *dosing pump*[9], so that a maximum heating period of 60 minutes is reached. The other models have integrated fuel tanks which permit heating periods of half an hour.

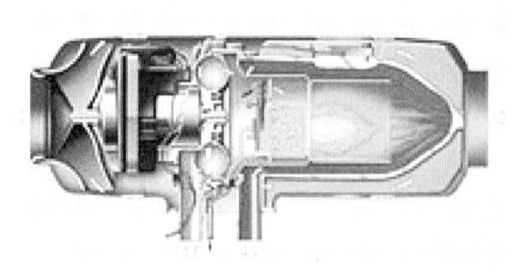

Figure 8.7.2.3: Cutaway[10] of Air Top 3500/5000 (Source: Webasto AG, Stockdorf)

Webasto has also taken into account increased demand for radio control operation. The Telestart T60 and the newest development, the T70 remote control units are now available as optional extras for all parking heater models. The new small magic T70 radio control for Webasto parking heaters activates the parking heater in the car whenever you need it from a distance of up to 600 m at the touch of button. The heating periods of the parking heater are variably programmable. A *retrofit kit*[11] for the Telestart T70 and the complete range of new accessories are available, and the remote control is suitable for retrofitting in all Thermo Top units with timer control.

Figure 8.7.2.4: Opel Frontera Limited (Source: Adam Opel AG, Rüsselsheim)

The benefit of a parking heater is undeniable and meanwhile proven by numerous tests of independent organisations. Scraping ice in the morning, frozen wiper blades and misted windows belong to the past.

¹ Standheizungen	² Verschleiß	³ Riss
⁴ Steuergerät	⁵ Fernsteuerung	⁶ Zusatzheizgerät
⁷ Kühlmittel-Kreislauf	⁸ Brennkammer (einer kraftstoff-betriebenen Standheizung)	⁹ Dosierpumpe
¹⁰ Schnittbild	¹¹ Nachrüst-Set	

9 Manufacturing Engineering

9.1 Automotive painting technologies

Improved quality, lower cost and less waste are being demanded from paint shop management. Furthermore, environmental legislation is calling for lower emissions. The motor industry is trying to square the circle.

Only when a totally new model goes into production, the OEMs may renew existing paint facilities. Because of huge investments, painting vehicles is expensive, *irrespective*[1] of the colour.

The Germans, Swedes and the British are spearheading the *transition*[2] towards more environmentally friendly facilities with water-based paints. Almost half of the *solvent*[3] was brought into being via the *base coat*[4]. It is that part of the system which has been the focus of water-based *coatings*[5].

Water-borne primers[6] are gradually beginning to *emerge*[7] with limited success. Water-borne *clear coats*[8] will take time to develop. Coatings with higher *solids*[9] content are alternatives to water, but they are leading to poorer *aesthetics*[10].

Figure 9.1.1: Painted calipers (Source: Continental Teves, Frankfurt)

Powder coating[11] is a second alternative for *primers*[12]. It has taken time *to catch on*[13] in Europe, although BMW is already working with powder clear coats. There is a disadvantage that remains unresolved: powder clear coat systems need to be even cleaner than powder primer. Another disadvantage has to be balanced with this, which includes higher stoving temperatures and a limited range of colours. However, the advantage of powder primers is the ability to *reclaim*[14] all unused *excess powder*[15]. After being filtered, this powder can be re-used. US manufacturers are prepared to utilise different coloured primers and top coats. European manufacturers prefer *colour-keyed*[16] processes which result in brighter and cleaner colours. Red and yellow have particularly poor *hiding power*[17], which has to be considered.

Figure 9.1.2: Automatical feeder[18] *for disc-brake pistons*[19] *(Source: Continental Teves, Frankfurt)*

BASF Lacke+Farben AG and Durr Systems *stand out for*[20] cooperating in the materials and processes used in the Mercedes Benz A Class plant at Rastatt, Germany. Their system employs a powder *slurry*[21] process for clear coat and *virtually*[22] *solvent-free*[23] systems with the target of optimally matching the optical appearance of steel body work and plastic attachments.

The advantage of such a powder slurry applied clear coat system is that there is no need for a completely new technology, *as opposed to*[24] powder coating. Furthermore, DaimlerChrysler has the option of installing the new system in other plants with comparatively little *outlay*[25]. However, powder based paints have not made the progress against *aqueous solutions*[26] that was once predicted, because consumers demand more metallic paints. Powder based paints on metallic surfaces create the effect, according to the intensity of the light, that their shading flips according to the angle from which they are viewed.

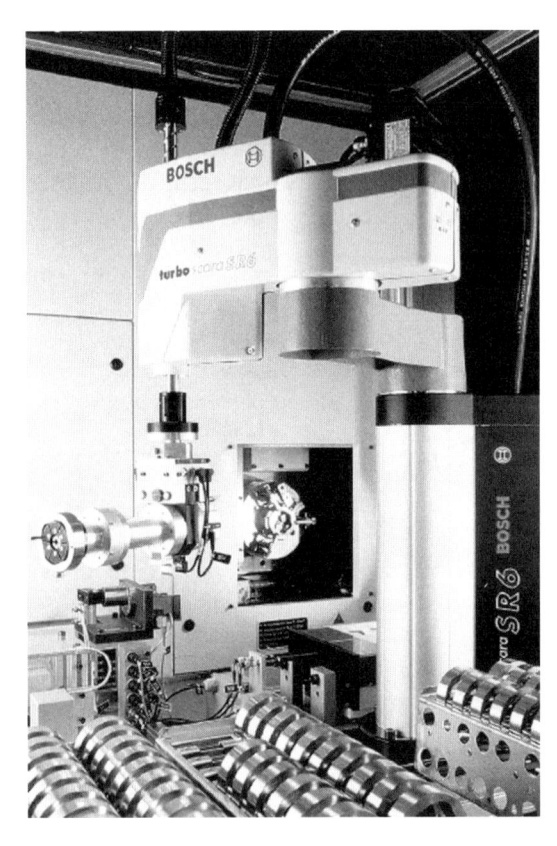

Figure 9.1.3: The new generation of Turboscara robots. In 1998 Bosch introduced a completely redesigned generation of its proven turboscara SR6 and SR8 series. Swivel-arm[27] robots, which are outstandingly robust and powerful, feature open control technology. A PC designed to meet the demands of industry enables improved visualization and data communication (Source: Robert Bosch GmbH, Stuttgart).

Therefore, this technology has been *superseded*[28] by paint finishes that glow and change colour with the light. PPG and DuPont are two of the paint suppliers which are offering this new type of finish, which is similar to the effect created when oil is spilled on water and is similar to that used on some banknotes. It utilises *light refraction*[29] between microscopic pieces of glass set in a layer no more than 1µm thick. For example, paints change from purple to green. However, there are still some disadvantages:
- It is proving very costly to use.
- It is unlikely to become popular until the price of the special pigment involved has dropped considerably.
- Quality cannot be retained.
- There are customer concerns about *chipping*[30], scratches, atmospheric pollution and bird droppings.

There are moves afoot to change the chemical composition of clear coats to improve resistance to acidic atmospheric conditions. Real life allows for a highly acidic bird dropping falling on to a car that has baked in the sun. Nissan, in parti-

cular, has formulated a recipe for artificial bird droppings. The patented formula of egg *albumen*[31], *nitrogen*[32] and water is now being used in the company's quality audit. To pass Nissan's quality test, owe has to proceed as follows:
- Apply the formula to a sample of painted body work.
- It is then cooked for an hour at 50 °C and 30 per cent *humidity*[33].
- The paint must be *blemish*[34]-free when the artificial bird droppings are washed off.

Normally it is possible to improve scratch resistance or resistance to *etching*[35], but not both. European clear coats tend to be *acrylic polymers*[36] crosslinked with *melamine*[37] *formaldehyde*[38] which *lacks*[39] etch performance. The race is on to replace the melamine with another material to improve etch performance. To overcome this problem, Volkswagen uses *isocyanate*[40] materials. Other car makers, however, are *reluctant*[41] to use isocyanate because of its potential link with asthma and other *respiration*[42] problems.

[1] ungeachtet; ohne Rücksicht auf	[2] Übergang	[3] Lösungsmittel
[4] Grundlackschicht	[5] Beschichtung; Überzug	[6] Grundierlacke auf Wasserbasis
[7] in Erscheinung treten	[8] Klarlackschichten	[9] Feststoffe
[10] Ästhetik	[11] Pulverbeschichtung; Pulverlackierung	[12] Grundierlacke
[13] Anklang finden	[14] wiedergewinnen; regenerieren	[15] überschüssiges Pulver
[16] farblich abgestimmt	[17] Deckkraft; Deckvermögen	[18] Automatische Zuführung
[19] Scheibenbrems-Kolben	[20] to stand out for sth.: sich auf etwas versteifen	[21] Schlamm
[22] tatsächlich; faktisch	[23] lösungsmittelfrei	[24] im Gegensatz zu
[25] Kostenaufwand	[26] wässrige Lösungen	[27] Schwenkarm; Gelenkhebel
[28] überflüssig	[29] Lichtbrechung	[30] absplittern
[31] Eiweiß	[32] Stickstoff	[33] Feuchtigkeit
[34] Schönheitsfehler; Fehlstellen	[35] Ätzung; abätzen	[36] Acryl-Polymerisat
[37] Melamin	[38] Formaldehyd; Methanal; Methylal; Formal	[39] mangeln
[40] Isocyanat	[41] abgeneigt	[42] Atmung

9.2 New glass forming process

With an award-winning idea for utilising a sophisticated glass forming process and a revolutionary power distribution system, Tunewell has broken through the cost barrier to the use of neon *discharge lamps*[1] in vehicles. The technology was presented to the automotive industry in a paper given at the SAE

Conference in Detroit in 1999. In many ways Neon discharge lamps are *superior*[2]:
- Neon lights can be manufactured using an adaptation of an existing process. This saves money on development costs.
- Speed of response is important in *brake lights*[3] and *longevity*[4].
- It must have the ability to *style*[5] in a wide variety of configurations.

The power distribution system is simple. It consists mainly of a thin, flat ribbon type cable which contains both power and signal wires and small individual *transformers*[6]. To provide power to various electrical features, it can be branched at junctions along its length. It runs on an *alternating current (AC)*[7] at a frequency of 50kHz, which is different to existing technology.

With regard to *power demand*[8] and *ancillaries*[9], Tunewell can demonstrate cost savings across a wide variety of applications. It offers a low cost alternative to large *copper*[10] based *wiring harnesses*[11], eliminating high voltage wires and large *ballasts*[12], *enabling*[13] multiplexed control, as well as *facilitating*[14] *fault*[15] reporting.

[1] Gasentladungslampen	[2] überlegen, souverän	[3] Bremslichter, Stopplichter
[4] Langlebigkeit	[5] stylen; designen	[6] Transformatoren
[7] Wechselstrom	[8] Energiebedarf	[9] Nebenaggregate
[10] Kupfer	[11] Kabelsätze; Kabelstränge	[12] Steuergeräte; Vorschaltgeräte
[13] möglich machen	[14] vereinfachen, erleichtern	[15] Fehler; Defekt

9.3 "Smart" core structures eclipse foam

Foam-filled structures are the traditional technology favoured by the automotive industry. Mass, cost and time savings and recycling benefits are found to be attractive. However, the *composite*[1] moulding industry is now being revolutionised by a technology which creates an "intelligent" *cavity*[2] for the *moulding resin*[3] process. The process is said to *surpass*[4] the traditional one due to massively lowering the cost of mass production operations of hollow *monocoque*[5] moulded structures. Typical products coming out of this new process are *spoilers*[6], *trunk lids*[7], *tractor*[8] roofs, *housings*[9] and *acoustic panels*[10]. Two main reasons why car companies are pouring their *funds*[11] into its further development and why designers will almost certainly discover new opportunities of application are: Firstly, the excellent control available to the *moulder*[12] enabling *autoclave*[13] quality at low cost. Secondly, tools are allowed to change their shape adaptively.

The key to the technology is a vacuum combined with the science of *particle hydraulics*[14], analogous to the production of vacuum-packed coffee. Within an evacuated mould cavity, a re-usable or *disposable*[15] *Lost Core Film (LCF)*[16] is pulled into the desired shape. Once in position the film is filled with *ash*[17] material exhibiting good particle hydraulics. Ash is then vibrated until it is as closely packed as possible. This process ensures complete structural integrity. A valve is then placed into the film and a vacuum pulled. The vacuum within the mould cavity is then released. What is left is a solid, simple light-mass particle-filled film. It is ready now to be incorporated within the resin transfer mould. The solid film is *wrapped*[18] with *impregnated*[19] *fibres*[20] which will form a wall in the cavity. By pulsing water at high frequency into a cavity, more water is pulsed into the cavity and in this way the volume of the cavity increases. Space is needed for the resin runner. Resin *runners*[21] are incorporated into the core component to facilitate mould *fitting*[22]. Runners are then placed into the mould and the resin introduced. This internal pressure also squeezes the resin. Once cured, the valve in the neck of the film is removed and the contents emptied out.

How low and cost efficient the process can be is shown by improving resin flow by demonstrating a change in dimension simply by adding cork strips to the core component tool. Another support is in the prevention of fibre *pinching*[23] at the *mould joints*[24] by making core tools slightly undersized in those areas, allowing the mould to be closed without pinching, and brought up to full size before resin *cures*[25].

What are the disadvantages of this new process?
- Polyurethane foam fillers are currently used for price reasons, with a tendency to *age*[26] and *blemishes*[27] appear which may lead to *sink*[28] holes within the component, thus leading to resin rich areas.
- Due to its thermal process, dimensional *integrity*[29] is difficult to achieve.
- Differences in the coefficients of thermal expansion of the two materials used can lead to structural weaknesses and aesthetic abnormalities.

The new process has already been proven in the manufacture of turbine blades and sailing ships. The next step is to develop the technology to make it accessible to mass production areas. Prior to the interest shown by the automotive industry the project had already received a SPUR (Support of Products Under Research) award from the UK's Department of Trade and Industry.

[1] Verbundwerkstoff	[2] Hohlraum; Aussparung	[3] Pressharz, Gussharz
[4] übertreffen	[5] einschalig; monocoque	[6] Windabweiser; Luftleitflügel
[7] Kofferraumdeckel	[8] Traktor; Zugfahrzeug	[9] Gehäuse
[10] Schall-Verkleidung	[11] Vermögen; Kapital	[12] Formmaschine
[13] Dampfdruckerhitzer; Druckhärtekessel	[14] "öldruckunterstützte" Körnung	[15] Wegwerf-, Einweg-
[16] Kernausschmelz-Schicht	[17] Asche	[18] umhüllt
[19] imprägniert	[20] Glasfaser	[21] Rohre; Krümmerrohre
[22] Anschlussstück	[23] quetschen	[24] Formspalt
[25] aushärten	[26] altern	[27] Fehlstellen
[28] Senke	[29] Vollständigkeit	

9.4 Advanced castings for low volume markets

Investment castings[1] are used in the aerospace industries for manufacturing many components used on the Airbus. In the automotive industry, to ensure that light alloy investment castings have mechanical properties which approach those of *forgings*[2], careful control of the casting process and new software is necessary to guarantee these properties. With the help of aerospace techniques applications in the low volume specialist road car market for the highest performance cars in motor sport, it is now possible to extract the best possible performance from investment.

Figure 9.4.1: Pallet system for automatic loading and unloading of castings on an assembly line (Source: Continental Teves, Frankfurt)

The new *confidential*[3] process improves the *directional*[4] *solidification*[5] of castings. When an alloy solidifies, a tree-like crystal is formed first. This technology reduces the space between the arms of the crystal. Furthermore, it produces a finer *eutectic*[6] structure in the material.

The technology has been applied to cylinder heads, engine blocks, *sumps*[7], gearboxes, gearbox housings, *bell housings*[8] and *brake calipers*[9].

A casting modelling computer software program called SOLSTAR, originally developed for modelling iron and steel casting, was sponsored to adapt and improve it for investment castings. Models created by using the software's own solid modelling capability are inputed as STL files. Thermal analysis is also used to predict defects, being displayed as X-ray like images. Based on empirical observations, the results are predicted by the program. The software works well with aluminium silicon casting alloys. Aeromet Corp., U.K., is working to improve its predictions on the casting of aluminium-copper based alloys which tend to have longer solidification times. It may also be used for making predictions of the performance of sand castings, which often have to include such *refinements*[10] as *insulated*[11] *sleeves*[12] on *feeders*[13], *cast iron*[14] *chills*[15], or regions of *silicon carbide*[16] sand to improve local thermal conductivity.

Motor sports customers, including leading names in Formula 1, Indy Series, Formula 3 and 3000 series, have *peculiar*[17] problems of "mushroom zones", which are peculiarities of the casting process. Existing computational fluid dynamic and plastic mould-filling software is unsuitable because they have not so far been able to solve these problems. Birmingham University, U.K., is investigating modelling of mould-filling and hopes to find a solution.

[1] Gussteile nach dem Wachsausschmelzgießverfahren	[2] Schmiedeteile	[3] vertraulich
[4] richtungsgebunden	[5] Verfestigung	[6] eutektisch
[7] Ölwanne	[8] Kupplungsgehäuse; Kupplungsglocke	[9] Bremssattel; Bremszange
[10] Verfeinerung; Veredelung	[11] isoliert	[12] Hülsen, Buchsen
[13] Angusse; Beschicker	[14] Gusseisen	[15] Gussformen; Kokillen
[16] Siliziumkarbid	[17] besonders	

9.5 New type of heat shields from lateral thinking

Heat build-up in the *engine bays*[1] of cars is becoming a major problem because of the increasing amount of equipment being included. To improve the fuel consumption and *axle load distribution*[2] of cars, the use of low mass shielding components is important. Additionally, engine noise has had to be blocked from the passengers.

A new type of heat shield material for underbody applications, which can be easily formed into complex shapes by using a simple mechanical manufacturing process, is an outstanding example of *lateral*[3] thinking. It is called Nimbus, if two sheets of aluminium are *comprised*[4]. Steel variants are called Cirrus. Furthermore, it has the considerable benefit of being acoustically dead. Nimbus is also a *poor conductor*[5] and acts as an effective barrier to radiated heat. It has thus been proven to be thermally extremely efficient. All these features are combined with good long term durability. The material is available in several forms. Nimbus can be combined with a *fibrous*[6] paper *filler*[7] for additional sound and heat insulation. To summarize, it is simple to manufacture, light and *resists*[8] vibration-*induced*[9] noise.

The key to the manufacturing process is systematically to bend the thin sheets of aluminium together over themselves in *interlocking*[10] *ridges*[11] so that they cannot *come apart*[12]. A resulting flat *two-ply*[13] sheet can subsequently be formed using a light press. The material absorbs bending stresses by slightly deforming each of the *folds*[14] without reducing structural or operational *integrity*[15]. This is necessary, because most heat shields have to take on complex shapes as they are formed around other local parts. Normally, problems arising from these forming operations include *wrinkling*[16] on *internal*[17] radii and *tearing*[18] on *external*[19] radii. This process has been patented.

Figure 9.5.1: High-quality plastic components in just 35 seconds. The valve carrier system VTS 02 enables the complex assembly of plastic assembly carriers and protective shields for the engine compartment in 3-shift production (Source: Robert Bosch GmbH, Stuttgart).

[1] Motorräume	[2] Achslastverteilung	[3] Quer-, seitlich
[4] bestehen aus	[5] schlechter Leiter	[6] faserig
[7] Füllmaterial	[8] widerstehen	[9] ausgelöst
[10] verriegeln, sperren, blockieren	[11] Druckkante; Knickkante	[12] auseinanderfallen
[13] zweilagen	[14] Falz; Biegung; Faltung	[15] Vollständigkeit
[16] schrumpeln	[17] innen liegend	[18] reißen, zerlegen
[19] außen liegend		

9.6 Modern coil and leaf spring manufacturing

Krupp Hoesch Federn (KHF) is a major producer of *coil springs*[1] and *leaf springs*[2]. Current state-of-the art materials have been pushed to their performance limits. Ambitious mass saving and performance targets have lead to the purchasing of *high-purity*[3], temperature-controlled, *micro-alloyed*[4] *fine grain spring steel*[5] and the use of it for a two-stage *peening*[6] process with *novel*[7] high temperature thermo-mechanical treatments. To benefit from the new technology *coil*[8] as an integral part of the production process, KHF is steadily increasing the performance of its steel suspension springs for car and truck manufacturers.

The current *strength*[9] is 1850 - 2000MPa for coil springs and 1600 to 1750MPa for leaf springs. The increase of coil springs to 2150-2300MPa and leaf springs to 1850-2000MPa would allow mass reductions of 26 and 24 per cent respectively.

The disadvantage is that at such high strengths chromium-silicon-vanadium steel grades used normally become very *brittle*[10], which makes spring surfaces *sensitive*[11] to *notching*[12] and, therefore, *diminishes*[13] *fatigue*[14] properties. The surface zone of the material is important for the *torsional*[15] and bending *stress*[16] to which coil and leaf springs are *subjected*[17]. To improve it, special protection of this area is necessary, *distingushing*[18] between *strengthening*[19] or *hardening*[20] treatments.

Shot peening[21] is the established method for increasing resistance to *incipient*[22] *surface cracks*[23]. The disadvantage is that shot peening treatment builds up *residual*[24] *compressive*[25] stresses in the surface zones of the material which *counteract*[26] the *tensile stresses*[27] occurring in the components under *load*[28].

To avoid this disadvantage, KHF has introduced a stress peening process in which springs are pre-loaded during treatment. This pre-load is in line with the operating load, and integrate this with normal *peening*[29] treatments, which build up much higher direction-orientated residual compressive stresses in sub-surface areas.

The different effects of normal stress peening is illustrated by the *cyclic*[30] load capacity of coil springs. Stress peening achieves four times the service life of normally peened springs.

A further significant increase in dynamic load capacity of coil and leaf springs will be achieved by a thermomechanical surface layer strengthening. KHF patented this new technology, which combines two shot peening treatments with a special heat treatment. Firstly, shot peening operation primarily targets plastic deformation and also strengthens the spring steel surface zone. The disdavantage of *imparting*[31] residual compressive stresses is of secondary importance here. Secondly, stress peening operation increases residual compressive stresses in the surface zone to the highest possible level. Thirdly, heat treatment *enhances*[32] the properties of the material in the plastically deformed surface zones due to *precipitation hardening*[33], *ageing*[34] and an increased tendency of the *tempered*[35] microstructure towards *polygonisation*[36].

Fatigue tests[37] show, with high temperature thermomechanical surface layer strengthening processes, that durability of coil springs can be increased by some 50 per cent and leaf springs by 80 per cent. It seems that only by *exploiting*[38] the potential of thermomechanical treatments, the further potential of steel for delivering the mass and performance expectations can be *unlocked*[39].

[1] Schraubenfedern	[2] Blattfedern	[3] Reinst-

⁴ mikrolegiert	⁵ feinkörniger Federstahl	⁶ kalthämmern
⁷ neuartig	⁸ Windung; Wicklung	⁹ Festigkeit
¹⁰ spröde, brüchig	¹¹ empfindlich	¹² Kerben; Einkerben
¹³ verringern	¹⁴ ermüdend	¹⁵ verdrehen, verwinden
¹⁶ Beanspruchung	¹⁷ ausgesetzt	¹⁸ unterscheiden
¹⁹ Versteifung; Verfestigung	²⁰ Erhärtung; Verhärten	²¹ kugelstrahlen
²² anfänglich	²³ Oberflächenrisse	²⁴ restlich
²⁵ Druckspannungs-	²⁶ entgegenwirken	²⁷ Zugbeanspruchungen
²⁸ Belastung	²⁹ kalt hämmern	³⁰ zyklisch
³¹ gewähren	³² unterstreichen	³³ Ausscheidungshärtung
³⁴ Alterung	³⁵ vorgespannt	³⁶ Vieleck
³⁷ Ermüdungstests	³⁸ auswerten	³⁹ freigeben

9.7 New injection moulding processes

Door panel *substrates*[1], *package trays*[2], *quarter panels*[3], *seat pans*[4]/backs, *spare tire covers*[5], *headliners*[6], and *sun visors*[7] require strong, *durable*[8] and lightmass substrates. These automotive components are obtained by using the *low-density*[9] *structural*[10] *reaction*[11] *injection moulding*[12] (LD- SRIM) process.

A typical production process for LD-SRIM substrates consists of several steps:
– Manually placing a thin *glass fibre*[13] *mat*[14] into a mould.
– Closing the mould.
– Injecting it with a two-part polyurethane system.
– In forming a structural *composite*[15] material, the glass fibre mat is *encapsulated*[16] by the polyurethane *resin*[17] during the *curing time*[18].
– The part is removed from the mould.
– Several *finishing operations*[19] are added.

Improvements are performed on several systems for further productivity gains and part cost savings:
– On the polyurethane chemical systems.
– On lower-density svstems which have been developed by material suppliers.
– On faster methods.
– On *internal*[20] *mould release*[21] technology with applications of *mould release agents*[22] to provide *multiple*[23] part releases.

The long fibre injection (LFI) process, introduced by Krauss-Maffei, is a newly developed process in automation technology to gain further improvements. A *rotary*[24] glass cutter is attached to a *mixhead*[25]. The glass is cut to the necessary length while polyurethane is poured into the mould. The LFI process varies the length and quantity of the delivered glass fibre, if desired. Finally, the *dispensing*[26] chamber is filled with liquid polyurethane at an *annular*[27] *portion*[28].

Figure 9.7.1: With the introduction of the MK60 at this time, Continental Teves has marketed the world's lightest electronic brake system EBS for passenger cars, supported by a new injection moulding process (Source: Continental Teves, Frankfurt)

Figure 9.7.2: Long Fibre Injection LFI Process Head (Source: Krauss Maffei, München)

Under *laminar*[29] conditions, the cut glass fibre is *propelled*[30] through the chamber, and at the same time the reacting polyurethane flows out of the annular dispensing chamber and *wets*[31] the cut glass fibre. A robot is necessary to control the LFI *pour*[32] pattern and *cycle time*[33] over the entire surface of the mould. A specific and *consistent*[34] pour pattern is necessary to produce a part with relatively *uniform*[35] glass-fibre distribution. To determine this pattern, pilot trials are necessary. Higher overall glass content is possible, if the flow requirement of the system is to be reduced.

For open pour moulding conditions, the LFI process requires SRIM polyurethane systems. These polyurethane systems are required to have an extended cycle time, which is necessary for the robot to move out of the *mould cavity*[36] and close the mould before the liquid polyurethane begins to expand.

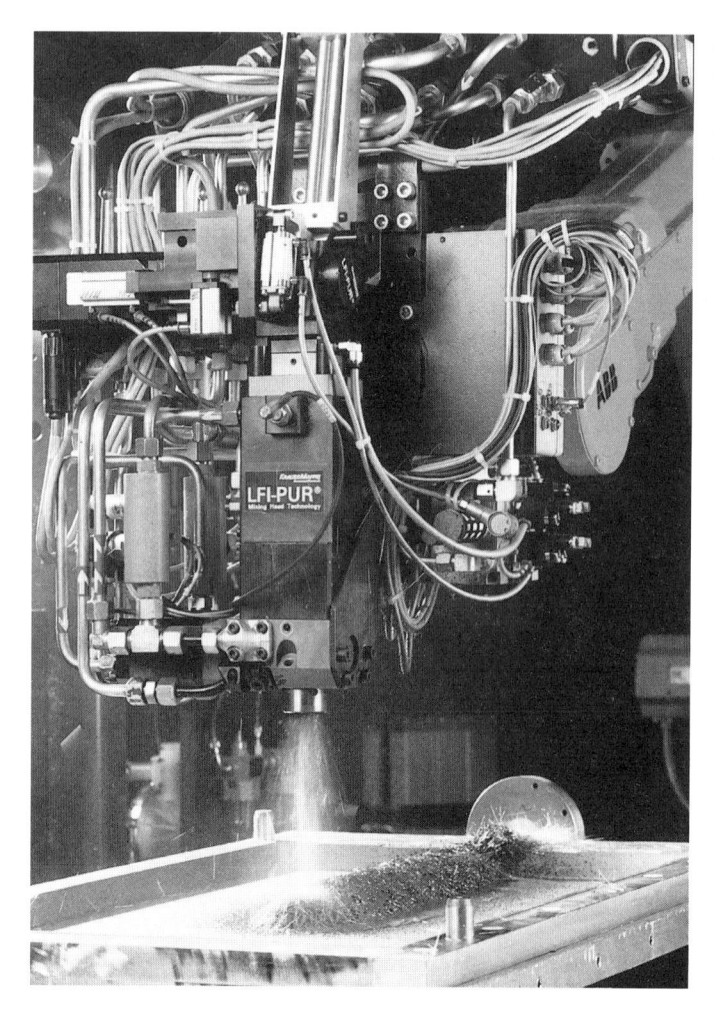

Figure 9.7.3: LFI-PUR Mixing Head Technology (Source: Krauss Maffei, München)

Since the LFI process incorporated robotic pour patterns, ensuring part *consistency*[37] and high productivity, design is more flexible by optimization of glass distribution in critical and noncritical areas.

In future, incorporation of this robot technology into a typical LD-SRIM moulding line would eliminate the manual loading of the glass mat into the mould and provide the potential for reduction of production moulds and/or labour per *moulding line*[38].

[1] Substrat; Träger	[2] Ablagefächer	[3] Seitenverkleidungen; Seitenwände
[4] Sitzwannen; Sitzschalen	[5] Ersatzreifenabdeckung	[6] Himmel; Dachverkleidungen
[7] Sonnenblenden	[8] haltbar; strapazierfähig	[9] Hochdruck-; niedrige Dichte
[10] strukurell; baulich	[11] Gegendruck	[12] Spritzgießen
[13] Glasfaser	[14] Matte	[15] Verbund
[16] eingekapselt; eingegossen	[17] Harz	[18] Aushärtungsdauer
[19] Feinbearbeitungsvorgänge; Endbearbeitung	[20] innen liegend	[21] Formtrennung
[22] Trennmittel	[23] vielfach	[24] drehend
[25] Mischkopf	[26] verteilen, austeilen	[27] ringförmig
[28] Teilmenge, Bereich	[29] stationär	[30] vorwärtsgetrieben
[31] sättigen; befeuchten	[32] strömen	[33] Taktzeit
[34] zähflüssig; fest	[35] gleichmäßig	[36] Formhohlraum
[37] Beständigkeit; Festigkeit	[38] Formpress- Band/Linie/Straße	

9.8 Sports car chassis manufactured with aluminium

The chassis of the Lotus Elise is manufactured from *bonded*[1] extruded aluminium structures and *alloy*[2] *sheetings*[3]. The sports car chassis of this aluminium intensive vehicle owes its manufacturing success to the *ingenuity*[4] and manufacturing skills of the Norwegian company Norsk Hydro Automotive.

The UK has been a substantial outlet for Norsk Hydro's products and the company is *bullish*[5] about its prospects and the advantages:

- Tooling costs are unbelievably low, each die costing only a few thousand pounds.
- Car manufacturing with use of extruded sections is now *predominant*[6], in the same way as the Fiat Multipla, which shows some similarities in production, like *spaceframe*[7] manufactured by using *rolled steel sections*[8].
- Multipla's production process is so fast that, if a new *derivative*[9] is required, it could be achieved in a matter of months. It shows this concept provides great potential for diversification.

The next new customers have been the "Opel Speedster" roadster, based on the Elise chassis and powered by a new two-litre engine and made of aluminium. As volume was not yet large enough to justify the cost of a *dedicated*[10] *extrusion facility*[11] in the UK, aluminium from Norway was extruded in Denmark and shipped to South Wales for *anodising*[12] and then to the Williamson road plant, Worcester, UK, for assembly. To justify the cost, there is a need to produce 20,000 tonnes of extruded material per year.

Figure 9.8.1: Hydraulic unit with aluminium part (Source: Continental Teves, Frankfurt)

A 2,200 tonne press is currently being used in the UK for extruded material to force the aluminium through dies at a temperature of 490 degrees Celsius. The acceptable range is 460-530 degrees Celsius. At lower temperatures, extrusions can be made more quickly, but at the expense of quality. However, the large *suspension turrets*[13] of the Elise are being produced at Alusuisse using a 100,000 tonne press, because they are too *substantial*[14] for the Norsk Hydro equipment. Sheet material is produced from 100% recycled aluminium, processed at 900 degrees Celsius. Electromagnets are used to remove steel *impurities*[15].

Figure 9.8.2: Opel Speedster (Source: Adam Opel AG, Rüsselsheim)

The Elise platform was originally designed as a chassis with no doors. As a result, the large chassis *rails*[16] provided a particular manufacturing challenge due to a fairly large *curved section*[17]. The end result was achieved by *stretching*[18] and pulling the components around a tool. A *mandrel*[19] was inserted into each rail to prevent the material *collapsing*[20].

Other critical areas included the suspension turrets. Potential crash damage is *catered for*[21] by a design which accommodates the *fitting*[22] of complete *replacement sections*[23]. Dealers who are unaware that repair is possible are reported to have *scrapped*[24] damaged chassis as a result. However, the matter is complicated: insurers will not allow repairs to use *structural adhesive*[25] and the chassis has to return to the factory for *bonding*[26].

The assembly process of Elise chassis starts with the picking of components using bar code readers. When a complete chassis has been picked, software issues the chassis number to which every part of the assembly process is then linked. Components are bonded automatically using a *heat-cured*[27] *epoxy-based glue*[28] which never cures outside the oven and can be stored for years. However, the disadvantage is that this kind of glue can absorb water, which turns to *stream*[29] during curing and can damage *joints*[30]. Bonding components is performed by a robot. The glue is applied in minutely metered amounts. Hand assembly onto a *jig*[31] completes the process.

[1] geklebt	[2] Legierung	[3] Blechverkleidung
[4] Einfallsreichtum	[5] in Haussestimmung	[6] vorherrschend
[7] Gitterrohrrahmen	[8] Walzprofilstahl	[9] Abkömmling
[10] neu eröffnet	[11] Strangpressanlage	[12] Eloxieren
[13] Radaufhängungsdom	[14] gewichtig	[15] Verunreinigungen
[16] Träger, Holme	[17] gekrümmter Abschnitt	[18] verlängern
[19] Dorn	[20] zusammenbrechen; versagen	[21] berücksichtigen
[22] Anschlussstück	[23] Austauschbereiche	[24] verschrottet
[25] Klebstoff für Strukturteile	[26] Kleben	[27] wärmeausgehärtet
[28] Klebstoff auf Epoxidbasis	[29] fließen	[30] Verbindungen
[31] Schablone		

9.9 Manufacturing processes and techniques

9.9.1 Component fabrication

Hot Forming

Hot forming[1] is used to improve body structure in relevant safety areas, with *gauges*[2] of between 0.8 and 3.0mm. The current process for automotive engineering includes applications, such as door reinforcements, *door intrusion beams*[3], bumper beams, *front shock tower reinforcement*[4] and *front floor cross-members*[5]. Tailored blanking can be used in this process to achieve lightmass parts with high *rigidity*[6]. The production of these components is computer controlled and fully automated. A problem is cost efficient surface treatment.

Laminate Material

The advantage of laminate material is the replacement of solid sheets of equal mechanical properties, whereby one can achieve a more than 5 kg mass saving. *Laminated steel*[7] *is comprised of*[8] a poly-propylene core *sandwiched between*[9] two thin outer sheets of steel. To receive equivalent mechanical properties, one has to take either a solid sheet of steel, which is 0.7mm thick, or a sandwich with a 0.76mm core and two 0.12mm thick steel sheets. The core acts as a spacer, keeping the outer surface away from the neutral axis when a bending load is applied to the laminate sheet. Laminate material is mainly used in high stress structural areas, like *dash panel insert*[10], *front floor center*[11] or *spare wheel well*[12].

Blow moulding technology

One of the first applications of carbon dioxide blowing technology for production of low density polyurethane foam automotive seating was implemented in a seat unit for the Fiat Uno and the world car Fiat Palio.

The advantage is the usage of physical processes rather than chemical reactions to reduce density. With water blowing 32kg/cbm were achieved, whereas with CO_2 blowing, 25% further mass reduction has been achieved, without compromise of comfort or foam durability. Further advantages are foams with higher surface *viscosity*[13], and a cleaner finish which is more suitable for *foam-in-fabric*[14] applications.

The disadvantage is that CO_2 produces a foam with a larger number of open cells, which tends to reduce stability. A new range of Polyurethane systems are necessary to ensure robust processing with CO_2 blowing.

Tubular Hydroforming

The new tubular hydroforming process is already well proven in the automotive industry generally and is used to replace stamped assemblies in order to reduce the number of parts and assembly operations, for example, for components ranging from *exhaust manifolds*[15], *exhaust pipes*[16], *engine cradles*[17] to *transmission shafts*[18], *subframes*[19], *IP beams*[20], *radiator supports*[21] and *crossmembers*[22].

In low pressure tube hydroforming the tube is *pre-bent*[23] to take up the longitudinal shape of the forming tool and internally pressured (typically to 600 bar) as the die closes. The pressure prevents the tube from collapsing as the two halves of the forming tool close on the tube to create the desired shape. Local expansion is limited to 2% and the outside periphery of the part must match the periphery of the initial tube.

High pressure tube hydroforming uses up to 10,000 bars in combination with *ram forces*[24]. As in low pressure, the tube is pre-bent to take up the basic shape of the die. However, the material is forced to the extremities of the forming tool by a combination of internal hydraulic pressure and axial forces applied to each end of the tube. As a result, up to a 50% expansion of the tube diameter is possible with minimal wall thinning. Indeed, it is the axial forces applied during the process that control the wall thickness. Examples for body in white components are *sills*[25], A pillars, C pillars, cross members and side *roof rails*[26].

What is the accurate forming process for high pressure tube hydroforming?
- 1st step: The basic tube is pre-bent on a conventional bending machine into a shape which is similar to the final shape of the part.
- 2nd step: The pre-bent part is placed into the lower tool. After the upper tool comes down and closes on the lower half, the tube is filled with a fluid. The pressure on the tube inner wall is increased to 2,000-10,000 bars which forces the tube to flow into the tool shape.
- 3rd step: The tube expands in to recesses using a combination of hydraulic pressure and axial ram forces. Two cylinders press the material from both ends. This minimises wall thinning, so a constant wall thickness can be achieved. Holes can be punched with tool inserts. Only one set of tools is needed for this process. In areas where the material flow is too high, local thinning may occur. In areas where the material flow is too low, cracks or wrinkles may occur.
- 4th step: The final component is removed from the die. After the part is taken out of the tools, cutting and controlling operations may be performed.

Advantages of the former process with stamped parts are mainly the following:
- Minimal section size for reducing part count, along with material and mass saving.
- Reduced number of joints.
- Materials of reduced gauge.
- Holes can be punched in the same process along with the forming of *nodes*[27] and *extrusions*[28] for connecting parts
- More efficient transfer of loads.
- Overall tooling costs are lower than for deep drawing.
- Repeat accuracy is very high.
- Wall thinning can be limited to 1-2%.
- Ability to produce extremely complex shapes in a single operation.
- High dimensional stability.
- Utilization of greater cross sections.
- Cold working effect increases yield strength.
- Smoother load flow.
- Fewer tooling sets required.
- Less assembly costs.

- Better utilization of package room.
- Greater material efficiency due to less local wall thinning.

There are, however, disadvantages of this process:
- Long cycle time[29].
- Pre-bending usually required.
- Material compression limited (*friction*[30]).
- Poor exposed surface quality.
- Sensitive to *buckling*[31] and *wrinkling*[32].
- Sensitive to die *lock*[33].
- *Seam welding*[34] required due to the absence of flanges.
- New solutions for joints necessary, e.g. combination of welding and form closure.

Advices from experts to prevent trouble:
- Tubular hydroformed parts have to be designed differently from regularly stamped parts. Therefore the manufacturing process should be determined prior to design.
- The smallest radii of the shape determine the level of internal pressure needed. Therefore they should be as large as possible.
- High attention has to be paid to die lock *sensitivity*[35]
- Today's available steel tubes (tubes with deep draw quality or isotropic steel) allow only a limited amount of elongation in longitudinal and transversal directions.
- If a section shape has to be varied over the length of the part, the percentage increase of the *circumference*[36] should not be higher than the maximum percentage elongation of the materials.
- Greater expansion in section *perimeter*[37] can be achieved if the two cylinders which seal the tube at the end push the part from the end during forming process. This allows additional "material flow" into areas where higher expansion is needed.
- Transitions between section shape changes should be designed as smooth as possible.

However, there are still problem areas which have to be considered:
- Formability of different grades of steel, especially the *boundary regions*[38] of expansion and *tightness*[39] of *radii*[40].
- Design of "triggers" for the controlled collapse of *crash resisting*[41] *members*[42].
- Joint design, especially in respect of joining together hydroformed components (e.g. laser welding).
- Effects of the process on surface coatings.

- Lengths of tubes, laser welded from materials of different gauges and/ or tensile strengths in order to precisely control design parameters, such as mass, strength and deformation within a single component.
- How thinner but stronger steels will behave.

The following additional improvements are suggested:
- *Custom^{43} rollformed^{44}* profiles can be used as semifinished products instead of standard shapes to reduce production costs.
- *Tailor^{45}* tubing could reinforce the parts locally and help to keep the mass at a minimum.

There follow some specifications of typical tube hydroforming machines, for example, of Hübner& Bauer company:
- *Cavity^{46}* diameter of 1.8 metres.
- *Clamping force^{47}* of 8,800 tonnes.
- Forming pressure of 4,200 bars.
- Axial forces of 200 tonnes.
- Max. tube diameter of 100mm.
- Max. tube wall thickness of 4mm.
- Part lengths 1,600 mm straight.

The latest research will allow designers to consider body in white components which are much more complex, calling for high degrees of deformation. Hydroforming involves using hydraulic pressure to help in the deformation of either the steel panel (*flexible forming^{48}*) or tube to take up the shape of a *die^{49}*.

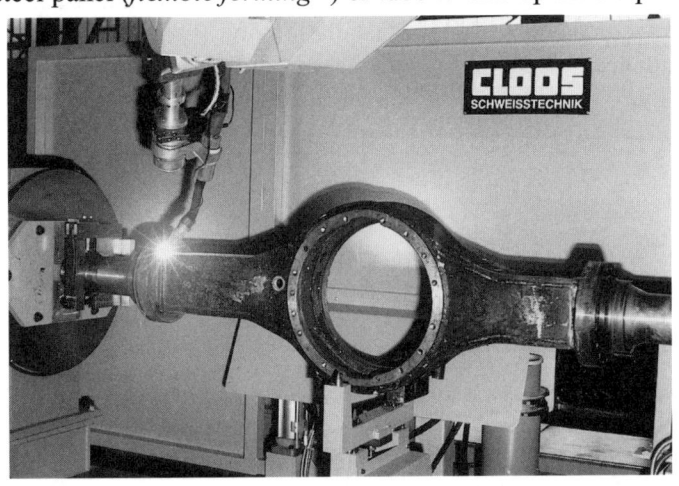

Figure 9.9.1.1: Fully automatic welding of truck axles (Source: Carl Cloos Schweisstechnik GmbH, Haiger)

^{1} Warmumformen; Heißformen	^{2} Blechstärke; Blechdicke	^{3} Türverstärkungsstrebe; Seitenaufprallschutz
^{4} Dom Verstärkung des Vorderachs-Stoßdämpfers	^{5} Querträger des vorderen Fußbodens	^{6} Steifigkeit
^{7} geschichteter Stahl	^{8} bestehen aus	^{9} eingeklemmt zwischen

[10] Armaturenbrett-Einlage	[11] Mitte des vorderen Fußbodens	[12] Ersatzradmulde; Reserveradwanne
[13] Flüssigkeitsgrad	[14] Einschäumen in Stoff/Gewebe	[15] Abgaskrümmer
[16] Abgaskrümmer	[17] Motorhilfsrahmen	[18] Verbindungswellen; Zwischenwellen
[19] Fahrschemel; Hilfsrahmen	[20] Armaturentafel-Träger	[21] Kühlerträger
[22] Querträger; Traverse; Spriegel	[23] vorgebogen	[24] Staukräfte
[25] Einstiegsschweller	[26] Dachlängsträger	[27] Knoten
[28] Strangpressteile	[29] Taktzeit	[30] Reibung
[31] Abknicken; Ausbeulen	[32] schrumpelig werden	[33] blockieren
[34] Nahtschweißung	[35] Abhängigkeit; Empfindlichkeit	[36] Umfang; Kreisumfang
[37] Rand; äußere Begrenzung	[38] Grenzbereiche	[39] Dichtheit
[40] Radien	[41] zusammenbruchbeständig	[42] Bauteile; Träger
[43] kundenspezifisch	[44] rollgeformt	[45] maßgeschneidert
[46] Hohlraum	[47] Spannkraft; Anpresskraft	[48] Anpassungsformen
[49] Form; Formwerkzeug		

9.9.2 Assembly processes

Weldbonding

The *body side outer assembly*[1] is *weldbonded*[2] to the body structure. It has an adhesive applied to its weld flanges prior to installation and spotwelding in the *framing*[3] assembly sequence. Weldbonding increases durability, *torsional rigidity*[4] and bending rigidity.

Figure 9.9.2.1:
Laserwelded safety
framework of Opel Zafira
(Source: Adam Opel AG,
Rüsselsheim)

Laser welding

The advantages of the laser technique are treatment of laserwelded parts with *hydroforming technique*[5], for example, manufacturing of axle components, and welding and cutting of thin gauge steel sheets by solid-state laser.

Weldability of each *weld seam*[6] depends on:
- Selection of the robotic system.
- The possibility to integrate the choosen robotic system into a welding station.
- The possibility to minimize gaps by optimized clamping systems.
- The orientation of the seam oriented to the dynamics of the robot movement.

Decision on the right laser welding system:
We have to differentiate between CO_2 laser and Nd:YAG laser techniques.
- The welding speed for the CO_2 laser is twice the speed for the Nd:YAG laser, caused by higher laser power and smaller *focal spot*[7].
- The process behaviour of the Nd:YAG laser is better, caused by a better absorption of its laser light, but the disadvantage of the Nd:YAG laser is its badly focused laser beam. Overall, due to wavelength, the interaction between laser beam and *shielding gas*[8] is less critical, if the Nd:YAG laser is used.

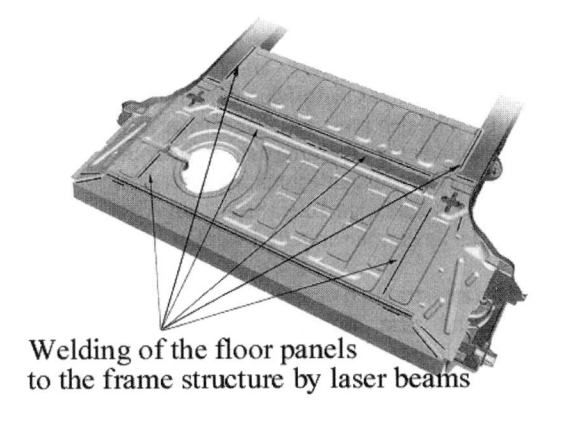

Figure 9.9.2.2: Laser beam welding of floor panels[9] to the frame structure (Source: ATZ, 3/2000)

Welding of the floor panels to the frame structure by laser beams

- The CO_2 laser has a wavelength of 10.6mm with power available up to 45 kW, whereas the Nd:YAG laser has a wavelength of 1.06mm with power available up to 3 kW. Electrical efficiency to optical power is up to 10% at the CO_2 laser, compared with 2% at the Nd:YAG laser.

- Available power of 2 to 6 kW for total sheet thicknesses of up to 3mm is necessary, which CO_2 can deliver.
- Beam guiding and focusing (mostly over a distance of up to 10m from laser source to robots).
- The Nd:YAG laser beam could be guided with an *optical fibre*[10], whereas the CO_2 laser beam has to be guided via a systems of mirrors. Therefore the flexibility of CO_2 beam guiding is low compared to Nd:YAG.
- Focusing of laser beams can be achieved by lens optics, mirrors or copper mirror focusing optic, depending on power up to 3kW or more.
- The smaller focal spot size of CO_2 systems (with sheet thickness of up to 3mm, diameter can be as low as 0.15mm) leads to higher welding speeds.

The following *nodes*[11] can be laserwelded:
- *Fender support rail*[12] with *shock tower reinforcement*[13], *skirt*[14], *A-pillar inner (panel) lower*[15] and *A-pillar inner (panel) upper*[16].
- *Side roof rail*[17] with A-pillar inner and door opening outer[18].
- Side roof rail with door opening outer.
- Side roof rail with B-pillar inner and door opening outer.
- Side roof rail with *quarter panel inner*[19].
- Side roof rail with *roof*[20].

Please take notice of the following suggestions from experts:
- Laser welding is not advantageous if the form is too complex. Redesigning of parts to obtain flat areas for weld seams is necessary in this case. Furthermore small radii to be welded should be avoided.
- Laser welding is not advantageous if the seams are too short.
- A decision has to be made for suitable welding sequence, seam length, overlapping dimension and welding speed for each node, because seams which require high quality or connecting parts of high stiffness have to be welded first.
- Body-in-white requires a robot system of high flexibility with a 6 axis. Avoid 5 axis robots or *gantry systems*[21].
- A low investment solution is positioning two welding robots next to the assembly line. The third one hangs above the middle of the assembly line to *incorporate*[22] the inner weld seams. However, there is a disadvantage: Processing time is mainly determined by time for *reorientation*[23] of the robots.
- A better solution is positioning 4 welding robots next to the assembly line. The 5th one hangs above the middle of the assembly line to incorporate the inner weld seams. An advantage of this solution is that there is a smaller processing time, because that time for reorientation of the robots in the front is used for carrying out welding tasks in the rear.

Figure 9.9.2.3: Special purpose device[24] for welding of belt pulleys[25] for passenger cars (Source: Carl Cloos Schweisstechnik GmbH, Haiger)

- Detailed safety requirements and costs for laser systems have to be taken into account.
- To ensure constant quality of the welding process, some parameters have to be monitored constantly: laser power, *velocity*[26] of the processing robot, cooling temperature of the laser and optic and flow of working gas.
- To ensure the quality of *lap joints*[27], the gap between joining partners has to be less than one tenth the thickness of the smaller sheet. In this case, the differences between two sheets should be less than factor 2. If this value is exceeded, the thicker sheet has to be the lower one and no gap is allowed. *Burrs*[28], *spatters*[29] and *chips*[30] have to be avoided between each sheet.

- Potential problem areas have to be taken into account, which could *be the focal length*[31] of the optic, the cooling system or minimum bending radius for an optical fibre of 300mm in length.

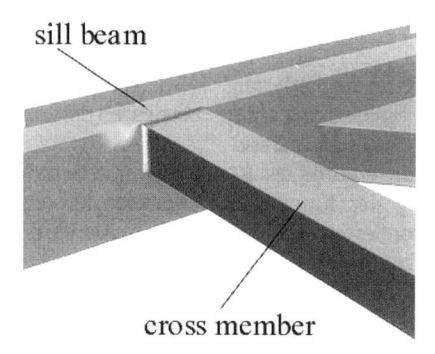

Figure 9.9.2.4: Laserwelding of sill beam[32] and crossmember[33] (Source: ATZ, 3/2000)

The following clamping problems and strategies have to be considered:
- To weld stamped parts to hydroformed parts, the gap has to be reduced without deformation to hydroformed parts by *clamping devices*[34]. This could be done using *clearence*[35] holes for *clamps*[36], or hydroformed parts could be designed as flat as possible in clamping areas to avoid deformation by distributing clamping forces.
- In the case of complex designs (e.g. door opening outer attached to side roof rail), it is proposed to separate the clamp to press and *counterforce*[37] parts in one step. Another possibility is to press a roll with springs to the sheet of metal (e.g. roof) running in front of the laser beam. A further solution could be to include the *fixturing*[38] task into the *loading tool*[39], by using *suckers*[40], magnets and forming *notches*[41].
- To reduce the travel of the robot system, the starting point of the weld sequences and weld positions (down, vertical or overhead) should be taken into consideration.

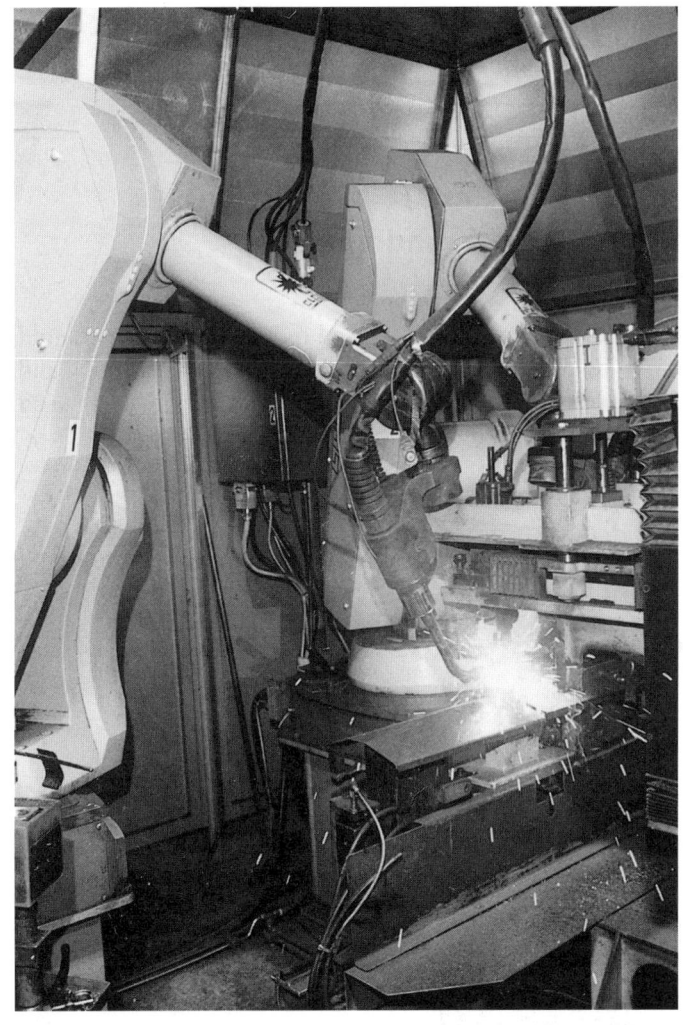

Figure 9.9.2.5: Welding of shock absorbing devices[42] *for different type of vehicles (Source: Carl Cloos Schweisstechnik GmbH, Haiger)*

[1] Zusammenbau Seitenwand-außen	[2] schweißgeklebt	[3] Karosserieaufbau
[4] Verdrehsteifigkeit	[5] Innenhochdruckumformen	[6] Schweißnaht
[7] Brennpunkt	[8] Schutzgas	[9] Bodenbleche
[10] Lichtwellenleiter	[11] Knotenpunkte	[12] Kotflügelhalterschiene
[13] Verstärkung Stoßfänger-Dom	[14] Schürze; Verkleidung	[15] A-Säule Innenblech unten
[16] A-Säule Innenblech oben	[17] Türöffnung außen	[18] Dachträger seitlich
[19] Seitenwandblech innen	[20] Dach	[21] Brückensysteme; Portalsysteme
[22] integrieren; einbinden	[23] Neuorientierung	[24] Sondervorrichtung
[25] Riemenscheiben	[26] Geschwindigkeit	[27] Überlappungsnähte
[28] Grate	[29] Schweißspritzer	[30] Splitter

³¹ Brennweite	³² Schweller; Türschweller	³³ Rahmenquerträger
³⁴ Spannvorrichtungen	³⁵ Freiraum; Spiel	³⁶ Spannpratzen; Zwingen
³⁷ Gegenkraft; Reaktion	³⁸ Befestigung	³⁹ beladende/ belastendeWerkzeug
⁴⁰ Sauger; Ansauger	⁴¹ Kerben	⁴² Dämpfungselemente

9.10 Cost and mass reduction modelling for manufacturing processes

There is a possibility of offering mass reduction and reduced costs. This could be shown by modelling. As modelling is always a *tradeoff*[1] between accuracy and efficiency, the following is an attempt to find the middle. Modelling is to be used as one tool in deciding which technologies to *discount*[2] and which are *persuasive*[3].

Figure 9.10.1: Production of injection components in India. For more than 40 years Bosch has held a strong position in India in the field of diesel injection equipment. In 1998 the company also began application engineering of components for gasoline injection (Source: Robert Bosch GmbH, Stuttgart).

Comparisons are made between material systems at a level of detail necessary to understand which technologies are the best short and long term solutions to a given problem. Models can be used to accomplish the following tasks:
- Simulate the costs of manufacturing products.

- Establish direct comparisons between material, process and design alternatives.
- Investigate the effects of changes in the process scenario on overall costs.
- Identify limiting process steps and parameters.
- Determine the *merits*[4] of specific process and design improvements.

As inputs into the modelling system, the most important onces are annual production volume and *production run*[5]. Due to the huge amount of parts, they have to be grouped and reresented by average or typical part classes: large, flat and *rectangular*[6]; medium *contoured*[7] with high *aspect ratio*[8]; and small parts.

Figure 9.10.2: Economic production requires individualized solutions. Assembly of diesel injection pumps at Bosch's Feuerbach plant show that zero defect assembly not only calls for fully automated work stations but also ergonomic design of work stations for performing special manual tasks. An assembly system from Bosch's Automation Technology division is used to produce these complex components.
(Source: Robert Bosch GmbH, Stuttgart).

In each category, an average part is defined based on surface area, thickness, mass, material *scrap*[9], production rate, material price, process types (stamping, moulding, etc.), labour requirement, machine cost, floor space required, power consumption, piece cost, tool cost, and assembly cost. The more classes that are used, the higher the accuracy of the output. Furthermore, simplifying assumptions have to be made for
- average steel price for all sorts of steels (mild, medium, high strength, *tailored blanks*[10], *laminate*[11] steel),
- an average price for type of joining of each vehicle design (spot welding for stamped sheet metal, weld-bonding for *spaceframes*[12], adhesive bonding for composite structures), and
- average price for various types of welding (spot, *fusion*[13], laser), bonding, etc.

The result is an average fabrication cost. Efforts to reduce costs must centre on reduction of mass and number of pieces, as mass is changed at the same rate as number of pieces and material cost, while being aware of production volume sensitivity. A change in annual production volume affects overall system cost, due to the higher utilization of fabrication and assembly plant.

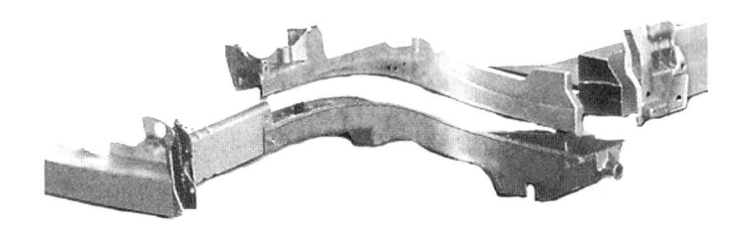

Figure 9.10.3: Some diecast parts[14] made of aluminium for spaceframe models (Source: ATZ, 3/2000)

The complex tasks of cost estimation can be reduced to a series of simpler estimating problems by breaking down total cost into variables (material, labour, energy, etc.) and *overhead cost*[15] elements (equipment, tooling, building, maintenance, overhead labour, cost of capital, etc.).

To present cost output, it is suggested to show manufacturing cost (sum of material, labour, equipment, tooling and other costs) for each case on the y-axis. Number of pieces and mass should be represented by lines or bars.

[1] Kompromiss	[2] ausschließen	[3] überzeugend
[4] Verdienste	[5] Herstellungslos	[6] rechtwinklig
[7] konturiert	[8] Höhen-Breiten-Verhältnis	[9] Schrott
[10] maßgeschneiderte Bleche	[11] Laminat; Schichtpressstoff	[12] Gitterrohrrahmen
[13] Schmelzschweißen	[14] Druckgussteile	[15] Fixkosten; allgemeine Kosten; indirekte Kosten

10 Information Technology Services

10.1 Hybrid software allows 3D working

Object-oriented hybrid software allows users to work in either 2D or 3D modes, so flexibility is its key advantage. Advanced surface and solids modelling package, *incorporating*[1] intelligent drawing technology, aimed at Windows 95/98/NT and Power Macintosh PC users, brings advanced capabilities to engineering departments. Ashlar Corp., which is well known and respected for a huge range of CAD systems, has released a new hybrid modeller, called Vellum Solids, in Europe. Data translation is a strong feature with versions for SolidWorks, AutoCAD, Alias and Pro/ENGINEER. Import options for using data exchange formats DWG, IGES and SAT (ACIS) are included.

[1] Integration			

Figure 10.1.1: Tasks at Styling. A sketch of Opel Speedster (Source: Adam Opel AG, Rüsselsheim)

10.2 Fluid flow modelling

In real turbulent flows, *eddies*[1] constantly appear and destroy each other, greatly affecting what goes on. It has long been recognised that modelling turbulent flow is at best an approximation. By tracking the flow of individual particles, it is possible to solve fluid flow problems which until now have completely *defied*[2] conventional computational fluid dynamics.

Modelling the motion of individual fluid particles has been prevented by computational power. The American Exa Corp. is currently offering Power-FLOW, using a Sun UltraSparc workstation. The Visual Instruction Set is used to speed graphics processing in the UltraSparc. But solution time is still long: a typical automotive problem will take about a day to solve on a 16 processor machine, or three days on a two processor machine.

It has long been known that if a car is designed with an *inclined*[3] *back window*[4], drag increases dramatically as the angle to the horizontal approaches 30 degrees, and then suddenly falls off again. This behaviour is clearly caused by two *vorticities*[5] which trail back from the top corners of the window. As the angle of the back window increases, the *vortices*[6] become stronger and stronger, until at 35 degrees they are completely destroyed by the turbulence generated by the rest of the window.

The company also *boasts*[7] that PowerFLOW took only one hour to set up a CD of 0.19, which was only 24% in error, much better than was achieved by anyone else. Presently, the software is only suitable for studies of flows passing at up to Mach 0.3. Beyond this speed, *compressibility*[8] has to be taken into account. To overcome this limitation, research partners work on it and intend to extend capabilities to Mach 1.3. Furthermore, the motor racing *fraternity*[9] want the addition of moving ground planes and rotating tyres. Other partners in Italy are engaged in extending the software to the study of reacting flows, for example in combustion.

The software has not yet been sold, but is licensed. A single processor machine has to be *purchased*[10] for around $18,200 for a year's licence, or $132,000 for use on a similar machine with eight processors.

[1] Wirbel	[2] herausgefordert	[3] geneigt
[4] Heckscheibe	[5] Verwirbelungen	[6] Wirbel
[7] prahlen, rühmen	[8] Zusammendrückbarkeit	[9] Zunft
[10] Anschaffung; Einkauf		

10.3 Limitations of Virtual Reality modelling

The way forward for Virtual Reality technology has been paved by way of presenting highly realistic simulations. Not every situation, however, *warrants*[1] its *expense*[2] and sophistication. Furthermore, manipulating the data is far from *straightforward*[3] for an engineer *trapped*[4] in a VR world. A two-dimensional computer screen *hampers*[5] the amazing advances made in 3D modelling software for investigating crash scenarios or fluid flow patterns within and around a vehicle.

A practical alternative was arrived at by scientists at Daimler-Benz Research, working in cooperation with the Mathematical Society (GMD). A screen, measuring about 2m by 1m, *emulates*[6] a *drawing board*[7] which is held in a simple wooden frame. The projected *image*[8], *diverted*[9] by a mirror located beneath the frame, appears *out of focus*[10] on the screen. However, as soon as the user puts on the special glasses provided, the projection appears as a three-dimensional image floating in space. A Silicon Graphics Reality Engine 3 is used as hardware.

The observer uses a special indicating and marking pen to manipulate the 3D virtual image. The pen incorporates rotation and zoom functions, and it can also remove components. The *exposure*[11] of critical areas is especially useful when working with crash simulations. The pen can also be used to cut *cross-sections*[12] through a virtual component to obtain information on critical *stress patterns*[13].

What tasks can be performed with these new VR glasses?
- Investigation of *swirl*[14] *break-off*[15] and turbulence formation in the engine *compression stroke*[16];
- injector jet[17] mixture formulation[18];
- *combustion*[19] analysis; and
- airflow analysis round the vehicle.

[1] garantiert	[2] Ausgaben	[3] einfach; direkt
[4] eingeschlossen, gefangen	[5] behindern	[6] emulieren
[7] Zeichenbrett	[8] Bild; Abbildung	[9] abgelenkt
[10] unscharf	[11] Freilegung; Aussetzung	[12] Querschnitte; Schnitte
[13] Spannungsverläufe	[14] Wirbel	[15] Abbruch
[16] Verdichtungstakt	[17] Einspritzdüse	[18] Mischung nach Formel
[19] Verbrennung		

10.4 Thermofluid analysis

Thermofluid analysis is said to offer new features which make software more powerful and easier to use.

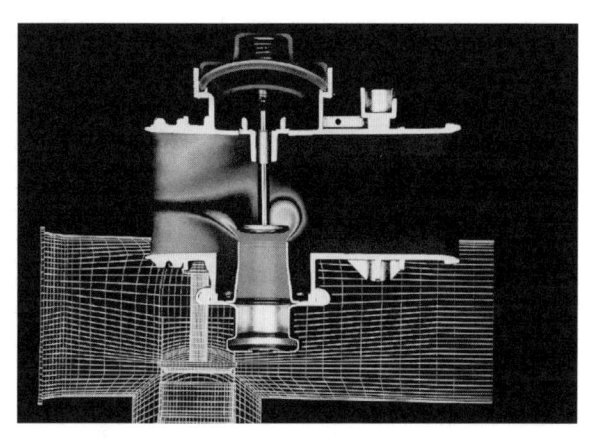

Figure 10.4.1: Computer simulations for product development. Computer simulations are indispensable[1] for the development of products. In this way, for instance, insight into flow behaviour and temperature dispersion[2] of an exhaust-gas recirculation valve[3] is gained (Source: Robert Bosch GmbH, Stuttgart).

Development of all *tetrahedral*[4] and surface trimmed *hexahedral*[5] *mesh*[6] handling capabilities has been a focal point of the latest version of STAR-CD, Release 3, or automatic mesh generators such as ICEM Tetra and SAMM. Simply by reducing the mesh generating time (by an *order of*[7] *magnitude*[8]), these new capabilities should reduce the *turnaround time*[9] of the overall analysis.

[1] unverzichtbar	[2] Feinverteilung	[3] Abgasrückführungsventil
[4] vierflächig; tetraedrisch	[5] sechsflächig	[6] Gitter; Netz
[7] je nach	[8] Wichtigkeit; Größe	[9] Umlaufzeit

11 Finance

11.1 The U.S. steelmarket

The automotive industry has always been a mixed *blessing*[1] for steelmakers. On the one hand, huge amounts of steel (nearly 17% of all produced domestically in the U.S.) is bought by General Motors Corp., Ford Motor Corp. and other carmakers, but on the other hand, these companies are *notorious for*[2] forcing steel companies to accept lower prices. Furthermore, steelmakers, still *stinging*[3] from the recent *surplus*[4] in cheaper imports, have had to pour money into new technologies. Their best hope is to make up in volume what they will lose from lower prices.

Huge online networks have been launched by GM and Ford, *in essence*[5], to force their suppliers and vendors to work together and cut waste. Under this network, GM will act as middleman, buying steel at *rock-bottom prices*[6] and reselling it cheaply to hundreds of *vendors*[7]. This step will be understood, as GM buys about five million tons of steel a year.

GM is *taking two stances*[8]: suppliers have to cooperate or lose GM's business entirely. Further cost cutting and slimmer profits are expected. Some firms will not survive the next *assault*[9] by the automotive industry. Industry observers expect

– more steel company *mergers*[10] to prevent *bankruptcy*[11], and
– *middlemen*[12] (currently steel service centers) who buy steel from the big producers and resell it to smaller buyers will be driven out of business.

When the Asian economy *declined*[13], cheaper imports flooded the steel market. The steel industry has fought much of the battle, and the fight isn't over yet. One of the industry's roughest periods has started. Steelmakers expected a great time for the domestic steel industry because of the booming national economy. Companies like U.S. Steel Corp., USX Corp., Bethlehem Steel Corp., Weirton Steel Corp, and LTV Corp., all big suppliers to carmakers, saw their quarterly profits drop and widespread *layoffs*[14] start, in order to cut employees from the payrolls. It is *claimed that*[15] illegal *dumping*[16] was *filed*[17].

A combination of U.S. government muscle and a *strengthening*[18] of the Asian economies began to put steelmakers back on the road to better profits. Many announced price increases on *flat-rolled steel*[19] scheduled to take effect with *shipments*[20] on Jan. 1, 2000.

[1] Segen	[2] berüchtigt wegen	[3] getroffen
[4] Überangebot	[5] im wesentlichen	[6] Schleuderpreise
[7] Verkäufer	[8] zwei Standpunkte beziehen	[9] Sturm; Angriff
[10] Fusionen	[11] Bankrott	[12] Zwischenhändler

[13] sinken, abfallen	[14] Personalabbau	[15] behaupten
[16] Dumping (von billigen Waren)	[17] zu den Akten gelegt	[18] verstärken; ausbauen
[19] Flachstahl	[20] Lieferungen	

11.2 Product costs and investment are important

Engineers always like to save money and development time. Cost is important, because imageleaders have to be seen on the streets in high volume. Therefore, Audi TT engineers, for example, have targeted to share 50 percent of the parts with the Audi A3 platform, to keep costs down.

However, at the start of production they met only 20-25 percent *commonality*[1] with the Audi A3 platform. The reason is that in decisions, product came ahead of cost. Anything that had a negative influence on the character of that car should not be selected according to *specification*[2]: but compromises were found. For example:
- The front *lock*[3], air-conditioning and *switch stalks*[4] are common to the A3.
- Almost all the exterior and interior parts are new, and much of the underfloor was also new due to the performance ambitions of the car.
- Some of the work that was original, such as in the engines, will end up on other group cars.

However, another 20 percent of the parts were developed from existing components used for the A3 and other Audi models using about 70 percent of the investments and 40-45 percent of the work:
- the unlocking mechanism is the same with A3, just with a different *lever*[5],
- the new front axle is an evolution of the one used on the A3,
- the dashboard module has the same crossbeam, but has been upgraded.

Investment[6] costs of tooling and assembling have to be considered, too. For example, Audi stamps, assembles and paints the body-in-white in Ingolstadt. As final assembly lines at Audi's plants at Ingolstadt and Neckarsulm in Germany are at full capacity, the plant in Gyor, Hungary, was chosen because it had space. The bodies are plastic-wrapped, loaded onto a train on pallets, and shipped overnight to Gyor. In Gyor, the pallets are taken off the train by a fork-lift and put on the final assembly line. Seats (Lear), bumpers and cockpit (Peguform), soft tops for convertible roofs (Edscha), and front-end modules (Mitras) are supplied from supplier manufacturing plants in Hungary.

Assembly takes seven to eight hours. Cars are shipped back to Ingolstadt the next night. About 850 people work on the TT at Ingolstadt and 500 assemble it in Gyor.

| [1] Gleichheit | [2] Lastenheft | [3] Schloss |
| [4] Schalthebel | [5] Bedienungshebel | [6] Investition; Anlage |

11.3 Carmakers' fight against recycling commission

In the coming days and weeks, the battle over the so-called "End of Life Vehicles" (ELV) *directive*[1], prepared by the European Commission in Brussels, will shift to the European Parliament's environment committee in Strasbourg, which is fearful of the damage caused by *dumping*[2] vehicle waste. Under the terms of the directive, from 2006 all cars in the EU must be taken back and recycled by manufacturers when they reach the end of their useful life. Furthermore, carmakers must recycle or re-use 80 percent of the vehicles' mass from that date, and take the cars free of charge. At issue is the European Commission's determination to make the directive *retro-active*[3]. This means carmakers will be *liable for*[4] meeting recycling costs for all 170m cars on Europe's roads, no matter how old they are, or where they were built.

Figure 11.3.1: Recyclable[5] assembly groups[6] (Source: Adam Opel AG, Rüsselsheim)

Europe's leading carmakers are planning a *rearguard*[7] action to *dilute*[8] or *amend*[9] legislation which, they claim, could leave them technically bankrupt. *Hostility to*[10] the measure is *likely to*[11] *prompt*[12] an *unprecedented*[13] lobbying effort in Strasbourg. The car industry finds itself fighting from a difficult corner. It supports the main *thrust*[14] of the legislation - the need to manufacture cars, from reusable materials - but not its *imposition*[15]. If they fail to persuade the European parliament to amend it, legal action appears *inevitable*[16]. That could *render*[17] the directive *unenforceable*[18], with carmakers going to court in all 15 member states to challenge it.

The European Commission has set itself on a collision course with the motor industry by proposing its *tough*[19] recycling legislation. The committee will be *urged*[20] to *back*[21] a compromise proposal, in which financial *liability*[22] for recycling old cars will be shared between carmakers, owners and *dismantling centres*[23]. Such a *concession*[24], however, is likely to prompt *fierce*[25] criticism from the Commission, which believes enough concessions have already been made to the car industry. Under German pressure, the imposition of the directive has already been delayed from 2001 to 2006.

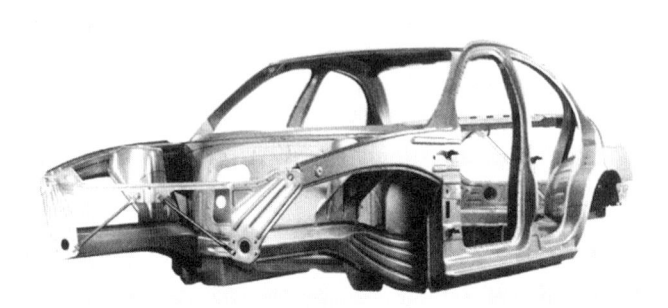

Figure 11.3.2: ULSAB (ATZ, 3/2000)

German carmakers are mobilising opposition to the directive. The German vehicle industry association (VDA) warns that the financial burden will have serious implications for all manufacturers and its smallest profits will decrease sharply. If *imposed*[26] in its current form, the directive will cost the car industry at least DM 20bn ($10.6bn) a year. The VDA has *commissioned*[27] *legal advice*[28] suggesting the retrospective element of the directive *contravenes*[29] both the German *penal law*[30] and the *Treaty*[31] of Rome.

The Commission is unimpressed. Only if the manufacturers are made financially liable for ensuring that vehicles can be re-used, will they have any *incentive*[32] to alter their design and production methods? Furthermore, they argue that end-of-life vehicles only impose a cost on the manufacturers if they have a negative value. Most of these cars (on average 12 years old) can generate income through recycling, with *salvaged*[33] components resold as spare parts.

Car manufacturers however say the industry cannot be held liable for cars engineered more than a decade ago. From Scandinavia to the Mediterranean today, *crushing machines*[34] will break up thousands of cars, working through an annual *tailback*[35] of 8m - 9m scrap vehicles. Forcing them to assume these costs could create an export trade in cars for recycling. They have *accused*[36] the Commission of *flouting*[37] laws.

Whichever side *emerges*[38] *victorious*[39] from the parliamentary process in Strasbourg, almost all new cars already on the market will meet the 2006 *threshold*[40] for recycling. Indeed, manufacturers such as Mercedes-Benz and Toyota are already using "*shredder residue*[41], mainly plastic and metal extracted from recycling, using this raw material for new components. The number of Europe's *scrapyards*[42] will certainly decrease rapidly.

Figure 11.3.3: The Mercedes SLA at Geneva Motor Show in spring 2000 (Source: Alexander Voos, Rüsselsheim)

[1] Richtlinie; Verordnung	[2] auskippen	[3] rückwirkend
[4] verantwortlich; haftbar	[5] recylingfähig	[6] Baugruppen
[7] Nachhut	[8] verdünnen; verwässern	[9] abändern; verbessern
[10] Feindschaft gegen	[11] könnte (dazu) führen; geeignet	[12] j-n veranlassen; dazu animieren, etwas zu tun
[13] beispiellos; noch nie dagewesen	[14] Schub; Druck	[15] Auferlegung (von Bedingungen)
[16] unvermeidlich	[17] (j-n, etwas) ... machen	[18] nicht einklagbar; nicht vollstreckbar
[19] aggressiv; hart	[20] vorantreiben; drängen	[21] unterstützen
[22] Verantwortlichkeit; Verpflichtung	[23] Demontagezentrum; Verwertungszentrum	[24] Entgegenkommen
[25] heftig	[26] verhängt; auferlegt	[27] abgenommen
[28] Rechtsberatung	[29] verstoßen	[30] Strafrecht
[31] Vertrag	[32] Anreiz; Ansporn	[33] wiederverwerten
[34] Grobzerkleinerungsmaschinen	[35] Rückstau	[36] beschuldigt
[37] missachten	[38] auftauchen; herauskommen	[39] siegreich
[40] Schwelle; Grenze	[41] Schredderabfall	[42] Autofriedhöfe; Schrottplätze

12 Plants

12.1 New Plant in Germany

The *foundation stone*[1] for a new automobile production plant for the 21st century was lain on February 8, 2000. Adam Opel AG celebrated the laying of the foundation stone for its new manufacturing plant in Rüsselsheim. In the presence of the *Federal Chancellor*[2] Gerhard Schröder, the *Federal Treasury Secretary*[3] Hans Eichel, the Minister of Social Affairs for Hesse, Marlies Mosiek-Urbahn, and the *Mayor*[4] of Rüsselsheim, Stefan Gieltowski, the *Chief Executive Officer*[5] of Adam Opel AG, Robert W. Hendry, and Rüsselsheim *Plant Manager*[6] Michael J. Wolf, underlined the significance of the DM 820 million investment for the company's future in general and the Rüsselsheim site in particular. Hendry stated: "Without doubt the construction of this new plant for the 21st century is the most important factor in our German investment program, which *envisages*[7] expenditure of DM 9 billion by the year 2004."

Boosting competitiveness

The new plant in Rüsselsheim will be one of the world's most modern automobile manufacturing plants and will, in the long term, *safeguard*[8] around 6000 jobs. All in all, 270,000 passenger cars are scheduled to be assembled on a joint production line, with *three-shift operation*[9].

Hendry went on to explain that Opel is the first carmaker to build a new plant with all its equipment and systems on an existing industrial site directly *adjacent to*[10] the current production location. Production will continue while the new plant is under construction. It is scheduled for completion in 2005, with the work being divided into three phases: the first begins with the laying of the foundation stone for the new production and *final assembly*[11] areas, which are scheduled to be roofed in by the end of September 2000 in order to ensure that installation of process equipment can *commence*[12]. In 2002, the first of the two model lines produced in Rüsselsheim should start to roll off the new production line. The second model will be added a year later. *Construction work*[13] will be *concluded*[14] in 2005 with completion of the new *paint shop*[15].

Utilizing resources

According to Robert W. Hendry, the basis for the decision was the opportunity to utilize the location's inherent advantages: in particular, these lie in the concentration of vehicle and component production, the *proximity*[16] to the International Technical Development Center, and direct contact with other vital corporate functions. As further bonus factors, Hendry mentioned the entire region's outstanding infrastructure and the highly experienced and qualified workforce available in Rüsselsheim.

Advanced logistical concept

The new production facility, which has been *erected*[17] directly adjacent to the current assembly plant, has an intelligent material-management system *at its disposal*[18] in order to permit smooth-running, *demand-oriented*[19] production processes.

Based on precisely planned production sequences, the required materials and components will be available at an exact time and at the correct assembly point.

This integrated logistics concept is promoted by the company in the form of its planned Supplier Park, which is located on site. Highly detailed fault prevention systems, which also involve the workforce, will ensure a consistently high level of quality in Opel production.

[1] Grundstein	[2] Bundeskanzler	[3] Bundesfinanzminister
[4] Bürgermeister	[5] Vorstandsmitglied	[6] Werksdirektor
[7] voraussehen	[8] sicherstellen	[9] 3-Schicht-Betrieb
[10] angrenzend; direkt neben	[11] Endmontage	[12] anfangen
[13] Bauarbeiten	[14] beenden	[15] Lackiererei
[16] Nähe; Nachbarschaft	[17] aufgerichtet	[18] jemanden zur Verfügung stehen
[19] bedarf-, nachfrageorientiert		

12.2 General Motors' new plant

The *stakes*[1] are high. To *loosen*[2] GMs' *grip*[3] on market segments, rival Ford Motor Corp. has launched a *salvo*[4] of full-sized sport-utilities in the past few years. GM is *fending off*[5] *stiff competition*[6] from competitors.

Figure 12.2.1: Production of sport-utility vans (Source: Adam Opel AG, Rüsselsheim)

If sport-utility sales stay on track, each GM car will provide a significant chunk of profits. Plants like Arlington, Texas, Silao, Mexico, or Janesville, however, have been *running flat*[7] out building Chevrolet Suburbans, Tahoes and GMC Yukons. Instead of relieving tight *supplies*[8], it is planning to spending $600 million on its plants for *full-size*[9] *sport-utility cars*[10]. GM spent its money mainly to improve quality and not for an extra unit of production.

Production of today's 1,160 sport-utilities per day can't be changed if production of the redesigned sport-utilities is launched in November 2000. A new paint shop would be necessary to increase production units by relieving the bottleneck there. However, the investment could be some of the best money GM has ever spent.

With the *changeover*[11] the *assembly line*[12] rate should be kept that high, which will be a challenge for the plant's engineers. The Janesville plant, for example, which also builds *medium-duty*[13] GM and Isuzu-brand trucks, normally operates with two 10-hour shifts, four days per week. However, overtime will add 10 hours to the weekly schedule of the 3,800 workers. That amounts to a fifth day of production.

Figure 12.2.2:Female worker on an assembly line (Source: Adam Opel AG, Rüsselsheim)

They have been ordered to increase quality on a vehicle that is also more complicated to build than its *predecessor*[14].

The new sport-utilities, which are based on the Chevrolet Silverado and GMC Sierra, have 25 percent fewer parts than their predecessors. Assembling should be easier, but there are some new *twists*[15]:
 − For example, sunroofs will be installed in the factory. The change requires new tooling and assembly line steps.
 − Another is an H-shaped underbody structure which engineers call "spider." The stamped-steel spider, which is designed to make the body more rigid, adds several assembly steps.

- Furthermore, it will apply 4,300 spot welds to the new Suburban, compared with 2,500 for the old model.
- Janesville's body shop also will fabricate almost all the *closure panels*[16] for the new sport-utilities, including the side doors, hood and rear *clamshell*[17] doors. On the 1999 models, these parts are supplied to the plant by Oxford Automotive in Indianapolis.

These are four reasons for Janesville's new *body shop*[18]. Its size, which is 240,000-square-metres, is twice that of the old one.

Figure 12.2.3: Modern manufacturing centre of thermoplastic components (Source: Krauss Maffei, München)

[1] Einsätze	[2] lockern	[3] Griff
[4] Salve	[5] abwehren	[6] scharfe Konkurrenz
[7] (business), auf niedrigen Touren laufen; auf Sparflamme kochen.	[8] Belieferungen	[9] Oberklasse
[10] Freizeitfahrzeuge	[11] Umstellung	[12] Fließband
[13] mittelschwer	[14] Vorgänger	[15] Verdrehungen
[16] Deckbleche; Abschlussbleche	[17] Muschelschale	[18] Karosserierohbau

13 Sales, Logistics and Distribution

13.1 Tax credits support sales

In the USA, all eyes are on General Motors' sales strategy for its EVI, which is offered to customers from 26 outlets in California and Arizona. Customers *lease*[1] rather than buy their EVIs.

Figure 13.1.1: GMs' EV1 (Source: Adam Opel AG, Rüsselsheim)

The EVI is a two-seater coupe, powered by 26 lead-acid batteries, *bristling with*[2] new technology and materials. It has all the features of a modern car: *twin*[3] airbags, *anti-lock brakes*[4], *power steering*[5] and air conditioning. Furthermore you can still plug in your *inductive charger*[6] even if you are standing in a pool of water and it is pouring with rain.

Lease payments are based on a $35,000 *price tag*[7], which the vehicle carries the equivalent of. Tax credit of 10% is given in California, and if you live within California's south coast air quality management district you qualify for a further 5% credit. Vehicles leased in Arizona qualify for a 60% reduction in annual registration fees, equivalent to 5% over the three-year lease.

However there are some costs which have to be paid additionally on top of that:
- For the privilege of being one of the first people to run an all-electric car, $520 and $620 a month has to be paid.
- The *charger*[8], which costs another $1,900 to buy, has to be installed.
- Electricity charges add $440 to the bill each year (a petrol car covering the same mileage would cost $720 a year).

Within the first month more than 70 EVIs went out from the 26 showrooms, although only 30 were scheduled to be leased. The *suspicion*[9] must be that this is more a fashion *fad*[10] than a genuine desire to go electric. If GM could maintain that lease rate, *pundits*[11] on both sides of the Atlantic would be proved wrong.

[1] mieten	[2] to b. with sth., von etwas gespickt sein	[3] doppelt
[4] ABS-Bremsanlage	[5] Hilfskraftlenkung	[6] induktives Aufladegerät
[7] Preisschild	[8] Ladegerät	[9] Verdacht
[10] Marotte	[11] Experten	

13.2 How to trim logistics costs

Nissan Motor Co. Ltd. wishes to trim logistics costs: in the *wake*[1] of cost-cutting decisions from its new Renault management, they have taken management control of Distribution and Auto Service Inc. of Los Angeles, which moves vehicles out of factories, cargo ships, ports and service centers across North America. Renault's global cost-cutting plans for Nissan are to trim 20 percent from total logistics costs over the next three years.

Nissan is a *minority*[2] owner, but will dictate prices for its handling and logistics services to Nissan's U.S. subsidiaries. Their objective is to get the best service for the lowest cost. Nissan will give a target price and the company will be responsible for hitting it. That means that no matter how great the inefficiency or how *unwise*[3] the request, Distribution and Auto Service would carry out the order and send Nissan the bill. If a Nissan sales region wanted the supplier to *expedite*[4] a shipment of cars, Nissan would pay the bill.

For this reason, within a shakeup, Nissan has put a new four-man management board in place for quality, purchasing and logistics. The executive vice president of the service company has been promoted to president and has been voted on the board. By putting executives from Nissan on the Distribution and Auto Service board, the supplier can turn down a request for cost reasons: for example, being able to tell a regional office that asks for something, that this requested way is too expensive and let's do it another way instead. It's easier to do things directly than to go through different layers. *Involvements*[5] will be easier now as own *CEO*[6].

[1] Kielwasser; Sog	[2] Minderheit	[3] unklug; töricht
[4] beschleunigen	[5] Beteiligungen	[6] Vorstandsmitglied (Chief Executive Officer)

14 Aftersales and Service

14.1 General

To answer *queries*[1] from customers quickly and accurately using dealership service staff, car manufacturers have to provide information on all new features and changes to previous models which are required for *maintenance*[2] and repairs. Improvements which are advantageous for customers and dealerships have to be emphasised. In addition, any differences between left-hand and *right-hand drive*[3] vehicles are described. Standard and special equipment car versions may vary as a result of market or legal requirements in individual countries.

Figure 14.1.1: Centre console with automatic transmission of the Fiat Punto (Source: Alexander Voos, Rüsselsheim)

If you buy a vehicle you will get an owner's manual, which should familiarize drivers with the *sophisticated*[4] technology and help them to handle their vehicles expertly. The manual is designed to be clearly laid-out and easily understood. The manual includes indications of dangers which may lead to vehicle damage if they are ignored, and it includes special information for the care and maintenance of vehicles. The service booklet is normally found in the *glove compartment*[5].

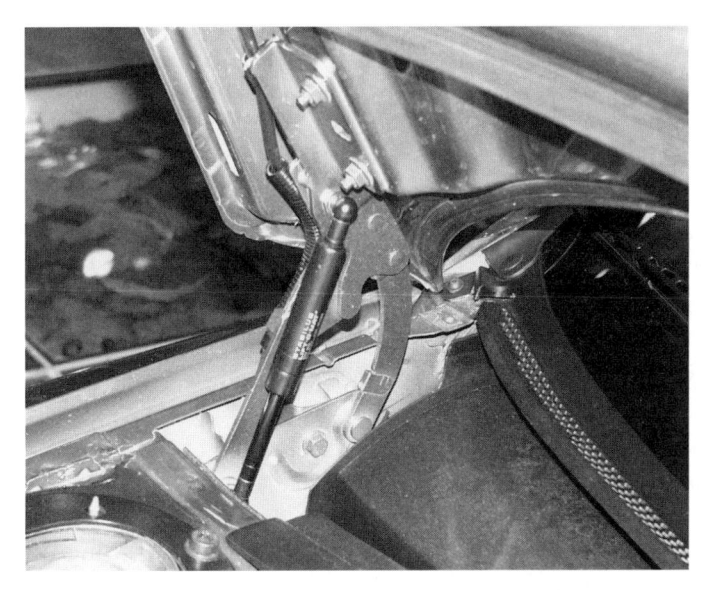

Figure 14.1.2: Bonnet hinge of the Peugeot 406 Coupé (Source: Alexander Voos, Rüsselsheim)

[1] Rückfragen; Fragen	[2] Instandhaltung; Wartung	[3] rechtsgelenkt; Rechtslenkung
[4] hoch entwickelt; hochmodern; ausgeklügelt	[5] Handschuhfach	

14.2 The interior

14.2.1 Instrument panel

Instrument panels consist of *instruments*[1]: ignition and starter switches with *steering column lock*[2], steering wheel adjustment, *horn pushes*[3], *levers for turn signals*[4], *headlamp flash*[5] and *dipped and main beam*[6], buttons for *cruise control*[7], side *ventilation jets*[8], *light switch*[9], *dimmer for instrument illumination*[10], switch for *fog tail lamp*[11], switch for *fog lamp*[12] ,*headlamp range adjustment wheel*[13] (if dipped beam is switched on, headlamp range has to be adjusted to suit vehicle load. Adjustments can be different for sedan, coupé, *station wagon*[14] with *level control*[15], or *delivery van*[16]), levers for windshield wipers and washer system, headlamp washer system, tailgate window washer system, buttons for multi-information display (e.g. time, date, outside temperature, radio, check control), switch for *hazard warning flashers*[17], heating and ventilation controls, switches for air circulation or air conditioning system, switch for heated rear window, *accessory socket*[18] or cigarette lighter, ashtrays, *tray*[19], *stowage compartment*[20], fuse box, radio, infotainment system, driver and front passenger airbags, glove compartment, release lever for engine hood, accelerator pedal, brake pedal and clutch pedal.

Figure 14.2.1.1: Cockpit of Opel Tigra (Source: Adam Opel AG, Rüsselsheim)

There are many control indicators illuminated during driving or parking on the instrument screen. These will remind or warn drivers, e.g. to fasten seat belts, brake system, oil pressure, preheating diesel engines, *anti-lock brake system*[21], electronic *immobilizer*[22], *alternator*[23], electronically controlled engine cooling, turn signal lamps, fog lamps, main beam, fog tail lamp, fuel level, airbag systems, belt tensioners, automatic transmission fault, traction control system, *trailer turn signal*[24], *tachometer*[25], *speedometer*[26], *odometer*[27], *trip odometer*[28], *engine temperature gauge*[29] and *fuel gauge*[30].

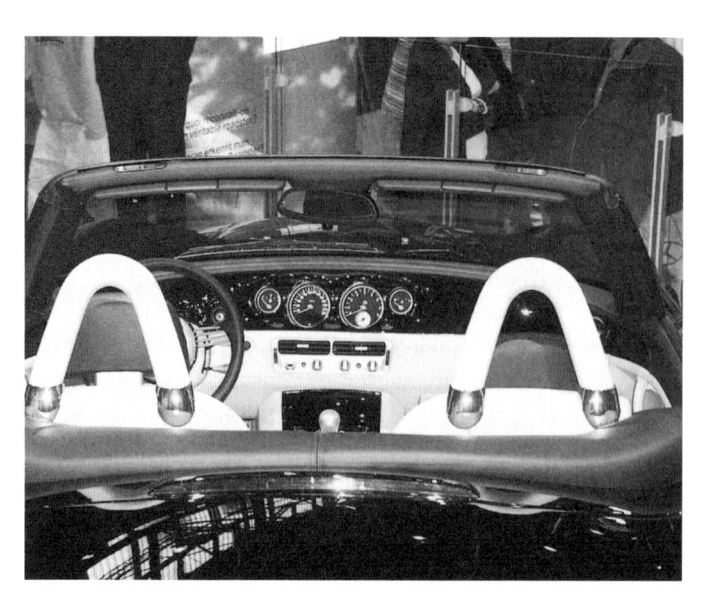

Figure 14.2.1.2: Interior of BMW Z8, seen at Geneva Motor Show in spring 2000 (Source: Alexander Voos, Rüsselsheim)

[1] Instrumente	[2] Lenkradsperre	[3] Signalhorntasten
[4] Schalter für Blinker	[5] Lichthupe	[6] Abblend- und Fernlicht
[7] Geschwindigkeitsregler	[8] Belüftungsdüsen	[9] Lichtschalter
[10] Dimmer für Instrumentenbeleuchtung	[11] Nebelschlussleuchte	[12] Nebelscheinwerfer
[13] Stellrad für Leuchtweitenregulierung	[14] Caravan	[15] Niveauregulierung
[16] Lieferwagen	[17] Warnblinker	[18] Zubehörsteckdose
[19] Ablagefach	[20] Ablagefach	[21] Antiblockiersystem
[22] Wegfahrsperre	[23] Lichtmaschine	[24] Anhängerblinker
[25] Drehzahlmesser	[26] Tachometer	[27] Kilometerzähler
[28] Tageskilometerzähler	[29] Kühlmittel-Temperaturanzeige	[30] Kraftstoffanzeige

14.2.2 Lighting

The information display and ashtray lights illuminate when the ignition is switched on. *Brightness*[1] can be adjusted with a *knurled knob*[2], reverse lamps come on when reverse gear is engaged, a courtesy lamp comes on when a door is opened (if the door is shut, the lamp goes out immediately or after a certain delay), and instrument illumination comes on with *exterior driving lamps*[3]. Reading lamps in the front or rear can be switched on if ignition is activated. The glove compartment is illuminated when the lid is open. The luggage compartment lamp comes on when the tailgate (trunk lid) is opened.

Figure 14.2.2.1: The extraordinary tailgate of the all-wheel-driven Renault Scenic AWD (Source: Alexander Voos, Rüsselsheim)

[1] Helligkeit	[2] Rändelrad	[3] Außenbeleuchtung

14.2.3 Seats

There are several possibilities to adjust the seat to driving or entry positions. *Lumbar support*[1] on front seats has to be adjusted by a handwheel, by pumping a hand pump or by pressing an air release knob.

Seat backrests have to be folded down by pulling up the release lever. *Thigh support*[2] is adjusted by raising and moving the front support pad. Front or rear head restraints have to be set to the position according to the heights of the driver or passenger.

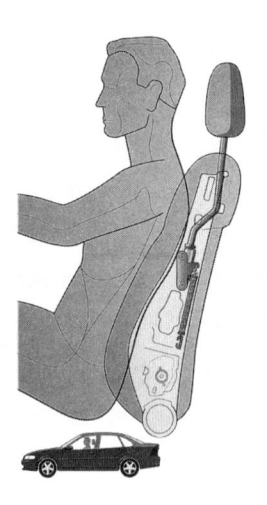

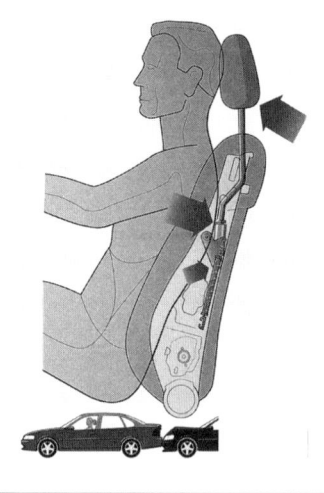

Figure 14.2.3.1: Active headrest[3] *(Source: Adam Opel AG, Rüsselsheim)*

| [1] Lendenwirbelstütze | [2] Oberschenkelauflage | [3] Aktive Kopfstütze |

14.2.4 Load compartment

The *load compartment floor*[1] is equipped with a *storage system*[2], consisting of several units.

Figure 14.2.4.1: Load compartment of Opel Corsa (Source: Adam Opel AG, Rüsselsheim)

For the Opel Corsa, for example, to remove left and right *floor cover*³, both *fastening buttons*⁴ have to be pressed, and the cover released from the *catch*⁵ to allow the cover to be removed. By turning the *locking pins*⁶ and pulling both *storage compartments*⁷ upwards, they can be removed.

The single-piece cover above the *spare wheel*⁸ is not fastened in order to facilitate straightforward removal. *Installation*⁹ is analogous *in reverse order*¹⁰.

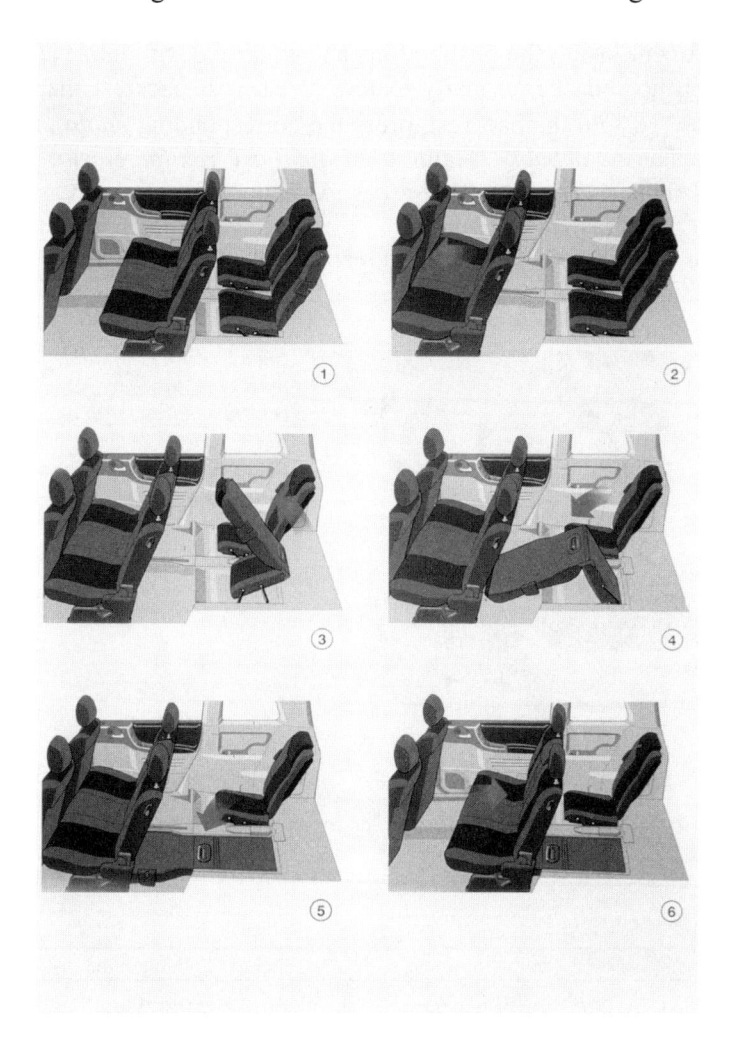

Figure 14.2.4.2: New seat system ("Flex7") of Opel Zafira (Source: Adam Opel AG, Rüsselsheim)

*Estate cars*¹¹ are standard-equipped with a *load compartment cover*¹². To snap it into a *guide*¹³ in the rear *quarter panel*¹⁴ *inner panel*¹⁵, first you have to pull the cover from its cassette. Then, the left and right *pins*¹⁶ of the cover have to be inserted horizontally into the guide, so that they *snap in towards the top*¹⁷ of the vehicle. Estates are also equipped with four lashing eyes (*lash lugs)*¹⁸ in the load department, which are fastened to the load compartment floor and are used for securing luggage and cargo by a luggage or safety net.

For transporting long objects, the luggage compartment can be enlarged if a rear seat backrest features a *loading ease*[19] by a fold-down rear seat backrest. Firstly, fold down the *centre armrest*[20] onto the seat cushion, then actuate the *flap*[21] *lock*[22], pulling the handle and *tilting* the cover *forwards*[23] and open the flap.

Another possibility is to *disengage*[24] one or both rear seat backrests to provide an *ample*[25] load compartment, using the pushbuttons and folding down onto the rear seat cushion. Saloon notchbacks normally feature a rear seat backrest that folds down in two halves. To fold the backrest, press the corresponding *knobs*[26] to the right and/or left. The *notchback*[27] features an *auxiliary reinforcement*[28] welded into the left and right *end panel*[29] floor areas to support rigidity by rear crash or load movements.

The *fastening*[30] of the *warning triangle*[31] of an Opel Corsa is solved by strapping it inside a pocket using rubber straps in the *tailgate inner panelling*[32].

Figure 14.2.4.3: Multiple function of the rear central headrest, seen on BMW Series 3 Touring (Source: Alexander Voos, Rüsselsheim)

[1] Laderaumboden	[2] Ablagesystem	[3] Deckel des Laderaumbodens
[4] Befestigungsknöpfe	[5] Verschluss; Arretierung	[6] Riegel; Anschlagstift
[7] Staufächer	[8] Ersatzrad	[9] Einbau
[10] in umgekehrter Reihenfolge	[11] Caravans	[12] Laderaumabdeckung
[13] Führung	[14] Seitenwand	[15] Innenverkleidung der Seitenwand
[16] Zapfen	[17] nach oben einhaken	[18] Verzurrösen
[19] hier: Durchlademöglichkeit	[20] Mittelarmlehne	[21] Klappe
[22] Verriegelung	[23] vorklappen	[24] ausrasten

[25] reichlich; genügend	[26] Knöpfe	[27] Stufenheck
[28] zusätzliche Verstärkung; Hilfs-; Zusatz-Verstärkung	[29] Rückwand; Verschlussblech	[30] Befestigung
[31] Warndreieck	[32] Innenverkleidung der Heckklappe	

14.2.5 Airbags

The front airbag system will be triggered if the ignition is switched on. When triggered, the front airbag inflates in milliseconds and forms a safety cushion for the driver and front passenger. The risk of injuries to the upper body and head will be reduced. Airbags inflate so quicky that they are often not noticed in an accident.

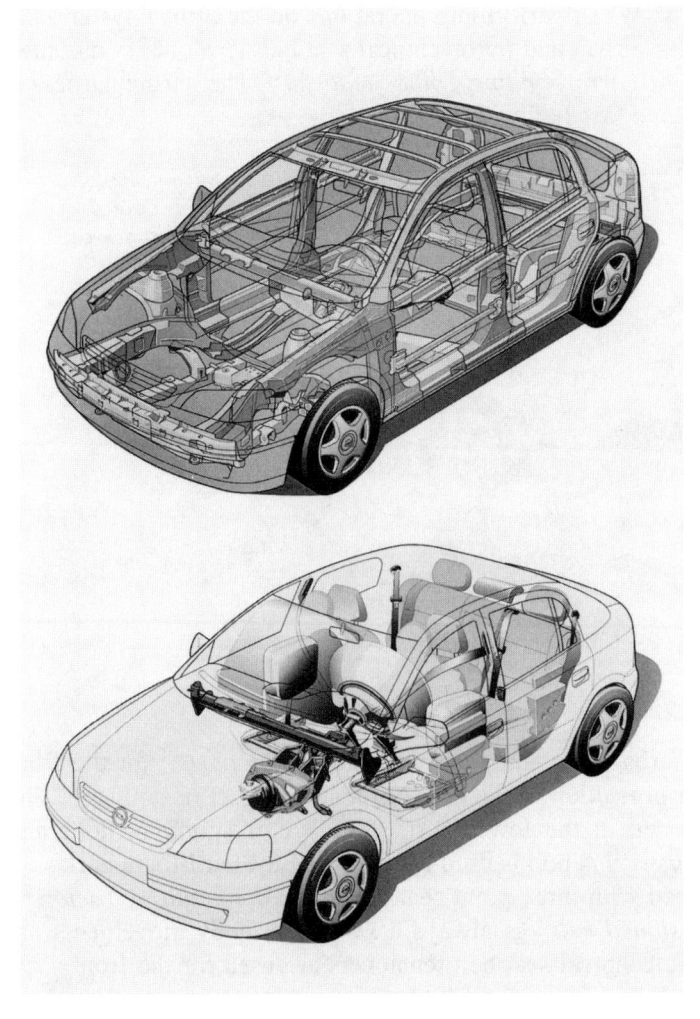

Figure 14.2.5.1: Safety by body structure, full-size airbags, pyrotechnically activated pretensioning device and side airbags of Opel Astra (Source: Adam Opel AG, Rüsselsheim)

All models are available with driver and passenger airbags in combination with *mechanical seat belt tensioners*[1] on front-seats. When the seat belt tensioner is deployed, the *belt lock*[2] is pulled back by a *pre-tensioned*[3] *spring*[4] in the corresponding *energy store*[5] via a *Bowden cable*[6] and *reverse pawl*[7]. This results in reduced *idle play*[8] in the shoulder and *lap belts*[9]. To avoid *unintentional*[10] deployment, the *safety fork*[11] always has to be inserted into the energy store when performing any operation on, and before removing, front seats.

For *saloons*[12], side airbag systems for the front seats are available. The airbag is integrated into the *outer backrest*[13] of the driver and passenger seats. An *appliqué*[14] with the word "Airbag" in coloured lettering identifies the airbags. The airbag is triggered depending on the severity of the accident and on the type of impact. The three-point seat belt must always be correctly fitted. When the side airbag is *deployed*[15], the *upholstery*[16] *tears*[17] open at the *seam*[18] to release it. In this case, the entire seat must always be replaced for safety reasons, as it is a single supplier part only. When performing operations on the airbag system, the *wiring harness plug*[19] for airbag and pyrotechnical seat belt tensioner is mounted in a *retainer*[20] beneath the *corresponding*[21] *outer seat rail*[22]. The wiring harness is routed beneath the seat and fastened with *cable ties*[23].

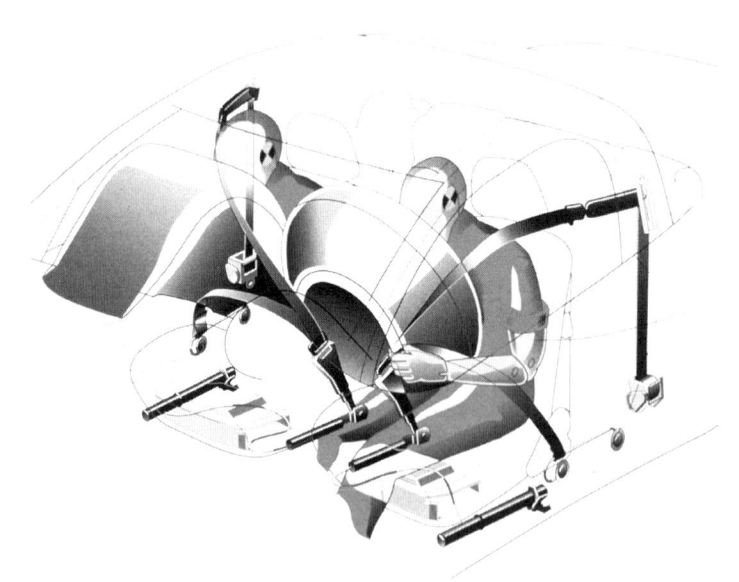

Figure 14.2.5.2: Safety through airbags (Source: Adam Opel AG, Rüsselsheim)

Vehicles with side airbags are equipped with *hard-foam parts*[24] for the front doors to add passenger protection in the event of a side impact or collision. The hard-foam part is inserted in the lower part of each corresponding door and *aligned*[25] with the *channels*[26]. A bolt is used for fastening the hard-foam part.

Vehicles are equipped with three-point seat belts *with automatic retractors*[27]. Although a *spring tensioned belt*[28] is always a *snug fit*[29], body movements are allowed. However, pyrotechnical seat belt tensioners are used for the front seats in vehicles with side airbags. These tensioners are fastened to the front seats at the height of the inner front-seat rail. Pyrotechnical systems are deployed selectively depending on the type of impact or collision. The control unit stores the number of deployments and must be replaced if the driver, passenger, or sideairbags are deployed.

Figure 14.2.5.3: A seat belt anchor fitting and belt guidance, seen on the Citroen Evasion (Source: Alexander Voos, Rüsselsheim)

[1] mechanische Gurtstraffer	[2] Gurtschloss	[3] vorgespannt
[4] Feder	[5] Kraftspeicher	[6] Bowdenzug
[7] Rücklauf-Sperrklinke	[8] Leerweg	[9] Beckengurt; Hüftgurt
[10] ungewollt	[11] Sicherungsgabel	[12] Limousinen
[13] Außenseite der Rückenlehne	[14] Aufnäher	[15] ausgelöst
[16] Sitzbezug	[17] reißen; zerreißen	[18] Naht
[19] Kabelsatzstecker	[20] Haltevorrichtung	[21] entsprechend
[22] äußere Sitzschiene	[23] Kabelbindern	[24] Hartschaumteile
[25] ausgerichtet	[26] Kanäle; Rinnen	[27] Aufroll- und Blockierautomatik
[28] federbelasteter Gürtel	[29] am Körper anliegen	

14.3 Chassis equipment

14.3.1 Brakes

Traffic safety is inextricably associated with brakes. There are some rules to ensure safe driving:

Wear of *brake pads*[1] must not exceed a certain limit. *Worn down*[2] brake pads to a minimum thickness will *squeal*[3]. Therefore regular maintenance is necessary.

After newly approved disc brake pads have been fitted, unnecessary hard braking is not allowed.

The braking system comprises two separate, *diagonally split*[4] *brake circuits*[5] to allow stopping of the vehicle if one brake circuit should fail. A regular check of the brake fluid level is necessary.

The mechanical hand brake acts on disc brakes or drum brakes on the rear wheels.

Figure 14.3.1.1: Chassis of Opel Zafira (Source: Adam Opel AG, Rüsselsheim)

During braking, the anti-lock brake system prevents the wheels from *locking*[6] by continuous monitoring of the vehicle's brake system and regulating the brake pressure as soon as a wheel shows a tendency to lock. In the event of heavy braking or even *full-on braking*[7] on *bends*[8] or when *swerving to avoid an obstacle*[9], the vehicle remains steerable. If the brake pedal is *pulsating*[10] with noise, the ABS is working. Even if pulsating, the brake pedal should be *fully depressed*[11] throughout the braking process by the driver.

Figure 14.3.1.2: CAD-made drawing of braking system. (Source: Continental Teves, Frankfurt)

All models are equipped with either front-wheel and rear-wheel *disc brakes*[12], or front-wheel disc brakes and rear-wheel drum brakes. Brake specifications correspond to the individual engine versions and body styles.

All models are equipped with ABS. The *hydraulic modulator*[13] is positioned in the engine compartment. The *control unit*[14] and *wiring harness plug*[15] are directly connected to the hydraulic modulator.

All models are equipped with a *brake proportioning valve*[16] at the rear-wheel brake. Depending on the model, the valve is either pressure- or *load-dependent*[17]. *Pressure-depending*[18] brake proportioning valves are installed to the side along the *latter part*[19] of the *rear brake lines*[20] in the area of the *rear axle*[21]. Load dependent brake proportioning valves are installed on the *vehicle underbody*[22] and connected to the rear axle via a spring. Load-dependent *compression*[23] of the rear axle is responsible for *proportioning*[24] the braking force accordingly.

[1] Bremsbeläge	[2] abgefahren; abgetragen	[3] Schleifgeräusche verursachen
[4] diagonal geteilt	[5] Bremskreise	[6] Blockieren
[7] Vollbremsung	[8] Kurven	[9] Ausweichmanöver
[10] pulsieren	[11] stark durchgetreten	[12] Scheibenbremsen
[13] Hydroaggregat	[14] Steuergerät	[15] Kabelsatzstecker
[16] Bremskraftregler	[17] lastabhängig	[18] druckabhängig
[19] im letzten Teil	[20] hintere Bremsleitungen	[21] Hinterachse
[22] Fahrzeugunterbau	[23] Einfederung	[24] zuteilen; dosieren; steuern

14.3.2 Wheels and tyres

In handling with wheels and *tyres*[1], the following rules are essential to observe to protect drivers and other road users:
– Only use suitable tyres and *rims*[2].
– New tyres should be fitted in pairs or sets. Tyres on one axle should be the same size, design, *make*[3] and *tread pattern*[4].
– Tyre inflation pressure has to be checked prior to any long journey when cold.
– Driving over *sharp edges*[5] has to be avoided to minimize the danger of tyre *blowout*[6].
– Regular checking of tyres for damage by *foreign bodies*[7], *punctures*[8], *cuts*[9], *cracks*[10], or *bulges*[11] in sidewalls to avoid *bursting*[12].
– Check *tread depth*[13] regularly. If a depth of 2-3 mm is reached, tyres should be replaced to avoid danger of aquaplaning.
– M+S tyres should be fitted on all wheels as they improve safety.

The meaning of tyre designation, e.g. 195/65 R15-84H: tyre width in mm (195), *aspect ratio*[14] in % (65), belt type (R= radial), rim diameter in inches (15), *load index*[15] (84), *speed code*[16] (H= up to 210 km/h).

If a wheel has to be changed for a *spare wheel*[17] or *temporary spare wheel*[18], a *jack*[19] has to be taken. The vehicle is raised by turning the *crank handle*[20] of the jack. Any replaced *defective*[21] tyre should be repaired and wheels *balanced*[22].

[1] Reifen	[2] Felgen	[3] hier: Fabrikat
[4] Profilausführung	[5] scharfe Kanten	[6] Platzen
[7] Fremdkörper	[8] Stiche	[9] Schnitte
[10] Risse	[11] Beulen	[12] Platzen
[13] Profiltiefe	[14] Querschnittsverhältnis	[15] Tragfähigkeits-Kennzahl
[16] Geschwindigkeits-Kennbuchstabe	[17] Ersatzrad	[18] Notrad
[19] Wagenheber	[20] Kurbel	[21] defekt
[22] ausgewuchtet		

14.3.3 Special safety features

In modern vehicles you will find some special safety features as standard equipment. A traction control system is one of them.

A traction control system prevents the *driving wheels*[1] from *spinning*[2], *irrespective*[3] of the road condition and *tyre grip*[4], by monitoring the rotational speed of all wheels and reduction of engine power output at spinning. If necessary, a spinning driving wheel can be braked to improve the vehicle's *directional control*[5], particularly on snow, ice, wet or slippery roads.

Figure 14.3.3.1.: Opel Zafira (Source: Adam Opel AG, Rüsselsheim)

This safety feature should not *tempt*[6] drivers into taking risks when driving, because safe driving can only be achieved through a responsible driving style.

By keeping the level at the rear of the vehicle up when heavily laden, handling will be significantly improved. This will be reached by a so-called *level control system*[7], with a pressure valve to be pumped up with a commercially available pump.

A *cruise control*[8] makes it possible to store and maintain constant speed. It is not recommended to use this feature *in heavy traffic*[9] or on *winding*[10], slippery or *greasy*[11] roads. The stored speed is erased when the ignition is switched off.

[1] Antriebsräder	[2] Durchdrehen	[3] unabhängig
[4] Griffigkeit der Reifen	[5] Fahrstabilität	[6] verleiten
[7] Niveauregulierung	[8] Geschwindigkeitsregler	[9] starker Verkehr
[10] kurvenreich	[11] schmierig	

14.3.4 Handling with caravans and trailers

The installation of *towing equipment*[1] is necessary to tow caravans or trailers. A removable *coupling ball bar*[2] will be fitted by removing the *sealing plug*[3] from the hole, checking the *tensioning*[4] and *inserting*[5] the coupling ball bar. If the anti-theft device is locked, vehicles may be driven. *A breakaway stopping cable*[6] has to be attached to an *eye*[7] in case caravan or trailers have their own brake.

The *permissible caravan/trailer load*[8], which is the difference between the *actual*[9] *gross mass*[10] of the caravan/trailer and the actual *coupling socket load*[11] with the caravan/trailer *coupled*[12], must not be exceeded. The coupling socket load is the load *exerted*[13] by the trailer/caravan on the *coupling ball*[14]. To check caravan/trailer load against *vehicle papers*[15], the *jockey wheel*[16] should not stand on the *weighing apparatus*[17]. In *mountainous territories*[18] and in *higher elevations*[19], a decrease of the engine output may not fully utilize permissible caravan/trailer loads.

Handling[20] is greatly influenced by the loading of the trailer/caravan. It is advised to use a *stabilizer*[21] to damp *rolling motions*[22] in the case of trailers/caravans with low *directional stability*[23]. During driving, *swaying*[24] of trailers/caravans is only to be prevented by slow driving. Starting on *inclines*[25] needs a high *engine speed*[26].

[1] Zugvorrichtung	[2] Kugelstange	[3] Verschlussstopfen
[4] Spannstellung	[5] Einsetzen	[6] Abreißseil
[7] Öse	[8] Zulässige Anhängelasten	[9] tatsächlich
[10] Gesamtgewicht	[11] Stützlast	[12] im angekoppelten Zustand; gekoppelt
[13] drücken	[14] Kupplungskugel	[15] Fahrzeugpapiere

[16] Bugrad	[17] Waage	[18] Gebirge
[19] größere Höhen	[20] Fahrverhalten	[21] Stabilisator
[22] Schlingerbewegungen	[23] Fahrstabilität	[24] pendeln; Pendelbewegungen
[25] Steigungen	[26] Motordrehzahl	

14.3.5 Steering

The EPS control unit features a new bracket in vehicles with EPS. It is normally positioned *level*[1] to the bracket behind the *fuse box*[2].

There are different types of steering wheels, depending on the equipment version: 2-*spoke*[3], 3-spoke or 4-spoke airbag steering wheels.

Figure 14.3.5.1: Cutaway of Electric Power Steering EPS (Source: Adam Opel AG, Rüsselsheim)

[1] eben; waagrecht	[2] Sicherungskasten	[3] Speichen

14.4 Heating, Ventilation, Air Conditioning

By mixing cold and hot air the temperature can be regulated without delay and held constant at all speeds. Temperature, *fan*[1] and air distribution (to *defrosters*[2], to front and rear foot area, to head area, or to provide *demisting*[3] of windows), can be adjusted mainly by *rotary switches*[4]. *Air circulation systems*[5] are switched on by pushing buttons. This prevents entry of outside air, so the system has to be switched on if unpleasant *odours*[6] *penetrate*[7] from outside.

The airflow can be directed as desired by *tilting*[8] and *swivelling*[9] the *fins*[10] of the *ventilation jets*[11]. To increase air supply, the fan has to be set to a higher speed. *Door window defroster vents*[12] can be used to direct air onto the windshield and onto the door windows.

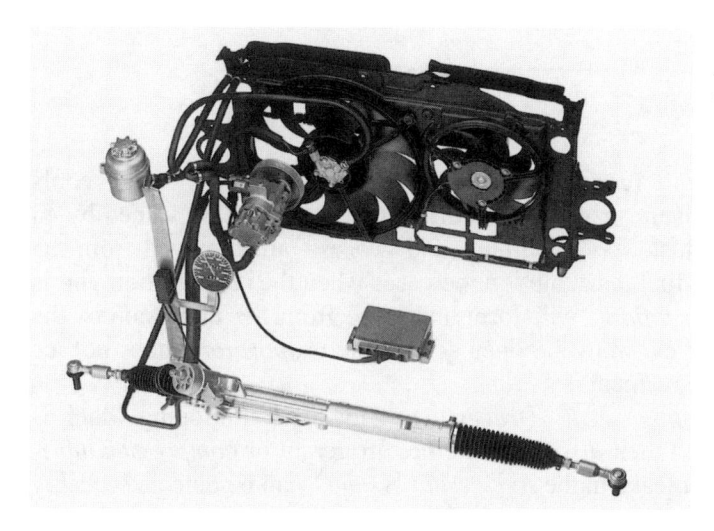

Figure 14.4.1: A hydraulic powered fan for the Audi A8 engine compartment (Source: ZF Friedrichshafen AG, Schwäbisch Gmünd)

The amount of heat is dependent on the engine temperature. For rapid warming of the passenger compartment, the temperature switch and the fan has to be set to the highest position and the air circulation should be switched on briefly.

Diesel engines are now standard-equipped with electric heater elements to *supersede*[13] the previous *fuel-powered*[14] ones. The advantages include a more *straightforward*[15] system design and immediate heat availability in the passenger department. The electric heater element is located in the lower half of the *vent housing*[16]. The central element consists of a *ceramic semi-conductor*[17] (PTC stones) which is supplied with *voltage*[18] via *contact plates*[19] to provide heat. The heat is introduced via *corrugated fins*[20] into the circulating airflow that *emerges*[21] through the *heating nozzles*[22]. As the engine temperature increases, the output of the electric heater element is reduced via the *engine control unit*[23]. The output is also modulated by the engine control unit in the event of *excessive load*[24] on the vehicle *electricity supply*[25], e.g. from too many active electrical consumers.

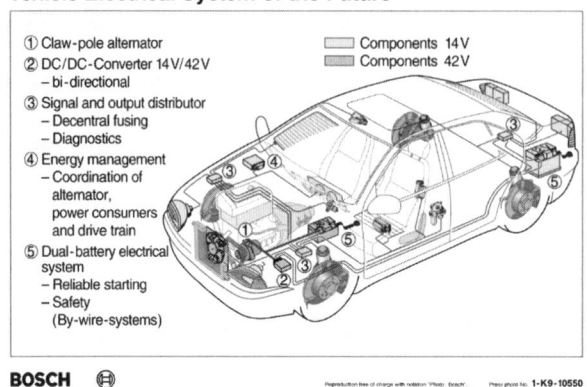

Figure 14.4.2: Vehicle electricity (Source: Robert Bosch GmbH, Stuttgart)

Vehicle Electrical System of the Future

① Claw-pole alternator
② DC/DC-Converter 14V/42V
  – bi-directional
③ Signal and output distributor
  – Decentral fusing
  – Diagnostics
④ Energy management
  – Coordination of alternator, power consumers and drive train
⑤ Dual-battery electrical system
  – Reliable starting
  – Safety
  (By-wire-systems)

Components 14V
Components 42V

BOSCH

The *refrigeration unit*[26] (compressor) of the *air conditioning system*[27] cools the air and removes moisture from it. The inflowing outside air is cleaned by an air filter. In this way, dust, *soot*[28], *pollen*[29] and *spores*[30] are removed from the inflowing air. However, fuel consumption increases when the refrigeration unit is on. Furthermore, *condensation*[31] will form and issue from the underside of the vehicle. At least one air exit must be open so that the *evaporator*[32] does not ice up due to a lack of air movement.

There is a *leak detecting agent*[33] (*tracer dye*[34]) for air conditioning which is located in the *dryer*[35] and then *dissolves*[36] in the refrigerant or *compressor lubricant*[37]. Even the smallest leaks in the *refrigerant system*[38] can be detected reliably by using *fluorescent*[39] colours. To detect the tracer dye a UV lamp and special glasses are needed.

[1] Gebläse	[2] Entfrostung	[3] Entfeuchtung
[4] Drehschalter	[5] Umluftsysteme	[6] Gerüche
[7] belästigen	[8] Kippen	[9] Schwenken
[10] Lamellen	[11] Belüftungsdüsen	[12] Seitenscheibenentfrosterdüsen
[13] verdrängen; überflüssig machen	[14] kraftstoffbetrieben	[15] einfach; unkompliziert
[16] Lüftungsgehäuse	[17] keramisches Halbleiterelement	[18] elektrische Spannung
[19] Kontaktbleche	[20] Wellrippen	[21] herauskommen; austreten
[22] Heizungsdüsen	[23] Motorsteuergerät	[24] zu hohe Belastung
[25] Stromversorgung	[26] Kälteteil	[27] Klimaanlage
[28] Ruß	[29] Pollen	[30] Sporen

³¹ Kondenswasser	³² Verdampfer	³³ Leckerkennungsmittel
³⁴ Signalfarbe	³⁵ Trockner	³⁶ auflösen
³⁷ Verdichter-Schmiermittel	³⁸ Kältemittelsystem	³⁹ fluoreszierend

14.5 Optional equipment, acccessories

Optional equipment[1] includes the Radio Navigation System, which is a combination of radio, CD player and navigation system, providing the driver with assistance for "negotiating" in traffic. It enables automatic travel route planning and *directional guidance*[2] without having to use conventional *maps*[3]. An up-to-date layout of the entire road network within a country, including city maps, is stored on a CD-ROM.

At the start of the journey, the driver enters the destination and activates "directional guidance". The system computes the current vehicle location on a continuous basis and provides instructions to the driver for the optimal route to the destination.

In the event that the system is no longer able to determine the vehicle location, the driver can enter the data manually.

Travel instructions are relayed over loudspeakers and on a display. A Global Positioning System GPS *receiving unit*[4] continuously computes the current vehicle location by means of a *gyro compass*[5] and the vehicle *odometer*[6] signal. The navigation computer compares the vehicle location against a digital street map stored on a CD ROM.

Figure 14.5.1:New type of rear mounted aerials, seen on BMW vehicles (Source: Alexander Voos, Rüsselsheim)

The aerial is usually installed on the rear roof, and an *amplifier*[7] is installed in the base of the aerial. The vehicle should be outdoors for *unimpeded reception*[8]. Poor reception, including *reception failure*[9], is possible in buildings, in tunnels, on ferries, etc.

Audio and visual information can be set for the desired language. In order to set the desired language, a language CD is necessary.

Other accessories are child seat safety system for the outer rear seats: such belts are *assemblied ex work*[10] or are *retrofitted*[11].

[1] Sonderausstattung	[2] Richtungsführung	[3] Straßenkarten
[4] Empfangseinheit	[5] Kreiselkompass	[6] Wegstreckenzähler; Kilometerzähler
[7] Verstärker	[8] ungestörter Empfang	[9] hier: Empfangsaussetzer
[10] werksseitig montiert	[11] nachträglich eingebaut	

14.6 Engine, attaching parts

The main differences between old and new engines are the *omission*[1] of *secondary air injection*[2]. Other new features include:

– *Engine control unit*[3] of *composite design*[4], instead of *printed circuit boards*[5]. The engine control unit is located, for example, in the *footwell*[6] of the passenger's side or in the engine compartment on the *cylinder head*[7].
– *Ignition module*[8] with *single ignition coils*[9] and integrated spark plug *connectors*[10] are in, *dual spark ignition coils*[11] are out.
– Modified *injection pattern*[12].
– New ripped *V-belt tensioner*[13].
– Improved *tank vent valve*[14].
– New *exhaust gas recirculation valve*[15] (mainly fitted directly onto the cylinder head).
– Heated *oxygen sensor*[16].
– *Catalytic converter*[17] with increased volume.
– The *fuel pressure regulator*[18] is no longer installed on the *fuel distributor pipe*[19], but is a component of the fuel tank, because the *fuel system has no return*[20].
– The composite-construction *engine control unit*[21] is *secured*[22] directly on the intake *manifold module*[23].
– New *flat-head pistons*[24] and *con-rods*[25] are of lightmass design.

Figure 14.6.1: Almost completely covered engine compartment of the Peugeot 607 (Source: Alexander Voos, Rüsselsheim)

But there are a lot of other new engine attaching parts found in the engine compartment. For examples:
- Knock sensor[26]
- Intake pipe pressure sensor[27]
- Crankshaft pulse pick-up[28]
- Intake air temperature sensor[29]
- Throttle valve potentiometer[30]
- Idle speed stepper motor[31]
- Coolant temperature sensor[32]
- Camshaft sensor[33]
- Hot film mass air flow meter[34]

Figure 14.6.2: New L850 engine of Opel Speedster (Source: Adam Opel AG, Rüsselsheim)

Between different engines there are important differences in size and type of components:
- *Toothed belt tensioner roller*[35]
- Diameter of *inlet valve head*[36], *valve stem*[37] and *cylinder bore*[38]
- *Length of stroke*[39]
- Elastomeric or liquid *seal*[40] of *oil pan gasket*[41]
- *Sheet-metal oil filter cartridge*[42] or *oil filter housing*[43] with an oil filter insert[44] as paper replacement cartridge[45]
- *Crescent oil pump*[46] or *rotor-type oil pump*[47]
- Conventional and improved-performance *coolant pump*[48]
- Cylinder head with external or internal *crankcase ventilation*[49]
- Intake manifold module with *uniform*[50], not variable, or variable *intake pipe*[51] lengths.
- Different engine management systems
- *Fuel feed lines*[52] and *fuel return lines*[53] with pressure regulator at the fuel distribution pipe, or use of fuel system without return (omission of the fuel return line in the engine compartment).

[1] Wegfall	[2] Sekundärlufteinblasung	[3] Motorsteuergerät
[4] Hybridbauweise	[5] Leiterplatten	[6] Fußraum
[7] Zylinderkopf	[8] Zündmodul	[9] Einzelzündspulen
[10] Zündkerzenstecker	[11] Doppelfunkenzündspulen	[12] geändertes Einspritzbild
[13] Keilrippenriemen-Spannvorrichtung	[14] Tankentlüftungsventil	[15] Abgasrückführventil
[16] beheizte Lambda-Sonde	[17] Katalysator	[18] Kraftstoffdruckregler
[19] Kraftstoffverteilerrohr	[20] rücklauffreies Kraftstoffsystem	[21] Motorsteuergerät in Hybridbauweise
[22] gesichert; befestigt	[23] Saugmodul	[24] Flachkolben
[25] Pleuelstangen	[26] Klopfsensor	[27] Fühler des Saugrohrdrucks
[28] Kurbelwellen-Impulsaufnehmer	[29] Sensor-Ansauglufttemperatur	[30] Drosselklappenpotentiometer
[31] Leerlaufschrittmotor	[32] Kühlmitteltemperatur-Sensor	[33] Nockenwellensensor
[34] Heißfilm-Luftmassenmesser	[35] Zahnriemen-Spannrolle	[36] Einlassventilteller
[37] Ventilschaft	[38] Zylinderbohrung	[39] Hublänge
[40] Dichtungsmittel	[41] Ölwannendichtung	[42] Blechölfilterpatrone
[43] Ölfiltergehäuse	[44] Ölfiltereinsatz	[45] Papierwechselpatrone
[46] Sichelölpumpe	[47] Rotorölpumpe	[48] Kühlmittelpumpe
[49] Kurbelgehäuseentlüftung	[50] einheitlich	[51] Saugrohr
[52] Kraftstoffvorlaufleitung	[53] Kraftstoffrücklaufleitung	

14.7 Exhaust systems

On vehicles with a catalytic converter, the following recommendations are given:
- *Leaded fuel*[1] will damage the converters and parts of the electronic systems.
- *Misfiring*[2], irregular engine running and significant loss of engine power indicate a fault in the ignition system and may damage catalytic converters.
- Frequent cold starts, actuation of the starter for an unnecessarily long time during starting, allowing the tank to become empty and starting the engine by pushing or towing lead to unburnt fuel entering the catalytic converter, which will become overheated and irreparably damaged.

The *proportion*[3] of *noxious*[4] materials in the *exhaust*[5], e.g. carbon monoxide CO, *hydrocarbons*[6] CH and *nitrogen oxides*[7] NO_x, is reduced to a minimum by correct proportion of these *poisonous constituents*[8], through design-related measures of *mixture formation system*[9] and ignition system. Electronic testing systems at dealers or authorized service operations permit rapid *diagnosis*[10] and *remedying of faults*[11].

[1] verbleiter Kraftstoff	[2] Fehlzündungen	[3] Anteil
[4] schädlich, giftig	[5] Abgas	[6] Kohlenwasserstoffe
[7] Stickoxide	[8] giftige Schadstoffe	[9] Gemischbildner
[10] Diagnose	[11] Korrektur von Fehlern	

14.8 Clutch, transmission

The transmission is fully synchronised and also has a synchronised reverse gear. There is a two-part transmission housing, which is sealed using a liquid sealing agent. The transmission can be identified using the labelling given on the housing for *output ratio*[1], year of production, current production number and part number, *barcode label*[2] for *production control*[3] in the manufacturing plants.

How does one operate a car with automatic *transmission*[4]?

The *selector level*[5] has to be shifted out of the "P" position only when the ignition is switched on and the brake pedal is depressed at the same time, thus preventing the vehicle from unintentionally driving off. A locking mechanism prevents the ignition key from being moved to any position other than "P".

How does manual transmission work?

The power in the transmission flows via the *drive shaft*[6] and the corresponding gears directly or via the *intermediate shaft*[7] to the *output shaft*[8]. The power is transmitted to the *differential*[9] and then on to the drive shafts via the *output gear set*[10].

[1] Abtriebsübersetzung	[2] Barcodeaufkleber	[3] Produktionssteuerung
[4] Getriebe	[5] Wählhebel	[6] Antriebswelle
[7] Zwischenwelle	[8] Abtriebswelle	[9] Ausgleichsgetriebe
[10] Abtriebsradsatz		

14.9 Electrical equipment, instruments

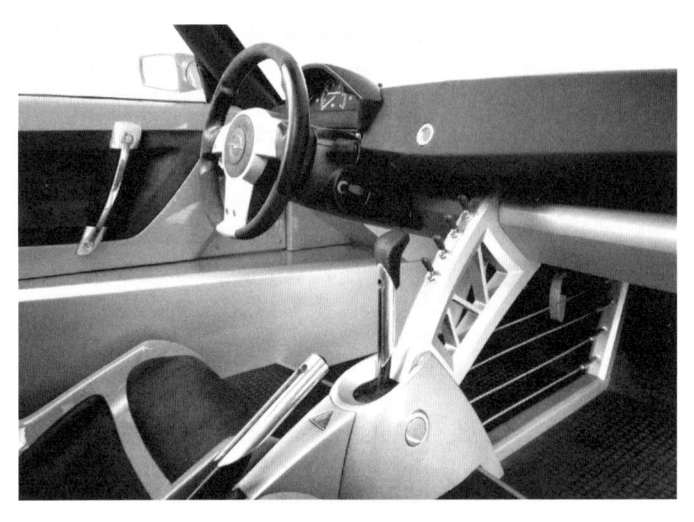

Figure 14.9.1: The passenger compartment of the Opel Speedster (Source: Adam Opel AG, Rüsselsheim)

An *anti-theft warning system*[1] includes a *glass breakage sensor*[2] and *tilt sensor*[3]. The vehicle interior is constantly monitored by an *ultrasound microphone*[4] when the warning system is switched on. Breaking a *glass pane*[5] activates sound in the ultrasound range. This sound is detected by the microphone, which then activates the anti-theft warning system via the control unit. The tilt sensor *triggers*[6] the alarm if the vehicle is raised but the tyres have not been lifted off the ground (e.g. for tyre theft).

Electrically adjustable^7 swing-out type rear windows^8 are activated using a *rocker switch^9* in the *switch console^{10}* for *front interior illumination^{11}*.

The fuse box is located in the vehicle passenger compartment. To exchange fuses, the *stowage compartment^{12}* normally has to be *swivelled down^{13}* to its *full extent^{14}*. A defective fuse can be recognized by its melted wire.

^{1} Diebstahlwarnanlage	^{2} Glasbruchsensor	^{3} Neigungsgeber; Winkelsensor
^{4} Ultraschall-Mikrofon	^{5} Glasscheibe	^{6} auslösen
^{7} elektrisch verstellbar	^{8} hinteres Ausstellfenster	^{9} Wipptaste
^{10} Schalterkonsole	^{11} vord. Innenraumbeleuchtung	^{12} Ablagefach
^{13} nach unten schwenken	^{14} voll und ganz	

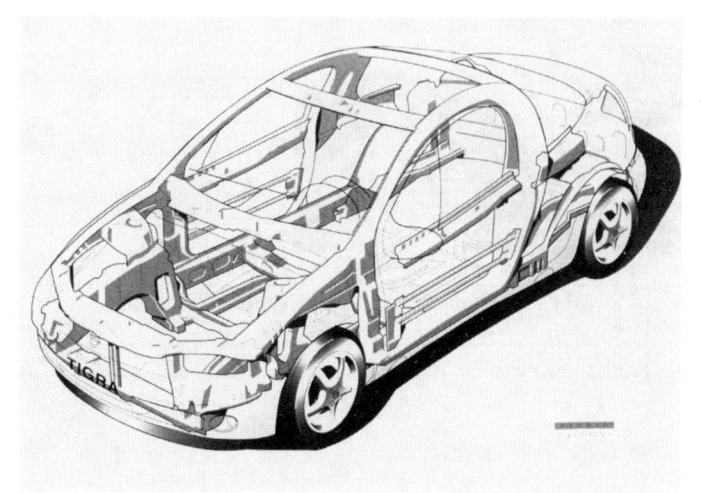

Figure 14.9.2: Safety framework of the Opel Tigra (Source: Adam Opel AG, Rüsselsheim)

14.10 Body parts

An open *front panelling^1* is designed for all models, being either *coarse grained^2* and unpainted or partly painted. Saloons or estates feature different rear panelling designs, depending on the equipment version. There are either square or oval *license plate lamps^3*.

Car models are standard equipment for *sill panels*[4] with a PVC *stone protector*[5] which is *painted*[6].

Figure 14.10.1: Rear entrance of VW Sharan with door sill and its cover (Source: Alexander Voos, Rüsselsheim)

[1] Frontverkleidung als offene Version	[2] genarbt; grobkörnig	[3] Kennzeichenleuchten
[4] Einstiegsschwellern	[5] Steinschlagschutz	[6] überlackiert

Appendix

Vocabulary German – English

German	English	Page
3-Schicht-Betrieb	three-shift operation	228
abändern; verbessern	amend	225
Abblend- und Fernlicht	dipped and main beam	235
Abblendlicht	low beam	172
Abbruch	break-off	221
abdichten	sealing	119, 153
abfallen; ansteigen	slope	71
Abgas	exhaust	255
Abgasgegendruck; Abgasstaudruck	exhaust back pressure	141
Abgaskrümmer	exhaust manifolds	206
Abgasrückführungsventil; Abgasrückführventil	exhaust-gas recirculation valve	221, 252
Abgasschalldämpfer	silencer	162
Abgasschalldämpfer; Auspufftopf	exhaust muffler	119
Abgassystem; Auspuffsystem	exhaust system	71
abgedichtet; eingeschweißt; versiegelt	sealed	133
abgefahren; abgetragen	worn down	243
abgelaufen; verfallen	expired	143
abgelenkt	diverted	221
abgeneigt	opposed	58
abgeneigt	reluctant	193
abgenommen	commissioned	226
abgeschirmt, entstört	shielded	87
abgeschliffen	sanded	116
abgesenkt	lowered	66
abgestrahlt	radiated	179
abgetrennt	segregated	126
Abhängigkeit; Empfindlichkeit	sensitivity	208
Abknicken; Ausbeulen	buckling	208
Abkömmling	derivative	203
Ablagefach	tray	235
Ablagefach	stowage compartment	235, 257
Ablagefächer	package trays	200
Ablagesystem	storage system	238
Ablaufplan	flow chart	62
ableiten; abführen	dissipating	84
ableiten; herleiten	deriving	127

ablenken	can head off	98
Abnutzung, Verschleiß, Erosion	abrasion	130
Abonnent (in)	subscriber	91, 121
Abreißseil	a breakaway stopping cable	247
absatzweise, periodisch auftretend	intermittently	164
Absaugung; Entlüftung	extraction	183
ABS-Bremsanlage	anti-lock brakes	232
Abschalter	cut-out	85
Abscheiderkolben	separator piston	153
Abschleppfahrzeug	tow-tractor (US: tow truck)	121
Abschleppfahrzeug; Abschleppwagen	breakdown lorry (wrecker truck)	16
absplittern	chipping	192
absteigend	descending	48
abstimmen; abgleichen	match	55
Abstreifer	scrapers	154
Abtriebsradsatz	output gear set	256
Abtriebsübersetzung	output ratio	255
Abtriebswelle	output shaft	256
abwehren	fending off	229
abweichen	departs	74
Achslastverteilung	axle load distribution	197
Achsschenkel	steering knuckles	71
Achswelle; Antriebswelle	drive shaft	143
Acrylnitril-Butadien-Styrol	abs	179
Acryl-Polymerisat	acrylic polymers	193
aggressiv; hart	tough	225
Aktien	shares	51
Aktiva; Deckungsforderungen; (Konkurs)masse, Betriebsvermögen	assets	
Aktive Kopfstütze	active headrest	238
Alarmanlage	alarm system	171
alarmieren	alert	90
Aldehyde	aldehydes	128
Algorithmus	algorithm	167
Allrad-Antrieb	all-wheel-drive	69
altern	age	195
alternd	ageing (GB), aging (US)	38
Alterung	ageing	199
Aluminium	aluminium (GB), aluminum (US)	81, 84
am Körper anliegen	snug fit	242
am laufenden Band produzieren (etwas)	churning out (to churn out sth.)	74
Anerkennen	validated	55
anfällig	vulnerable	44
anfangen	commencing, commence	127, 228
anfänglich	incipient	199
angetrieben	powered	66
Angleich-Drehpunkt, Angleichregler	torque control fulcrum	175
angrenzend	adjoining	183

angrenzend; direkt neben	adjacent to	228
Anguss; Beschicker	feeders	197
Anhaltspunkte	cues	80
Anhängefahrzeug	towed vehicle	16
Anhänger	trailer	16
Anhängerblinker	trailer turn signal	236
Anhänger-Zugmaschine	trailer towing vehicle	16
Anklang finden	to catch on	190
Annahme; Übernahme	adoption	95
Anpassungsformen	flexible forming	209
anregen	whet	44
Anreiz; Ansporn	incentive	226
Anschaffung; Einkauf	purchased	220
Anschlussstück	fitting	195, 205
Anschuldigung	allegation	37
anspornen	spur	137
Ansprechverhalten des Motors (auf Drosselklappenbefehle)	throttle response	144
Anspringtemperatur; Ansprechtemperatur	light-off temperature	141
anstacheln	juice	
Anteil	proportion	255
anthropometrische Beständigkeit	anthropometric consistency	79
Antiblockiersystem	anti-lock brake system	236
Antrieb; Antriebsstrang	drive line	122
Antrieb; Getriebe	transmission	71
Antriebsräder	driving wheels	246
Antriebsstrang (Motor + Getriebe)	powertrain	65
Antriebswelle	drive shaft	176, 256
Anwendungsspezifischer integrierter Schaltkreis	asic (application-specific integrated circuit)	170
Aramidfaser; AFK-Faser	aramid fibres	85
Arbeitskosten	cost of labour	105
Armaturenanlage	dashboard	133
Armaturenbrett; Instrumententafel	instrument panel	87
Armaturenbrett-Einlage	dash panel insert	206
Armaturentafel, Instrumentenbrett	instrument-panel	65
Armaturentafel-Träger	ip beams	206
A-Säule Innenblech oben	a-pillar inner (panel) upper	212
A-Säule Innenblech unten	a-pillar inner (panel) lower	212
Asche	ash	195
Ästhetik	aesthetics	190
Asynchronmotor; Induktionsmotor	asynchronous motor	125
Atmung	respiration	193
Ätzung; abätzen	etching	193
auf etwas zurückgreifen	hark back to (to hark back to sth.)	80
auf niedrigen Touren laufen; auf Sparflamme kochen.	running flat (business)	230
auf Zug beansprucht	trailing	132

Aufbau; Architektur	architecture	56
aufblasbar	inflatable	154
aufblasen, aufblähen	inflate	90, 135
aufbürden, auferlegen	imposed	171
Auferlegung (von Bedingungen)	imposition	225
aufgeben	ditched	
aufgenommen; geschluckt	absorbed	134
aufgerichtet	erected	229
aufgezeigt	drawn up	
Aufhängungsquerträger	suspension crossmembers	182
Auflader; Verdichter; Kompressor	supercharger	81
auflösen	dissolves	250
Auflösungsprozess	solution process	156
aufmöbeln	revamping	
Aufnäher	appliqué	242
aufnehmen, schlucken	absorbing, absorb	130, 163
Aufprallbelastung, Stoßbelastung	impact loads	65
Aufroll- und Blockierautomatik	with automatic retractors	242
Aufsteck-Dichtungen	cap seals	154
auftauchen; herauskommen	emerges	226
Auftrieb geben	boost	
aufweisen, beinhalten	feature	171
Aufwertung	upgrades	87
Aufwickeltrommel	winding drum	132
Ausdauer; Durchhaltevermögen	perseverance	120
auseinander fallen	come apart	198
auseinander nehmen, zerlegen.	dismantling	48
Ausformzeit	demould time	179
Ausführung	finish	49
Ausgaben	expense	220
Ausgänge	outlets	132
ausgedacht; entwickelt	conceived	172
ausgefallen	offbeat	75
ausgelagert	remoted	93
ausgelöst	induced	197
ausgelöst	deployed	242
ausgerichtet	aligned	242
ausgesetzt	subjected	199
ausgestellt	showcased	137
ausgewuchtet	balanced	246
Ausgleichsgetriebe	differential	256
Ausgleichswelle	balance shaft	69
Ausgleichswelle	counterbalance shaft	85
aushalten, tragen	bear	65
aushärten	cures	195
Aushärteöfen	hardening furnaces	174
Aushärteprozess	curing process	114
Aushärtungsdauer	curing time	200

auskippen	dumping	225
Auslass; Auspuff	exhaust	119
Auslasskanäle	exhaust passages	139
auslösen; zünden	trigger	171, 256
ausplaudern, preisgeben	divulge	37
Auspuffrohre	exhaust pipes	206
Auspuffrohrleitung	exhaust pipe	162
ausrasten	disengage	240
Ausscheidungshärtung	precipitation hardening	199
ausschließen	discount	216
außen liegend	external	198
Außenbeleuchtung	exterior driving lamps	237
Außenform	exterior	56
Außenhaut	outer skin	84
Außenseite der Rückenlehne	outer backrest	242
äußere Sitzschiene	outer seat rail	242
äußerste; hier: maximum	ultimate	105, 172
Aussetzung; Einwirkung	exposure	161
Ausstattung	equipment	56
Ausstattung; Ausrüstung	features	54
ausstoßen	expels	134
ausstoßen, emittieren	emit	127
Austauschbereiche	replacement sections	205
ausüben (eine Kraft, einen Einfluss)	exert	92
Ausübung des Prämienrechts; Optionsausübung	option	51
ausverkauft	sold out	
Ausweichmanöver	swerving to avoid an obstacle	244
auswerten	exploiting	199
Auswölbung	buckle	88
Autofriedhöfe; Schrottplätze	scrapyards	226
automatische Zuführung	automatical feeder	191
Autopanne	breakdown	91
Axialkolben-Verteilereinspritzpumpe	axial piston distributor pump	152
Bankrott	bankruptcy	223
Barcodeaufkleber	barcode label	255
Bariumoxid	baryta	178
Bauarbeiten	construction work	228
Baugruppen	assembly groups	225
baut zusammen	assembles	22
Bauteile; Träger	members	208
Beanspruchung	stress	199
Becken (menschl.)	pelvis	135
Beckengurt; Hüftgurt	lap belts	242
bedarf-, nachfrageorientiert	demand-oriented	229
Bedienung; Steuerung, Betätigung	actuation	95
Bedienungshebel	lever	224

263

beeinträchtigen	impair	160
beeinträchtigen (etwas)	detract from (to detract from sth.)	71
beenden	concluded	228
Befestigung	fastening	240
Befestigung, Aufnahme	fixture, fixing, fixturing	63, 114, 214
Befestigungsknöpfe	fastening buttons	239
befürworten	advocates	48
begonnen, gestartet, angefangen	commenced	177
begraben	bury	49
begrenzen	limit	37
behaupten	claimed that	223
beheizte Lambda-Sonde	heated oxygen sensor	252
behindern	hampers	220
behinderte Autofahrer	disabled drivers	98
beinhaltet	featured	167
beispiellos; noch nie dagewesen	unprecedented	42, 225
beitragen, beisteuern	contributing	51
beladende/ belastendeWerkzeug	loading tool	214
Belag	facing	161
belästigen	penetrate	249
Belastung	load	199
Belegungserkennung-Sensoren	occupant detection sensors	171
Beleidigung	insult	37
Belieferungen	supplies	230
Belüftungen, Lüfter	vents	132
Belüftungsdüsen	ventilation jets	235, 249
bemustert; stichprobenweise überprüft	sampled	63
Benzin saufend	gas-guzzling	
Benzin, Ottokraftstoff, „Sprit"	gas; gasoline	
Benzol	benzene	120
Bequemlichkeit	convenience	124
Beratungspodium	advisory panel	79
Bereich	branch	89
berüchtigt wegen	notorious for	223
berücksichtigen	catered for	205
beschäftigen; mit befassen	engages	52
beschichtet	coated	163
Beschichtung	film	173
Beschichtung; Überzug; Ummantelung	coating	178, 190
Beschlag; Befeuchtung	demity	105
Beschlagentfernungsfunktion; Entfeuchtungsfunktion	demist function	99
beschleunigen	speed	44
beschleunigen	hasten	125
beschleunigen (etwas)	expedite	233
Beschleunigungsmesser	accelerometers	171
beschuldigt	accused	226
besonders	peculiar	197

Beständigkeit; Festigkeit	consistency	202
bestehen (aus etw.); bestehen aus	comprises	125
bestehen aus	comprised; comprised of	197, 206
bestrafen	penalized	105
bestücken	populating	87
Beteiligungen	involvements	233
Betonmischer-Lkw, Transportbetonmischer	concrete-mixer lorries	15
Betriebsart; Modus	mode	97
Betriebstemperatur	operating temperatures	178
Beulen	bulges	245
bevorstehend; in Kürze erscheinend.	forthcoming	80
Bewerber; Wettbewerber	contestant	120
Bewertung des Vermessungssystems	measurement systems evaluation	62
Bewertungen	ratings	48
Biegebeanspruchung; Biegelast	bending load	143
Biegemoment	bending moment	154
biegesteifer Einbau	flexurally stiff mounting	65
Biegesteifigkeit	bending stiffness	110
Biegevermögen	bendability	173
Bienenwabe; Wabenkörper	honeycomb	110
bieten	bidding	
Bild; Abbildung	image	221
Blase	bubble	150
blasgeformt	blow-moulded	159
Blattfedern	leaf springs	198
Blech	sheet metal	60, 63
Blech/Kunststoff-Formteil, Verbundbauteil	sheet moulding composite (smc)	116
Blechdicke, Blechstärke	gauge (GB); gage (US)	110, 205
Blechölfilterpatrone	sheet-metal oil filter cartridge	254
Blechverkleidung	sheetings	203
bleifrei	non-leaded	160
Blei-Säure Batterien	lead-acid batteries	122
Blende; Klappe	flap	49
Blinker	turn indicators	70
Blinker; Fahrtrichtungsanzeiger	indicators	69
blockieren	lock	208
Blockieren	locking	244
Blütezeit	heyday	38
Bodenblech	floorpan	177
Bodenbleche	floor panels	211
Bodenfläche	floor space	56
Bodengruppe	floor assembly	65
Bogen	arc	172
Bojen	buoys	123
Bordwand, Seitenwand	gate	105
Bowdenzug	bowden cable	242

Brandgefahr	fire hazard	128
Bremsanlagen mit Antiblockiersystem	anti-lock braking systems	96
Bremsbeläge	brake pads	243
Bremseingriff	braking intervention	97
Bremsen	brake; brakes	71
Bremseneingriff	brake intervention	96
Bremskraftregler	brake proportioning valve	245
Bremskreise	brake circuits	244
Bremslichter, Stopplichter	brake lights	194
Bremssattel; Bremszange	brake calliper (GB); brake caliper (US)	85, 196
Bremsscheiben	brake discs (GB); brake disks (US)	80
Bremsung mit Energierückgewinnung	regenerative braking	127
Brennkammer (einer mit Kraftstoff betriebenen Standheizung)	combustion chamber	188
Brennpunkt	focal spot	211
Brennstoff-Zelle	fuel-cell	50
Brennweite	focal length	214
Bruchdehnung, Reißdehnung	elongation at fracture	105
Brückensysteme; Portalsysteme	gantry systems	212
Brückenzug	platform road train	16
Bugrad	jockey wheel	247
Bund, Flansch	collar	100
bündeln	harness	156
Bundesfinanzminister	federal treasury secretary	228
Bundeskanzler	federal chancellor	228
Bundesvorschriften/-normen	federal standards	51
Bürgermeister	mayor	228
Busanhänger	bus trailer	16
Caravan; Wohnwagen	caravan (GB); house trailer (US)	16
Chemie	chemistry	173
chlorsulfoniertes Polyethylen	chlorosulphonated polyethylene	178
Coupe Styling Studie	concept coupe vehicle	114
Dach	roof	212
Dachhaut	roof panels	106
Dachhimmel	headliners	179, 184
Dachhimmel; Dachverkleidung	roof lining	133
Dachlängsträger	roof rails	207
Dachträger seitlich	side roof rail	212
dagegen wirken	militating against	124
Dampfdruck	vapour pressure	134
Dampfdruckerhitzer; Druckhärtekessel	autoclave	194
Dämpfungselemente	shock absorbing devices	215
darstellen	constitutes	49
darstellen, ausmachen	constitutes	65
das ist ein bisschen viel verlangt!	that's a tall order	74

German	English	Page
das Wichtigste; die Hauptsache	essence	97
Daseinsberechtigungen; raison d'etre	appealing	120
Datenknotenpunkte	data nodes	88
Dauerproben	fatigue tests	165
dazu kommen	to get round to	109
Deckbleche, Abschlussbleche	closure panels	117, 231
Deckel des Laderaumbodens	floor cover	239
Deckkraft; Deckvermögen	hiding power	191
defekt	defective	246
Dehnung, Verlängerung	elongation	173
Dellen	dents	107
Demontagezentrum; Verwertungszentrum	dismantling centres	226
den Hof machen; um j-s Gunst werben	courting; fig: to court s.o.'s favour	
denkbar	conceivable	123
der Tatsache Rechnung tragen	take account of the fact	98
deutlich	distinct	
Diagnose	diagnosis	255
diagonal geteilt	diagonally split	244
dicht über die Oberfläche dahingleiten	skimming over the surface	157
Dichtheit	tightness	208
Dichtmaterial; Dichtungsmasse	sealant	84
Dichtungen	gaskets	173
Dichtungsmittel	seal	254
Diebstahlwarnanlage	anti-theft warning system	256
digitales Modell/ Attrappe	digital mockup	55
Dimmer für Instrumentenbeleuchtung	dimmer for instrument illumination	235
Direkteinspritzung; Zylindereinspritzung	direct-injection	68
diskret; digital	discrete	177
Diversifizierung; Verschiedenartigkeit	diversification	73
Dividentenpapiere	equity	
Docht	wick	134
Dollar (N.Am)	bucks	73
Dom – Verstärkung des Vorderachs-Stoßdämpfers	front shock tower reinforcement	205
Doppelfunkenzündspulen	dual spark ignition coils	252
doppelt	twin	232
doppelt gekrümmt/gerundet	double-curvature	122
Doppelzündung	dual ignition	81
Dorn	mandrel	205
Dosierpumpe	dosing pump	187
drehen	pivot	80
drehend	rotary	200
Drehkolbenpumpe	rotary pump	175
Drehkurbel	cranks	131
Drehmaschine	rotary machine	63
Drehmaschine	lathe	161
Drehmoment	torque	96

Drehschalter	rotary switches	249
Drehschwingungs-	torsional vibration	183
Drehstromgenerator; Drehstrom-Lichtmaschine	alternator	119, 183
Drehzahlmesser	tachometer	236
Dreiwege-Katalysator; Katalysator mit Lambda-Sonde; Selektivkatalysator	three-way catalytic converter	141
dringend (notwendig), unerlässlich	imperative	73
Drosselklappengehäuse	throttle body	184
Drosselklappenpotentiometer	throttle valve potentiometer	253
drosseln	throttle	94
Drosselventil; Drosselklappe	throttle	85
druckabhängig	pressure-depending	245
drücken	exerted	247
Druckguss	die casting; pressure casting	81, 106, 108
Druckgussteile	diecast parts	218
Druckkante; Knickkante	ridges	198
Druckspannungs-	compressive	199
Druckventil	delivery valve	176
Dumping (von billigen Waren)	dumping	223
Dünnflüssigkeit	low viscosity	114
dünnwandig	thin-walled	118
durch die Struktur übertragener Schall	structure-borne sound	178
Durchdrehen	spinning	246
Durchdringung	penetration	114
Durchdringung	permeation	159
durchgefärbt	moulded-in-colour	117
durchgestochene Löcher	pierced holes	63
Durchlademöglichkeit	loading ease	240
Durchlässigkeit; Porosität	permeability	160
durchlöchert	perforated	163
duroplastische Kunststoffe	thermosets	108
Düse; Mundstück	nozzle	138, 150
Düsenträger; Düsenhalter	nozzle holder	150
eben; waagerecht	level	248
Edelstahl; rostfreier Stahl	stainless steel	111
Ehrfurcht gebietend	awe-inspiring	137
Ehrlichkeit	honesty	52
Eifer	zeal	
Eigen-; eigen	inherent	105, 120
Eigenkapital (hier: Wert)	equity capital	51
Eigenspannngen; innere Spannungen	internal stresses	105
eigenwillig	headstrong	41
Einbau	onboard	119
Einbau	installation	239
einbinden; integrieren	incorporate	69
Eindringen; Eingriff	invasion	130

eine ganze Menge	whole lot	
einfach; direkt; unkompliziert	straightforward	220, 249
Einfallsreichtum	ingenuity	203
Einfederung	compression	245
Einfederungsanschläge	jounce bumpers	183
Eingangskanäle	inlet ports	142
eingearbeitet	incorporated	60
eingebunden	involved	56
Eingebung	inspiration	58
eingekapselt; eingegossen	encapsulated	200
eingeklemmt zwischen	sandwiched between	206
eingeschlossen, gefangen	trapped	220
eingestellt; justiert	adjusted	141
einheitlich	uniform	254
Einkauf	purchasing	56
Einlasskrümmer; Ansaugkrümmer	intake manifold	106
Einlasskrümmer; Ansaugkrümmer; Ansaugrohr	air intake manifold; air distributor	114, 180, 184
Einlassventilteller	inlet valve head	254
Einlaufkanäle; Saugkanäle	intake ports	138
Einnahmen	revenues	
einrichten	set-up	63
Einrichtungen; Ausstattungen	devices	170
Einsätze	stakes	229
Einschalenbauweise, Monocoque-Bauweise	monocoque design	108
einschalig; monocoque	monocoque	194
Einschäumen in Stoff/Gewebe	foam-in-fabric	206
Einschnapp-Passung/-Sitz	snap-fits	112
einsetzen	applying	130
Einsetzen	inserting	247
Einspritzdüse	injector jet	221
Einspritzdüsen	injectors	85, 136
Einspritzstrahl	injection beam	149
Einspritzventil	injection nozzle	150
Einstellschraube für Vollbelastung	full-load adjusting screw	176
Einstellschrauben	aiming screws	64
Einstiegsschweller	rocker panel; rocker section	258
Einstiegsschweller, Türschweller	sill; door sill; sill panel	181, 207
Einstiegszone	boarding zones	
Einzelhandel	retail	126
Einzelwiderstand	dent resistance	107
Einzelzündspulen	single ignition coils	252
einzigartig	unique	51
Eiweiß	albumen	193
eklatant, himmelschreiend	blatant	52
elastische Verbindung	flex joint	182
Elastizitätsmodul	young's modulus	105, 108

elektrisch verstellbar	electrically adjustable	257
elektrische Ladungsdruckkontrolle/-steuerung	electrical charge pressure control	69
elektrische Spannung	voltage	249
elektrischer Strom	electrical current; electric current	119, 124
Elektrolyt; Säure	electrolyte	125
elektromagnetische Kräfte	electromagnetic forces	171
elektromagnetisches Ventil	solenoid valve	144, 152, 165
Elektronisches Stabilitätsprogramm (ESP)	electronic stability management	167
Eloxieren	anodising	203
emittieren; ausstoßen	emit	159
Empfangsaussetzer	reception failure	252
Empfangseinheit	receiving unit	251
empfindlich	delicate	186
empfindlich	sensitive	199
empfindlich, feinfühlig	sensitive	186
Empfindlichkeit	susceptibility	175
emulieren	emulates	221
Emulsion	emulsion	156
Endlackierung	finish	121
Endmontage	final assembly	228
Energiebedarf	power demand	194
Energieerzeugung	power generation	124
Entfeuchtung	demisting	249
Entfrostung	defrosters	249
Entgegenkommen	concession	226
entgegentreten, gekontert	countered	168
entgegenwirken	counteract	154, 199
enthüllen	unveil (a face, monument etc.)	38, 68
enthüllen, verraten	reveal (sth.)	52, 65
Enthüllen; Bekanntgabe	disclosures	87
entkoppeln	decoupling	55
entleeren, auslaufen	drain	170
entscheidend	crucial	185
entsorgen	discarded	104
entsprechend	corresponding	242
entwickeln, erschließen	exploit	93
Entwicklungszeiten; Vorlaufzeiten	lead times	54
Epichlorohydrin	epichlorohydrin	179
Erfahrung	expertise	54
erfassen	capture	172
Erfindungsgabe; Einfallsreichtum	ingenuity	109
Ergänzung	complement	141
Erhärtung; Verhärten	hardening	199
erleben; sich unterziehen	undergoing	173
ermüdend	fatigue	199
Ermüdung	fatigue	102, 134, 177

Ermüdungstests	fatigue tests	199
ernannt (offiziell)	nominated	56
erobern, gewinnen	capture	54
errichten	erected	137
Ersatzrad	spare wheel	239, 246
Ersatzradmulde; Reserveradwanne	spare wheel well	206
Ersatzreifenabdeckung	spare tire covers	200
erste Gehversuche unternehmen	rolled out	76
Erwartung	expectancy	58
Erwerb	acquisitions	41
erwerben	acquired	51
Ethylalkohol	ethanol	
Ethylen-Acryl-Elastomer	ethylene acrylic elastomer	178
Ethylen-Propylen-Dien-Monomer	ethylene propylene diene monomer	179
eutektisch	eutectic	196
Experten	pundits	233
exzentrisch	eccentric	143
Fabrikat	make	245
Fach, Ablage	tray	101
fahrbare Bohrtürme	mobile drilling derricks	15
Fahrdynamikregelsystem	stability management system (psm)	167
Fahrgastraumabdeckung; Verdeckhülle	tonneau cover	116
Fahrgestell mit Fahrerhaus	chassis-cab	121
Fahrgestell; Fahrwerk	running gear	122
Fahrrad mit Hilfsmotor (Moped, Mofa)	moped	16
Fahrschemel; Hilfsrahmen; Unterrahmen	subframe; underframe; wheel-suspension raft; chassis auxiliary frame	84, 206
Fahrspurbreite	track-width	122
Fahrstabilität	directional control	246
Fahrstabilität	directional stability	247
Fahrtrichtungsanzeiger; Blinker	direction indicators	94
Fahrverhalten	handling	247
Fahrwerk	chassis	23, 50
Fahrzeuggastraum, Fahrzeuginnenraum; Interieur	interior	56
Fahrzeuginnenraum	car interior	178
Fahrzeugklimaregelung	climate control	88
Fahrzeuglinien; hier: Automodelle	carline	54
Fahrzeugpapiere	vehicle papers	247
Fahrzeugunterbau	vehicle underbody	245
falsch	improperly	64
Faltdach	folding roof	66
Falz; Biegung; Faltung	folds	198
fantasiereich; phantastisch	fanciful	80
farblich abgestimmt	colour-keyed	191
faserig	fibrous	197
faserverstärkt	fibre-reinforced	81

Feder	spring	242
Federbein	spring-strut	65
Federbeine	struts	67
Federbeine; Radaufhängungsbeine	suspension struts	71
federbelasteter Gürtel	spring tensioned belt	242
Federisolierung; Blattfeder-Zwischenlagen	spring isolators	183
Fehler; Defekt	fault	194
Fehler; Störungen	faults	88
Fehlstellen	blemishes	195
Fehlzündung; Aussetzer	misfire, misfiring, backfire; ignition fault	139, 255
fein	subtly	169
Feinbearbeitungsvorgänge; Endbearbeitung	finishing operations	200
Feindschaft gegen	hostility to	225
feinkörniger Federstahl	fine grain spring steel	198
Feinverteilung	dispersion	221
Feldeffekt-Transistoren, MOS-Transistoren; MOSFETs	fets (field effect transistors)	170
Felgen	rims	245
Fernlicht	high beam	172
Fernsteuerung	remote control	186
Fertigungslosgröße für Versuch, Erprobung	production trial run	62
Fertigungssteuerung	production control	62
fertig werden mit	to cope with	125
fest, formstabil, steif	rigid	131
fest; hart	firm	135
Festigkeit	strength	165, 199
Festkörper-	solid state	134
Feststoffe	solids	190
Feststoffe; Partikel, Ruß	particulate matter	128
fett	rich	141
Feuchtigkeit	dampness	64
Feuchtigkeit	moisture	114
Feuchtigkeit	humidity	193
Feuerwehr-, Lösch-Fahrzeug	fire fighting vehicles	15
Fixkosten; allgemeine Kosten; indirekte Kosten	overhead cost	218
Flachbandkabel	flat ribbon cables	87
flacher/ebener Unterboden	flat under body	86
Flachkolben	flat-head pistons	252
Flachstahl	flat-rolled steel	223
Flammenausbreitung	flame spread	118
Flaute, Abwärtsbewegung	downturn	
Fliehgewicht	flymass	175
Fließband	assembly line	230
Fließbild	flow sheet	173

fließen	stream	205
fließgepresst; stranggepresst	extruded	172
Fließpressen	extrusion	159
Fließvermögen	flowability	179
Fluchtungsfehler; Achsversatz	misalignment	153
Flügel; Schaufel	vanes	139
fluoreszierend	fluorescent	250
Fluorieren	fluorination	159
Flüssigkeitsgrad	viscosity	206
folglich; auf diese Weise	thus	92
foltern	racked	75
Form; Formwerkzeug	mould	63
Form; Formwerkzeug	die	209
Formaldehyd; Methanal; Methylal; Formal	formaldehyde	193
Formänderungsfestigkeit; Fließgrenze, Streckgrenze	yield strength	105
formgefräst; profilgefräst	profiled	86
formgepresst	moulded	172
Formhohlraum	mould cavity	202
Formmaschine	moulder	194
Formmaschine; Formhersteller	moulder	101
Formpress-/Spritzguss-Maschine	moulding machines	63
Formpress-Band/Linie/Straße	moulding line	203
Formpressen mit Einlegeteilen	insert moulding	157
formschlüssig	positively-engaged	182
Formspalt	mould joints	195
Formtrennung	mould release	200
Formwerkzeuge	production dies	60
forschend untersuchen; (eine Angelegenheit) erforschen	probe	
Forschung	research	56
Forschung und Entwicklung	r&d	57
fossile Brennstoffe	fossil fuels	120
freigeben	unlocked	199
Freilegung; Aussetzung	exposure	221
Freiraum; Spiel	clearence	214
Freizeitfahrzeug	SUV (sport utility vehicle)	167
Freizeitfahrzeug, Fun-Fahrzeug, sportlicher Pick-up	sport utility vehicle, sport-utility car	73, 230
Fremdkörper	foreign bodies	245
Frequenz, Häufigkeit	frequency	65
Frequenzlötmaschinen	wave solder machines	63
Fresnel-Linsenscheinwerfer	fresnel spots	171
Frontverkleidung als offene Version	front panelling	257
frühzeitig	prematurely	58
Fuge; Spalt; Schließlinie	shut line	67
Fügen	joining	114
Fügeverbindungen, Gelenke	joints	108

Fühler des Saugrohrdrucks	intake pipe pressure sensor	253
Führung	guide	239
Füllmaterial	filler	197
Füllstandsfühler	level sensor	171
fünfstufig	five-speed	71
Funke	spark	15
Fusionen	mergers	223
Fuß; unteres Ende	lower end	165
Fußraum	footwell	252
Fußraumkonstruktion	footwell structure	98
Gänsehaut	goose pimples	132
Garantie	warranty	86
garantiert	warrants	220
garnieren	trimming	133
Gasentladungslampen	discharge lamps	193
Gasentladungs-Scheinwerfer	high intensity discharge (hid) lamps	172
gasförmig	gaseous	119
Gaspedal	accelerator	95
geändertes Einspritzbild	modified injection pattern	252
Gebirge	mountainous territories	247
Gebläse	fan	95, 133, 249
gebunden	tied	160
geeicht	calibrated	59
gefährlich	hazardous	128
gefangen	trapped	141
gegen etwas wirken	militates against	156
Gegenbewegung	opposing movement	142
Gegendruck	reaction	200
Gegenkraft; Reaktion	counterforce	214
Gehäuse	casing	165
Gehäuse	housings	194
Gehörgefühl	auditory sensation	179
geklebt	bonded	108, 203
gekrümmter Abschnitt	curved section	205
Gel	gel	186
Geld	dough	
Gelenkbus	articulated bus	16
Gelenk-Deichselanhänger	drawbar trailer	16
Gelenke	links	131
gelenkig	articulating	79
geloben	vows	157
gelötet	soldered	63
gemeinsame Fahrzeugbenutzung	car-sharing	121
gemeinsame Versorgungsleitung	common rail	152
Gemeinschaftsunternehmen	joint venture	22, 51
gemessen an	rated on	54
Gemisch	compound	64

Gemischbildner	mixture formation system	255
Gemischbildung; Kraftstoffaufbereitung	mixture formation	147
genarbt; grobkörnig	coarse grained	257
geneigt	inclined	220
Geräuschdämpfung, Schalldämpfung	attenuation	178
Geräuschpegel	noise level	177
geringfügig	minor	105
Gerüche	odours	249
Gesamtgewicht	gross mass	247
geschichtet	stratified	152
geschichteter Stahl	laminated steel	206
geschmiedet	forged	85
geschnitzt	carved	172
Geschwindigkeit	velocity	168, 213
Geschwindigkeits-Kennbuchstabe	speed code	246
Geschwindigkeitsregler	cruise control	235, 247
gesichert; befestigt	secured	252
gesintert	sintered	105
gespannt	stretched	132
Gespanntheit; Verspannung	tenseness	134
gestartet, lanciert	launched	
Gestell, Träger	cradle	107
Getriebe	transmission	255
Getriebe; Getriebegehäuse	gearbox	69
Getriebegehäuse	gearbox casing	84
getroffen	stinging	223
gewagt, verwegen	daring	73
gewählt, ergriffen, verabschiedet	adopted	
gewähren	imparting	199
gewaltig	formidable	42
Gewebe	fabric	154
gewebt	woven	186
gewellt; geriffelt	corrugated	160
gewichtig	substantial	204
gewickelt	wound	132
Gewinde; Schraubengang	thread	100, 155
Gewinnspanne	profit margin	
Giermomentenregelung	yaw stability control	169
Gierratesensor	yaw rate sensor	169
Gierwinkelgeschwindigkeit; Giergeschwindigkeit	yaw velocity	168
Gierwinkelsensor; Gierwinkelaufnehmer	yaw sensor	168
giftige Schadstoffe	poisonous constituents	255
Gitter; Netz	mesh	222
Gitterrohrrahmen	spaceframe	203, 217
Glanz	brightness	114
glänzend	glossy	117

Glasbruchsensor	glass breakage sensor	256
Glasfaser	fibreglass, fibres	186, 195
Glasfaser	glass fibre	200
glasfaserverstärkt	glassfibre reinforced	165
Glasscheibe	glass pane	256
Gleichheit	commonality	224
gleichmacherisch	egalitarian	
gleichmäßig	uniform	202
Gleichstrom	dc	171
Gleichstrom-Gleichstrom	dc-dc	122
Gong; Läutewerk	chime	171
Graphit	graphite	160
Grate	burrs	213
Grauguss	gray cast iron	82
greifbar, konkret	tangible	110
Grenzbereiche	boundary regions	208
Griff	handle	66
Griff	grip	229
Griffigkeit der Reifen	tyre grip	246
Grobzerkleinerungsmaschinen	crushing machines	226
größere Höhen	higher elevations	247
Großhandel	wholesale	95, 120
Großraumlimousine; Großraumfahrzeug	minivans	73
Grube	pit	
Grundierlacke	primers	190
Grundierlacke auf Wasserbasis	water-borne primers	190
Grundlackschicht	basecoat, base coat	114, 190
Grundstein	foundation stone	228
Gruppierung, Angebot	lineup	44
Gültigkeitserklärung; Validierung	validation	51
Gummimischung	rubber compound	156
Gurtgehäuse	belt housing	101
Gurtschloss	belt lock	242
Gurtstraffer; Gurtstrammer	seatbelt tensioners	66
Gusseisen	cast iron	82, 197
Gussform; Gießform	die	105
Gussformen; Kokillen	chills	197
Gussteile nach dem Wachsausschmelzgießverfahren	investment castings	196
gut zusammen passend	compatible	59
haftende/klebende Lauffläche	gripping tread	155
Haftreibungsbeiwert	coefficient of friction	153
halbkugelförmig	hemispherical	183
Halbleiter	semi-conductor	134
Halt; Sicherung	retention	170
haltbar; strapazierfähig	durable (of material)	54

haltbar; strapazierfähig	durable	200
Halter	bracket	63
Halterung, Träger, Stütze	module support	65
Haltevorrichtung	retainer	242
Handel	merchandising	38
Handschuhfach	glove compartment	235
Handschuhkasten	glove boxes	87
Handwerker	artisans	77
Härte	hardness	178
Härteöfen	hardening furnaces	111
Hartmetall	carbide	161
Hartschaumteile	hard-foam parts	242
Harz	resin	200
hauchdünn	knife-edge	180
Haupt-	primary	79
Hauptbereiche	prime zones	117
Hauptbremszylinder	brake master cylinder	96
Hauptschallquellen	primary sound sources	180
Hauptzulieferer; Komplettsystemlieferant	tier one suppliers	158
Hebel	levers	131
Heckklappe	tailgate	71
Heckklappe	rear hatch	84
Heckscheibe	back window	220
heftig	fierce	226
heimisch	domestic	133
Heißfilm-Luftmassenmesser	hot film mass air flow meter	253
heiter; zuversichtlich.	sanguine (of temperament); (of views, policy etc.)	48
Heizungs-, Lüftungs- und Klimatisierungssysteme	hvac systems	132
Heizungsdüsen	heating nozzles	249
Helligkeit	brightness	237
herausfinden	figure out (to figure it out)	52
herausgefordert	defied	219
herauskommen; austreten	emerges	249
herausragend, überragend	superior to	106
Herrschaft	reign	117
Herstellungslos	production run	217
herumpfuschen	tinker	73
herumschleichen	on the prowl; to be on the prowl	44
Hilfskraftlenkung	power steering	232
Hilfsrahmen, Fahrschemel	subframe	65
Himmel; Dachverkleidungen	headliners	200
hin- und hergehend, wechselnd	reciprocating	174
Hinterachse	rear axle	245
hintere Bremsleitungen	rear brake lines	245
hintere Radspur, hintere Spurweite	rear track	71
hinterer Kotflügel; hinteres Schutzblech	rear fender	67

hinteres Ausstellfenster	swing-out type rear windows	257
Hintergrundgeräuschpegel	background-noise level	177
Hinterkante	low trailing edge	71
Hinterspritzen; Verstärken; Hinterschäumung	backing	178
Hitzebeständigkeit	heat resistance	114
hoch beschleunigen, hoch fahren (Motor)	rev; revving; rev-up; revving-up	95
hoch entwickelt; hochmodern; ausgeklügelt	sophisticated	234
hoch beansprucht	highly-stressed	108
hochdichtes Polyethylen	hdpe	159
Hochdruck-; niedrige Dichte	low-density	200
Hochdruck-Seite	high-side	170
hochentwickelt; raffiniert	sophisticated	132
hochfein	ultrafines	119
hochfester Stahl (HSS)	high-strength steel	65
hochglanz	high-gloss	49
höchst; unschlagbar	supreme	93
höchste Reinheit	high purity	106
Höhen-Breiten-Verhältnis	aspect ratio	217
Höhepunkte; Glanzlichter	highlights	127
Hohlkolben	concave-pistons	142
Hohlprofile	hollow sections	114
Hohlraum; Aussparung	cavity	133, 181, 194, 209
Hohlwelle	quill shaft	143
Holdinggesellschaft; Dachgesellschaft	holding company	51
Hubkolbenmotor mit Innenverbrennung (Abk. ICE/IC)	piston engines	15
Hublänge	length of stroke	254
Hubraum; Zylinderinhalt	displacement	70
Hubscheibe	camplate	174
Hüfte	hip	52
Hülsen, Buchsen	sleeves	197
Hutablage; Heckablage; Kofferraumbrücke	rear package tray	88
Hybridbauweise	composite design	252
Hydroaggregat	hydraulic modulator	245
im angekoppelten Zustand; gekoppelt	coupled	247
im Entstehen	creating	137
im Gegensatz zu	as opposed to	191
im letzten Teil	latter part	245
im unteren Drehzahlbereich	low-low	139
im Wesentlichen	in essence	223
imponierend, eindrucksvoll	striking; strikingly	81, 120
imponiert	imposing	
Importkontingent	import quotas	

imprägniert	impregnated	195
in der Größenordnung von	of the order of	101
in die Höhe schnellen	soaring	45
in die Höhe schnellen (Preise)	soar	
in einem Durchgang	single pass	161
in Erscheinung treten	emerge	171, 190
in Haussestimmung	bullish	203
in Reihe/Serie geschaltet	series-connected	122
in umgekehrter Reihenfolge	in reverse order	239
in Zaum halten	curb	44
induktives Aufladegerät	inductive charger	232
innen liegend	internal	198, 200
Innenhochdruckumformen	hydroforming technique	211
Innenraum-, Fahrgastraum-Temperatur	cabin temperature	99
Innenverkleidung	interior trim	178
Innenverkleidung der Heckklappe	tailgate inner panelling	240
Innenverkleidung der Seitenwand	inner panel	239
innerer, luftundurchlässiger Mantel	inner air-proof liner	154
Insassen	occupants	67
Instandhaltung; Wartung	maintenance	234
Instrumente	instruments	235
Instrumententafel-Querträger	ip crossbeams	105
Instrumententräger; Armaturenbretthalter	instrument panel support	106
Integration	incorporating	219
integrieren, einbeziehen	integrates	96
integrieren; einbinden	incorporate	212
integrierte Variante	integral variant	122
Investition; Anlage	investment	224
ionisiert	ionized	119
Isocyanat	isocyanate	193
isoliert	insulated	197
Jahresproduktion	annual production	
je nach	order of	222
jemanden zur Verfügung stehen	at its disposal	229
j-n veranlassen; dazu animieren, etwas zu tun	prompt	225
Kabelbindern	cable ties	242
Kabelsätze, Kabelstränge	wiring harnesses	92, 194
Kabelsatzstecker	wiring harness plug	242, 245
Kabriolett	convertible	16
kalt hämmern	peening	199
Kältekammerverfahren	cold chamber process	105
Kältemittelsystem	refrigerant system	250
Kälteteil	refrigeration unit	250
kalt gezogen	cold drawn	85

kalthämmern	peening	198
kämpferisch	combative	41
Kanal; Anschluss	port	139
Kanalauslegung; Führung	ducting	114
Kanäle	ducts	88
Kanäle; Rinnen	channels	242
Kanalreinigungs-Fahrzeug	sewer cleaning vehicle	16
Karkasse, Unterbau	carcass	158
Karosserie	body	50
Karosserie; Aufbau	bodywork	67, 111, 112, 177
Karosserieaufbau	framing	210
Karosserie-Gelenkfestigkeit	body joint strength	
Karosserien	bodies	23
Karosserierohbau	body shop	231
Karosserierohbau; Rohbau	body structure	84
Karosserietraglager	body mounts	183
Katalysator	catalyst; catalytic converter; catalyser (GB); catalyzer (US)	51, 102, 162, 252
Kautschukmischung	rubber compound	154
kegelförmig; konisch	tapered	70
kehren	sweep	155
Keilrippenriemen-Spannvorrichtung	ripped v-belt tensioner	252
Kennzeichenleuchten	license plate lamps	257
keramisches Halbleiterelement	ceramic semi-conductor	249
Kerben	notches	215
kerben; einkerben	notching	199
Kernausschmelz-Schicht	lost core film (lcf)	194
Kettenantriebsrad	drive sprocket	144
Kielwasser; Sog	wake	233
Kieselerde; Quarz	silica	156
Kilometerzähler	odometer	236
Kindersitzerkennung	child seat recognition	88
Kippen	tilting	249
Kissen; Polster	cushions	82
Klappe	flap	240
klappern	rattling	130
Klarlackschichten	clear coats	190
kleben; festkleben, einkleben	bonding	84, 156, 205
Klebstoff auf Epoxidbasis	epoxy-based glue	205
Klebstoff für Strukturteile	structural adhesive	205
Klebstoff; Klebemittel	adhesives	84
klebstoffbeschichtet	adhesive lined	118
klein; unbedeutend	minor	155
kleine Fische	small fries	44
Klimaanlage	air conditioning system	250
Klopfsensor	knock sensor	253
Knautschzonen	crumple zones	111, 174

Knöpfe	knobs	240
Knoten	nodes	207
Knotenpunkte	nodes	108, 212
Köder	baits	
Kofferraum, Gepäckraum	boot (GB); trunk (US)	67
Kofferraumdeckel	deck lid; rear deck lid; boot lid (GB); luggage-compartment lid (GB); trunk lid (US); trunk deck US); baggage-compartment lid (US)	106, 115, 194
Kohle führend	carboniferous	119
Kohlendioxid	carbon dioxide	51
Kohlenmonoxid	carbon monoxide	51, 128
Kohlenstofffaser	carbon fibre	81
Kohlenwasserstoffe	hydrocarbons	51, 255
Kohlenwasserstoffverbindungen	hydrocarbons	119, 126
Kolben	pistons	173
Kolben; Stempel	plunger	176
Kolbenmulde; Ventiltasche	piston relief	139
Kolbenrückholfeder	plunger spring	176
Kolbenstangendichtung	piston rod seal	166
Kolbenwelle	plunger shaft	142
Kombi; Variant; Caravan;	estate car (GB); station wagon (US)	235, 239
kommt vor wie/erscheint wie...	have seemed like	73
kompakte Großraumlimousine	compact van	123
Komponentenentwicklungspläne	development plans	54
Kompromiss	trade-off; tradeoff	155, 216
Kondenswasser	condensation	250
könnte (dazu) führen; geeignet	likely to	225
konsequent; verständlich	coherent	
Konstellationen	situations	182
Kontaktbleche	contact plates	249
Kontaktwiderstand; Übergangswiderstand	contact resistance	171
konturiert	contoured	217
Konzern	combine	
konzipiert	formulated	118
Kopfstütze	headrest	101
Kornbildung; Kristallbildung	crystallising	173
Körnung (öldruckunterstützt)	particle hydraulics	194
Korossionsbeständigkeit	corrosion-resistance	106
Korrektur von Fehlern	remedying of faults	255
Korrekturhebel	corrector lever	176
Korrosionsbeständigkeit	corrosion- resistance	107
Kostenaufwand	outlay	191
Kotflügel; Schutzbleche	wings	84
Kotflügelhalterschiene	fender support rail	212
Kraftfahrzeug	power driven vehicles	16
Kraftfahrzeugindustrie	motor industry	15
kräftig	beefy	

Kraftmaschine mit Innenverbrennung	internal combustion engines	120
Kraftrad	power driven cycles	16
Kraftspeicher	energy store	242
Kraftstoff-Systemintegrität	fuel system integrity	
Kraftstoffanzeige	fuel gauge	236
Kraftstoff betrieben (m.)	fuel-powered	249
Kraftstoffdruckregler	fuel pressure regulator	252
Kraftstoff-Einfüllstutzen	fuel-filler neck	159
Kraftstoffeinspritzpumpe	injection pump	174
Kraftstoffförderpumpe	fuel-supply pump	176
Kraftstofffüllstandsgeber; Tankgeber	fuel level sensor	159
Kraftstoffleitung	fuel lines	158, 160
Kraftstoffrücklaufleitung	fuel return lines	254
Kraftstoff sparend	fuel efficiency	51
Kraftstoffverdunstung	evaporative emissions	128
Kraftstoffverdunstungsabsaugsystem; Gaspendelanlage	refueling vapour recovery system	159
Kraftstoffverteilerrohr	fuel distributor pipe	252
Kraftstoffvorlaufleitung	fuel feed lines	254
Kraftstoffzuleitungen	fuel lines	159
Kraftstoffzusätze	fuel additives	119
Kraftwagen	motor vehicles	16
Kraftwerk	power station	120
Kratzer, Narbe	scar	174
krebserregend	carcinogenic	119
Kredit	credits	
Kreiselkompass	gyro compass	251
Kreuzung	cross-breed	74
Kreuzung	crossing	74
Kreuzungen	junctions	82
Kriechstrombeständigkeit	resistance to creepage	105
Krümmerrohr; Vorrohr	header pipe	162
Kügelchen; Perlen	beads	116
Kugelstange	coupling ball bar	247
kugelstrahlen	shot peening	199
Kühlbleche; Kühlkörper	heat sinking	87
Kühlergrill/-Gitter	grille; grill; radiator grill; front grill	49, 63
Kühlerträger	radiator supports	206
Kühlerverstärkungen	grille reinforcements	106
Kühlmittelkreislauf	coolant circuit	188
Kühlmittelpumpe	coolant pump	254
Kühlmittelsysteme	coolant systems	114
Kühlmittel-Temperaturanzeige	engine temperature gauge	236
Kühlmitteltemperatur-Sensor	coolant temperature sensor	253
Kühlplatten, Kühlbleche	heat sinks	186
kundenspezifisch	custom	209
Kunstfaser	synthetic fibre	154
Kunststoffspritzgussmaschinen	plastic injection moulding machines	63

Kupfer	copper	115, 194
Kupplungen	clutches	100
Kupplungsgehäuse; Kupplungsglocke	bell housings	196
Kupplungskugel	coupling ball	247
Kurbel	crank handle	246
Kurbelfenster; Hebefenster	roll-up windows	182
Kurbelgehäuseentlüftung	crankcase ventilation	254
Kurbelwellen-Impulsaufnehmer	crankshaft pulse pick-up	253
Kurven	bends	244
Kurvenfahrten mit Höchstwerten	maximum-rate cornering	98
kurvenreich	winding	247
Kurvenscheinwerfer; Kurvenleuchten	swivelling headlights	80
kurz und dick	stubby	75
Kurzschluss	short-circuit	88, 95
Lackierbandstraßen	paint lines	114
Lackiererei	paint shop	228
Lackierprozess	paint processes	114
Lackware	lacquerware	77
Ladedruck; Ladeluftdruck	boost pressure	139
Ladegerät	charger	122, 232
Ladeklappe; Heckklappe	tailgate	86
Ladeklappe; Kombi-Hecktüre	hatchback	76, 115
Ladeklappen; oben/unten angeschlagene Heckklappen	liftgate	116
Ladeluftkühlung	charge air cooling	69
Laderaumabdeckung	load compartment cover	239
Laderaumboden	load compartment floor	238
Ladungswechsel	charge cycle	139
Lage, Schicht	ply	182
Lager	bearings	153
Lager; Lagerfläche	inventory	
Lager; Stützlager; Halter, Halterungen	mounts	71
Lagerbestände	inventories	157
Lagerung	mounting	65
Lagerungen	bracketry	115
Laie	layman	95
Lamellen	fins	249
Laminat; Schichtpressstoff	laminate	217
Lampe	bulb	171
Landesverrat	treason	73
Langlebigkeit	longevity	194
Längslenker; Zugstange; Zugstrebe	trailing arm	67, 85
Längsträger, Rahmenlängsträger	side members	65
Längsträger, Zugstangen	trailing arms	115
Langzeitverbindung	long-lasting bond	160
Laserstrahlschweißen	laser welding	110
lastabhängig	load-dependent	245

Lastabschaltung	load dump	170
Lastanhänger	goods trailer	16
Lastenheft	specification	224
Lastkraftwagen (Lkw)	lorry (GB); truck (US)	15, 16
Lauf mit gewünschter Stückzahl	run at rate	61
Laufrichtung	direction of travel	182
Laufringe	races	100
Laufspiel	running clearances	153
lebenserhaltend	sustainable	158
lebensfähig	viable	123
lebenswichtig	vital	54
Leckerkennungsmittel	leak detecting agent	250
Leergewicht	unladen mass, kerb mass (GB); curb mass (US)	67
Leergewicht	curb mass (US)	70
Leergewicht	kerb mass (GB)	50
Leerlaufdrehzahl	idle speed	182
Leerlauffeder	idling spring	176
Leerlaufkennkurven	idling characteristics	144
Leerlaufschrittmotor	idle speed stepper motor	253
Leerlauf-Umleitventil	idle air bypass valve	184
Leerweg	idle play	242
Legierung	alloy	203
leichte Nutzfahrzeuge	light goods vehicles	121
Leichtlastwagen mit Pritsche	pickup; pickup truck	44, 73
Leistungsbeschreibungen	material specifications	62
Leistungsprüfstand	dynamometer	50
Leitbleche, Ablenkbleche; Abweiser	baffles	182
Leiterfolie	conductive foil	133
Leiterplatten	printed circuit boards	252
Leiterplatten; gedruckte Schaltungen	circuit boards	63
Leiterrahmen	ladder frame	142
leitfähige Mischungen/Ansätze	conductive formulations	114
Lendenwirbel	lumbar vertebra	135
Lendenwirbelsäule	lumbar spine	79
Lendenwirbelstütze; Lordosenstütze	lumbar support	79, 238
Lenkeinschlag; Radeinschlag; Lenkwinkel	steering angle	82
Lenker; Beine, Streben	struts	85
Lenkradgerüst; Lenkradgestelle	steering wheel frames	105
Lenkrad-Kerne/Innenringe	steering wheel cores	104
Lenkradsperre	steering column lock	235
leuchtender Punkt (auf dem Bildschirm)	blip	96
leugnen, dementieren, abstreiten	denies	37
Lichtbrechung	light refraction	192
Lichthupe	headlamp flash	235
Lichtmaschine	alternator	236
Lichtschalter	light switch	235

Lichtstrom	lumens; luminous flux; light flux	172
Lichtverteilung	beam pattern	172
Lichtwellenleiter	optical fibre (GB); optical fiber (US)	212
lieber als	rather than	83
Lieferungen	shipments	223
Lieferwagen	delivery van; commercial van; delivery lorry (GB); delivery truck (US); delivery wagon (US)	235
Limousine; geschlossener Pkw	limousine; saloon (GB); sedan (US); coach (US)	16, 68, 242
Linienbus	urban bus	16
Lippe; Falz	lip	86
Listenpreis	list price	121
Lkw-Anhänger	truck trailers	23
lockern	loosen	229
Lösungsmittel	solvent	190
lösungsmittelfrei	solvent-free	191
Lötmittel	flux	63
Luftblase	bubble	64
Luftfeuchtigkeit	humidity	64, 99
Luftkanäle	air ducts	179
Luftkästen; Luftspeicher	plenum chambers	133
Luftkühler; Wasserkühler	radiator	102
Luftschall; durch Luft übertragener Schall	airborne noise	181
Lüftungsgehäuse	vent housing	249
Luftwiderstand; Strömungswiderstand	drag	71
machen (j-n, etwas)	render	225
mächtig	mighty	44
magerer	leaner	141
Magerkonzept (mit magerer Verbrennung)	lean burn concept	141
Magnesium-Druckguss	die cast magnesium	105
Magnesiumlegierungen	magnesium alloys	106
Magnetventil für Kraftstoffabschaltung	fuel-cutoff solenoid	176
mangeln	lacks	193
Marke	brand	51
Marken; Eigentum	proprietary	164
Markenname, Markenbezeichnung	brand name	22
Marotte	fad	233
Massenschluss, Erdschluss	shorted to ground	89
maßgeschneidert	customed	186
maßgeschneidert	tailored	209
maßgeschneiderte Bleche	tailored blanks	217
Maßhaltigkeit, Formbeständigkeit	dimensional stability	165
Matte	mat	163, 200
mechanische Gurtstraffer	mechanical seat belt tensioners	242
Mechanismus, Mechanik	gears	115

Mehrfachpol; Vielpol	multi-conductor	87
Mehrstufenplan	multiphase plan	124
Mehrzweckfahrzeug	multi purpose vehicle	167
Meilen pro Galone	mpg (Miles per Gallon)	
Meilensteine; Projektkontrollen	milestones	56
Melamin	melamine	193
Merkmale; Eigenschaften	features	87
Messing	brass	115
Messstab	dipstick	50
Metallgussteile	metal castings	63
Metalloxid-Halbleiter, MOS	mos (metal oxide semiconductor)	170
Methodik	methodology	164
Methylalkohol	methanol	123
Meute	pack	
mieten	lease	232
Mikrofaser	microfibre	183
mikrolegiert	micro-alloyed	198
Mikroporen	micropores	133
Minderheit	minority	233
Mischkopf	mixhead	200
Mischung nach Formel	mixture formulation	221
missachten	flouting	226
mit Abgasturbolader	turbocharged	67
mit etwas beginnen.	embarking on (something)	
mit etwas Schritt halten	keep pace with	131
mit j-m uneins sein	at odds with (to be at o. with s.o.)	185
Mitnehmer	drivers	170
Mitnehmerscheibe; Antriebsscheibe	driving disc	176
Mitte des vorderen Fußbodens	front floor centre	206
Mittelarmlehne	centre armrest	240
mittelschwer	medium-duty	230
mitten in/unter	amid	117
Modell; Pilot	pilot	60
modern, modisch	fashionably	121
möglich machen	enabling	194
Montageplatte	bed-plate	183
Montagestraße, Fließband	assembly line	56
Montieren durch Stoßen/Drücken	push-fit	171
Motor mit Innenverbrennung	internal-combustion engines	51
Motor mit innerer Verbrennung	ic-engine	121
Motoraufhängungen	engine mounts	183
Motorblöcke	engine blocks	106
Motordrehzahl	engine speed	247
Motoren	engines	23
Motor-Getriebe-Einheiten; Antriebsgruppe	powerplants	103
Motorhaube	bonnet (GB); hood (US); engine cowl	64, 115

Motorhaube; Kühlerhaube	engine bonnet (GB); engine hood (US)	106
Motorhilfsrahmen	engine cradles	206
Motorlager	engine mount	182
Motorrad	motor cycle	16
Motorraum-; motornah	underbonnet	112
Motorräume	engine bays	197
Motorroller	scooter	16
Motorsteuergerät	engine control unit	249, 252
Motorsteuergerät in Hybridbauweise	composite-construction engine control unit	252
Motorträger; Motorhilfsrahmen	engine cradles	115
Mulde; Vertiefung	recess	66
Muldenkipper (Schwerst-Lkw)	dumpers	15
Müllwagen	garbage truck	16
Muschelschale	clamshell	231
Muster	samples	59
Muster; Proben	specimens	157
Musterbeispiel	paradigm	101
nach oben einhaken	snap in towards the top	239
nach unten schwenken	swivelled down	257
Nachbehandlungssysteme	aftertreatment systems	119
nachfolgend	subsequent	108
Nachfolgenden	followers	100
Nachfüllen (des Tanks/ der Zellen)	replenishment	124
Nachgiebigkeit; Elastizität	resilience	179
nachhallend, reflektierend	reverberant	183
Nachhut	rearguard	225
nachkommen (einer Bitte)	comply	59
Nachrüst-Set	retrofit kit	188
nachschleifen	regrind	159
Nachtanken; Auftanken	refueling	128
nachträglich eingebaut	retrofitted	252
nachwachsend	regenerative	125
Nähe; Nachbarschaft	proximity	162, 228
Naht	seam	242
nahtlos	seamless	54
Nahtschweißung	seam welding	208
Nebelscheinwerfer	fog lamp	235
Nebelschlussleuchte	fog tail lamp	235
Nebenaggregate	ancillaries	194
Nebenstraßen	secondary roads	82
Nebenverbraucher	accessories	122
Neigung (zu etwas neigen)	proneness	106
Neigungsgeber; Winkelsensor	and tilt sensor	256
nervös	skittish	44
neu eröffnet	dedicated	203

neu; neuartig	novel	131, 141, 171, 198
Neuorientierung	reorientation	213
nicht angezapft/angebohrt	untapped	185
nicht ausführlicher sein können	it is not possible to elaborate	102
nicht einklagbar; nicht vollstreckbar	unenforceable	225
nicht glaubwürdig.	unreliable	15
nichtleitend	dielectric	130
Niederdruck; druckarm	low pressure	171
Niederdruckgefälle	low pressure differential	166
niedrig	poor	144
niedrige Dichte	low-density	122
Niveauregulierung	level control; level control system	235, 247
Niveauregulierungsanlage	levelling system	165
Nobelklasse; für höhere Ansprüche	upmarket	37
Nockenscheibe; Kurvenscheibe	cam plate	176
Nockenstößel	followers	142
Nockenwelle	camshaft	85, 143, 173
Nockenwellensensor	camshaft sensor	253
Noppenriemen	knobbed belt	182
Notdienst	emergency services	90
Notrad	temporary spare wheel	246
notwendig machen; fordern (etwas)	necessitated	71
nüchtern, sachlich	sober	75
Nut; Fuge	groove	154
Nutzfahrzeuge	commercial vehicles (cv)	17
Nutzfahrzeug-Standard	cv-standard	122
Nutzkraftwagen (Nkw)	commercial vehicles	16
Nutzkraftwagen-Kombi (Nkw-Kombi)	truck station wagon	16
Nutzwertanalyse	efficiency analysis	58
oben hängendes Ventil	ohv	145
Oberbau; Aufbau	superstructure	84
oberer Windschutzscheibenrahmen; vorderer Dachquerträger	windshield header rail	66
Oberflächen	surface	61
Oberflächenbeschaffenheit mit 1A Qualität	class a surface finish	115
Oberflächenbeschaffenheit; Oberflächengüte	surface finish	161
Oberflächengeschwindigkeit	surface velocity	180
oberflächenmontiert	surface-mounted	87
Oberflächenrisse	surface cracks	199
Oberklasse	full-size	230
Oberleitungsbus (O-Bus)	trolley bus	16
Oberschenkelauflage	thigh support	238
offener Stromkreis	open-circuit	95
Öffnung; Ausschnitt	apertures	181
Öffnungsdauer	opening duration	143

Ölfiltereinsatz	oil filter insert	254
Ölfiltergehäuse	oil filter housing	254
Ölraffinerien	refineries	126
Ölwanne	sump	85, 142, 196
Ölwannendichtung	oil pan gasket	254
optische Kanäle	optical channels	92
organisch	organic	119
Öse	eye	247
oxidiert	oxidized	111
Ozon	ozone	102
Palette	pallet	63
Papierwechselpatrone	paper replacement cartridge	254
Pedalbetätigungseinheit	pedal actuation unit	165
Pedalweg	pedal travel	82
pendeln; Pendelbewegungen	swaying	247
Pendler; Berufspendler	commuter	120
Personal	staff	58
Personalabbau	layoffs	223
Personenkraftwagen (Pkw)	passenger car	16
Persönlichkeit	personality	57
pfeilförmig	arrow-shaped	80
Pfütze/Lache verursachen	pools	128
Phasenverschiebung	phase shifting	143
Pkw-Kombi; Kombi	station wagon	16
Pläne finanzieren	finance schemes	
Platinen, Stanzteile	blanks	110
Platzen	blowout	245
Platzen	bursting	245
Pleuelstangen	con-rods	252
Pollen	pollen	250
Polsterung; Aufpolsterung	padding	130
polyaromatische Kohlenwasserstoffe	polyaromatic hydrocarbons	119
Polystyrol (PS)	polystyrene	114
Polyvinylidenfluorid	pvdf	160
prahlen, rühmen	boasts	220
Prallblech; Blende	baffle	163
Preisschild	price tag	50, 232
Pressharz, Gussharz	moulding resin	194
Pressteil; Ziehteil	pressing	132
Pritschenaufbau	platform body	121
Produktionssteuerung	production control	255
Produktsortiment; Produktprogramm	product range	86
Profil	tread	154
Profilausführung	tread pattern	245
Profiltiefe	tread depth	245
Protest (lautstarker)	outcry	48
Prototypenfahrzeuge	prototype vehicles	55

provozieren; hervorrufen	provoked	98
Prüfstand	test stand	144
Prüfstand, Teststand	rig	174
pulsieren	pulsating	244
Pulverbeschichtung; Pulverlackierung	powder coating systems; powder coating	114, 190
Pulverklarlackschicht	powder clearcoat	114
Quarts	quarts	146
quer	transversely	163
Quer-, Diagonal-, Schräg-	diagonal	65
Quer-, seitlich	lateral	197
quer, transversal	transversal	168
Querbeschleunigungsaufnehmer, -sensoren	lateral accelerometers	82
Querlenker	wishbones	67, 85
Querlenker	transverse links	115
Querlenker; Führungslenker	control arms	81, 182
Querschnitte; Schnitte	cross-sections	221
Querschnittsverhältnis	aspect ratio	246
Querträger	crossmember	65
Querträger des vorderen Fußbodens	front floor crossmembers	205
Querträger; Traverse; Spriegel	crossmembers	206
quetschen	pinching	195
quietschen, knarren, knarzen	squeak	179
Radaufhängungsdom	suspension turrets	204
Radaufhängungslager; Fahrwerkslager	suspension bushings	183
Radaufhängungssystem; Federungssystem	suspension systems	153
Radialkolben-Verteilereinspritzpumpe	radial piston distributor injection pump	139
Radien	radii	208
Radius	radius	156
Rahmenlängsträger	frame rail	182
Rahmenquerträger	crossmember	213
Rand; äußere Begrenzung	perimeter	208
Rand; Grenze	verge	147
Rändelrad	knurled knob	237
rattern, vibrieren	judder	173
Rauigkeit	roughness	108
Rechtfertigungen	justifications	94
Rechtsberatung	legal advice	226
rechtsgelenkt; Rechtslenkung	right-hand drive	234
rechtwinklig, rechteckig	rectangular	65, 217
Rechtwinkligkeit	perpendicularity	63
recylingfähig	recyclable	225
Reduktionskatalysator	reduction catalytic converter	141
Reformeranlage	reformer system	125

Regelkreis, Regelschleife	loop	170
Regelventil	regulating valve	176
Regen-Erkenner/Aufspürer/Sensor	rain detectors	99
regieren	reign	93
Regler	modulators	82, 96
Reglerfeder	governor spring	176
Reibung	friction	153, 173, 208
Reibungsverluste; mechanische Verluste	frictional losses	132
reichlich; genügend	ample	240
Reichweite	range	50
Reichweite; Aktionsradius	range	120
Reifen (sing.), Reifen (pl)	tire, tires (US)	
Reifen (sing.), Reifen (pl)	tyre, tyres (GB)	245
Reifen mit Notlaufeigenschaften	"run-flat" tyre	155
Reifenaufstandsfläche	tyre's footprint	155
Reiheneinspritzpumpen	inline pumps	150
Reinst-	high-purity	198
Reisebus	long distance coach	16
reißen, zerlegen	tearing	198
reißen; zerreißen	tears	242
reizen; Anziehungskraft ausüben	justifications	120
Relaissteuerung	relay control	171
Resonator; Reflexionsschalldämpfer	resonator	163
restlich	residual	199
Richtlinie; Verordnung	directive	225
Richtungsführung	directional guidance	251
richtungsgebunden	directional	196
Riegel; Anschlagstift	locking pins	239
Riemenantrieb	belt drive	125
Riemenscheiben	belt pulleys	213
Riesen	giants	
Ring; Umgehung	orbital path	132
ringförmig	annular	201
Riss	tear	186
Risse	cracks	245
robust, stabil	rugged	170
robuster	sturdier	128
Rohblöcke, Barren	ingots	173
Rohre; Krümmerrohre	runners	195
rohrförmige Verstärkung in der A-Säule	tubular a-pillar reinforcements	65
Rollenstößel	roller followers	100
rollgeformt	rollformed	209
Rollkörper	rollers	174
Rollwiderstand	resistance to rolling	154
Röntgen	x-ray	173
Rotorölpumpe	rotor-type oil pump	254

Rückenlehne; Sitzlehne	backrest	135
Rückenschmerzen	backache	134
Rückfragen; Fragen	queries	234
Rückführung	recirculation	81
Rückgrat	backbone	73
Rückkehrzeitpunkt der getätigten Investitionen	return of investment	56
rücklauffreies Kraftstoffsystem	fuel system has no return	252
Rücklauf-Sperrklinke	reverse pawl	242
Rückstau	tailback	226
Rückwand; Verschlussblech	end panel	240
rückwirkend	retro-active	225
Ruf	reputation	54, 106
Rumpf; Oberkörper	torso	79
runde Rohlinge	round blanks	161
rundlaufend; konzentrisch	coaxial	160
Ruß	soot	120, 147, 250
Rußausstoß	soot emissions	138
rutschen, gleiten	slipping	100
rutschen; gleiten	skidding	154
Sach-, Fachkenntnis	expertise	51
Salve	salvo	229
Sandguss	sand-cast	161
Sattelanhänger	semi-trailer	16
Sattelkraftfahrzeug	articulated vehicle	16
Sattelzug	double road train	16
Sattelzugmaschine	semi-trailer towing vehicle	16
sättigen; befeuchten	wets	201
Sauerstoff	oxygen	124
Saugdruck-Seite	low-side	170
Sauger; Ansauger	suckers	214
Saugmodul	intake manifold module	252
Saugrohr	intake pipe	254
schäbig, minderwertig	shoddy	41
Schablone	jig	205
schädlich, giftig	noxious	255
Schadstoff	contaminant	119
Schalldämmung	soundproofing	137
Schalldämpfung; Unterdrückung; Schwächung	suppression	179
schalltot; nicht reflektierend	anechoic	183, 184
Schall-Verkleidung/- Beplankung	acoustic panels	194
Schalter	switches	93
Schalter für Blinker	levers for turn signals	235
Schalterkonsole	switch console	257
Schalthebel	switch stalks	224
Schalthebel; Einrückhebel	shift lever	82

Schalthebel; Schaltknüppel	gear lever	94
Schaltkreise	circuits	88
scharfe Kanten	sharp edges	245
scharfe Konkurrenz	stiff competition	229
schaukeln	rocks	135
schäumend	bubbly	74
schäumendes Polyurethan	foaming pu	131
Scheibenbremse	disc brake (GB); disk brake (US)	245
Scheibenbremsen-Bremsbelag	disc brake pads	173
Scheibenbrems-Kolben	disc-brake pistons	191
Scheinwerfereinstellung	headlamp aiming	63
Scheinwerferspiegel	headlamp reflectors	114
Schellen, Halter	clips	130
scheuern, reiben	scuffing	174
Scheune	barn	75
Schichten	layers	154
Schichtladung	stratified charge	147
schieben, wegschieben	drift	169
Schlagfestigkeit	impact resistance	165
Schlamm	slurry	191
schlank	lean	56
Schläuche	hoses	118
schlechter Leiter	poor conductor	197
Schleifgeräusche verursachen	squeal	243
Schleuderpreise	rock-bottom prices	223
Schlingerbewegungen	rolling motions	247
Schloss	lock	224
Schlupfregelung, automatische Schlupfregelung	traction control	95
Schmalbandbrummen	narrow band hum	125
Schmelzschweißen	fusion	217
Schmiedeteile	forgings	196
schmierig	greasy	247
schneckenförmiges Stellglied	helical actuator	142
Schneidkante; riskant	cutting-edge	38
Schneidwerkzeug	cutting tool	63
schnell, glatt, lebhaft	briskly	
schnell; wendig	nippy	121
Schnittbild	cutaway; sectional view	188
Schnitte	cuts	245
schnittig	sleek	74
Schnittstellen	interfaces	56
schnüffeln	sniffing	
Schönheitsfehler; Fehlstellen; Schönheitsfehler (pl)	blemish; blemishes (pl)	63, 193
Schottwand; Querwand	bulkhead	177
schrauben, winden	thread	98
Schraubenfeder	coil spring	85, 198

293

Schraubverbindungen	screw connections	65
Schredderabfall	shredder residue	226
Schrittmotor	stepper motor	95
Schrott	scrap	104, 159, 217
schrullig	whimsical	44
schrumpeln; schrumpelig werden	wrinkling	198, 208
Schub; Druck	thrust	225
Schürze; Verkleidung	skirt	212
Schutzgas	shielding gas	211
Schutztülle; Abdichtstulpe	grommet	171
schwefelfreies Benzin	sulphur-free gasoline	125
Schwefelgehalt	sulphur content	119
Schwefeln	sulphonation	159
Schweißbarkeit	weldability	105
Schweißgeklebt	weldbonded	210
Schweißnaht	weld seam	211
Schweißspritzer	spatters	213
Schwelle; Fig: (very close) vor der Tür	doorstep	41
Schwelle; Grenze	threshold	123, 226
Schwellenwerte; Grenzwerte	threshold values	151
Schweller; Türschweller	sill beam	213
Schwenkarm; Gelenkhebel	swivel-arm	192
schwenkbar; klappbar	hinged	67
Schwenken	swivelling	249
schwer entflammbar, feuerhemmend	flame retardant	118
schwer verdaulich; schwerfällig	stodgy	73
Schwerpunkt	focal point	155
Schwingung	oscillation	179
Schwingungsfrequenz	resonance frequency	179
Schwingungsmessgerät	vibrometer	184
Schwung; Impuls	momentum	123
Schwungmasse; Fliehgewicht	flymass	176
Schwungmassenantriebsrad	flymass drive gear	176
Schwungmassenprüfstand	dynamometer	162
sechsflächig	hexahedral	222
Segen	boon	98
Segen	blessing	223
Seitenführungskräfte	cornering force	98
Seitenscheibenentfrosterdüsen	door window defroster vents	249
Seitenverkleidungen; Seitenwände	quarter panels	200
Seitenwand	quarter panel	239
Seitenwandblech innen	quarter panel inner	212
Seitenwände	side panels	65
seitlich, quer	laterally; lateral	143, 169
Sekundärlufteinblasung	secondary air injection	252
selbstführender Antrieb	self-locating drive	182
Senke	sink	63, 195
sensibel; anfällig	susceptible	153

Sensor-Ansauglufttemperatur	intake air temperature sensor	253
sequentielle Gangschaltung	sequential-shift	71
serielle Schnittstelle	serial interface	170
Servicefreundlichkeit	serviceability	88
sich auf etwas versteifen	stand out for (to stand out for sth.)	191
sich entscheiden	opting	160
sich entschieden haben	opted	81
sich etwas zunutze machen; aus etwas Vorteil ziehen	turned to account	96
Sichelölpumpe	crescent oil pump	254
sichern	secure	66
sicherstellen	safeguard	228
Sicherungsgabel	safety fork	242
Sicherungskasten	fuse box	248
Siebe	sieves	141
siegreich	victorious	226
Signalfarbe	tracer dye	250
Signalhorntasten	horn pushes	235
Silizium; Silicium	silicon	170
Siliziumkarbid	silicon carbide	197
sinken, abfallen	declined	223
Sitzaufnahme; Sitzträger	seat base	135
Sitzbezug	upholstery	242
Sitzfehler	seat defection	79
Sitzgestelle	seat frames	105
Sitzkissen	seat cushion	79
Sitzlehne	back rest	134
Sitzlehne, Rückenlehne	seat backs	66
Sitzlehnenneigungswinkel	seatback angle	79
Sitzlehnenverstellung; Rückenlehnenverstellung	backrest adjustment	82
Sitzrahmen; Sitzgestelle	seat frames	84
Sitzschale	seat pan	101
Sitzungsraum	boardroom	48
Sitzwannen; Sitzschalen	seat pans	200
Skeptiker	sceptics	65
sofort; unverzüglich	instant	87
Sonderausstattung	optional equipment	251
Sondervorrichtung	special purpose device	213
sondieren; untersuchen	probe	173
Sonnenblenden	sun visors	200
Sonnenkollektor	solar panel	133
Sorten	grades	114
Soundsystem; Audioanlage	audio system	93
Spalt	gap	114
Spannhebel; Klemmhebel	tensioning lever	176
Spannkraft; Anpresskraft	clamping force	209
Spannpratzen; Zwingen	clamps	214

Spannstellung	tensioning	247
Spannungsanalysen	stress analysis	60
Spannungsverläufe	stress patterns	221
Spannvorrichtungen	clamping devices	214
spazieren fahren; davon profitieren	ride	44
Speichen	spoke	248
Speichereinspritzsystem	accumulator injection system	136
Speichereinspritzung	accumulator injection	152
Spender; Dosierbehälter	dispenser	128
Sperrschicht/Zonenübergang-Temperaturen	junction temperatures	186
spezifisches Gewicht; Raumgewicht	specific gravity	114
spiralverzahnt, bogenverzahnt	spiral cut	182
Spleißung; Naht	splicing	158
Splitter	chips	213
Sporen	spores	250
Sprachsteuerung; Sprachbedienung	voice activation	93
springen	leap	157
spritzgegossen	injection moulded	113
Spritzgießen	injection moulding	200
Spritzgussteile	injection mouldings	115
Spritzgussteile; Blasformteile	blow mouldings	114
spröde	brittle	64
spröde, brüchig	brittle	199
Spurdifferenzgeometrie, Lenkdifferenzgeometrie der Lenkanlage	"ackermann" geometry	98
Stabilisator	stabilizer	247
Stabilitätsverbesserung	stability enhancement	95
Stahl mit Zinkschicht	of zinc-coated steel	108
Stahlguss	steel castings	109
Stammbaum, Herkunft	pedigrees	43
Standheizungen	parking heaters	186
Stanzwerkzeug	stamping die	63
Stapel	stack	50
stark durchgetreten	fully depressed	244
starke Gegenreaktion	backlash	58
starker Verkehr	in heavy traffic	247
starr	rigidly	65
Starrachse	beam axle	85
Starr-Deichselanhänger	rigid drawbar trailer	16
stationär	laminar	201
Staufächer	storage compartments	239
Staukräfte	ram forces	206
steht in Eingriff mit	engaged	132
Steifigkeit	rigidity	105, 206
Steifigkeit	stiffness	108, 165
steigend, wachsend	mounting	37
steigern	stepped up	

Steigungen	inclines	247
Steinschlagschaden	stone chipping	115
Steinschlagschutz	stone protector	258
Stellglieder	actuators	98
Stellrad für Leuchtweitenregulierung	headlamp range adjustment wheel	235
Stellung; Haltung; Position	posture	79
Stellwerk	actuator mechanism	143
Steuerdose; Kapsel	capsule	172
Steuergerät	control unit	186, 245
Steuergeräte; Vorschaltgeräte	ballasts	194
Steuerhebel; Einstellhebel	control lever	176
Steuerriemenabdeckung	timing belt covers	180
Stiche	punctures	245
Stickoxide	nitrogen oxides	255
Stickstoff	nitrogen	193
Stickstoffoxid (NOx)	nitrogen oxide	51
Stickstoffoxide	oxides of nitrogen	128
Stilistik, Formgebung, Gestaltung	styling	56
Stimmung	vein	75
Stirnseite; Vorderseite	front end	122
stöchiometrisches Kraftstoff-Luft-Verhältnis (ideales Verhältnis; Lambda = 1)	stoichiometric air-fuel ratio	141
Stoß aufnehmend	impact-absorbing	130
Stoßdämpfer	shock absorbers	85
Stoßdämpfer; Stoßstangen	bumpers	107
Stoßdämpferhalterungen	shock absorber mountings	67
Stoßdämpferkolben; Arbeitskolben	damper piston	153
Stoßdämpferstange	damper rods	153
Stoßfänger-Abdeckung	bumper covers	86
Strafrecht	penal law	226
Strahlungswärme	radiant heat	132
Strangpressanlage	extrusion facility	203
Strangpressteile	extrusions	207
Straßenausleuchtung	beam pattern	64
Straßenkarten	maps	251
Streckgrenze, Fließgrenze	yield strength	172
Streu-Lastwagen	salt, grit and sand spreader (gritting truck)	16
Streuungen; Schwankungen	variations	164
stromaufwärts	upstream	163
stromaufwärts; gegen den Strom	upstream	
strömen	pour	202
stromgesteuert	current-controlled	170
Stromkreise; elektrische Schaltungen	circuits	170
Strömungslinien	flow lines	63
Strömungswiderstand	drag	86
Stromversorgung	mains supply	122
Stromversorgung	electricity supply	249

Strudel; Wirbel	swirl	138
Struktur, Aufbau; Gerippe	structure	65
Strukturintegrität	structural integrity	130
strukurell; baulich	structural	200
Stufenheck	notchback	240
Stupsnase, stupsnasig	snub-nose, snub-nosed	75
Sturm; Angriff	assault	223
Stützlast	coupling socket load	247
stylen; designen	style	194
Styrol-Budadien	styrene-butadiene	156
Substrat; Träger	substrates	200
subtil, raffiniert	subtle	97
subventioniert, bezuschusst	subsidised	84
Suche	quest	154, 174
Summgeräusche, Brummtöne	humming noises	179
synthetisches Benzin	synthetic gasoline	123
Tachometer	speedometer	236
Tageskilometerzähler	trip odometer	236
Takt	phase	81
Taktsignale	clock signals	88
Taktzeit	cycle time	202, 208
Talkum	talc	179
Tankentlüftungsventil	tank vent valve	252
Tankstelle	filling station	91
tatsächlich	actual	247
tatsächlich; faktisch	virtually	191
Tauglichkeit	capability	62
technische Beratung; Beratung	consultancy	110
technischer Ruß	carbon black	156, 160
Teflon (Polytetrafluorethylen)	ptfe	154
Teilchen; Körnchen	particulates	119
Teile mit Körnung	parts grained	61
Teilmenge, Bereich	portion	201
Telematik	telematics	89
Teppichrückseite; Teppichunterseite	under carpet	184
Testgelände; Versuchsgelände; Prüffelder	proving grounds	177
Tiefenprofil	depth profile	173
tieftemperaturmäßig	cryogenically	127
Tochterunternehmen; Tochtergesellschaft	subsidiary	35, 37
Todesopfer	fatalities	
toll	groovy	44
Torsionskraft	torsional force	143
tragende Bauteile; Stützglieder	supporting members	181
Träger	substrate	178
Träger, Holme	rails	205

Träger; Halterung	carrier	100
Träger; Holm	member	65
Trägerbefestigung; Sattelbefestigung	cradle mounts	183
Trägerplatte	carrying plate	168
Tragfähigkeits-Kennzahl	load index	246
Traktor; Zugfahrzeug	tractor	16, 23, 194
Transformatoren	transformers	194
Treibhauseffekt	greenhouse effect	151
Treibhausgas	greenhouse gas	128
Trennmittel	mould release agents	200
Trennwand	partition	163
tribologische Eigenschaften	tribological properties	153
Trick	gimmick	
Trockner	dryer	250
Tropfen; Tröpfchen	droplets	147
Tüchtigkeit	prowess	30
Türbleche, Türblätter	the door panels	130
Türblechverkleidung	door panel lining	179
Turboantrieb	turbocharging	32
Turbulenzen, Luftwirbel	buffeting	66
Türholm, Türsäule	door pillars	181
Türöffnung außen	door opening outer	212
Türschweller; Einstiegsschweller	door sill; doorsill	65, 81
Türverstärkungsstrebe; Seitenaufprallschutz	door intrusion beams	205
Überangebot	surplus	223
übereinstimmen mit	coincides with	179
Übereinstimmung; Einhaltung	compliance	61
überflüssig	redundant	88
überflüssig	superseded	192
Überfülle	plethora	81, 94
Übergang	crossover	74
Übergang	transition	190
übergreifen	encroache	130
überholen, instandsetzen	overhaul	38
überlackiert	painted	258
überladen (zu viel berechnet)	overcharged	
überlagert	superimposed	177
Überlandlinienbus	interurban coach	16
Überlappungsnähte	lap joints	213
überlegen, souverän	superior	194
übermäßig	excess	134
übermäßig lang	lengthy	139
übernehmen, annehmen	adopted	95
übernommen	adopted	174
Überrollbügel	rollover bars	65

Überschlagspannung; Durchbruchspannung	breakdown voltage	171
überschüssiges Pulver	excess powder	191
Überströmventil	overflow valve	176
übertreffen	outperform	113, 186
übertreffen	surpass	141, 194
übertrieben	exaggerated	73
Überwachung, Kontrolle	monitoring	61, 91
überwinden	overcome	97, 115
überzeugend	persuasive	58, 216
Ultraschall-Mikrofon	ultrasound microphone	256
umbördeln um 180 Grad	hemming process	108
Umfang; Kreisumfang	circumference	132, 208
umfassen	embrace	80
umfassend	comprehensive	54
Umformungskosten	transformation cost	105
umgebend; einfassend	surrounding	97
umgebendes Lichtniveau	ambient light level	99
Umgebungsluft; Außenluft	ambient air	134
Umgehungleitung	bypass	163
umhüllt	wrapped	195
Umlaufzeit	turnaround time	222
Umleitung; Ablenkung	diversion	94
Umluftsysteme	air circulation systems	249
ummantelt; umhüllt	wrapped	137
Umordnung, Neuordnung	rearrangement	58
Umstellung	changeover	230
Umweg	circuitous route	163
Umweltbelastung	environmental loading	114
unabhängig	irrespective	246
unbemannt	unmanned	121
undurchlässig	impermeable	181
Unfähigkeit	inability	124
ungeachtet; ohne Rücksicht auf	irrespective	190
ungenügend	inadequate	58
ungeschichtet; unkaschiert	unlaminated	179
ungestörter Empfang	unimpeded reception	252
ungewollt	unintentional	242
ungünstig; nachteilig	adversely	175
unklug; töricht	unwise	233
unkompliziert	straightforward	124
unmerklich; verschwindend gering	imperceptibly	135
unscharf	out of focus	221
unter Überprüfung	under review	87
unter- und übersteuern	under and oversteer	168
Unterboden	underbody	71
unterdrückt; gedämpft	suppressed	88
Unterdruckunterstützung	vacuum servo	95

untere Fläche	sub-surface	173
untergebracht	housed	127
untergeordnete/niedrige Schmiereigenschaften	inferior lubricity	174
Unterkante	bottom edge	132
unterscheiden	distingushing	199
Unterschenkelverletzungen	lower leg injuries	98
Untersetzungsgetriebe; Zwischengetriebe	reduction gear	132
unterstreichen	underscore	42
unterstreichen	enhances	199
unterstützen	back	225
Unterstützung	support	62
untersuchen; beobachten	surveying	143
Untersuchung	inquiry	37
Untersuchungen	surveys	54
Untertitel	subheaded	15
unvermeidlich	inevitable	109, 225
unvermeidlich; zwangsläufig	inevitably	143
Unverträglichkeit	incompatibility	86
Unverwechselbarkeit; Deutlichkeit	distinctiveness	73
unverzichtbar	indispensable	221
unwirtschaftlich, unrentabel	uneconomic	37
Unwucht; Gleichgewichtsstörungen	imbalances	85
Unzen	ounces	146
UV-Beständigkeit	uv stability	114
Ventile	valves	94
Ventilhub	valve lift	143
Ventilschaft	valve stem	254
Ventilsteuerung	valve operation	143
Ventilsteuerzeiten	valve timing	142
verändern	altering	143
verankert	anchored	65
verantwortlich; haftbar	liable for	225
Verantwortlichkeit; Verpflichtung	liability	225
Verarbeitbarkeit	processability	165
verbessern	enhance; enhancing	153, 172
Verbindung, Mischung	compound	130
Verbindung; Mischung; Zusammensetzung	compounds	178
Verbindungen	jumpers	160
Verbindungen	joints	205
Verbindungselemente	fasteners	130
Verbindungstücke	connectors	114
Verbindungswellen; Zwischenwellen	transmission shafts	206
verblassen	fading	73
verbleites Kraftstoff	leaded fuel	255
verborgen	concealed	133

Verbrennung	combustion	221
Verbund-	composite	200
Verbundbauteil, Blech/Kunststoff-Formteil	sheet moulding compound	113
verbunden	allied	50
Verbundlenker-Hinterachse	twist beam rear axle	82
Verbundwerkstoff	composite material	66, 110, 178, 194
Verdacht	suspicion	233
verdächtig	suspected	119
Verdampfer	evaporator	250
Verdeck; Klappverdeck; Faltdach	hood	66
verdecken	masks	184
Verdichter-Schmiermittel	compressor lubricant	250
Verdichtung	ignition	15
Verdichtungstakt	compression stroke	221
Verdienste	merits	217
verdrängen; überflüssig machen	supersede	249
verdrehen	twist	66
verdrehen, verwinden	torsional	199
Verdrehsteifigkeit	torsional rigidity	210
Verdrehsteifigkeit, Verwindungssteifigkeit	torsional stiffness	65
verdrehte, verdrillte	twisted cable	89
Verdrehungen	twists	230
verdünnen; verwässern	dilute	225
vereinfachen, erleichtern	facilitating	194
verfeinern; veredeln	refining	89
Verfeinerung; Veredelung	refinements	197
Verfestigen, Erstarren; Verfestigung	solidification	105, 196
verflüchtigen	fleeting	73
verfolgen	pursue	126
Verfolgung	pursuit	61, 117
Verformung	deformation	65
verführerisch	seductive	120
Vergehen	offence	37
verglast	glazed	133
Vergleichbarkeit	comparability	15
verhängt; auferlegt	imposed	226
verhärtet	hardened	174
verheerende Folgen	disastrous consequences	126
Verhindern	hampered	30
verhindern	impede	182
verjazzen (ein Stück)	jazz up	74
Verkäufer	vendor	60, 223
Verkehrsstau	traffic jams	92
Verkleidung; Aussenverkleidung	fascias	117
Verkleidungen, Verschalungen	fairings	131

Verkleidungsteile, Verblendungsteile	facing parts	179
verlängern	stretching	205
verlassen; aufgeben	abandon	49
verleiten	tempt	247
Verlustfaktor	loss factor	179
Vermögen; Kapital	funds	194
vermuten	presume	98
vermutlich	presumably	91
verriegeln, sperren, blockieren	interlocking	198
Verriegelung	lock	240
Verriegelung; Sperren, Verblockung	interlocking	65
verringern	diminishes	199
Verrippungen	ribbings	105
Verschlechterung; Beschädigung; Zerstörung	deterioration	175
Verschleiß, Abnutzung; Abrieb	wear	154, 173, 174, 186
verschlossen	tight-lipped	158
Verschluss; Arretierung	catch	239
Verschlussstopfen	sealing plug	247
verschmolzen	fused	130
verschmutzen, verunreinigen	contaminate	128
Verschmutzer	pollutants	102
verschrottet	scrapped	205
versetzt angeordnet	staggered	81
versiegeln, konservieren	seal	130
Versprechen	pledge	151
verstärken; ausbauen	strengthening	223
Verstärker	amplifier	252
verstärkt	reinforced	66
Verstärkung	boost	85
Verstärkung Stoßfänger-Dom	shock tower reinforcement	212
Versteifung; Verfestigung	strengthening	199
Versteifungsrippen	stiffening ribs	101
verstellbare Turbine	variable turbine	85
verstellbarer Turbolader	variable turbocharger	139
Versteller	timing device	176
Verstellhebelwelle	control lever shaft	176
Verstellmuffe; Regelhülse	control sleeve	176
Verstopfung	congestion	92
verstoßen	contravenes	226
Versuchspressen	try out presses	60
verteilen, austeilen	dispensing	201
verteilen; zerstreuen	dissipates	128
Verteilereinspritzpumpen	distributor pumps	174
Vertrag	treaty	226
vertraulich	confidential	196
vertraut	intimate	110

Verunreinigungen	impurities	204
verwechseln, durcheinander bringen	confound	98
verwindungssteif, verdrehsteif	rigid	65
Verwirbelungen	vorticities	220
verwirren (den Gegner usw.)	confounded	65
Verzerrung	distortions	37
verzichtet	dispensed with	164
Verzurrösen	lash lugs	239
Vieleck	polygonisation	199
vielfach	multiple	200
vielseitig	versatile	177
Vielseitigkeit; Wandelbarkeit	versatility	92
Vielzwecklastkraftwagen	general purpose goods vehicle	16
vierfach	quadruple	81
vierflächig; tetraedrisch	tetrahedral	222
viskoelastische Schwerschicht	septum	179
voll und ganz	full extent	257
Vollbremsung	full-on braking	244
vollendet	accomplished	89
vollendet	accomplished	139
Vollständigkeit	integrity	97, 195, 198
vom Anfang an	from the outset	126
von etwas abhängen	hinge on	174
von etwas strotzen	bristling with (to b. with sth.)	232
vorantreiben; drängen	urged	225
vorausgesehen	envisaged	154
voraussehen	anticipated	117
voraussehen	envisage	139, 228
Vorbaustruktur	front-end structure	65
vordere Innenraumbeleuchtung	front interior illumination	257
Vorgänger; Vorläufermodell	predecessor	153, 230
vorgebogen	pre-bent	206
vorgespannt	tempered	199
vorgespannt	pre-tensioned	242
vorherrschend	predominant	203
Vorhersagesystem	predictive system	92
Vorhub	preliminary stroke	138
vorklappen	forwards	240
Vorkommen	occurring	54
Vorrichtungen	fixtures	60
vorschreiben	stipulated	165
Vorschub	feed	161
Vorspannung	prestrain	108
Vorstand; Vorstandsgremium	management board	70
Vorstandsmitglied	chief executive officer	228
Vorstandsmitglied	CEO (Chief Executive Officer)	233
vorstehend	prominent	79
Vorteil; Plus	asset	51

Vorteile	gains	42
vorübergehend, zeitweise	temporarily	141
vorübergehend; vergänglich	transient	96
vorwärts getrieben	propelled	201
Waage	weighing apparatus	247
Wabenkörper	honeycomb	130
Wabenkörper	monolith	163
Wabenkörper-Struktur	monolithic structure	131
Wagenheber	jack	246
Wählhebel	selector level	255
wahrnehmen	perceive	101, 115
Wahrscheinlichkeit	likelihood	65
Walzprofilstahl	rolled steel sections	203
Waren; Artikel; Gebrauchsgüter	commodities	15
warm verrippt, warm versickt	hot ribbing	108
Wärmeausdehnung	thermal expansion	114
wärmeausgehärtet	heat-cured	205
Wärmebeständigkeit	heat resistance	114
wärmeleitend	thermally conductive	186
Wärmeleitfähigkeit; Wärmeleitvermögen	thermal conductivity	107, 186
Warmschrumpfschlauch; Aufschrumpfschlauch	heat-shrinkable tubing	118
Warmumformen; Heißformen	hot forming	205
Warnblinker	hazard warning flashers	235
Warndreieck	warning triangle	240
Wartung	maintenance	54
Wasserstoff	hydrogen	50, 123, 124
Wasserwaage	level	64
wässrige Lösungen	aqueous solutions	191
wechselnd; hin- und hergehend	alternating	135
Wechselstrom	ac (alternating current)	88, 124
Wechselstrom	alternating current (ac)	194
Wechselwirkungen	interactions	56
Wegfahrsperre	immobilizer	236
Wegfall	omission	252
wegstecken, verstecken	tucked away	125
Wegstreckenzähler; Kilometerzähler	odometer	251
Wegwerf-, Einweg-	disposable	194
Weißrauschen; weißes Rauschen	white noise	184
weiterführen	pursues	37
Welle	shaft	100
Wellenspitzen	wave crests	88
Wellrippen	corrugated fins	249
Werksdirektor	plant manager	228
werksseitig montiert	assemblied ex work	252
Werkzeug	tool	61

Wertminderung; Wertverlust	depreciation	105
wichtig	essential	177
Wichtigkeit; Größe	magnitude	222
widerspiegeln	reflecting	50
Widerspruch	contradiction	178
Widerstand	resistance	130, 170
widerstandsfähig	toughened	66
widerstehen	resist	157, 197
Widerwille, Abneigung	reluctances	115
wie angegossen passen	fit as snugly	130
wieder auffüllen	replenish	124
Wiederaufbereitungsfähigkeit	recyclability	105
wiederbeleben; sich erholen	reviving	
wiedergewinnen; regenerieren	reclaim	191
wiederverwerten	salvaged	226
Wiege zu Grabe tragen	cradle-to-grave	48
Windabweiser; Luftleitflügel	spoilers	194
Windschutz, Windschott	windbreak	66
Windschutzscheibe	windscreen (GB); screen (GB); windshield (US)	50
Windstöße, Böen	blasts	132
Windung; Wicklung	coil	198
Winkel	several angles	63
Winkelbleche, Knotenbleche	gusset plates	66
Wipptaste	rocker switch	257
Wirbel	eddies	219
Wirbel	vortices	220
Wirbel	swirl	221
Wirbelsäule; Rückgrat	spinal column	135
Wirkungsgrad	efficiency	124
Wirkungsverlust; Schwund; Nachlassen der Wirkung	fade	82
Wohlstand	prosperity	
Wohnwagen	caravan; camper; house trailer	23
Wolfram	tungsten	161
wuchtig	massive	115
zähflüssig; fest	consistent	202
zahlungsunfähig	insolvent	41
Zahnrad	gear	100, 132
Zahnrad mit Geradverzahnung; Stirnrad	spur gear	132
Zahnriemen-Spannrolle	toothed belt tensioner roller	254
Zapfen	pins	239
Zeichenbrett	drawing board	221
zeitgenössisch	contemporary	171
zerhacken	chopping	95
Zerreißfestigkeit; Zugfestigkeit	tensile strength	105
Zerstäuber	diffuser	71

zerstreuen; zerstäuben	diffuse	133
Ziegel; Stein	brick	141
Ziehwinkel	draft angle	105
Ziel	objective	79
Ziele	targets	54
Zischgeräusch	hissing noise	184
zögernd	halting	40
Zollgebühren	tariffs	
Zonenübergang; Sperrschicht	junction	134
zu den Akten gelegt	filed	223
zu hohe Belastung	excessive load	249
zuallererst	first and foremost	84
Zubehör	accessories	23
Zubehörsteckdose	accessory socket	235
Zugbeanspruchungen	tensile stresses	199
zugeführt; eingeleitet	fed	168
Zugfestigkeit	tensile strength	172, 174
Zugmaschinen	towing vehicles	16
Zugmaschinenzug	drawbar tractor combination	16
Zugvorrichtung	towing equipment	247
Zuladung	payload	121
zulässig; genehmigt	permitted	88
zulässige Anhängelasten	permissible caravan/trailer load	247
zulässiges Gesamtgewicht, ZGG	gross vehicle mass	15
zum Schauen auffordern	appealing looks	120
zum Spielen aufgelegt; (wild) ausgelassen; verspielt	playful	74
zum Unternehmen gehörend	captive	37
Zündfähigkeit	inflammability	106
Zündkerzenstecker	spark plug connectors	252
Zündmodul	ignition module	252
Zündpille (für Airbags)	squibs	170
Zündung	internal combustion	15
Zunft	fraternity	220
zur Folge haben; mit sich bringen	entails	125
zurückkehren	reverts	141
Zusammenarbeit	tie-ups	41
zusammenarbeiten	collaborating	79
Zusammenbau Seitenwand außen	body side outer assembly	210
zusammenbrechen; versagen	collapsing	205
zusammenbruchbeständig	crash resisting	208
Zusammendrückbarkeit	compressibility	186, 220
zusammenfallen, entleeren	deflate	135
Zusammenfassung, Handbuch	compendium	15
Zusammensetzung	composition	141
Zusatzmittel; Wirkstoffe	additives	173
Zusatzheizgerät	auxiliary heating	187

zusätzliche Verstärkung; Hilfs-; Zusatz-Verstärkung	auxiliary reinforcement	240
Zuschlagskosten	excess cost	106
Zustand	state	143
zuteilen; dosieren; steuern	proportioning	245
Zuverlässigkeit	reliability	62
Zwang	coercion	58
Zwänge	constraints	56
zwei obenliegende Nockenwellen	twin overhead camshafts	145
zwei Standpunkte beziehen	taking two stances	223
zwei, doppelt	twin	65
zwei Lagen	two-ply	198
zwingen	slaving	99
Zwischenhändler	middlemen	223
Zwischenkühler	intercooler	81
Zwischenlösung	interim solution	165
Zwischenwelle	intermediate shaft	256
zyklisch, periodisch	cyclic	143, 199
Zylinderbohrung	cylinder bore	254
Zylindereinlass	intakes	86
Zylinderkopf	cylinder head	252
Zylinderkopfdeckel	cylinder head covers	106

Vocabulary English – German

English	German	Page
"Ackermann" geometry	Spurdifferenzgeometrie, Lenkdifferenzgeometrie der Lenkanlage	98
abandon	verlassen; aufgeben	49
abrasion	Abnutzung, Verschleiß, Erosion	130
abs	Acrylnitril-Butadien-Styrol	179
absorbed	aufgenommen; geschluckt	134
absorbing, absorb	aufnehmen, schlucken	130, 163
ac (alternating current)	Wechselstrom	88, 124
accelerator	Gaspedal	95
accelerometers	Beschleunigungsmesser	171
accessories	Nebenverbraucher	122
accessories	Zubehör	23
accessory socket	Zubehörsteckdose	235
accomplished	vollendet	89, 139
accumulator injection	Speichereinspritzung	152
accumulator injection system	Speichereinspritzsystem	136
accused	beschuldigt	226
acoustic panels	Schall-Verkleidung/- Beplankung	194
acquired	erwerben	51
acquisitions	Erwerb	41
acrylic polymers	Acryl-Polymerisat	193
active headrest	aktive Kopfstütze	238
actual	tatsächlich	247
actuation	Bedienung; Steuerung, Betätigung	95
actuator mechanism	Stellwerk	143
actuators	Stellglieder	98
additives	Zusatzmittel; Wirkstoffe	173
adhesive lined	m. Klebstoff beschichtet	118
adhesives	Klebstoff; Klebemittel	84
adjacent to	angrenzend; direkt neben	228
adjoining	angrenzend	183
adjusted	eingestellt; justiert	141
adopted	gewählt, ergriffen, verabschiedet	
adopted	übernommen, angenommen	95, 174
adoption	Annahme; Übernahme	95
adversely	ungünstig; nachteilig	175
advisory panel	Beratungspodium	79
advocates	befürworten	48
aesthetics	Ästhetik	190
aftertreatment systems	Nachbehandlungssysteme	119
age	altern	195
ageing	Alterung	199
ageing (GB), aging (US)	alternd	38

aiming screws	Einstellschrauben	64
air circulation systems	Umluftsysteme	249
air conditioning system	Klimaanlage	250
air ducts	Luftkanäle	179
air intake manifold; air distributor	Einlasskrümmer; Ansaugkrümmer; Ansaugrohr	114, 180, 184
airborne noise	durch Luft übertragener Schall	181
alarm system	Alarmanlage	171
albumen	Eiweiß	193
aldehydes	Aldehyde	128
alert	alarmieren	90
algorithm	Algorithmus	167
aligned	ausgerichtet	242
allegation	Anschuldigung	37
allied	verbunden	50
alloy	Legierung	203
all-wheel-drive	Allrad-Antrieb	69
altering	verändern	143
alternating	wechselnd; hin- und hergehend	135
alternating current (ac)	Wechselstrom	194
alternator	Drehstromgenerator; Drehstrom-Lichtmaschine; Lichtmaschine	119, 183, 236
aluminium (GB), aluminum (US)	Aluminium	81, 84
ambient air	Umgebungsluft; Außenluft	134
ambient light level	umgebendes Lichtniveau	99
amend	abändern; verbessern	225
amid	mitten in/unter	117
ample	reichlich; genügend	240
amplifier	Verstärker	252
anchored	verankert	65
ancillaries	Nebenaggregate	194
and tilt sensor	Neigungsgeber; Winkelsensor	256
anechoic	schalltot; nicht reflektierend	183, 184
annual production	Jahresproduktion	
annular	ringförmig	201
anodising	Eloxieren	203
anthropometric consistency	anthropometrische Beständigkeit	79
anticipated	voraussehen	117
anti-lock brake system	Antiblockiersystem	236
anti-lock brakes	ABS-Bremsanlage	232
anti-lock braking systems	Bremsanlagen mit Antiblockiersystem	96
anti-theft warning system	Diebstahlwarnanlage	256
apertures	Öffnung; Ausschnitt	181
a-pillar inner (panel) lower	A-Säule Innenblech unten	212
a-pillar inner (panel) upper	A-Säule Innenblech oben	212
appealing	Daseinsberechtigungen; raison d'etre	120
appealing looks	zum Schauen auffordern	120
appliqué	Aufnäher	242

applying	einsetzen	130
aqueous solutions	wässrige Lösungen	191
aramid fibres	Aramidfaser; AFK-Faser	85
arc	Bogen	172
architecture	Aufbau; Architektur	56
arrow-shaped	pfeilförmig	80
articulated bus	Gelenkbus	16
articulated vehicle	Sattelkraftfahrzeug	16
articulating	gelenkig	79
artisans	Handwerker	77
as opposed to	im Gegensatz zu	191
ash	Asche	195
asic (application-specific integrated circuit)	anwendungsspezifischer integrierter Schaltkreis	170
aspect ratio	Höhen-Breiten-Verhältnis	217
aspect ratio	Querschnittsverhältnis	246
assault	Sturm; Angriff	223
assembles	baut zusammen	22
assemblied ex work	werksseitig montiert	252
assembly groups	Baugruppen	225
assembly line	Montagestraße, Fließband	56, 230
asset	Vorteil; Plus	51
assets	Aktiva; Deckungsforderungen; (Konkurs-)Masse, Betriebsvermögen	
asynchronous motor	Asynchronmotor; Induktionsmotor	125
at its disposal	jemandem zur Verfügung stehen	229
at odds with (to be at o. with s.o.)	mit j-m uneins sein	185
attenuation	Geräuschdämpfung, Schalldämpfung	178
audio system	Soundsystem; Audioanlage	93
auditory sensation	Gehörgefühl	179
autoclave	Dampfdruckerhitzer; Druckhärtekessel	194
automatical feeder	automatische Zuführung	191
auxiliary heating	Zusatzheizgerät	187
auxiliary reinforcement	zusätzliche Verstärkung; Hilfs-; Zusatz-Verstärkung	240
awe-inspiring	Ehrfurcht gebietend	137
axial piston distributor pump	Axialkolben-Verteilereinspritzpumpe	152
axle load distribution	Achslastverteilung	197
back	unterstützen	225
back rest	Sitzlehne	134
back window	Heckscheibe	220
backache	Rückenschmerzen	134
backbone	Rückgrat	73
background-noise level	Hintergrundgeräuschpegel	177
backing	Hinterspritzen; Verstärken; Hinterschäumung	178
backlash	starke Gegenreaktion	58
backrest	Rückenlehne; Sitzlehne	135

backrest adjustment	Sitzlehnenverstellung; Rückenlehnenverstellung	82
baffle	Prallblech; Blende	163
baffles	Leitbleche, Ablenkbleche; Abweiser	182
baits	Köder	
balance shaft	Ausgleichswelle	69
balanced	ausgewuchtet	246
ballasts	Steuergeräte; Vorschaltgeräte	194
bankruptcy	Bankrott	223
barcode label	Barcodeaufkleber	255
barn	Scheune	75
baryta	Bariumoxid	178
basecoat, base coat	Grundlackschicht	114, 190
beads	Kügelchen; Perlen	116
beam axle	Starrachse	85
beam pattern	Lichtverteilung	172
beam pattern	Straßenausleuchtung	64
bear	aushalten, tragen	65
bearings	Lager	153
bed-plate	Montageplatte	183
beefy	kräftig	
bell housings	Kupplungsgehäuse; Kupplungsglocke	196
belt drive	Riemenantrieb	125
belt housing	Gurtgehäuse	101
belt lock	Gurtschloss	242
belt pulleys	Riemenscheiben	213
bendability	Biegevermögen	173
bending load	Biegebeanspruchung; Biegelast	143
bending moment	Biegemoment	154
bending stiffness	Biegesteifigkeit	110
bends	Kurven	244
benzene	Benzol	120
bidding	bieten	
blanks	Platinen, Stanzteile	110
blasts	Windstöße, Böen	132
blatant	eklatant, himmelschreiend	52
blemish; blemishes (pl)	Schönheitsfehler; Fehlstellen; Schönheitsfehler (pl)	63, 193
blemishes	Fehlstellen	195
blessing	Segen	223
blip	leuchtender Punkt (auf dem Bildschirm)	96
blow mouldings	Spritzgussteile; Blasformteile	114
blow-moulded	blasgeformt	159
blowout	Platzen	245
boarding zones	Einstiegszone	
boardroom	Sitzungsraum	48
boasts	prahlen, rühmen	220

bodies	Karosserien	23
body	Karosserie	50
body joint strength	Karosserie-Gelenkfestigkeit	
body mounts	Karosserietraglager	183
body shop	Karosserierohbau	231
body side outer assembly	Zusammenbau Seitenwand außen	210
body structure	Karosserierohbau; Rohbau	84
bodywork	Karosserie; Aufbau	67, 111, 112, 177
bonded	geklebt	108, 203
bonding	kleben; festkleben, einkleben	84, 156, 205
bonnet (GB); hood (US); engine cowl	Motorhaube	64, 115
boon	Segen	98
boost	Auftrieb geben	
boost	Verstärkung	85
boost pressure	Ladedruck; Ladeluftdruck	139
boot (GB); trunk (US)	Kofferraum, Gepäckraum	67
bottom edge	Unterkante	132
boundary regions	Grenzbereiche	208
bowden cable	Bowdenzug	242
bracket	Halter	63
bracketry	Lagerungen	115
brake calliper (GB); brake caliper (US)	Bremssattel; Bremszange	85, 196
brake circuits	Bremskreise	244
brake discs (GB); brake disks (US)	Bremsscheiben	80
brake intervention	Bremseneingriff	96
brake lights	Bremslichter, Stopplichter	194
brake master cylinder	Hauptbremszylinder	96
brake pads	Bremsbeläge	243
brake proportioning valve	Bremskraftregler	245
brake; brakes	Bremsen	71
braking intervention	Bremseingriff	97
branch	Bereich	89
brand	Marke	51
brand name	Markenname, Markenbezeichnung	22
brass	Messing	115
breakaway stopping cable	Abreißseil	247
breakdown	Autopanne	91
breakdown lorry (wrecker truck)	Abschleppfahrzeug; Abschleppwagen	16
breakdown voltage	Überschlagsspannung; Durchbruchspannung	171
break-off	Abbruch	221
brick	Ziegel; Stein	141
brightness	Glanz	114
brightness	Helligkeit	237
briskly	schnell, glatt, lebhaft	
bristling with (to b. with sth.)	von etwas strotzen	232
brittle	spröde, brüchig	64, 199

bubble	Luftblase; Blase	64, 150
bubbly	schäumend	74
buckle	Auswölbung	88
buckling	Abknicken; Ausbeulen	208
bucks	Dollar (N.Am)	73
buffeting	Turbulenzen, Luftwirbel	66
bulb	Lampe	171
bulges	Beulen	245
bulkhead	Schottwand; Querwand	177
bullish	in Haussestimmung	203
bumper covers	Stoßfänger-Abdeckung	86
bumpers	Stoßdämpfer; Stoßstangen	107
buoys	Bojen	123
burrs	Grate	213
bursting	Platzen	245
bury	begraben	49
bus trailer	Busanhänger	16
bypass	Umgehungsleitung	163
cabin temperature	Innenraum-, Fahrgastraum-Temperatur	99
cable ties	Kabelbinder	242
calibrated	geeicht	59
cam plate	Nockenscheibe; Kurvenscheibe	176
camplate	Hubscheibe	174
camshaft	Nockenwelle	85, 143, 173
camshaft sensor	Nockenwellensensor	253
can head off	ablenken	98
cap seals	Aufsteck-Dichtungen	154
capability	Tauglichkeit	62
capsule	Steuerdose; Kapsel	172
captive	zum Unternehmen gehörend	37
capture	erfassen	172
capture	erobern, gewinnen	54
car interior	Fahrzeuginnenraum	178
caravan (GB); house trailer (US)	Caravan; Wohnwagen	16
caravan; camper; house trailer	Wohnwagen	23
carbide	Hartmetall	161
carbon black	technischer Ruß	156, 160
carbon dioxide	Kohlendioxid	51
carbon fibre	Kohlenstofffaser	81
carbon monoxide	Kohlenmonoxid	51, 128
carboniferous	Kohle führend	119
carcass	Karkasse, Unterbau	158
carcinogenic	krebserregend	119
carline	Fahrzeuglinien; hier: Automodelle	54
carrier	Träger; Halterung	100
carrying plate	Trägerplatte	168
car-sharing	gemeinsame Fahrzeugbenutzung	121

carved	geschnitzt	172
casing	Gehäuse	165
cast iron	Gusseisen	82, 197
catalyst; catalytic converter; catalyser (GB); catalyzer (US)	Katalysator	51, 102, 162, 252
catch	Verschluss; Arretierung	239
catered for	berücksichtigen	205
cavity	Hohlraum; Aussparung	133, 181, 194, 209
centre armrest	Mittelarmlehne	240
CEO (Chief Executive Officer)	Vorstandsmitglied	233
ceramic semi-conductor	keramisches Halbleiterelement	249
changeover	Umstellung	230
channels	Kanäle; Rinnen	242
charge air cooling	Ladeluftkühlung	69
charge cycle	Ladungswechsel	139
charger	Ladegerät	122, 232
chassis	Fahrwerk	23, 50
chassis-cab	Fahrgestell mit Fahrerhaus	121
chemistry	Chemie	173
chief executive officer	Vorstandsmitglied	228
child seat recognition	Kindersitzerkennung	88
chills	Gussformen; Kokillen	197
chime	Gong; Läutewerk	171
chipping	absplittern	192
chips	Splitter	213
chlorosulphonated polyethylene	chlorsulfoniertes Polyethylen	178
chopping	zerhacken	95
churning out (to churn out sth.)	am laufenden Band produzieren (etwas)	74
circuit boards	Leiterplatten; gedruckte Schaltungen	63
circuitous route	Umweg	163
circuits	Stromkreise; elektrische Schaltungen; Schaltkreise	88, 170
circumference	Umfang; Kreisumfang	132, 208
claimed that	behaupten	223
clamping devices	Spannvorrichtungen	214
clamping force	Spannkraft; Anpresskraft	209
clamps	Spannpratzen; Zwingen	214
clamshell	Muschelschale	231
class a surface finish	Oberflächenbeschaffenheit mit 1A Qualität	115
clear coats	Klarlackschichten	190
clearence	Freiraum; Spiel	214
climate control	Fahrzeugklimaregelung	88
clips	Schellen, Halter	130
clock signals	Taktsignale	88
closure panels	Deckbleche, Abschlussbleche	117, 231
clutches	Kupplungen	100

coarse grained	genarbt; grobkörnig	257
coated	beschichtet	163
coating	Beschichtung; Überzug; Ummantelung	178, 190
coaxial	rundlaufend; konzentrisch	160
coefficient of friction	Haftreibungsbeiwert	153
coercion	Zwang	58
coherent	konsequent; verständlich	
coil	Windung; Wicklung	198
coil spring	Schraubenfeder	85, 198
coincides with	übereinstimmen mit	179
cold chamber process	Kältekammerverfahren	105
cold drawn	kaltgezogen	85
collaborating	zusammenarbeiten	79
collapsing	zusammenbrechen; versagen	205
collar	Bund, Flansch	100
colour-keyed	farblich abgestimmt	191
combative	kämpferisch	41
combine	Konzern	
combustion	Verbrennung	221
combustion chamber	Brennkammer (einer mit Kraftstoff betriebenen Standheizung)	188
come apart	auseinander fallen	198
commenced	begonnen, gestartet, angefangen	177
commencing, commence	anfangen	127, 228
commercial vehicles	Nutzkraftwagen (Nkw)	16, 17
commissioned	abgenommen	226
commodities	Waren; Artikel; Gebrauchsgüter	15
common rail	gemeinsame Versorgungsleitung	152
commonality	Gleichheit	224
commuter	Pendler; Berufspendler	120
compact van	kompakte Großraumlimousine	123
comparability	Vergleichbarkeit	15
compatible	gut zusammen passend	59
compendium	Zusammenfassung, Handbuch	15
complement	Ergänzung	141
compliance	Übereinstimmung; Einhaltung	61
comply	nachkommen (einer Bitte)	59
composite	Verbund-	200
composite design	Hybridbauweise	252
composite material	Verbundwerkstoff	66, 110, 178, 194
composite-construction engine control unit	Motorsteuergerät in Hybridbauweise	252
composition	Zusammensetzung	141
compound	Gemisch; Verbindung, Mischung	64, 130
compounds	Verbindung; Mischung; Zusammensetzung	178
comprehensive	umfassend	54
compressibility	Zusammendrückbarkeit	186, 220

compression	Einfederung	245
compression stroke	Verdichtungstakt	221
compressive	Druckspannungs-	199
compressor lubricant	Verdichter-Schmiermittel	250
comprised; comprised of	bestehend aus	197, 206
comprises	bestehen (aus etw.); bestehen aus	125
concave-pistons	Hohlkolben	142
concealed	verborgen	133
conceivable	denkbar	123
conceived	ausgedacht; entwickelt	172
concept coupe vehicle	Coupe Styling Studie	114
concession	Entgegenkommen	226
concluded	beenden	228
concrete-mixer lorries	Betonmischer-Lkw, Transportbetonmischer	15
condensation	Kondenswasser	250
conductive foil	Leiterfolie	133
conductive formulations	leitfähige Mischungen/Ansätze	114
confidential	vertraulich	196
confound	verwechseln, durcheinander bringen	98
confounded	verwirren (den Gegner usw.)	65
congestion	Verstopfung	92
connectors	Verbindungstücke	114
con-rods	Pleulstangen	252
consistency	Beständigkeit; Festigkeit	202
consistent	zähflüssig; fest	202
constitutes	darstellen, ausmachen	49, 65
constraints	Zwänge	56
construction work	Bauarbeiten	228
consultancy	technische Beratung; Beratung	110
contact plates	Kontaktbleche	249
contact resistance	Kontaktwiderstand; Übergangswiderstand	171
contaminant	Schadstoff	119
contaminate	verschmutzen, verunreinigen	128
contemporary	zeitgenössisch	171
contestant	Bewerber; Wettbewerber	120
contoured	konturiert	217
contradiction	Widerspruch	178
contravenes	verstoßen	226
contributing	beitragen, beisteuern	51
control arms	Querlenker; Führungslenker	81, 182
control lever	Steuerhebel; Einstellhebel	176
control lever shaft	Verstellhebelwelle	176
control sleeve	Verstellmuffe; Regelhülse	176
control unit	Steuergerät	186, 245
convenience	Bequemlichkeit	124
convertible	Kabriolett	16

coolant circuit	Kühlmittel-Kreislauf	188
coolant pump	Kühlmittelpumpe	254
coolant systems	Kühlmittelsysteme	114
coolant temperature sensor	Kühlmitteltemperatur-Sensor	253
copper	Kupfer	115, 194
cornering force	Seitenführungskräfte	98
corrector lever	Korrekturhebel	176
corresponding	entsprechend	242
corrosion-resistance	Korrosionsbeständigkeit	106, 107
corrugated	gewellt; geriffelt	160
corrugated fins	Wellrippen	249
cost of labour	Arbeitskosten	105
counteract	entgegenwirken	154, 199
counterbalance shaft	Ausgleichswelle	85
countered	entgegen treten, gekontert	168
counterforce	Gegenkraft; Reaktion	214
coupled	im angekoppelten Zustand; gekoppelt	247
coupling ball	Kupplungskugel	247
coupling ball bar	Kugelstange	247
coupling socket load	Stützlast	247
courting; fig: to court s.o.'s favour	den Hof machen; um j-s Gunst werben	
cracks	Risse	245
cradle	Gestell, Träger	107
cradle mounts	Trägerbefestigung; Sattelbefestigung	183
cradle-to-grave	Wiege zu Grabe tragen	48
crank handle	Kurbel	246
crankcase ventilation	Kurbelgehäuseentlüftung	254
cranks	Drehkurbel	131
crankshaft pulse pick-up	Kurbelwellen-Impulsaufnehmer	253
crash resisting	zusammenbruchbeständig	208
creating	im Entstehen	137
credits	Kredit	
crescent oil pump	Sichelölpumpe	254
cross-breed	Kreuzung	74
crossing	Kreuzung	74
crossmember	Querträger; Rahmenquerträger; Traverse; Spriegel	65, 206, 213
crossover	Übergang	74
cross-sections	Querschnitte; Schnitte	221
crucial	entscheidend	185
cruise control	Geschwindigkeitsregler	235, 247
crumple zones	Knautschzonen	111, 174
crushing machines	Grobzerkleinerungsmaschinen	226
cryogenically	tieftemperaturmäßig	127
crystallising	Kornbildung; Kristallbildung	173
cues	Anhaltspunkte	80
curb	in Zaum halten	44
curb mass (US)	Leergewicht	70

cures	aushärten	195
curing process	Aushärteprozess	114
curing time	Aushärtungsdauer	200
current-controlled	stromgesteuert	170
curved section	gekrümmter Abschnitt	205
cushions	Kissen; Polster	82
custom	kundenspezifisch	209
customed	maßgeschneidert	186
cutaway; sectional view	Schnittbild	188
cut-out	Abschalter	85
cuts	Schnitte	245
cutting tool	Schneidwerkzeug	63
cutting-edge	Schneidkante; riskant	38
cv-standard	Nutzfahrzeug-Standard	122
cycle time	Taktzeit	202, 208
cyclic	zyklisch, periodisch	143, 199
cylinder bore	Zylinderbohrung	254
cylinder head	Zylinderkopf	252
cylinder head covers	Zylinderkopfdeckel	106
damper piston	Stoßdämpferkolben; Arbeitskolben	153
damper rods	Stoßdämpferstange	153
dampness	Feuchtigkeit	64
daring	gewagt, verwegen	73
dash panel insert	Armaturenbrett-Einlage	206
dashboard	Armaturenanlage	133
data nodes	Datenknotenpunkte	88
dc	Gleichstrom	171
dc-dc	Gleichstrom-Gleichstrom	122
deck lid; rear deck lid; boot lid (GB); luggage-compartment lid (GB); trunk lid (US); trunk deck US); baggage-compartment lid (US)	Kofferraumdeckel	106, 115, 194
declined	sinken, abfallen	223
decoupling	entkoppeln	55
dedicated	neu eröffnet	203
defective	defekt	246
defied	herausgefordert	219
deflate	zusammenfallen, entleeren	135
deformation	Verformung	65
defrosters	Entfrostung	249
delicate	empfindlich	186
delivery valve	Druckventil	176
delivery van; commercial van; delivery lorry (GB); delivery truck (US); delivery wagon (US)	Lieferwagen	235
demand-oriented	bedarf-, nachfrageorientiert	229
demist function	Beschlagentfernungsfunktion; Entfeuchtungsfunktion	99

demisting	Entfeuchtung	249
demity	Beschlag; Befeuchtung	105
demould time	Ausformzeit	179
denies	leugnen, dementieren, abstreiten	37
dent resistance	Einzelwiderstand	107
dents	Dellen	107
departs	abweichen	74
deployed	ausgelöst	242
depreciation	Wertminderung; Wertverlust	105
depth profile	Tiefenprofil	173
derivative	Abkömmling	203
deriving	ableiten; herleiten	127
descending	absteigend	48
deterioration	Verschlechterung; Beschädigung; Zerstörung	175
detract from (to detract from sth.)	beeinträchtigen (etwas)	71
development plans	Komponentenentwicklungspläne	54
devices	Einrichtungen; Ausstattungen	170
diagnosis	Diagnose	255
diagonal	Quer-, Diagonal-, Schräg-	65
diagonally split	diagonal geteilt	244
die	Gussform; Gießform, Form; Formwerkzeug	105, 209
die cast magnesium	Magnesium-Druckguss	105
die casting; pressure casting	Druckguss	81, 106, 108
diecast parts	Druckgussteile	218
dielectric	nichtleitend	130
differential	Ausgleichsgetriebe	256
diffuse	zerstreuen; zerstäuben	133
diffuser	Zerstäuber	71
digital mockup	digitales Modell/ Attrappe	55
dilute	verdünnen; verwässern	225
dimensional stability	Maßhaltigkeit, Formbeständigkeit	165
diminishes	verringern	199
dimmer for instrument illumination	Dimmer für Instrumentenbeleuchtung	235
dipped and main beam	Abblend- und Fernlicht	235
dipstick	Messstab	50
direct-injection	Direkteinspritzung; Zylindereinspritzung	68
direction indicators	Fahrtrichtungsanzeiger; Blinker	94
direction of travel	Laufrichtung	182
directional	richtungsgebunden	196
directional control	Fahrstabilität	246
directional guidance	Richtungsführung	251
directional stability	Fahrstabilität	247
directive	Richtlinie; Verordnung	225
disabled drivers	behinderte Autofahrer	98
disastrous consequences	verheerende Folgen	126

disc brake (GB); disk brake (US)	Scheibenbremse	245
disc brake pads	Scheibenbremsen-Bremsbelag	173
discarded	entsorgen	104
disc-brake pistons	Scheibenbrems-Kolben	191
discharge lamps	Gasentladungslampen	193
disclosures	Enthüllen; Bekanntgabe	87
discount	ausschließen	216
discrete	diskret; digital	177
disengage	ausrasten	240
dismantling	auseinander nehmen, zerlegen	48
dismantling centres	Demontagezentrum; Verwertungszentrum	226
dispensed with	verzichtet	164
dispenser	Spender; Dosierbehälter	128
dispensing	verteilen, austeilen	201
dispersion	Feinverteilung	221
displacement	Hubraum; Zylinderinhalt	70
disposable	Wegwerf-, Einweg-	194
dissipates	verteilen; zerstreuen	128
dissipating	ableiten; abführen	84
dissolves	auflösen	250
distinct	deutlich	
distinctiveness	Unverwechselbarkeit; Deutlichkeit	73
distingushing	unterscheiden	199
distortions	Verzerrung	37
distributor pumps	Verteilereinspritzpumpen	174
ditched	aufgeben	
diversification	Diversifizierung; Verschiedenartigkeit	73
diversion	Umleitung; Ablenkung	94
diverted	abgelenkt	221
divulge	ausplaudern, preisgeben	37
domestic	heimisch	133
door intrusion beams	Türverstärkungsstrebe; Seitenaufprallschutz	205
door opening outer	Türöffnung außen	212
door panel lining	Türblechverkleidung	179
door panels	Türbleche, Türblätter	130
door pillars	Türholm, Türsäule	181
door sill; doorsill	Türschweller; Einstiegsschweller	65, 81
door window defroster vents	Seitenscheibenentfrosterdüsen	249
doorstep	Schwelle; Fig: (very close) vor der Tür	41
dosing pump	Dosierpumpe	187
double road train	Sattelzug	16
double-curvature	doppelt gekrümmt/gerundet	122
dough	Geld	
downturn	Flaute, Abwärtsbewegung	
draft angle	Ziehwinkel	105
drag	Luftwiderstand; Strömungswiderstand	71, 86

drain	entleeren, auslaufen	170
drawbar tractor combination	Zugmaschinenzug	16
drawbar trailer	Gelenk-Deichselanhänger	16
drawing board	Zeichenbrett	221
drawn up	aufgezeigt	
drift	schieben, wegschieben	169
drive line	Antrieb; Antriebsstrang	122
drive shaft	Achswelle; Antriebswelle	143, 176, 256
drive sprocket	Kettenantriebsrad	144
drivers	Mitnehmer	170
driving disc	Mitnehmerscheibe; Antriebsscheibe	176
driving wheels	Antriebsräder	246
droplets	Tropfen; Tröpfchen	147
dryer	Trockner	250
dual ignition	Doppelzündung	81
dual spark ignition coils	Doppelfunkenzündspulen	252
ducting	Kanalauslegung; Führung	114
ducts	Kanäle	88
dumpers	Muldenkipper (Schwerst-Lkw)	15
dumping	auskippen	225
dumping	Dumping (von billigen Waren)	223
durable	haltbar; strapazierfähig	200
durable (of material)	haltbar; strapazierfähig	54
dynamometer	Leistungsprüfstand	50
dynamometer	Schwungmassenprüfstand	162
eccentric	exzentrisch	143
eddies	Wirbel	219
efficiency	Wirkungsgrad	124
efficiency analysis	Nutzwertanalyse	58
egalitarian	gleichmacherisch	
electrical charge pressure control	elektrische Ladungsdruckkontrolle/-steuerung	69
electrical current; electric current	elektrischer Strom	119, 124
electrically adjustable	elektrisch verstellbar	257
electricity supply	Stromversorgung	249
electrolyte	Elektrolyt; Säure	125
electromagnetic forces	elektromagnetische Kräfte	171
electronic stability management	Elektronisches Stabilitätsprogramm (ESP)	167
elongation	Dehnung, Verlängerung	173
elongation at fracture	Bruchdehnung, Reißdehnung	105
embarking on (something)	mit etwas beginnen	
embrace	umfassen	80
emerge	in Erscheinung treten	171, 190
emergency services	Notdienst	90
emerges	auftauchen; herauskommen	226
emerges	herauskommen; austreten	249

emit	ausstoßen, emittieren	127, 159
emulates	emulieren	221
emulsion	Emulsion	156
enabling	möglich machen	194
encapsulated	eingekapselt; eingegossen	200
encroache	übergreifen	130
end panel	Rückwand; Verschlussblech	240
energy store	Kraftspeicher	242
engaged	steht in Eingriff mit	132
engages	beschäftigen; mit befassen	52
engine bays	Motorräume	197
engine blocks	Motorblöcke	106
engine bonnet (GB); engine hood (US)	Motorhaube; Kühlerhaube	106
engine control unit	Motorsteuergerät	249, 252
engine cradles	Motorhilfsrahmen	206
engine cradles	Motorträger; Motorhilfsrahmen	115
engine mount	Motorlager	182
engine mounts	Motoraufhängungen	183
engine speed	Motordrehzahl	247
engine temperature gauge	Kühlmittel-Temperaturanzeige	236
engines	Motoren	23
enhance; enhancing	verbessern	153, 172
enhances	unterstreichen	199
entails	zur Folge haben; mit sich bringen	125
environmental loading	Umweltbelastung	114
envisage	voraussehen	139, 228
envisaged	vorausgesehen	154
epichlorohydrin	Epichlorohydrin	179
epoxy-based glue	Klebstoff auf Epoxidbasis	205
equipment	Ausstattung	56
equity	Dividentenpapiere	40
equity capital	Eigenkapital (hier: Wert)	51
erected	aufgerichtet; errichtet	137, 229
essence	das Wichtigste; die Hauptsache	97
essential	wichtig	177
estate car (GB); station wagon (US)	Kombi; Variant; Caravan;	235, 239
etching	Ätzung; abätzen	193
ethanol	Ethylalkohol	45
ethylene acrylic elastomer	Ethylen-Acryl-Elastomer	178
ethylene propylene diene monomer	Ethylen-Propylen-Dien-Monomer	179
eutectic	eutektisch	196
evaporative emissions	Kraftstoffverdunstung	128
evaporator	Verdampfer	250
exaggerated	übertrieben	73
excess	übermäßig	134
excess cost	Zuschlagskosten	106
excess powder	überschüssiges Pulver	191
excessive load	zu hohe Belastung	249

exert	ausüben (eine Kraft, einen Einfluss)	92
exerted	drücken	247
exhaust	Abgas; Auslass; Auspuff	119, 255
exhaust back pressure	Abgasgegendruck; Abgasstaudruck	141
exhaust manifolds	Abgaskrümmer	206
exhaust muffler	Abgasschalldämpfer; Auspufftopf	119
exhaust passages	Auslasskanäle	139
exhaust pipe	Auspuffrohrleitung	162
exhaust pipes	Auspuffrohre	206
exhaust system	Abgassystem; Auspuffsystem	71
exhaust-gas recirculation valve	Abgasrückführungsventil; Abgasrückführventil	221, 252
expectancy	Erwartung	58
expedite	beschleunigen (etwas)	233
expels	ausstoßen	134
expense	Ausgaben	220
expertise	Sach-, Fachkenntnis; Erfahrung	51, 54
expired	abgelaufen; verfallen	143
exploit	entwickeln, erschließen	93
exploiting	auswerten	199
exposure	Aussetzung; Einwirkung	161
exposure	Freilegung; Aussetzung	221
exterior	Außenform	56
exterior driving lamps	Außenbeleuchtung	237
external	außen liegend	198
extraction	Absaugung; Entlüftung	183
extruded	fließgepresst; stranggepresst	172
extrusion	Fließpressen	159
extrusion facility	Strangpressanlage	203
extrusions	Strangpressteile	207
eye	Öse	247
fabric	Gewebe	154
facilitating	vereinfachen, erleichtern	194
facing	Belag	161
facing parts	Verkleidungsteile, Verblendungsteile	179
fad	Marotte	233
fade	Wirkungsverlust; Schwund; Nachlassen der Wirkung	82
fading	verblassen	73
fairings	Verkleidungen, Verschalungen	131
fan	Gebläse	95, 133, 249
fanciful	fantasiereich; phantastisch	80
fascias	Verkleidung; Aussenverkleidung	117
fashionably	modern, modisch	121
fasteners	Verbindungselemente	130
fastening	Befestigung	240
fastening buttons	Befestigungsknöpfe	239

fatalities	Todesopfer	
fatigue	ermüdend	199
fatigue	Ermüdung	102, 134, 177
fatigue tests	Dauerproben	165
fatigue tests	Ermüdungstests	199
fault	Fehler; Defekt	194
faults	Fehler; Störungen	88
feature	aufweisen, beinhalten	171
featured	beinhaltet	167
features	Ausstattung; Ausrüstung	54
features	Merkmale; Eigenschaften	87
fed	zugeführt; eingeleitet	168
federal chancellor	Bundeskanzler	228
federal standards	Bundesvorschriften/-normen	51
federal treasury secretary	Bundesfinanzminister	228
feed	Vorschub	161
feeders	Anguss; Beschicker	197
fender support rail	Kotflügelhalterschiene	212
fending off	abwehren	229
fets (field effect transistors)	Feldeffekt-Transistoren, MOS-Transistoren; MOSFETs	170
fibreglass, fibres	Glasfaser	186, 195
fibre-reinforced	faserverstärkt	81
fibrous	faserig	197
fierce	heftig	226
figure out (to figure it out)	herausfinden	52
filed	zu den Akten gelegt	223
filler	Füllmaterial	197
filling station	Tankstelle	91
film	Beschichtung	173
final assembly	Endmontage	228
finance schemes	Pläne finanzieren	
fine grain spring steel	feinkörniger Federstahl	198
finish	Ausführung	49
finish	Endlackierung	121
finishing operations	Feinbearbeitungsvorgänge; Endbearbeitung	200
fins	Lamellen	249
fire fighting vehicles	Feuerwehr-, Lösch-Fahrzeug	15
fire hazard	Brandgefahr	128
firm	fest; hart	135
first and foremost	zuallererst	84
fit as snugly	wie angegossen passen	130
fitting	Anschlussstück	195, 205
five-speed	fünfstufig	71
fixture, fixing, fixturing	Befestigung, Aufnahme	63, 114, 214
fixtures	Vorrichtungen	60
flame retardant	schwer entflammbar, feuerhemmend	118

flame spread	Flammenausbreitung	118
flap	Blende; Klappe	49
flap	Klappe	240
flat ribbon cables	Flachbandkabel	87
flat under body	flacher/ebener Unterboden	86
flat-head pistons	Flachkolben	252
flat-rolled steel	Flachstahl	223
fleeting	verflüchtigen	73
flex joint	elastische Verbindung	182
flexible forming	Anpassungsformen	209
flexurally stiff mounting	biegesteifer Einbau	65
floor assembly	Bodengruppe	65
floor cover	Deckel des Laderaumbodens	239
floor panels	Bodenbleche	211
floor space	Bodenfläche	56
floorpan	Bodenblech	177
flouting	missachten	226
flow chart	Ablaufplan	62
flow lines	Strömungslinien	63
flow sheet	Fließbild	173
flowability	Fließvermögen	179
fluorescent	fluoreszierend	250
fluorination	Fluorieren	159
flux	Lötmittel	63
flymass	Schwungmasse; Fliehgewicht	175, 176
flymass drive gear	Schwungmassenantriebsrad	176
foam-in-fabric	Einschäumen in Stoff/Gewebe	206
foaming pu	schäumendes Polyurethan	131
focal length	Brennweite	214
focal point	Schwerpunkt	155
focal spot	Brennpunkt	211
fog lamp	Nebelscheinwerfer	235
fog tail lamp	Nebelschlussleuchte	235
folding roof	Faltdach	66
folds	Falz; Biegung; Faltung	198
followers	Nachfolgenden	100
followers	Nockenstößel	142
footwell	Fußraum	252
footwell structure	Fußraumkonstruktion	98
foreign bodies	Fremdkörper	245
forged	geschmiedet	85
forgings	Schmiedeteile	196
formaldehyde	Formaldehyd; Methanal; Methylal; Formal	193
formidable	gewaltig	42
formulated	konzipiert	118
forthcoming	bevorstehend; in Kürze erscheinend.	80
forwards	vorklappen	240

fossil fuels	fossile Brennstoffe	120
foundation stone	Grundstein	228
frame rail	Rahmenlängsträger	182
framing	Karosserieaufbau	210
fraternity	Zunft	220
frequency	Frequenz, Häufigkeit	65
fresnel spots	Fresnel Linsenscheinwerfer	171
friction	Reibung	153, 173, 208
frictional losses	Reibungsverluste; mechanische Verluste	132
from the outset	vom Anfang an	126
front end	Stirnseite; Vorderseite	122
front floor centre	Mitte des vorderen Fußbodens	206
front floor crossmembers	Querträger des vorderen Fußbodens	205
front interior illumination	vordere Innenraumbeleuchtung	257
front panelling	Frontverkleidung als offene Version	257
front shock tower reinforcement	Dom – Verstärkung des Vorderachs-Stoßdämpfers	205
front-end structure	Vorbaustruktur	65
fuel additives	Kraftstoffzusätze	119
fuel distributor pipe	Kraftstoffverteilerrohr	252
fuel efficiency	Kraftstoff sparend	51
fuel feed lines	Kraftstoffvorlaufleitung	254
fuel gauge	Kraftstoffanzeige	236
fuel level sensor	Kraftstoffüllstandsgeber; Tankgeber	159
fuel lines	Kraftstoffleitung	158, 160
fuel lines	Kraftstoffzuleitungen	159
fuel pressure regulator	Kraftstoffdruckregler	252
fuel return lines	Kraftstoffrücklaufleitung	254
fuel system has no return	rücklauffreies Kraftstoffsystem	252
fuel system integrity	Kraftstoffsystem-Integrität	
fuel-cell	Brennstoff-Zelle	50
fuel-cutoff solenoid	Magnetventil für Kraftstoffabschaltung	176
fuel-filler neck	Kraftstoff-Einfüllstutzen	159
fuel-powered	mit Kraftstoff betrieben	249
fuel-supply pump	Kraftstoffförderpumpe	176
full extent	voll und ganz	257
full-load adjusting screw	Einstellschraube für Vollbelastung	176
full-on braking	Vollbremsung	244
full-size	Oberklasse	230
fully depressed	stark durchgetreten	244
funds	Vermögen; Kapital	194
fuse box	Sicherungskasten	248
fused	verschmolzen	130
fusion	Schmelzschweißen	217
gains	Vorteile	42
gantry systems	Brückensysteme; Portalsysteme	212

gap	Spalt	114
garbage truck	Müllwagen	16
gas; gasoline	Benzin, Ottokraftstoff, „Sprit"	
gaseous	gasförmig	119
gas-guzzling	Benzin saufend	
gaskets	Dichtungen	173
gate	Bordwand, Seitenwand	105
gauge (GB); gage (US)	Blechdicke, Blechstärke	110, 205
gear	Zahnrad	100, 132
gear lever	Schalthebel; Schaltknüppel	94
gearbox	Getriebe; Getriebegehäuse	69
gearbox casing	Getriebegehäuse	84
gears	Mechanismus, Mechanik	115
gel	Gel	186
general purpose goods vehicle	Vielzwecklastkraftwagen	16
giants	Riesen	
gimmick	Trick	
glass breakage sensor	Glasbruchsensor	256
glass fibre	Glasfaser	200
glass pane	Glasscheibe	256
glassfibre reinforced	glasfaserverstärkt	165
glazed	verglast	133
glossy	glänzend	117
glove boxes	Handschuhkasten	87
glove compartment	Handschuhfach	235
goods trailer	Lastanhänger	16
goose pimples	Gänsehaut	132
governor spring	Reglerfeder	176
grades	Sorten	114
graphite	Graphit	160
gray cast iron	Grauguss	82
greasy	schmierig	247
greenhouse effect	Treibhauseffekt	151
greenhouse gas	Treibhausgas	128
grille reinforcements	Kühlerverstärkungen	106
grille; grill; radiator grill; front grill	Kühlergrill/-Gitter	49, 63
grip	Griff	229
gripping tread	haftende/klebende Lauffläche	155
grommet	Schutztülle; Abdichtstulpe	171
groove	Nut; Fuge	154
groovy	toll	44
gross mass	Gesamtgewicht	247
gross vehicle mass	zulässiges Gesamtgewicht ZGG	15
guide	Führung	239
gusset plates	Winkelbleche, Knotenbleche	66
gyro compass	Kreiselkompass	251
halting	zögernd	40

hampered	Verhindern	30
hampers	behindern	220
handle	Griff	66
handling	Fahrverhalten	247
hardened	verhärtet	174
hardening	Erhärtung; Verhärten	199
hardening furnaces	Härteöfen; Aushärteöfen	111, 174
hard-foam parts	Hartschaumteile	242
hardness	Härte	178
hark back to (to hark back to sth.)	auf etwas zurückgreifen	80
harness	bündeln	156
hasten	beschleunigen	125
hatchback	Ladeklappe; Kombi-Hecktüre	76, 115
have seemed like	kommt vor wie/erscheint wie...	73
hazard warning flashers	Warnblinker	235
hazardous	gefährlich	128
hdpe	hochdichtes Polyethylen	159
header pipe	Krümmerrohr; Vorrohr	162
headlamp aiming	Scheinwerfereinstellung	63
headlamp flash	Lichthupe	235
headlamp range adjustment wheel	Stellrad für Leuchtweitenregulierung	235
headlamp reflectors	Scheinwerferspiegel	114
headliners	Dachhimmel	179, 184
headliners	Himmel; Dachverkleidungen	200
headrest	Kopfstütze	101
headstrong	eigenwillig	41
heat resistance	Hitzebeständigkeit	114
heat resistance	Wärmebeständigkeit	114
heat sinking	Kühlbleche; Kühlkörper	87
heat sinks	Kühlplatten, Kühlbleche	186
heat-cured	wärmeausgehärtet	205
heated oxygen sensor	beheizte Lambda-Sonde	252
heating nozzles	Heizungsdüsen	249
heat-shrinkable tubing	Warmschrumpfschlauch; Aufschrumpfschlauch	118
helical actuator	schneckenförmiges Stellglied	142
hemispherical	halbkugelförmig	183
hemming process	umbördeln um 180 Grad	108
hexahedral	sechsflächig	222
heyday	Blütezeit	38
hiding power	Deckkraft; Deckvermögen	191
high beam	Fernlicht	172
high intensity discharge (hid) lamps	Gasentladungs-Scheinwerfer	172
high purity	höchste Reinheit	106
higher elevations	größere Höhen	247
high-gloss	hochglanz	49
highlights	Höhepunkte; Glanzlichter	127
highly-stressed	hoch beansprucht	108

high-purity	Reinst-	198
high-side	Hochdruck-Seite	170
high-strength steel	hochfester Stahl (HSS)	65
hinge on	von etwas abhängen	174
hinged	schwenkbar; klappbar	67
hip	Hüfte	52
hissing noise	Zischgeräusch	184
holding company	Holdinggesellschaft; Dachgesellschaft	51
hollow sections	Hohlprofile	114
honesty	Ehrlichkeit	52
honeycomb	Bienenwabe; Wabenkörper	110
honeycomb	Wabenkörper	130
hood	Verdeck; Klappverdeck; Faltdach	66
horn pushes	Signalhorntasten	235
hoses	Schläuche	118
hostility to	Feindschaft gegen	225
hot film mass air flow meter	Heißfilm-Luftmassenmesser	253
hot forming	Warmumformen; Heißformen	205
hot ribbing	warm verrippt, warm versickt	108
housed	untergebracht	127
housings	Gehäuse	194
humidity	Luftfeuchtigkeit; Feuchtigkeit	64, 99, 193
humming noises	Summgeräusche, Brummtöne	179
hvac systems	Heizungs-, Lüftungs- und Klimatisierungssysteme	132
hydraulic modulator	Hydroaggregat	245
hydrocarbons	Kohlenwasserstoffe	51, 255
hydrocarbons	Kohlenwasserstoffverbindungen	119, 126
hydroforming technique	Innenhochdruckumformen	211
hydrogen	Wasserstoff	50, 123, 124
ic-engine	Motor mit innerer Verbrennung	121
idle air bypass valve	Leerlauf-Umleitventil	184
idle play	Leerweg	242
idle speed	Leerlaufdrehzahl	182
idle speed stepper motor	Leerlaufschrittmotor	253
idling characteristics	Leerlaufkennkurven	144
idling spring	Leerlauffeder	176
ignition	Verdichtung	15
ignition module	Zündmodul	252
image	Bild; Abbildung	221
imbalances	Unwucht; Gleichgewichtsstörungen	85
immobilizer	Wegfahrsperre	236
impact loads	Aufprallbelastung, Stoßbelastung	65
impact resistance	Schlagfestigkeit	165
impact-absorbing	Stoß aufnehmend	130
impair	beeinträchtigen	160
imparting	gewähren	199

impede	verhindern	182
imperative	dringend (notwendig), unerlässlich	73
imperceptibly	unmerklich; verschwindend gering	135
impermeable	undurchlässig	181
import quotas	Importkontingent	37
imposed	aufbürden, auferlegen	171
imposed	verhängt; auferlegt	226
imposing	imponiert	
imposition	Auferlegung (von Bedingungen)	225
impregnated	imprägniert	195
improperly	falsch	64
impurities	Verunreinigungen	204
in essence	im Wesentlichen	223
in heavy traffic	starker Verkehr	247
in reverse order	in umgekehrter Reihenfolge	239
inability	Unfähigkeit	124
inadequate	ungenügend	58
incentive	Anreiz; Ansporn	226
incipient	anfänglich	199
inclined	geneigt	220
inclines	Steigungen	247
incompatibility	Unverträglichkeit	86
incorporate	integrieren; einbinden	69, 212
incorporated	eingearbeitet	60
incorporating	Integration	219
indicators	Blinker; Fahrtrichtungsanzeiger	69
indispensable	unverzichtbar	221
induced	ausgelöst	197
inductive charger	induktives Auflagegerät	232
inevitable	unvermeidlich	109, 225
inevitably	unvermeidlich; zwangsläufig	143
inferior lubricity	untergeordnete/niedrige Schmiereigenschaften	174
inflammability	Zündfähigkeit	106
inflatable	aufblasbar	154
inflate	aufblasen, aufblähen	90, 135
ingenuity	Einfallsreichtum	203
ingenuity	Erfindungsgabe; Einfallsreichtum	109
ingots	Rohblöcke, Barren	173
inherent	Eigen-; eigen	105, 120
injection beam	Einspritzstrahl	149
injection moulded	spritzgegossen	113
injection moulding	Spritzgießen	200
injection mouldings	Spritzgussteile	115
injection nozzle	Einspritzventil	150
injection pump	Kraftstoffeinspritzpumpe	174
injector jet	Einspritzdüse	221
injectors	Einspritzdüsen	85, 136

inlet ports	Eingangskanäle	142
inlet valve head	Einlassventilteller	254
inline pumps	Reiheneinspritzpumpen	150
inner air-proof liner	innerer, luftundurchlässiger Mantel	154
inner panel	Innenverkleidung der Seitenwand	239
inquiry	Untersuchung	37
insert moulding	Formpressen mit Einlegeteilen	157
inserting	Einsetzen	247
insolvent	zahlungsunfähig	41
inspiration	Eingebung	58
installation	Einbau	239
instant	sofort; unverzüglich	87
instrument panel	Armaturenbrett; Instrumententafel	87
instrument panel support	Instrumententräger; Armaturenbretthalter	106
instrument-panel	Armaturentafel, Instrumentenbrett	65
instruments	Instrumente	235
insulated	isoliert	197
insult	Beleidigung	37
intake air temperature sensor	Sensor-Ansauglufttemperatur	253
intake manifold	Einlasskrümmer; Ansaugkrümmer	106
intake manifold module	Saugmodul	252
intake pipe	Saugrohr	254
intake pipe pressure sensor	Fühler des Saugrohrdrucks	253
intake ports	Einlaufkanäle; Saugkanäle	138
intakes	Zylindereinlass	86
integral variant	integrierte Variante	122
integrates	integrieren, einbeziehen	96
integrity	Vollständigkeit	97, 195, 198
interactions	Wechselwirkungen	56
intercooler	Zwischenkühler	81
interfaces	Schnittstellen	56
interim solution	Zwischenlösung	165
interior	Fahrzeuggastraum, Fahrzeuginnenraum; Interieur	56
interior trim	Innenverkleidung	178
interlocking	verriegeln, sperren, blockieren	198
interlocking	Verriegelung; Sperren, Verblockung	65
intermediate shaft	Zwischenwelle	256
intermittently	absatzweise, periodisch auftretend	164
internal	innen liegend	198, 200
internal combustion	Zündung	15
internal combustion engines	Kraftmaschine mit Innenverbrennung	120
internal-combustion engines	Motor mit Innenverbrennung	51
internal stresses	Eigenspannngen; innere Spannungen	105
interurban coach	Überlandlinienbus	16
intimate	vertraut	110
invasion	Eindringen; Eingriff	130

inventories	Lagerbestände	157
inventory	Lager; Lagerfläche	
investment	Investition; Anlage	224
investment castings	Gussteile nach dem Wachsausschmelzgießverfahren	196
involved	eingebunden	56
involvements	Beteiligungen	233
ionized	ionisiert	119
ip beams	Armaturentafel-Träger	206
ip crossbeams	Instrumententafel-Querträger	105
irrespective	unabhängig	246
irrespective	ungeachtet; ohne Rücksicht auf	190
isocyanate	Isocyanat	193
it is not possible to elaborate	nicht ausführlicher sein können	102
jack	Wagenheber	246
jazz up	verjazzen (ein Stück)	74
jig	Schablone	205
jockey wheel	Bugrad	247
joining	Fügen	114
joint venture	Gemeinschaftsunternehmen	22, 51
joints	Fügeverbindungen, Gelenke	108
joints	Verbindungen	205
jounce bumpers	Einfederungsanschläge	183
judder	rattern, vibrieren	173
juice	anstacheln	
jumpers	Verbindungen	160
junction	Zonenübergang; Sperrschicht	134
junction temperatures	Sperrschicht/Zonenübergang-Temperaturen	186
junctions	Kreuzungen	82
justifications	Rechtfertigungen	94
justifications	reizen; Anziehungskraft ausüben	120
keep pace with	mit etwas Schritt halten	131
kerb mass (GB)	Leergewicht	50
knife-edge	hauchdünn	180
knobbed belt	Noppenriemen	182
knobs	Knöpfe	240
knock sensor	Klopfsensor	253
knurled knob	Rändelrad	237
lacks	mangeln	193
lacquerware	Lackware	77
ladder frame	Leiterrahmen	142
laminar	stationär	201
laminate	Laminat; Schichtpressstoff	217
laminated steel	geschichteter Stahl	206

lap belts	Beckengurt; Hüftgurt	242
lap joints	Überlappungsnähte	213
laser welding	Laserstrahlschweißen	110
lash lugs	Verzurrösen	239
lateral	Quer-, seitlich	197
lateral accelerometers	Querbeschleunigungsaufnehmer, -sensoren	82
laterally; lateral	seitlich, quer	143, 169
lathe	Drehmaschine	161
latter part	im letzten Teil	245
launched	gestartet, lanciert	
layers	Schichten	154
layman	Laie	95
layoffs	Personalabbau	223
lead times	Entwicklungszeiten; Vorlaufzeiten	54
lead-acid batteries	Blei-Säure-Batterien	122
leaded fuel	verbleiter Kraftstoff	255
leaf springs	Blattfedern	198
leak detecting agent	Leckerkennungsmittel	250
lean	schlank	56
lean burn concept	Magerkonzept (mit magerer Verbrennung)	141
leaner	magerer	141
leap	springen	157
lease	mieten	232
legal advice	Rechtsberatung	226
length of stroke	Hublänge	254
lengthy	übermäßig lang	139
level	eben; waagerecht	248
level	Wasserwaage	64
level control; level control system	Niveauregulierung	235, 247
level sensor	Füllstandsfühler	171
levelling system	Niveauregulierungsanlage	165
lever	Bedienungshebel	224
levers	Hebel	131
levers for turn signals	Schalter für Blinker	235
liability	Verantwortlichkeit; Verpflichtung	225
liable for	verantwortlich; haftbar	225
license plate lamps	Kennzeichenleuchten	257
liftgate	Ladeklappen; oben/unten angeschlagene Heckklappen	116
light goods vehicles	leichte Nutzfahrzeuge	121
light refraction	Lichtbrechung	192
light switch	Lichtschalter	235
light-off temperature	Anspringtemperatur; Ansprechtemperatur	141
likelihood	Wahrscheinlichkeit	65
likely to	könnte (dazu) führen; geeignet	225
limit	begrenzen	37

limousine; saloon (GB); sedan (US); coach (US)	Limousine; geschlossener Pkw	16, 68, 242
lineup	Gruppierung, Angebot	44
links	Gelenke	131
lip	Lippe; Falz	86
list price	Listenpreis	121
load	Belastung	199
load compartment cover	Laderaumabdeckung	239
load compartment floor	Laderaumboden	238
load dump	Lastabschaltung	170
load index	Tragfähigkeits-Kennzahl	246
load-dependent	lastabhängig	245
loading ease	Durchlademöglichkeit	240
loading tool	beladende/ belastende Werkzeug	214
lock	blockieren	208
lock	Verriegelung; Schloss	224, 240
locking	Blockieren	244
locking pins	Riegel; Anschlagstift	239
long distance coach	Reisebus	16
longevity	Langlebigkeit	194
long-lasting bond	Langzeitverbindung	160
loop	Regelkreis, Regelschleife	170
loosen	lockern	229
lorry (GB); truck (US)	Lastkraftwagen (Lkw)	15, 16
loss factor	Verlustfaktor	179
lost core film (lcf)	Kernausschmelz-Schicht	194
low beam	Abblendlicht	172
low pressure	Niederdruck; druckarm	171
low pressure differential	Niederdruckgefälle	166
low trailing edge	Hinterkante	71
low viscosity	Dünnflüssigkeit	114
low-density	Hochdruck-; niedrige Dichte	122, 200
lower end	Fuß; unteres Ende	165
lower leg injuries	Unterschenkelverletzungen	98
lowered	abgesenkt	66
low-low	im unteren Drehzahlbereich	139
low-side	Saugdruck-Seite	170
lumbar spine	Lendenwirbelsäule	79
lumbar support	Lendenwirbelstütze; Lordosenstütze	79, 238
lumbar vertebra	Lendenwirbel	135
lumens; luminous flux; light flux	Lichtstrom	172
magnesium alloys	Magnesiumlegierungen	106
magnitude	Wichtigkeit; Größe	222
mains supply	Stromversorgung	122
maintenance	Instandhaltung; Wartung	54, 234
make	Fabrikat	245
management board	Vorstand; Vorstandsgremium	70

mandrel	Dorn	205
maps	Straßenkarten	251
masks	verdecken	184
massive	wuchtig	115
mat	Matte	163, 200
match	abstimmen; abgleichen	55
material specifications	Leistungsbeschreibungen	62
maximum-rate cornering	Kurvenfahrten mit Höchstwerten	98
mayor	Bürgermeister	228
measurement systems evaluation	Bewertung des Vermessungssystems	62
mechanical seat belt tensioners	mechanische Gurtstraffer	242
medium-duty	mittelschwer	230
melamine	Melamin	193
member	Träger; Holm	65
members	Bauteile; Träger	208
merchandising	Handel	38
mergers	Fusionen	223
merits	Verdienste	217
mesh	Gitter; Netz	222
metal castings	Metallgussteile	63
methanol	Methylalkohol	123
methodology	Methodik	164
micro-alloyed	mikrolegiert	198
microfibre	Mikrofaser	183
micropores	Mikroporen	133
middlemen	Zwischenhändler	223
mighty	mächtig	44
milestones	Meilensteine; Projektkontrollen	56
militates against	gegen etwas wirken	156
militating against	dagegen wirken	124
minivans	Großraumlimousine; Großraumfahrzeug	73
minor	geringfügig, klein; unbedeutend	105, 155
minority	Minderheit	233
misalignment	Fluchtungsfehler; Achsversatz	153
misfire, misfiring, backfire; ignition fault	Fehlzündung; Aussetzer	139, 255
mixhead	Mischkopf	200
mixture formation	Gemischbildung; Kraftstoffaufbereitung	147
mixture formation system	Gemischbildner	255
mixture formulation	Mischung nach Formel	221
mobile drilling derricks	fahrbare Bohrtürme	15
mode	Betriebsart; Modus	97
modified injection pattern	geändertes Einspritzbild	252
modulators	Regler	82, 96
module support	Halterung, Träger, Stütze	65
moisture	Feuchtigkeit	114

momentum	Schwung; Impuls	123
monitoring	Überwachung, Kontrolle	61, 91
monocoque	einschalig; monocoque	194
monocoque design	Einschalenbauweise, Monocoque-Bauweise	108
monolith	Wabenkörper	163
monolithic structure	Wabenkörper-Struktur	131
moped	Fahrrad mit Hilfsmotor (Moped, Mofa)	16
mos (metal oxide semiconductor)	Metalloxid-Halbleiter, MOS	170
motor cycle	Motorrad	16
motor industry	Kraftfahrzeugindustrie	15
motor vehicles	Kraftwagen	16
mould	Form; Formwerkzeug	63
mould cavity	Formhohlraum	202
mould joints	Formspalt	195
mould release	Formtrennung	200
mould release agents	Trennmittel	200
moulded	formgepresst	172
moulded-in-colour	durchgefärbt	117
moulder	Formmaschine	194
moulder	Formmaschine; Formhersteller	101
moulding line	Formpress-Band/Linie/Straße	203
moulding machines	Formpress-/Spritzguss-Maschine	63
moulding resin	Pressharz, Gussharz	194
mountainous territories	Gebirge	247
mounting	Lagerung	65
mounting	steigend, wachsend	37
mounts	Lager; Stützlager; Halter, Halterungen	71
mpg (Miles per Gallon)	Meilen pro Galone	
multi purpose vehicle	Mehrzweckfahrzeug	167
multi-conductor	Mehrfachpol; Vielpol	87
multiphase plan	Mehrstufenplan	124
multiple	vielfach	200
narrow band hum	Schmalbandbrummen	125
necessitated	notwendig machen; fordern (etwas)	71
nippy	schnell; wendig	121
nitrogen	Stickstoff	193
nitrogen oxide	Stickstoffoxid (NOx)	51
nitrogen oxides	Stickoxide	255
nodes	Knoten	207
nodes	Knotenpunkte	108, 212
noise level	Geräuschpegel	177
nominated	ernannt (offiziell)	56
non-leaded	bleifrei	160
notchback	Stufenheck	240
notches	Kerben	215
notching	kerben; einkerben	199

notorious for	berüchtigt wegen	223
novel	neu; neuartig	131, 141, 171, 198
noxious	schädlich, giftig	255
nozzle	Düse; Mundstück	138, 150
nozzle holder	Düsenträger; Düsenhalter	150
objective	Ziel	79
occupant detection sensors	Belegungserkennung-Sensoren	171
occupants	Insassen	67
occurring	Vorkommen	54
odometer	Wegstreckenzähler; Kilometerzähler	236, 251
odours	Gerüche	249
of the order of	in der Größenordnung von	101
of zinc-coated steel	Stahl mit Zinkschicht	108
offbeat	ausgefallen	75
offence	Vergehen	37
ohv	oben hängendes Ventil	145
oil filter housing	Ölfiltergehäuse	254
oil filter insert	Ölfiltereinsatz	254
oil pan gasket	Ölwannendichtung	254
omission	Wegfall	252
on the prowl; to be on the prowl	herumschleichen	44
onboard	Einbau	119
open-circuit	offener Stromkreis	95
opening duration	Öffnungsdauer	143
operating temperatures	Betriebstemperatur	178
opposed	abgeneigt	58
opposing movement	Gegenbewegung	142
opted	sich entschieden haben	81
optical channels	optische Kanäle	92
optical fibre (GB); optical fiber (US)	Lichtwellenleiter	212
opting	sich entscheiden	160
option	Ausübung des Prämienrechts; Optionsausübung	51
optional equipment	Sonderausstattung	251
or spare wheel well	Ersatzradmulde; Reserveradwanne	206
orbital path	Ring; Umgehung	132
order of	je nach	222
organic	organisch	119
oscillation	Schwingung	179
ounces	Unzen	146
out of focus	unscharf	221
outcry	Protest (lautstarker)	48
outer backrest	Außenseite der Rückenlehne	242
outer seat rail	äußere Sitzschiene	242
outer skin	Außenhaut	84
outlay	Kostenaufwand	191

outlets	Ausgänge	132
outperform	übertreffen	113, 186
output gear set	Abtriebsradsatz	256
output ratio	Abtriebsübersetzung	255
output shaft	Abtriebswelle	256
overcharged	überladen (zu viel berechnet)	
overcome	überwinden	97, 115
overflow valve	Überströmventil	176
overhaul	überholen, instandsetzen	38
overhead cost	Fixkosten; allgemeine Kosten; indirekte Kosten	218
oxides of nitrogen	Stickstoffoxide	128
oxidized	oxidiert	111
oxygen	Sauerstoff	124
ozone	Ozon	102
pack	Meute	
package trays	Ablagefächer	200
padding	Polsterung; Aufpolsterung	130
paint lines	Lackierbandstraßen	114
paint processes	Lackierprozess	114
paint shop	Lackiererei	228
painted	überlackiert	258
pallet	Palette	63
paper replacement cartridge	Papierwechselpatrone	254
paradigm	Musterbeispiel	101
parking heaters	Standheizungen	186
particle hydraulics	Körnung (öldruckunterstützt)	194
particulate matter	Feststoffe; Partikel, Ruß	128
particulates	Teilchen; Körnchen	119
partition	Trennwand	163
parts grained	Teile mit Körnung	61
passenger car	Personenkraftwagen (Pkw)	16
payload	Zuladung	121
peculiar	besonders	197
pedal actuation unit	Pedalbetätigungseinheit	165
pedal travel	Pedalweg	82
pedigrees	Stammbaum, Herkunft	43
peening	kalt hämmern	199
peening	kalthämmern	198
pelvis	Becken (menschl.)	135
penal law	Strafrecht	226
penalized	bestrafen	105
penetrate	belästigen	249
penetration	Durchdringung	114
perceive	wahrnehmen	101, 115
perforated	durchlöchert	163
perimeter	Rand; äußere Begrenzung	208

permeability	Durchlässigkeit; Porosität	160
permeation	Durchdringung	159
permissible caravan/trailer load	zulässige Anhängelasten	247
permitted	zulässig; genehmigt	88
perpendicularity	Rechtwinkligkeit	63
perseverance	Ausdauer; Durchhaltevermögen	120
personality	Persönlichkeit	57
persuasive	überzeugend	58, 216
phase	Takt	81
phase shifting	Phasenverschiebung	143
pickup; pickup truck	Leichtlastwagen mit Pritsche	44, 73
pierced holes	durchgestochene Löcher	63
pilot	Modell; Pilot	60
pinching	quetschen	195
pins	Zapfen	239
piston engines	Hubkolbenmotor mit Innenverbrennung (Abk. ICE/IC)	15
piston relief	Kolbenmulde; Ventiltasche	139
piston rod seal	Kolbenstangendichtung	166
pistons	Kolben	173
pit	Grube	
pivot	drehen	80
plant manager	Werksdirektor	228
plastic injection moulding machines	Kunststoffspritzgussmaschinen	63
platform body	Pritschenaufbau	121
platform road train	Brückenzug	16
playful	zum Spielen aufgelegt; (wild) ausgelassen; verspielt	74
pledge	Versprechen	151
plenum chambers	Luftkästen; Luftspeicher	133
plethora	Überfülle	81, 94
plunger	Kolben; Stempel	176
plunger shaft	Kolbenwelle	142
plunger spring	Kolbenrückholfeder	176
ply	Lage, Schicht	182
poisonous constituents	giftige Schadstoffe	255
pollen	Pollen	250
pollutants	Verschmutzer	102
polyaromatic hydrocarbons	polyaromatische Kohlenwasserstoffe	119
polygonisation	Vieleck	199
polystyrene	Polystyrol (PS)	114
pools	Pfütze/Lache verursachen	128
poor	niedrig	144
poor conductor	schlechter Leiter	197
populating	bestücken	87
port	Kanal; Anschluss	139
portion	Teilmenge, Bereich	201
positively-engaged	formschlüssig	182
posture	Stellung; Haltung; Position	79

pour	strömen	202
powder clearcoat	Pulverklarlackschicht	114
powder coating systems; powder coating	Pulverbeschichtung; Pulverlackierung	114, 190
power demand	Energiebedarf	194
power driven cycles	Kraftrad	16
power driven vehicles	Kraftfahrzeug	16
power generation	Energieerzeugung	124
power station	Kraftwerk	120
power steering	Hilfskraftlenkung	232
powered	angetrieben	66
powerplants	Motor-Getriebe-Einheiten; Antriebsgruppe	103
powertrain	Antriebsstrang (Motor + Getriebe)	65
pre-bent	vorgebogen	206
precipitation hardening	Ausscheidungshärtung	199
predecessor	Vorgänger; Vorläufermodell	153, 230
predictive system	Vorhersagesystem	92
predominant	vorherrschend	203
preliminary stroke	Vorhub	138
prematurely	frühzeitig	58
pressing	Pressteil; Ziehteil	132
pressure-depending	druckabhängig	245
prestrain	Vorspannung	108
presumably	vermutlich	91
presume	vermuten	98
pre-tensioned	vorgespannt	242
price tag	Preisschild	50, 232
primary	Haupt-	79
primary sound sources	Hauptschallquellen	180
prime zones	Hauptbereiche	117
primers	Grundierlacke	190
printed circuit boards	Leiterplatten	252
probe	forschend untersuchen; (eine Angelegenheit) erforschen	
probe	sondieren; untersuchen	173
processability	Verarbeitbarkeit	165
product range	Produktsortiment; Produktprogramm	86
production control	Fertigungssteuerung	62
production control	Produktionssteuerung	255
production dies	Formwerkzeuge	60
production run	Herstellungslos	217
production trial run	Fertigungslosgröße für Versuch, Erprobung	62
profiled	formgefräst; profilgefräst	86
profit margin	Gewinnspanne	
prominent	vorstehend	79
prompt	j-n veranlassen; dazu animieren, etwas zu tun	225

proneness	Neigung (zu etwas neigen)	106
propelled	vorwärts getrieben	201
proportion	Anteil	255
proportioning	zuteilen; dosieren; steuern	245
proprietary	Marken; Eigentum	164
prosperity	Wohlstand	
prototype vehicles	Prototypenfahrzeuge	55
proving grounds	Testgelände; Versuchsgelände; Prüffelder	177
provoked	provozieren; hervorrufen	98
prowess	Tüchtigkeit	30
proximity	Nähe; Nachbarschaft	162, 228
ptfe	Teflon (Polytetrafluorethylen)	154
pulsating	pulsieren	244
punctures	Stiche	245
pundits	Experten	233
purchased	Anschaffung; Einkauf	220
purchasing	Einkauf	56
pursue	verfolgen, durchführen	126
pursues	weiterführen	37
pursuit	Verfolgung	61, 117
push-fit	Montieren durch Stoßen/Drücken	171
pvdf	Polyvinylidenfluorid	160
quadruple	vierfach	81
quarter panel	Seitenwand	239
quarter panel inner	Seitenwandblech innen	212
quarter panels	Seitenverkleidungen; Seitenwände	200
quarts	Quarts	146
queries	Rückfragen; Fragen	234
quest	Suche	154, 174
quill shaft	Hohlwelle	143
r&d	Forschung und Entwicklung	57
races	Laufringe	100
racked	foltern	75
radial piston distributor injection pump	Radialkolben-Verteilereinspritzpumpe	139
radiant heat	Strahlungswärme	132
radiated	abgestrahlt	179
radiator	Luftkühler; Wasserkühler	102
radiator supports	Kühlerträger	206
radii	Radien	208
radius	Radius	156
rails	Träger, Holme	205
rain detectors	Regen-Erkenner/Aufspürer	99
ram forces	Staukräfte	206
range	Reichweite	50
range	Reichweite; Aktionsradius	120

rated on	gemessen an	54
rather than	lieber als	83
ratings	Bewertungen	48
rattling	klappern	130
reaction	Gegendruck	200
rear axle	Hinterachse	245
rear brake lines	hintere Bremsleitungen	245
rear fender	hinterer Kotflügel; hinteres Schutzblech	67
rear hatch	Heckklappe	84
rear package tray	Hutablage; Heckablage; Kofferraumbrücke	88
rear track	hintere Radspur, hintere Spurweite	71
rearguard	Nachhut	225
rearrangement	Umordnung, Neuordnung	58
receiving unit	Empfangseinheit	251
reception failure	Empfangsaussetzer	252
recess	Mulde; Vertiefung	66
reciprocating	hin- und hergehend, wechselnd	174
recirculation	Rückführung	81
reclaim	wiedergewinnen; regenerieren	191
rectangular	rechtwinklig, rechteckig	65, 217
recyclability	Wiederaufbereitungsfähigkeit	105
recyclable	recylingfähig	225
reduction catalytic converter	Reduktionskatalysator	141
reduction gear	Untersetzungsgetriebe; Zwischengetriebe	132
redundant	überflüssig	88
refinements	Verfeinerung; Veredelung	197
refineries	Ölraffinerien	126
refining	verfeinern; veredeln	89
reflecting	widerspiegeln	50
reformer system	Reformeranlage	125
refrigerant system	Kältemittelsystem	250
refrigeration unit	Kälteteil	250
refueling	Nachtanken; Auftanken	128
refueling vapour recovery system	Kraftstoffverdunstungsabsaugsystem; Gaspendelanlage	159
regenerative	nachwachsend	125
regenerative braking	Bremsung mit Energierückgewinnung	127
regrind	nachschleifen	159
regulating valve	Regelventil	176
reign	Herrschaft	117
reign	regieren	93
reinforced	verstärkt	66
relay control	Relaissteuerung	171
reliability	Zuverlässigkeit	62
reluctances	Widerwille, Abneigung	115
reluctant	abgeneigt	193

remedying of faults	Korrektur von Fehlern	255
remote control	Fernsteuerung	186
remoted	ausgelagert	93
render	machen (j-n, etwas)	225
reorientation	Neuorientierung	213
replacement sections	Austauschbereiche	205
replenish	wieder auffüllen	124
replenishment	Nachfüllen (des Tanks/ der Zellen)	124
reputation	Ruf	54, 106
research	Forschung	56
residual	restlich	199
resilience	Nachgiebigkeit; Elastizität	179
resin	Harz	200
resist	widerstehen	157, 197
resistance	Widerstand	130, 170
resistance to creepage	Kriechstrombeständigkeit	105
resistance to rolling	Rollwiderstand	154
resonance frequency	Schwingungsfrequenz	179
resonator	Resonator; Reflexionsschalldämpfer	163
respiration	Atmung	193
retail	Einzelhandel	126
retainer	Haltevorrichtung	242
retention	Halt; Sicherung	170
retro-active	rückwirkend	225
retrofit kit	Nachrüst-Set	188
retrofitted	nachträglich eingebaut	252
return of investment	Rückkehrzeitpunkt der getätigten Investitionen	56
rev; revving; rev-up; revving-up	hoch beschleunigen, hoch fahren (Motor)	95
revamping	aufmöbeln	39
reveal (sth.)	enthüllen, verraten	52, 65
revenues	Einnahmen	
reverberant	nachhallend, reflektierend	183
reverse pawl	Rücklauf-Sperrklinke	242
reverts	zurückkehren	141
reviving	wiederbeleben; sich erholen	
ribbings	Verrippungen	105
rich	fett	141
ride	spazieren fahren; davon profitieren	44
ridges	Druckkante; Knickkante	198
rig	Prüfstand, Teststand	174
right-hand drive	rechtsgelenkt; Rechtslenkung	234
rigid	fest, formstabil, steif	131
rigid	verwindungssteif, verdrehsteif	65
rigid drawbar trailer	Starr-Deichselanhänger	16
rigidity	Steifigkeit	105, 206
rigidly	starr	65

rims	Felgen	245
ripped v-belt tensioner	Keilrippenriemen-Spannvorrichtung	252
rock-bottom prices	Schleuderpreise	223
rocker panel; rocker section	Einstiegsschweller	258
rocker switch	Wipptaste	257
rocks	schaukeln	135
rolled out	erste Gehversuche unternehmen	76
rolled steel sections	Walzprofilstahl	203
roller followers	Rollenstößel	100
rollers	Rollkörper	174
rollformed	rollgeformt	209
rolling motions	Schlingerbewegungen	247
rollover bars	Überrollbügel	65
roll-up windows	Kurbelfenster; Hebefenster	182
roof	Dach	212
roof lining	Dachhimmel; Dachverkleidung	133
roof panels	Dachhaut	106
roof rails	Dachlängsträger	207
rotary	drehend	200
rotary machine	Drehmaschine	63
rotary pump	Drehkolbenpumpe	175
rotary switches	Drehschalter	249
rotor-type oil pump	Rotorölpumpe	254
roughness	Rauigkeit	108
round blanks	runde Rohlinge	161
rubber compound	Gummimischung	156
rubber compound	Kautschukmischung	154
rugged	robust, stabil	170
run at rate	Lauf mit gewünschter Stückzahl	61
run-flat tyre	Reifen mit Notlaufeigenschaften	155
runners	Rohre; Krümmerrohre	195
running clearances	Laufspiel	153
running flat (business)	auf niedrigen Touren laufen; auf Sparflamme kochen.	230
running gear	Fahrgestell; Fahrwerk	122
safeguard	sicherstellen	228
safety fork	Sicherungsgabel	242
salt, grit and sand spreader (gritting truck)	Streu-Lastwagen	16
salvaged	wiederverwerten	226
salvo	Salve	229
sampled	bemustert; stichprobenweise überprüft	63
samples	Muster	59
sand-cast	Sandguss	161
sanded	abgeschliffen	116
sandwiched between	eingeklemmt zwischen	206
sanguine (of temperament); (of views, policy etc.)	heiter; zuversichtlich	48

scar	Kratzer, Narbe	174
sceptics	Skeptiker	65
scooter	Motorroller	16
scrap	Schrott	104, 159, 217
scrapers	Abstreifer	154
scrapped	verschrottet	205
scrapyards	Autofriedhöfe; Schrottplätze	226
screw connections	Schraubverbindungen	65
scuffing	scheuern, reiben	174
seal	Dichtungsmittel	254
seal	versiegeln, konservieren	130
sealant	Dichtmaterial; Dichtungsmasse	84
sealed	abgedichtet; eingeschweißt; versiegelt	133
sealing	abdichten	119, 153
sealing plug	Verschlussstopfen	247
seam	Naht	242
seam welding	Nahtschweißung	208
seamless	nahtlos	54
seat backs	Sitzlehne, Rückenlehne	66
seat base	Sitzaufnahme; Sitzträger	135
seat cushion	Sitzkissen	79
seat defection	Sitzfehler	79
seat frames	Sitzgestelle	105
seat frames	Sitzrahmen; Sitzgestelle	84
seat pan	Sitzschale	101
seat pans	Sitzwannen; Sitzschalen	200
seatback angle	Sitzlehnenneigungswinkel	79
seatbelt tensioners	Gurtstraffer; Gurtstrammer	66
secondary air injection	Sekundärlufteinblasung	252
secondary roads	Nebenstraßen	82
secure	sichern	66
secured	gesichert; befestigt	252
seductive	verführerisch	120
segregated	abgetrennt	126
selector level	Wählhebel	255
self-locating drive	selbstführender Antrieb	182
semi-conductor	Halbleiter	134
semi-trailer	Sattelanhänger	16
semi-trailer towing vehicle	Sattelzugmaschine	16
sensitive	empfindlich, feinfühlig	186, 199
sensitivity	Abhängigkeit; Empfindlichkeit	208
separator piston	Abscheiderkolben	153
septum	viskoelastische Schwerschicht	179
sequential-shift	sequentielle Gangschaltung	71
serial interface	serielle Schnittstelle	170
series-connected	in Reihe/Serie geschaltet	122
serviceability	Servicefreundlichkeit	88
set-up	einrichten	63

several angles	Winkel	63
sewer cleaning vehicle	Kanalreinigungs-Fahrzeug	16
shaft	Welle	100
shares	Aktien	51
sharp edges	scharfe Kanten	245
sheet metal	Blech	60, 63
sheet moulding composite (smc)	Blech/Kunststoff-Formteil, Verbundbauteil	116
sheet moulding compound	Verbundbauteil, Blech/Kunststoff-Formteil	113
sheetings	Blechverkleidung	203
sheet-metal oil filter cartridge	Blechölfilterpatrone	254
shielded	abgeschirmt, entstört	87
shielding gas	Schutzgas	211
shift lever	Schalthebel; Einrückhebel	82
shipments	Lieferungen	223
shock absorber mountings	Stoßdämpferhalterungen	67
shock absorbers	Stoßdämpfer	85
shock absorbing devices	Dämpfungselemente	215
shock tower reinforcement	Verstärkung Stoßfänger – Dom	212
shoddy	schäbig, minderwertig	41
short-circuit	Kurzschluss	88, 95
shorted to ground	Massenschluss, Erdschluss	89
shot peening	kugelstrahlen	199
showcased	ausgestellt	137
shredder residue	Schredderabfall	226
shut line	Fuge; Spalt; Schließlinie	67
side members	Längsträger, Rahmenlängsträger	65
side panels	Seitenwände	65
side roof rail	Dachträger seitlich	212
sieves	Siebe	141
silencer	Abgasschalldämpfer	162
silica	Kieselerde; Quarz	156
silicon	Silizium; Silicium	170
silicon carbide	Siliziumkarbid	197
sill beam	Schweller; Türschweller	213
sill; door sill; sill panel	Einstiegsschweller, Türschweller	181, 207
single ignition coils	Einzelzündspulen	252
single pass	in einem Durchgang	161
sink	Senke	63, 195
sintered	gesintert	105
situations	Konstellationen	182
skidding	rutschen; gleiten	154
skimming over the surface	dicht über die Oberfläche dahingleiten	157
skirt	Schürze; Verkleidung	212
skittish	nervös	44
slaving	zwingen	99
sleek	schnittig	74

sleeves	Hülsen, Buchsen	197
slipping	rutschen, gleiten	100
slope	abfallen; ansteigen	71
slurry	Schlamm	191
small fries	kleine Fische	44
snap in towards the top	nach oben einhaken	239
snap-fits	Einschnapp-Passung/-Sitz	112
sniffing	schnüffeln	41
snub-nosed	stupsnasig	75
snug fit	am Körper anliegen	242
soar	in die Höhe schnellen (Preise)	
soaring	in die Höhe schnellen	45
sober	nüchtern, sachlich	75
solar panel	Sonnenkollektor	133
sold out	ausverkauft	
soldered	gelötet	63
solenoid valve	elektromagnetisches Ventil	144, 152, 165
solid state	Festkörper-	134
solidification	Verfestigen, Erstarren; Verfestigung	105, 196
solids	Feststoffe	190
solution process	Auflösungsprozess	156
solvent	Lösungsmittel	190
solvent-free	lösungsmittelfrei	191
soot	Ruß	120, 147, 250
soot emissions	Rußausstoß	138
sophisticated	hoch entwickelt; hochmodern; ausgeklügelt	234
sophisticated	hoch entwickelt; raffiniert	132
soundproofing	Schalldämmung	137
spaceframe	Gitterrohrrahmen	203, 217
spare tire covers	Ersatzreifenabdeckung	200
spare wheel	Ersatzrad	239, 246
spark	Funke	15
spark plug connectors	Zündkerzenstecker	252
spatters	Schweißspritzer	213
special purpose device	Sondervorrichtung	213
specific gravity	spezifisches Gewicht; Raumgewicht	114
specification	Lastenheft	224
specimens	Muster; Proben	157
speed	beschleunigen	44
speed code	Geschwindigkeits-Kennbuchstabe	246
speedometer	Tachometer	236
spinal column	Wirbelsäule; Rückgrat	135
spinning	Durchdrehen	246
spiral cut	spiralverzahnt, bogenverzahnt	182
splicing	Spleißung; Naht	158
spoilers	Windabweiser; Luftleitflügel	194
spoke	Speichen	248

spores	Sporen	250
sport utility vehicle, sport-utility car	Freizeitfahrzeug, Fun-Fahrzeug, sportlicher Pick-up	73, 230
spring	Feder	242
spring isolators	Federisolierung; Blattfeder-Zwischenlagen	183
spring tensioned belt	federbelasteter Gürtel	242
spring-strut	Federbein	65
spur	anspornen	137
spur gear	Zahnrad mit Geradverzahnung; Stirnrad	132
squeak	quietschen, knarren, knarzen	179
squeal	Schleifgeräusche verursachen	243
squibs	Zündpille (für Airbags)	170
stability enhancement	Stabilitätsverbesserung	95
stability management system (psm)	Fahrdynamikregelsystem	167
stabilizer	Stabilisator	247
stack	Stapel	50
staff	Personal	58
staggered	versetzt angeordnet	81
stainless steel	Edelstahl; rostfreier Stahl	111
stakes	Einsätze	229
stamping die	Stanzwerkzeug	63
stand out for (to stand out for sth.)	sich auf etwas versteifen	191
state	Zustand	143
station wagon	Pkw-Kombi; Kombi	16
steel castings	Stahlguss	109
steering angle	Lenkeinschlag; Radeinschlag; Lenkwinkel	82
steering column lock	Lenkradsperre	235
steering knuckles	Achsschenkel	71
steering wheel cores	Lenkrad-Kerne/Innenringe	104
steering wheel frames	Lenkradgerüst; Lenkradgestelle	105
stepped up	Steigern	
stepper motor	Schrittmotor	95
stiff competition	scharfe Konkurrenz	229
stiffening ribs	Versteifungsrippen	101
stiffness	Steifigkeit	108, 165
stinging	getroffen	223
stipulated	vorschreiben	165
stodgy	schwer verdaulich; schwerfällig	73
stoichiometric air-fuel ratio	stöchiometrisches Kraftstoff-Luft-Verhältnis (ideales Verhältnis; Lambda = 1)	141
stone chipping	Steinschlagschaden	115
stone protector	Steinschlagschutz	258
storage compartments	Staufächer	239
storage system	Ablagesystem	238
stowage compartment	Ablagefach	235, 257

straightforward	einfach; direkt; unkompliziert	124, 220, 249
stratified	geschichtet	152
stratified charge	Schichtladung	147
stream	fließen	205
strength	Festigkeit	165, 199
strengthening	verstärken; ausbauen	223
strengthening	Versteifung; Verfestigung	199
stress	Beanspruchung	199
stress analysis	Spannungsanalysen	60
stress patterns	Spannungsverläufe	221
stretched	gespannt	132
stretching	verlängern	205
striking; strikingly	imponierend, eindrucksvoll	81, 120
structural	strukurell; baulich	200
structural adhesive	Klebstoff für Strukturteile	205
structural integrity	Strukturintegrität	130
structure	Struktur, Aufbau; Gerippe	65
structure-borne sound	durch die Struktur übertragener Schall	178
struts	Federbeine	67
struts	Lenker; Beine, Streben	85
stubby	kurz und dick	75
sturdier	robuster	128
style	stylen; designen	194
styling	Stilistik, Formgebung, Gestaltung	56
styrene-butadiene	Styrol-Budadien	156
subframe	Hilfsrahmen, Fahrschemel	65
subframe; underframe; wheel-suspension raft; chassis auxiliary frame	Fahrschemel; Hilfsrahmen; Unterrahmen	84, 206
subheaded	Untertitel	15
subjected	ausgesetzt	199
subscriber	Abonnent(in)	91, 121
subsequent	nachfolgend	108
subsidiary	Tochterunternehmen; Tochtergesellschaft	35, 37
subsidised	subventioniert, bezuschusst	84
substantial	gewichtig	204
substrate	Träger	178
substrates	Substrat; Träger	200
sub-surface	untere Fläche	173
subtle	subtil, raffiniert	97
subtly	fein	169
suckers	Sauger; Ansauger	214
sulphonation	Schwefeln	159
sulphur content	Schwefelgehalt	119
sulphur-free gasoline	schwefelfreies Benzin	125
sump	Ölwanne	85, 142, 196
sun visors	Sonnenblenden	200

supercharger	Auflader; Verdichter; Kompressor	81
superimposed	überlagert	177
superior	überlegen, souverän	194
superior to	herausragend, überragend	106
supersede	verdrängen; überflüssig machen	249
superseded	überflüssig	192
superstructure	Oberbau; Aufbau	84
supplies	Belieferungen	230
support	Unterstützung	62
supporting members	tragende Bauteile; Stützglieder	181
suppressed	unterdrückt; gedämpft	88
suppression	Schalldämpfung; Unterdrückung; Schwächung	179
supreme	höchst; unschlagbar	93
surface	Oberflächen	61
surface cracks	Oberflächenrisse	199
surface finish	Oberflächenbeschaffenheit; Oberflächengüte	161
surface velocity	Oberflächengeschwindigkeit	180
surface-mounted	oberflächenmontiert	87
surpass	übertreffen	141, 194
surplus	Überangebot	223
surrounding	umgebend; einfassend	97
surveying	untersuchen; beobachten	143
surveys	Untersuchungen	54
susceptibility	Empfindlichkeit	175
susceptible	sensibel; anfällig	153
suspected	verdächtig	119
suspension bushings	Radaufhängungslager; Fahrwerkslager	183
suspension crossmembers	Aufhängungsquerträger	182
suspension struts	Federbeine; Radaufhängungsbeine	71
suspension systems	Radaufhängungssystem; Federungssystem	153
suspension turrets	Radaufhängungsdom	204
suspicion	Verdacht	233
sustainable	lebenserhaltend	158
SUV (sport utility vehicle)	Freizeitfahrzeug	167
swaying	pendeln; Pendelbewegungen	247
sweep	kehren	155
swerving to avoid an obstacle	Ausweichmanöver	244
swing-out type rear windows	hinteres Ausstellfenster	257
swirl	Strudel; Wirbel	138
swirl	Wirbel	221
switch console	Schalterkonsole	257
switch stalks	Schalthebel	224
switches	Schalter	93
swivel-arm	Schwenkarm; Gelenkhebel	192
swivelled down	nach unten schwenken	257
swivelling	Schwenken	249

swivelling headlights	Kurvenscheinwerfer; Kurvenleuchten	80
synthetic fibre	Kunstfaser	154
synthetic gasoline	synthetisches Benzin	123
tachometer	Drehzahlmesser	236
tailback	Rückstau	226
tailgate	Heckklappe	71
tailgate	Ladeklappe; Heckklappe	86
tailgate inner panelling	Innenverkleidung der Heckklappe	240
tailored	maßgeschneidert	209
tailored blanks	maßgeschneiderte Bleche	217
take account of the fact	der Tatsache Rechnung tragen	98
taking two stances	zwei Standpunkte beziehen	223
talc	Talkum	179
tangible	greifbar, konkret	110
tank vent valve	Tankentlüftungsventil	252
tapered	kegelförmig; konisch	70
targets	Ziele	54
tariffs	Zollgebühren	
tear	Riss	186
tearing	reißen, zerlegen	198
tears	reißen; zerreißen	242
telematics	Telematik	89
tempered	vorgespannt	199
temporarily	vorübergehend, zeitweise	141
temporary spare wheel	Notrad	246
tempt	verleiten	247
tenseness	Gespanntheit; Verspannung	134
tensile strength	Zugfestigkeit	105, 172, 174
tensile stresses	Zugbeanspruchungen	199
tensioning	Spannstellung	247
tensioning lever	Spannhebel; Klemmhebel	176
test stand	Prüfstand	144
tetrahedral	vierflächig; tetraedrisch	222
that's a tall order	das ist ein bisschen viel verlangt!	74
thermal conductivity	Wärmeleitfähigkeit; Wärmeleitvermögen	107, 186
thermal expansion	Wärmeausdehnung	114
thermally conductive	wärmeleitend	186
thermosets	duroplastische Kunststoffe	108
thigh support	Oberschenkelauflage	238
thin-walled	dünnwandig	118
thread	Gewinde; Schraubengang	100, 155
thread	schrauben, winden	98
three-shift operation	3-Schicht-Betrieb	228
three-way catalytic converter	Dreiwege-Katalysator; Katalysator mit Lambda-Sonde; Selektivkatalysator	141
threshold	Schwelle; Grenze	123, 226

threshold values	Schwellenwerte; Grenzwerte	151
throttle	drosseln	94
throttle	Drosselventil; Drosselklappe	85
throttle body	Drosselklappengehäuse	184
throttle response	Ansprechverhalten des Motors (auf Drosselklappenbefehle)	144
throttle valve potentiometer	Drosselklappenpotentiometer	253
thrust	Schub; Druck	225
thus	folglich; auf diese Weise	92
tied	gebunden	160
tier one suppliers	Hauptzulieferer; Komplettsystemlieferant	158
tie-ups	Zusammenarbeit	41
tight-lipped	verschlossen	158
tightness	Dichtheit	208
tilting	Kippen	249
timing belt covers	Steuerriemenabdeckung	180
timing device	Versteller	176
tinker	herumpfuschen	73
tire, tires (US)	Reifen (sing.), Reifen (pl)	
to catch on	Anklang finden	190
to cope with	fertigwerden mit	125
to get round to	dazu kommen	109
tonneau cover	Fahrgastraumabdeckung; Verdeckhülle	116
tool	Werkzeug	61
toothed belt tensioner roller	Zahnriemen-Spannrolle	254
torque	Drehmoment	96
torque control fulcrum	Angleich-Drehpunkt, Angleichregler	175
torsional	verdrehen, verwinden	199
torsional force	Torsionskraft	143
torsional rigidity	Verdrehsteifigkeit	210
torsional stiffness	Verdrehsteifigkeit, Verwindungssteifigkeit	65
torsional vibration	Drehschwingungs-	183
torso	Rumpf; Oberkörper	79
tough	agressiv; hart	225
toughened	widerstandsfähig	66
towed vehicle	Anhängefahrzeug	16
towing equipment	Zugvorrichtung	247
towing vehicles	Zugmaschinen	16
tow-tractor (US: tow truck)	Abschleppfahrzeug	121
tracer dye	Signalfarbe	250
track-width	Fahrspurbreite	122
traction control	Schlupfregelung, automatische Schlupfregelung	95
tractor	Traktor; Zugfahrzeug	16, 23, 194
trade-off; tradeoff	Kompromiss	155, 216
traffic jams	Verkehrsstau	92
trailer	Anhänger	16

trailer towing vehicle	Anhänger-Zugmaschine	16
trailer turn signal	Anhängerblinker	236
trailing	auf Zug beansprucht	132
trailing arm	Längslenker; Zugstange; Zugstrebe	67, 85
trailing arms	Längsträger, Zugstangen	115
transformation cost	Umformungskosten	105
transformers	Transformatoren	194
transient	vorübergehend; vergänglich	96
transition	Übergang	190
transmission	Antrieb; Getriebe	71, 255
transmission shafts	Verbindungswellen; Zwischenwellen	206
transversal	quer, transversal	168
transverse links	Querlenker	115
transversely	quer	163
trapped	eingeschlossen, gefangen	220
trapped	gefangen	141
tray	Fach, Ablage, Ablagefach	101, 235
tread	Profil	154
tread depth	Profiltiefe	245
tread pattern	Profilausführung	245
treason	Landesverrat	73
treaty	Vertrag	226
tribological properties	tribologische Eigenschaften	153
trigger	auslösen; zünden	171, 256
trimming	garnieren	133
trip odometer	Tageskilometerzähler	236
trolley bus	Oberleitungsbus (O-Bus)	16
truck station wagon	Nutzkraftwagen-Kombi (Nkw-Kombi)	16
truck trailers	Lkw-Anhänger	23
try out presses	Versuchspressen	60
tubular a-pillar reinforcements	rohrförmige Verstärkung in der A-Säule	65
tucked away	wegstecken, verstecken	125
tungsten	Wolfram	161
turbocharged	mit Abgasturbolader	67
turbocharging	Turboantrieb	32
turn indicators	Blinker	70
turnaround time	Umlaufzeit	222
turned to account	sich etwas zunutze machen; aus etwas Vorteil ziehen	96
twin	zwei, doppelt	65, 232
twin overhead camshafts	zwei obenliegende Nockenwellen	145
twist	verdrehen	66
twist beam rear axle	Verbundlenker-Hinterachse	82
twisted cable	verdrehte, verdrillte	89
twists	Verdrehungen	230
two-ply	zwei Lagen	198
tyre grip	Griffigkeit der Reifen	246

tyre, tyres (GB)	Reifen (sing.), Reifen (pl)	245
tyre's footprint	Reifenaufstandsfläche	155
ultimate	äußerste; hier: maximum	105, 172
ultrafines	hochfein	119
ultrasound microphone	Ultraschall-Mikrofon	256
under and oversteer	unter- und übersteuern	168
under carpet	Teppichrückseite; Teppichunterseite	184
under review	unter Überprüfung	87
underbody	Unterboden	71
underbonnet	Motorraum-; motornah	112
undergoing	erleben; sich unterziehen	173
underscore	unterstreichen	42
uneconomic	unwirtschaftlich, unrentabel	37
unenforceable	nicht einklagbar; nicht vollstreckbar	225
uniform	einheitlich	254
uniform	gleichmäßig	202
unimpeded reception	ungestörter Empfang	252
unintentional	ungewollt	242
unique	einzigartig	51
unladen mass, kerb mass (GB); curb mass (US)	Leergewicht	67
unlaminated	ungeschichtet; unkaschiert	179
unlocked	freigeben	199
unmanned	unbemannt	121
unprecedented	beispiellos; noch nie dagewesen	42, 225
unreliable	nicht glaubwürdig.	15
untapped	nicht angezapft/angebohrt	185
unveil (a face, monument etc.)	enthüllen	38, 68
unwise	unklug; töricht	233
upgrades	Aufwertung	87
upholstery	Sitzbezug	242
upmarket	Nobelklasse; für höhere Ansprüche	37
upstream	stromaufwärts	163
upstream	stromaufwärts; gegen den Strom	
urban bus	Linienbus	16
urged	vorantreiben; drängen	225
uv stability	UV-Beständigkeit	114
vacuum servo	Unterdruckunterstützung	95
validated	Anerkennen	55
validation	Gültigkeitserklärung; Validierung	51
valve lift	Ventilhub	143
valve operation	Ventilsteuerung	143
valve stem	Ventilschaft	254
valve timing	Ventilsteuerzeiten	142
valves	Ventile	94
vanes	Flügel; Schaufel	139

vapour pressure	Dampfdruck	134
variable turbine	verstellbare Turbine	85
variable turbocharger	verstellbarer Turbolader	139
variations	Streuungen; Schwankungen	164
vehicle papers	Fahrzeugpapiere	247
vehicle underbody	Fahrzeugunterbau	245
vein	Stimmung	75
velocity	Geschwindigkeit	168, 213
vendor	Verkäufer	60, 223
vent housing	Lüftungsgehäuse	249
ventilation jets	Belüftungsdüsen	235, 249
vents	Belüftungen, Lüfter	132
verge	Rand; Grenze	147
versatile	vielseitig	177
versatility	Vielseitigkeit; Wandelbarkeit	92
viable	lebensfähig	123
vibrometer	Schwingungsmessgerät	184
victorious	siegreich	226
virtually	tatsächlich; faktisch	191
viscosity	Flüssigkeitsgrad	206
vital	lebenswichtig	54
voice activation	Sprachsteuerung; Sprachbedienung	93
voltage	elektrische Spannung	249
vortices	Wirbel	220
vorticities	Verwirbelungen	220
vows	geloben	157
vulnerable	anfällig	44
wake	Kielwasser; Sog	233
warning triangle	Warndreieck	240
warrants	garantiert	220
warranty	Garantie	86
water-borne primers	Grundierlacke auf Wasserbasis	190
wave crests	Wellenspitzen	88
wave solder machines	Frequenzlötmaschinen	63
wear	Verschleiß, Abnutzung; Abrieb	154, 173, 174, 186
weighing apparatus	Waage	247
weld seam	Schweißnaht	211
weldability	Schweißbarkeit	105
weldbonded	Schweißgeklebt	210
wets	sättigen; befeuchten	201
whet	anregen	44
whimsical	schrullig	44
white noise	Weißrauschen; weißes Rauschen	184
whole lot	eine ganze Menge	
wholesale	Großhandel	95, 120
wick	Docht	134

windbreak	Windschutz, Windschott	66
winding	kurvenreich	247
winding drum	Aufwickeltrommel	132
windscreen (GB); screen (GB); windshield (US)	Windschutzscheibe	50
windshield header rail	oberer Windschutzscheibenrahmen; vorderer Dachquerträger	66
wings	Kotflügel; Schutzbleche	84
wiring harness plug	Kabelsatzstecker	242, 245
wiring harnesses	Kabelsätze, Kabelstränge	92, 194
wishbones	Querlenker	67, 85
with automatic retractors	Aufroll- und Blockierautomatik	242
worn down	abgefahren; abgetragen	243
wound	gewickelt	132
woven	gewebt	186
wrapped	ummantelt; umhüllt	137, 195
wrinkling	schrumpeln; schrumpelig werden	198, 208
x-ray	Röntgen	173
yaw rate sensor	Gierratesensor	169
yaw sensor	Gierwinkelsensor; Gierwinkelaufnehmer	168
yaw stability control	Giermomentenregelung	169
yaw velocity	Gierwinkelgeschwindigkeit; Giergeschwindigkeit	168
yield strength	Formänderungsfestigkeit; Fließgrenze, Streckgrenze	105, 172
young's modulus	Elastizitätsmodul	105, 108
zeal	Eifer	

Pictures and Sources

Die nachfolgend aufgeführten Firmen haben durch Bereitstellung von Bildmaterial und Druckschriften die Ausgestaltung des Buches unterstützt. Meinen herzlichen Dank dafür.

- Adam Opel AG, Rüsselsheim
- Audi AG, Ingolstadt
- Cloos Schweißtechnik, Haiger
- Continental Teves AG, Frankfurt
- DaimlerChrysler AG, Stuttgart
- Ford AG, Köln
- Krauss-Maffei GmbH, München
- Robert Bosch GmbH, Stuttgart
- Thyssen-Krupp Stahl AG, Duisburg
- Volkswagen AG, Wolfsburg
- Webasto AG, Stockdorf bei München
- ZF Friedrichshafen AG, Schwäbisch Gmünd

Folgende Personen haben durch Ihr Engagement diesem Buch mit zum Erfolg verholfen. Ich danke ihnen hierfür herzlich.

- Andreas Baier
- Erika Grieshober-Treber
- Kimo Kosunen
- Alexander Voos
- Adrian Zürl

Für die eigenen Recherchen über Suchmaschinen sind beispielsweise nachfolgende Webseiten sowie Links zu den einzelnen Automobilfirmen und Lieferanten interessant (in alphabetischer Reihenfolge sortiert):
http://biz.yahoo.com/ic/n/carmfg.html; http://money.cnn.com;
http://www.automotivedigest.com; http://www.autonews.com;
http://www.autonewseurope.com; http://www.auto-motor-und-sport.de;
http://www.einnews.com; http://www.faz.net; http://www.fourin.com;
http://www.internationalbusinessstrategies.com; http://www.just-auto.com;
http://www.langzeittest.de; http://www.motortrend.com; http://www.rmi.org;
http://www.segmenty.com; http://www.siemensvdo.com;
http://www.theautochannel.com; http://www.vision-asia.com;
http://www.roadandtravel.com; http://www.whatcar.com

Bibliography

1. Motor Vehicle Market
Automotive Engineering International (Oct. 98)
Bielefsky, Dan; Marsh Peter (21.07.99), London: Financial Times
Burt, Tim (2.7.99), Detroit: Financial Times
Burt, Tim (11.1.2000), Detroit: Financial Times
Burt, Tim (12.1.2000), Detroit: Financial Times
Coutinho, Eneida (25.Jan. 2000); Die brasilianischen Autowerke: Die Welt
FAZ, 11.1.2000
Financial Times (Dec 15,1999)
Ford und Opel (22.Jan. 2000); Die Welt
Frankfurter Neue Presse (13.1.2000), Frankfurt
Frankfurter Rundschau (6.1.2000), Frankfurt
Handelsblatt (12.1.2000), Detroit
Handelsblatt (6.1.2000)
Ihlwan, Moon (24.1.2000), Seoul: Business Week
International Herald Tribune (11.1.2000), Detroit
James, Barry (11.9.1997): Herald Tribune
Karnitschnig, Matt (January 24, 2000), Detroit: Business Week
Kervin, Kathleen (Jan 10, 2000), Detroit: Business Week
L. White, Gregory; Miller, Scott (11.1.2000): The Wall Street Journal
Larner, Monica (Oct. 19, 1998), Modena: Business Week
Naughton, Keith; LowT Miller, Karen; Woellert, Lorraine; Kerwin, Kathleen, (Aug. 9, 1999), Detroit, Frankfurt, Washington : Business Week
ON am Sonntag (8.1.2000)
Recklinghäusener Zeitung (8.1.2000)
Roberts, Dexter (17.1.2000), Changchun: Business Week
Start in den Autofrühling (10.3.2000): VDI Nachrichten
Süddeutsche Zeitung (12.1.2000), München
Süddeutsche Zeitung (13.1.2000), München
Tatsachen u. Zahlen aus der Kraftverkehrswirtschaft (1998), 62. Auflage, Frankfurt: VDA,
Thornton, Emily (10.1.2000), Tokyo: Business Week
Weernink, Wim Oude (June 7, 1999): Automotive News Europe

2. Enterprise Marketing Strategies and Politics
Ball, Jeffrey; Biddle, Frederic M. (Nov. 12, 1999), Detroit: Wall Street Journal
Birch, Stuart (Nov. 1999): Automotive Engineering International
Bishop, Roger (Sept. 1998); European Automotive Design
Boudette, Neal (Nov. 19-20, 1999), Wall Street Journal Europe
Buchholz, Kami (Nov.1999): Automotive Engineering International
Burt, Tim (26.07.1999), London: Financial Times
Chappel, Lindsey (Oct. 25, 1999), Automotive News Europe
DaimlerChryslser (1999); Geschäftsbericht
Ewing, Jack; Thornton, Emily (Dec. 13, 1999), Frankfurt, Tokyo: Business Week
Halliday, Jean (Nov.1, 1999): Automotive news
Harney, Alexandra (Nov. 24, 1999); Tokyo: Financial Times
Harney, Alexandra (07.01.2000), London: Financial Times
Hightech (2/2000);Heiliger Schein: DM
Hsieh, Paul I; Lee, Robert Eugene (Aug. 1999): Automotive Engineering International
Kerwin, Kathleen (Febr. 28, 2000), At Ford...; Detroit: Business Week

Motavalli, Jim (23.07.1999), New York: New York Times
Rossant, John (March 27, 2000); European Business, Paris: Business Week
Shirouzu, Norihiko; Williams, Michael (Nov. 15, 1999), Tokyo: Wall Street Journal Europe

3. Strategical Operational Planning
Adcock, Ian; Bishop, Roger (Sept. 1998), Inside the Ford Focus; European Automotive Design
Advanced Product Quality Planning and Control Plan (June 1994): Chrysler, Ford and GM Corp.
Arthur D. Little Inc.; Boghani,Ashok B. (Nov. 1998): Automotive Engineering International
Birch, Stuart (Oct. 1998), Ford Focus: Automotive Engineering International
Birch, Stuart (June 1999), Automotive Engineering International
Burman, Richard (Aug./Sept. 1994); Manufacturing Sytems: Automotive Engineer
Direktvertrieb im Interent (12/30/1999). Frankfurter Allgemeine
Dunkel, Monika (12/16/1999) EU: Wirtschaftswoche
Joint Venture in der Automobiltechnik (21.3.2000): Süddeutsche Zeitung
Prozesse (5/1999), Automotive Engineering Partners
Vollradt, K. (12.11.1999); Zulieferer werden Komplett-Dienstleister: VDI Nachrichten
Zürl, Karl-Heinz (1997), Confidence in Dealing with Conferences, Discussions, and Speeches, Oldenbourg-Verlag

4. Carmakers' Portfolio
Audi A2 (Sonderausgabe 2000): ATZ, MTZ
Automobil/Umwelt (28.4.2000): VDI Nachrichten
Ball, Jeffrey (Jan 27, 2000), DaimlerChrysler, The Wall Street Journal
Birch, Stuart (Oct. 1999), Automotive Engineering International
Birch, Stuart (Nov. 1999), Automotive Engineering International
Burt, Tim (Jan 27, 2000), BMW, Financial Times
Chew, Edmund (Nov. 8, 1999), A2 features: Automotive News Europe
Eckert, Vera (21.3.2000); Rund ums Auto bleibt Stahlbranche führend: Handelsblatt Nr. 57
Ponticel,Patrick (Oct. 1999), Automotive Engineering International
Robinson, Aaron (Oct.18, 1999), Automotive News

5. Styling
Armstrong, Larry; Echikson, William; Noughton, Keith; Thornton,Emily; Woodruff, David (21.9.1998), Brüssel, Detroit, Frankfurt, Los Angeles, Tokio: Business Week
Büchling; Jens (1/2000), Produkte-Styling: Automotive Engineering Partners
Goppelt, Gernot (2000); Interior Design in der Praxis: MTZ; ATZ
Mackenzie, Angus (March 20, 2000); Autos: Business Week
Wernle; Bradford (19.9.1999), London: Automotive News Europe

6. Advanced Engineering
Aachener Kolloquium (2/2000), ATZ Automobiltechnische Zeitschrift
Adcock, Ian (Sept. 1998); European Automotive Design
Adcock, Ian (Nov. 1998); European Automotive Design
Adcock, Ian (May 1999); European Automotive Design
Automobil Electronics (2000); Innovationen durch Elektronik: ATZ
Birch, Stuart (April 1999), Automotive Engineering International
Birch, Stuart (Nov. 1999), Automotive Engineering International
Bishop, Roger (Nov. 1998); European Automotive Design
Buchholz, Kami (Dec. 1998), Detroit: Automotive Engineering International
Canusa Systems (Sept. 1998), European Automotive Design
Daniels, Jeff (Sept. 1998); European Automotive Design

Daniels, Jeff (Nov. 1998); European Automotive Design
Demmler, Al (Dec. 1998), Automotive Engineering International
Einspritzsysteme werden zur Schlüsseltechnik (3.4.2000): Frankfurter Allgemeine Zeitung, Frankfurt
Gary W. Pollak, email: gary@sae.org
Holt, Dan (Jan. 2000), Car of 2100: Automotive Engineering International
Holt, Dan (Jan. 2000), Telematics: Automotive Engineering International
Kragtwijk, Simon P; Langerak, Nico A.J. (Oct. 1998), Automotive Engineering International
Murphy, John (Sept. 1998); European Automotive Design
Shelley, Tom (Nov. 1998); European Automotive Design
Thompson, Tony (Nov. 1999), Observer Newspaper

7. Alternative Propulsion
Beutler, Maik; Schmidt, Margaret (3/2000); Alternative Automobilkonzepte;Erdgas: ATZ
Birch, Stuart (April 1999); Automotive Engineering International
Boblenz, Hanno (4/2000); Öko? Logisch!, Alternative Antriebe: Firmen Auto
Global Partners (4/2000); Fiat Multipla Hybrid Power; neue Antriebskonzepte von Ford: ATZ/MTZ
Harvey, Michael (30.10.1999), Financial Times
Kittler, Eberhard (15.4.2000), mot-technik
Nadol, Christiane (23.3.2000); Brennstoffzellen: Die Telebörse 13/2000
Sauer, Hans Dieter (2.6.2000); Öko-Kraftstoff vom Bauernhof: VDI Nachrichten
Wasserstoff an Bord erzeugen (19.1.2000): KFT

8. Product Engineering
Adcock, Ian (Summer 1997); European Automotive Design
Adcock, Ian (Sept. 1998); European Automotive Design
Adcock, Ian (Nov. 1998); European Automotive Design
Bishop, Roger (Nov. 1998); European Automotive Design
Boonchanta, Pipon; Bovonsomat, Pakorn; Siangsanorh, Somchai (Oct. 1999); Automotive Engineering International
Brady, Diane; Port, Ottis (9.8.1999), Greenwich, New York: Business Week
Buchholz, Kami (Oct. 1999), Detroit: Automotive Engineering International
Burgess, Peter (Summer 1997), European Automotive Design
Climate Control (Aug/Sep. 1994): Automotive Engineer
Collier, Andrew (09/29/1999) Business in the Net Economy: The Daily Telegraph
Durchbruch für die FPC-Technik (01/11/2000): Mainspitze
Fletcher, Mark (Summer 1997); European Automotive Design
Global Partners (4/2000); Dichtungen, Abgassysteme, Standheizungen: ATZ/MTZ
Jacobson, Marcus (Aug./Sept. 1994) Tire Developments: Automotive Engineer
Jost, Kevin (Oct. 1998), Intelligent Vehicles: Automotive Engineering International
Jost, Kevin (Oct. 1999), New Car:-Highlights: Automotive Engineering International
Leonhard, Dr. Rolf (Oct. 1999); With Gasoline Direct Injection Motronic MED7 from Bosch; Presentation to the 54th Automotive Press Conference, Schwieberdingen: Robert Bosch GmbH
Lewis, Anthony (Summer 1997); European Automotive Design
Luis, Antony (Summer 1997); European Automotive Design
Murphy, John (Summer 1997), European Automotive Design
Murphy, John (Nov. 1998), European Automotive Design
Opel 100 years (11/1999); The Zafira, ATZ Automobiltechnische Zeitschrift Worldwide
Rechtin, Mark (Jan. 10, 2000); Shifting gears: Automotive News
Russel, Eric (Sept 1994) Vehicle Communications Automotive Engineer
Science and Technology (Aug,09.1999) Business Week

Scott, David (Summer 1997); European Automotive Design
Shelley, Tom (Summer 1997); European Automotive Design
Tait, Nikki (11/08/1999) US Car: Financial Times
Uhlig, Robert (11/29/1999) German Computer Steers Car: The Daily Telegraph
Ward, Marc (11/29/1999) Fiat Lights: The Daily Telegraph
Winterhagen, Johannes (1/2000); Euromold 1999: Automotive Engineering International

9. Manufacturing Engineering
Adcock, Ian (Oct. 1999); European Automotive Design
Crosse, Jesse (June 1998); FT World Automotive Manufacturing
DaimlerChrysler (4/2000); Genetische Programme zur Robotersteuerung: ATZ/MTZ
Fischer, Hans-Georg (17.1.2000); Porsches Porzellan hält: Focus
Fletcher, Mark (Summer 1997); European Automotive Design
Gerspacher, M; Leopold, F; Mathes, G.; Metzger,O.; Tyler, R. (5.5.2000); Ein Weg zur 90 Gramm CO_2 Emission pro Kilometer am Beispiel des G90; Adam Opel AG, Rüsselsheim
Hightech-Materialbearbeitung (28.4.2000): VDI Nachrichten
Kippels, Dietmar (11.Febr. 2000); Opel stärkt die Fertigung: VDI Nachrichten
Messe Euroguss in Sindelfingen (28.4.2000): VDI Nachrichten
Langton, Ray (Aug/Sept. 1994), Manufactoring Processes, Automotive Engineer
Pelts, Gregory A; Rothacker, Andreas H. (June 1998); Automotive Engineering International
Pilgrim,Ralf (3/2000); Fügetechnik-Produktion: ATZ
Rother, Mike; Shook, John (Jan. 2000), Manufacturing solutions: Automotive Engineering International
Shelley, Tom (Summer 1997); European Automotive Design
Siebenlist, J. (2.6.2000); Kunststoffe: VDI Nachrichten
VDI-Nachrichten Nr. 37 (12.9.1997)
Vollradt, Klaus (12.5.2000), Aluminium: VDI Nachrichten
Vorderachsträger für Astra und Zafira (April 2000): Bänder, Bleche, Rohre
Wirtschaft im Revier (1/1998)

10. Information Technology Services
Bishop, Roger (Sept. 1998), European Automotive Design
Dölle, Andrea (1/2000); Prozesse; Management: Automotive Engineering Partners
EDS Update (I/2000); Solid Modelling Technik: EDS Informationstechnologie und Service GmbH, Rüsselsheim
Grafenberger, Peter (4/2000); Simulation der Motorkühlung mit 3D-Strömungsberechnung: ATZ/MTZ
Shelley, Tom (Sept. 1998), European Automotive Design
Scharf, Achim (19.5.2000), Engineering per Internet: VDI Nachrichten
Tag der Karosserie (2/2000); ATZ Automobiltechnische Zeitschrift
Tönshoff, H.K. (4/2000); Datenmodell zum Informationsaustausch: Konstruktion, VDI-EKV
Voigt, A (5/2000); E-Commerce Lösungen: Konstruktion, Springer/VDI-Verlag
Voxel-News (Issue 1/1998); Tecoplan Informatik GmbH

11. Finance
Altautoregelung (10.5.2000): Opel Post, Rüsselsheim
Burt, Tim (19.11.1999), Financial Times
Carrey, John (Dez. 27, 1999) American News, Detroit: Business Week
Coleman, Brian (June 16, 1999) May Sales Data The Wall Street Journal Europe
Dunne, Nancy (Febr. 12, 2000); Stong car sales, Washington: Financial Times
Karnitschnig, Matthew (March 6, 2000); European Business, Frankfurt: Business Week
Matthews, Robert Guy (29.Nov..1999), The Wall Street Journal Europe

12. Plants
Assembly plants in Europe (Jan. 2000); Automotive News Europe
Hannover Messe Industrie (17.3.2000); Oberflächentechnik; Laser: VDI Nachrichten
Pressetext (1999), Rüsselsheim: Adam Opel AG
Robinson, Aaron (Oct. 18,1999), Automotive News
Stahl bringt Wachstum (31.3.2000): VDI Nachrichten

13. Sales, Logistic and Distribution
Chew, Edmund (28.9.98), Automotive News Europe
Global Partners (4/2000); Unterschiedliche länderspezifischen Kundenwünsche: ATZ/MTZ
Rose, Bernd (10.3.2000); Logistik, Supply-Chain-Management kappt die Lieferzeiten im Automobilbau: VDI Nachrichten

14. Aftersales and Service
Bedienung, Sicherheit, Wartung (Sept. 1999), Rüsselsheim: Adam Opel AG
Chappell, Lindsay (Nov 1,1999), Automotive News
English, Bob (Oct. 18,1999), Automotive News
Produkthaftung in der Automobilindustrie (Mai 2000); Hyatt Hotel, Köln: VDI Bildungswerk

Zuerl & Books

www.lernen-lehren.de
www.hanser.de
Borner Str. 12 D-64569 Nauheim
info@zuerl.com
Tel.: 06152/960200, Fax: 06152/960203

Lesen und Lernen mit Freude

Wir bieten für Sie an:

- Zuerl & Books ... und wie Sie damit auch richtig Geld verdienen können. Das Beratungsgespräch wird Sie überzeugen.
- Übersetzungen (u.a. Bücher, Präsentationen, Bewerbungen) in Sprachen Ihrer Wahl
- Effektive und günstige Sprachreisen nach England (Plymouth) und China (Beijing).
    - Individualkurse und Zertifikatskurse an prämierten Sprachschulen
    - mit netten und erfahrenen Lehrkräften und sehr gutem Preis-Leistungs-Verhältnis
- Fernlehrgänge Englisch und Chinesisch für das nebenberufliche Studium zu Hause

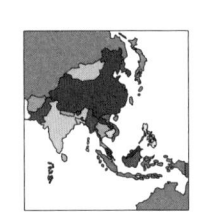

Für SCHULE, BETRIEB UND BÜRO
Für Maschinenbau, Automobilbau, IT, Qualitätsmanagement und Wirtschaft

Der Erfolg ist mit unseren Büchern und bei unserem Service kurzfristig spürbar. Für Jung und Alt.

Lassen Sie sich umgehend von uns ein persönliches Angebot unterbreiten. Sie werden von Qualität und Preis begeistert sein.